CHRONICLES OF
STEPHEN FOSTER'S FAMILY

The "Old Folks at Home," William Barclay Foster
and his wife Eliza Clayland Tomlinson

Chronicles of

STEPHEN FOSTER'S FAMILY

BY

Evelyn Foster Morneweck

ILLUSTRATED FROM
CONTEMPORARY PAINTINGS, PHOTOGRAPHS
AND PRINTS

VOLUME I

Published for the
FOSTER HALL COLLECTION
by the
UNIVERSITY OF PITTSBURGH PRESS

1944

PRINTED IN U.S.A., BY DAVIS & WARDE, INC., PITTSBURGH, PA.

To my father, Morrison Foster

FOREWORD

GRATEFUL acknowledgment is made here to Josiah Kirby Lilly, of Indianapolis, Indiana, founder of the Foster Hall Collection, whose love for Stephen Foster's music and interest in all that pertains to his life have made possible the publication of these *Chronicles of Stephen Foster's Family*.

The author does not presume to call this book a literary work. It is simply a compilation of notes and letters and personal recollections that we hope will bring a message of kinship to many admirers of Stephen Foster, and also to members of the Foster clan who have been widely separated by time and space. I have incorporated a great deal of what I fear will seem like tedious detail in the way of dates, lists of names, expenditures, and trips. But some of these items may be helpful in settling disputed points in the life of Stephen Foster, or other persons, and have been put on record here for possible future reference. Certain bits of source material may be of aid to Foster students, or of use to some historical novelist in building up a narrative in biographical or romantic form woven around particular events in the life of Stephen Collins Foster, or other individuals presented in these pages. I hope that no errors appear in this account that might cause annoyance or confusion in the family records of any friends of the Foster family brought into the story.

I am exceedingly grateful for the generous, untiring assistance I have received from Fletcher Hodges, Jr., Curator of the Foster Hall Collection, University of Pittsburgh. Mr. Hodges patiently went through the entire manuscript, checking every item back against its source, making many corrections and additions, and revising various conclusions of my own that could not be fully supported by contemporary records.

I would like to express my thanks for the great help received from Mr. Lilly's staff of workers in Indianapolis, including: Dorothy J. Black, secretary; Mary A. Wilson and Mrs. Broward Busard, who typed the manuscript; Eli Messenger, Frank C. Springer, Jr.,

Katharine Bell, Mrs. Donaldson Brown, and Lucile Davis, assistants.

Members of the Foster Hall staff at the University of Pittsburgh gave much assistance. The careful research work and conscientious proofreading of Henry W. Koropal are deeply appreciated. Louise Hauser, Lenora B. Groenert, Brooks N. Sipes, Mrs. William U. Follansbee III, and Mrs. B. B. Corson all shared in the editing of this book.

My husband, Alfred C. Morneweck, also assisted in editorial work.

For many valuable items of information, notes, and corrections, I am indebted to John Tasker Howard, of Glen Ridge, N. J., author of *Stephen Foster—America's Troubadour, Ethelbert Nevin, Our American Music, Our Contemporary Composers,* and other authoritative works on American music and musicians.

Amongst the good friends who have furnished me with important information are the late Walter R. Whittlesey, of the Library of Congress, Washington, D. C., and his daughter, Mrs. Katharine W. Copley; Alfred Reed Hamilton, Jr., of Ligonier, Pa., grandson of "Billy" Hamilton; Irene Stewart, former head of the Reference Department, Carnegie Library of Pittsburgh; the late Judge James R. Macfarlane, of Pittsburgh; Mrs. Marion M. Davis, of Glendale, Fla.; the late Joseph Muller, of Closter, N. J.; Mrs. R. E. Good (Marian Bigler Good), of Patton, Pa., granddaughter of William Bigler, elected governor of Pennsylvania in 1851, and grandniece of the other "Bigler Boy," John Bigler, elected governor of California the same year; Mrs. Alexander Nelson (Eliza McCandless, daughter of "Steve" McCandless), of Atlantic City, N. J.; Mrs. William B. McIlvaine (Julie Murray LeMoyne McIlvaine, daughter of Julia Murray LeMoyne), of Hubbard Woods, Ill.; Harmar Denny, Jr., and George A. Brown, of Pittsburgh; Dr. Frederick Kinsman, of Bryant Pond, Me.; Edward G. Fletcher, of the University of Texas; Elliott Shapiro, of New York City; Dr. Raymond Walters, president of the University of Cincinnati, author of *Stephen Foster: Youth's Golden Gleam,* which contains a wealth of new, documented material on Stephen Foster's life in Cincinnati; Mrs. Edith W. Howry (granddaughter of Judge John Rowan), of Louisville, Ky.; Lorena Callahan, of Louisville; Dr. Weir C. Ketler, president of Grove City College, Grove City, Pa.; Helen B.

Stuckslager, of McKeesport, Pa.; Dr. Elsie Murray and the late Jessie Welles Murray, of Athens, Pa.; Mrs. J. W. Chase (Edith Foster Chase), of St. Clair, Minn.; Mrs. Thornton Oakley, of Villanova, Pa.; Rose Demorest, librarian in charge of the Pennsylvania Room, Carnegie Library of Pittsburgh; Mrs. James F. Mulkearn, librarian of the Darlington Memorial Library, University of Pittsburgh; Agnes Lynch Starrett, of the University of Pittsburgh; Captain Frederick Way, Jr., of Sewickley, Pa.; Clarence W. Evans, of Wilmington, Del.; May Beale (a relative of Susan Pentland), of Wilkinsburg, Pa.; Franklin Taylor Nevin (a descendant of "Father" John Taylor), of Cambridge, Mass.; Louisa Miller, of Blairsville, Pa.; Mrs. James W. Arnold, Curator at "My Old Kentucky Home," Bardstown, Ky.; Reverend Albert E. Stuart, minister of the Upper Octorara Presbyterian Church, Parkesburg, Pa.; John Wilson Townsend, of Lexington, Ky., author of *Kentucky: Mother of Governors, Kentucky in American Letters: 1784-1912,* and many valuable historical papers on Kentucky history; Annie D. Flower, of Hazelwood, Pittsburgh, Pa.; the late Louis P. Kleber, of Saxonburg, Pa., son of Augustus Kleber, and nephew of Henry Kleber; Franklin F. Holbrook, director of the Historical Society of Western Pennsylvania, Pittsburgh; Edwin Y. Dobson, Superintendent of Records, Recorder of Deeds, Allegheny County, Pittsburgh; the late William Scott, former secretary of the Allegheny County Planning Commission, Pittsburgh; and Sidney S. McKay, of Pittsburgh.

Foster relatives who have given me important information include Alice Buchanan Ewing, of Bryn Mawr, Pa., the late Maskell Ewing, Jr., of Philadelphia, Mrs. Robert E. Brooke (Cornelia L. Ewing), of Birdsboro, Pa., Robert K. Cassatt, of Philadelphia, Mrs. John B. Thayer III (Lois B. Cassatt), of Haverford, Pa.—all descendants of Ann Eliza Foster; my brother, William B. Foster, of Pittsburgh, son of Morrison Foster; Henrietta Crosman (Mrs. Maurice Campbell), of Pelham Manor, N. Y., William Foster Thornton, Jr., of San Gabriel, Calif., Mrs. Mary Thornton Dodge, of San Gabriel, Calif., John Sayles, of Pelham Manor, N.Y.—descendants of Henrietta Angelica Foster; Lois Butterfield, of Atlantic City, N. J., and the late Henry Butterfield, grandchildren of Henry Baldwin Foster; Mrs. Jessie Welsh Rose, of Pittsburgh, granddaughter of Stephen C.

Foster; Miss Ethel Smith and Mrs. Charles Davis Clark (Bertha Smith), of Philadelphia, daughters of Gilead Smith; Mrs. Joseph H. Harper (Maria Daugherty), of Fort Bragg, N. C., descended from the "Fighting Parson," the Reverend William Foster; William Galbraith-Smith, of Cleveland, Ohio, a descendant of "Uncle John" Struthers; Mrs. Annie Stark McDaniel Foster, of Little Rock, Ark., widow of Benjamin Smith Foster, a descendant of John Foster, second son of Alexander Foster; Henry L. Sawyers, of Maryville, Mo., and the Reverend James Sumner Cotton, of Grove City, Pa., descendants of Violet Foster Scott, a daughter of Alexander Foster; and Dr. John Clayland, of Brooklyn, N. Y.

The names of other persons, who kindly permitted me to quote from their published writings, are mentioned in the pages of these Chronicles.

Many individuals assisted in the technical details of printing this book. I am especially grateful to Thomas C. Pears III and Mary W. Dickson, of the printing firm of Davis & Warde, Inc., Pittsburgh; C. C. Goodrich and Robert A. Twente, both of Indianapolis, Ind., and Thomas M. Jarrett, of the University of Pittsburgh, who prepared many of the illustrations; and T. Ward Hunter, of Bellevue, Pa., who designed the end papers.

It is a pleasure to acknowledge the fine work of the University of Pittsburgh Press, under the able leadership of Lawrence E. Irwin, who designed this book and supervised the many details of editing and printing. He was assisted by Wendell Gullion, Dorothy M. Bridge, Leah Hauser, and the late Helen E. Reed.

The index was compiled by Sarah Margaret Hodges, of Pittsburgh.

Many of the illustrations are included through the courtesy of relatives, friends, and correspondents. My cousin, Alice Buchanan Ewing, of Bryn Mawr, Pa., permitted me to use five pictures: Edward Young Buchanan and his wife, Ann Eliza Foster Buchanan, facing page 50; William B. Foster, Jr., facing page 142; Jessie Lightner Foster, facing page 556; four brothers and sisters of Stephen Foster, facing page 565. My brother, William B. Foster, of Pittsburgh, is the owner of the portraits of William and Eliza Foster, facing page 158, and Dunning McNair Foster, facing page 159. Washington and Jefferson College, of Washington, Pa., loaned the

picture of Jefferson College, facing page 195. The late Louis
P. Kleber, of Saxonburg, Pa., sent me the photograph of his uncle,
Henry Kleber, facing page 202. The picture of Robert Peebles
Nevin, facing page 203, is included through the courtesy of his
daughter, Mrs. Thomas A. Standish, of Sewickley, Pa. The sketch of
the steamboat *J. M. White,* facing page 275, was obtained from
Floyd C. Shoemaker, secretary of the State Historical Society of
Missouri, Columbia, Mo. The photograph of Rachel Keller Woods,
facing page 282, is reproduced through the co-operation of Mrs.
Sarepta Kussart, of Pittsburgh, and Rose Demorest, librarian in
charge of the Pennsylvania Room, Carnegie Library of Pittsburgh.
Eleanor S. Wilby, librarian of the Historical and Philosophical
Society of Ohio, Cincinnati, Ohio, sent me the two prints of early
Cincinnati, facing pages 306 and 307. Mrs. William B. McIlvaine
(Julie Murray LeMoyne McIlvaine), of Hubbard Woods, Ill., has
permitted the use of three pictures: "Homewood," facing page 323;
Julia Nancy Murray, facing page 330; and "Julia's Valentine," fac-
ing page 331. The photograph of my father, Morrison Foster, fac-
ing page 362, belonged to my cousin, the late Maskell Ewing, Jr.,
of Philadelphia. Mrs. R. E. Good (Marian Bigler Good), of Patton,
Pa., loaned the photograph of the Bigler boys (her grandfather and
his two brothers), facing page 392. I am indebted to John O'Connor,
Jr., acting director of the Department of Fine Arts, Carnegie
Institute, Pittsburgh, for the use of the portrait of Stephen Foster
by George Lafayette Clough, facing page 424. The sketch of the
Gaskill House, Warren, Ohio, facing page 521, is the work of the
late Joseph Muller, of Closter, N. J. My cousin, Henrietta Crosman
(Mrs. Maurice Campbell), of Pelham Manor, N. Y., sent me the
photographs of her mother and herself, facing page 553. The photographs of the statue of Stephen Foster and his grave, facing page
564, were taken by E. J. Kloes, city photographer of Pittsburgh.
Mrs. Benjamin R. B. Townsend, of Sewickley, Pa., loaned the
photograph of her uncle, James H. Park, facing page 572. The
photograph of the interior of the Stephen C. Foster Memorial, University of Pittsburgh, facing page 581, was taken by the Trinity Court
Studio, of Pittsburgh. The original of Map B2 (Lawrenceville,
from a map of Pittsburgh published by Robert Patterson, Decem-

ber 24, 1816), reproduced following page 632, is from the records of the War Department, now in the custody of the National Archives, Washington, D. C. The outline copy of the Foster cottage and the outline drawing of the "Ford purchase," following page 632, were made by my cousin, Sidney S. McKay, of Pittsburgh.

Many of the illustrations have been reproduced from books, magazines, or newspapers. In such cases, credit for the source is given on the page bearing the illustration.

Evelyn Foster Morneweck

Detroit, Michigan
October 23, 1943

PUBLICATION OF THIS BOOK

IS MADE POSSIBLE BY THE GENEROSITY OF

JOSIAH KIRBY LILLY OF INDIANAPOLIS

FOUNDER OF THE FOSTER HALL

COLLECTION

TABLE OF CONTENTS

VOLUME I

	Page
FOREWORD	vii
LIST OF ILLUSTRATIONS	xvii
BEFORE 1814	1
LAWRENCEVILLE AND THE YOUNG FOLKS AT HOME, 1814-1832	10
ALLEGHENY TOWN, 1833-1845	88
ALL MERRY, ALL HAPPY AND BRIGHT, 1846-1854	289

VOLUME II

LIST OF ILLUSTRATIONS	vii
ALL MERRY, ALL HAPPY AND BRIGHT, 1846-1854 (CONTINUED)	371
CLOUDS OF SORROW, 1855-1864	459
WHAT CAME AFTERWARDS	566
APPENDICES	607
I. THE DESCENDANTS OF WILLIAM BARCLAY FOSTER AND ELIZA CLAYLAND FOSTER, WITH BRIEF NOTES ON OTHER BRANCHES OF THE FAMILY	607
ADDITIONAL GENEALOGICAL INFORMATION	629
II. THE BIRTHPLACE OF STEPHEN C. FOSTER	630
III. GRANT'S HILL IRONWORKS	664
IV. MEMORIALS AND TRIBUTES TO STEPHEN COLLINS FOSTER	666
CORRECTIONS	740
INDEX	743

LIST OF ILLUSTRATIONS

VOLUME I

The "Old Folks at Home," William Barclay Foster
and his wife Eliza Clayland Tomlinson — *frontispiece*

The White Cottage — *facing page* 24

The steamboat *Enterprise* in 1815 — 25

The Reverend Edward Young Buchanan and his wife
Ann Eliza Foster — 50

"Pittsburgh Quick Step" — 51

"Federal Hill" at Bardstown, "My Old Kentucky Home,"
and Judge John Rowan — 58

"Cotton Plantation," by H. Lewis — 59

Letter from Eliza C. Foster to her son William, May 14, 1832 — 86

Professor John Kelly and the Reverend Joseph Stockton — 102

Minstrel songs of Stephen Foster's boyhood: "My Long
Tail Blue," "Coal-Black Rose," "Jim Crow," "Zip Coon" — 103

Letter from William B. Foster, Sr., to his son William,
September 3, 1841 — 110

William B. Foster, Jr. (Brother William) — 142

"Cairo, Mouth of the Ohio," by H. Lewis — 143

William B. Foster, Sr., painted by William Cogswell,
and his wife Eliza, painted by a Mr. Clifford — 158

Dunning McNair Foster — 159

"Map of the New York and Erie Railroad" — 194

Jefferson College at Canonsburg, 1840 — 195

xvii

Augustus A. Addams and Henry Kleber   202

Robert Peebles Nevin and John Desmond Scully   203

The *Jacob Strader,* a western steamboat of the 1850's   258

"Steamboat Wooding at Night," by H. Lewis   259

"Maria Bach Waltz"—one of Stephen Foster's early
    attempts at composition   266

Manuscript of Stephen Foster's first song,
    "Open Thy Lattice, Love"   267

William B. Foster, Jr.'s home in Towanda; and his children,
    William B. Foster, III, and Charlotte Frances Foster
    (Mrs. Henry Reed)   274

The steamboat *J. M. White*   275

"Belle of the Allegheny," an unpublished fragment
    from Stephen Foster's notebook   275

Susan Pentland and Rachel Keller Woods   282

Manuscript of "The Five Nice Young Men"   283

Cincinnati about 1846   306

Cincinnati in the 1850's   307

Early editions of Foster songs: "Old Uncle Ned,"
    "Oh! Susanna," "Old Folks at Home,"
    "Willie We Have Missed You"   314

"Memphis, Tennessee," by H. Lewis   315

Broadsides of the 1850's: "Gentle Annie" and
    "Jeanie with the Light Brown Hair"   322

"Homewood," residence of the Honorable William Wilkins   323

Julia Nancy Murray   330

"Julia's Valentine," sent to Julia Nancy Murray
    by Richard Cowan about 1851   331

First headquarters of Firth, Pond & Co., Stephen's publishers   354

Early editions of Foster songs: "Farewell My Lilly Dear,"
   "Old Folks at Home," "The Glendy Burk,"
   "Gentle Lena Clare"   355

Morrison Foster about 1849   362

Manuscript of "For Thee, Love, for Thee"   363

VOLUME II

Stephen Foster, from a tintype found among his letters;
   and Stephen Foster and George Cooper, from a tintype
   taken in New York City late in 1863   *facing page* 376

Broadsides: "Camptown Races" and "Fairy Belle"   377

The Bigler boys: William, Governor of Pennsylvania in 1851;
   John, Governor of California in 1851; and George   392

Manuscript of "The Wife"   393

New Orleans   396

Stephen Foster's daughter Marion   397

Songsters of the middle 1800's: *The Love and Sentimental
   Songster* and *The American Dime Song Book*   404

Henry Baldwin Foster and Morrison Foster, 1849   405

First draft of "My Old Kentucky Home"   408

Early editions of Foster songs: "Old Dog Tray," "My Old
   Kentucky Home," "Willie My Brave," "Ellen Bayne"   409

Two portraits of Stephen Foster: by George Lafayette Clough
   and Thomas Hicks   424

Map of the Cleveland and Pittsburgh Railroad   425

The Social Orchestra   444

Waters' Golden Harp and *The Sparkling Stream*   445

List of Illustrations

Early editions of Foster songs: "Old Black Joe,"
  "Come Where My Love Lies Dreaming," "Jeanie with the
  Light Brown Hair," "Linger in Blissful Repose"   452

St. Louis   453

Pittsburgh   504

Stephen Foster's melodeon   505

Major Jesse Thornton, his wife Henrietta Foster Wick,
  and their two sons, William Foster and Dunning Foster   508

Manuscript of "Down by the Gate"   509

Stephen Foster, from an original daguerreotype taken
  June 12, 1859, and the letter to Morrison Foster that
  accompanied it   516

Harriet Buchanan, Eliza Wick, and Charlotte Foster   517

Original manuscript of "The Glendy Burk"   520

The Gaskill House, Warren, Ohio   521

Clark's School Visitor, May, 1862   540

Broadsides published during the Civil War:
  "Beautiful Dreamer" and "Bring My Brother Back to Me"   541

Clement L. Vallandigham, Charles W. Couldock and his
  daughter Eliza, and Matthew I. Stewart   548

Josiah Kirby Lilly   549

Marion Foster Welch, Stephen Foster's daughter   552

Henrietta Crosman and her mother, Mary Wick Crosman   553

Morrison Foster about 1865, his wife Jessie Lightner,
  and their daughter Evelyn Louise   556

Morrison Foster and his wife Rebecca Snowden, in 1903;
  and their children, William Barclay Foster and
  Evelyn Foster Morneweck   557

List of Illustrations xxi

Statue of Stephen Foster, formerly in Highland Park, Pittsburgh
(now located in Schenley Park), and his grave 564

Brothers and sisters of Stephen Foster: Henry, Morrison, Ann
Eliza Foster Buchanan, and Henrietta Foster Wick Thornton 565

Jessie Welsh Rose, granddaughter of Stephen Foster 568

The three grandchildren of Stephen Foster: Matthew
Wiley Welsh; Jessie and Maybelle Welsh about 1899 569

The Stephen C. Foster Memorial Home, Pittsburgh, and
James H. Park 572

The house at the forks of the road in 1934 before its
removal from Pittsburgh 573

Foster Hall, Indianapolis, Indiana 580

The Stephen C. Foster Memorial on the campus of the
University of Pittsburgh 581

Maps and other illustrations relating to the birthplace
of Stephen Foster *following page* 632

Map A—Lawrenceville in 1814

Map B—Original map of the outlots, Lawrenceville, 1815-1816

Map B2—Lawrenceville, from a map of Pittsburgh published by
Robert Patterson, December 24, 1816

Map C—The outlots, 1815-1816; certified copy made in 1885

Map D—Lawrenceville in 1882

Map E—Robert E. McGowin's 1847 copy of William B. Foster's
original plan of Lawrenceville

Map F—Lawrenceville, from Robert E. McGowin's 1852 map of
Pittsburgh

Map G—The Robert Bell plan of the Malcolm Leech property, 1864

Map H—A portion of Lawrenceville, 1900

Accounts of Morrison Foster's visit to Lawrenceville

Article from the *Pittsburgh Sun*, February 17, 1927

Outline drawings of the White Cottage and the house at the forks of
the road

CHRONICLES OF
STEPHEN FOSTER'S FAMILY

Before 1814

THESE are the simple, everyday chronicles of an average Pennsylvania family in the days following the Revolution and in the nineteenth century. One cannot but marvel at the few years which elapsed after the Revolutionary War before the wilderness west of the Allegheny Mountains was converted into a dwelling place that was safe and secure, where settlers laid their hearthstones and built their homesteads without fear. With amazing rapidity, the Indians' narrow trails through the forests were widened by these indomitable pioneers into roads for the passage of oxcarts and Conestoga wagons laden down with incoming settlers and their goods; and great stagecoaches, traveling on schedules, hurried passengers from one firmly established settlement to another.

When William Barclay Foster and his wife, Eliza Clayland Tomlinson Foster, journeyed over the mountains from Baltimore to Pittsburgh in 1807, they were probably as safe from attack by savages or highwaymen as they would have been traveling from Boston to New York, or even from London to Liverpool.

Just west of Pittsburgh, the wilderness began again; in 1812, only two hundred miles to the northwest, Indians and hostile British threatened the life of every settler. But, sixteen years later, the Western Reserve was almost as safe and peaceful as an English countryside. When Eliza Foster came to Pittsburgh in 1807, the little village was hardly more than a frontier trading post. In 1821, however, she called it "town," and could write to her daughter Charlotte, "Pittsburgh looks dirty and smoky, there is no pleasure in it." Twenty years more, and all the Indians were gone from neighboring Ohio. William Dean Howells, recalling his childhood along the Miami Canal, says that in the early 1840's when he was a boy living in Hamilton, Ohio, he "saw the last of the Ohio Indians

1

passing through the town in the three canal boats which carried the small remnant of their nation southward and westward, out of the land that was to know them no more forever!"

Thus, in surroundings which so recently had been the scene of bloody massacres, William and Eliza Foster established a serene and peaceful home, their days untroubled except by the inescapable sorrows and cares that are the natural heritage of every mortal under the sun. They were not divided then—they worked together, played together, sang together and wept together. The mother and father of that family held fast each child's hand through the swift current of the years, and by precept and example, bound brothers and sisters close to each other with lifelong ties of loyalty and love.

It is not surprising that Stephen C. Foster's music is so purely American in character, for when he was born in 1826, the families of both his mother and father had been American for over one hundred years. His grandfather, James Foster, served through the Revolutionary War. James Foster's remains are laid in the cemetery at Poland, Ohio, in the plot of the Struthers family; the last years of James Foster's life were spent with his daughter Mary, who had married John Struthers, the much loved "Uncle Struthers" of Stephen's boyhood. When Stephen visited Poland as a child, James Foster and his daughter Mary were buried in the churchyard of the old Poland Presbyterian Church, and the great flat slab of stone covering his soldier-grandfather's grave was a familiar sight to little Stephen. Sometime during the 1860's, the remains of all the Struthers family, including James Foster, were removed to the new Poland Cemetery, and the ancient stone marks the spot today. The slab bears the following inscription.

IN MEMORY OF

JAMES FOSTER

WHO DEPARTED THIS LIFE

7 APRIL, 1814

AGED 76 YEARS AND 1 DAY.

"This spot contains the ashes of the just,
Who sought no honour and betrayed no trust.
His worth he proved in every path he trod;
An honest man is the noblest work of God."

James Foster was the eldest son of Alexander Foster, who emigrated from county Londonderry, Ireland, about the year 1725, and settled first in Freehold, Monmouth County, New Jersey; later, about 1728, Alexander Foster removed to Little Britain Township, Lancaster County, Pennsylvania. He had three sons, James, William, and John, and five daughters. (See Appendix I.) James Foster was born April 6, 1738. At the outbreak of the Revolution, he enrolled with the Liberty Company of Londonderry Volunteers, a fiery band of fighters of Irish and Scotch-Irish blood, commanded by Captain James Cook. He is listed as a private in Captain Samuel Hays' company, Tenth Pennsylvania Regiment, from 1777 to 1781. Sometime thereafter, he joined a Virginia regiment, and was present at the siege of Yorktown and the surrender of Cornwallis. John Foster, according to tradition, also served in the Revolution, and afterwards removed to Tennessee where he lived and died and left a large number of descendants. James Foster's brother, William, born in 1740, graduated from the College of New Jersey in 1764 and was installed as pastor of the Presbyterian congregations of Upper Octorara and Doe Run, in Chester County, Pennsylvania, in 1768. The Reverend William Foster was a Revolutionary patriot, and while his brothers, James and John, served in the ranks, William Foster rode about the country recruiting men for the Continental Army, and aroused such resentment amongst the British that at one time they placed a price upon his head. They did not succeed in capturing the courageous minister, however, because he and his family were kept hidden by members of his congregation in their houses or barns.

In 1766, James Foster married Ann Barclay, also of Lancaster County. She was the daughter, or granddaughter, of William Barclay, a Revolutionary soldier serving in the Pennsylvania line. Soon after the war started, James and Ann moved to Berkeley County, Virginia, where some of Ann's relatives were living. Their son William Barclay Foster, father of Stephen, was born there September 7, 1779. About a year after the close of the war, James Foster moved his family to Washington County, Pennsylvania, where many Scotch-Irish farmers had settled. They were almost all of them firm Presbyterians, with a great respect for learning, and it was not long before a little log college was started at Canonsburg, with Dr. John McMillan as the first president. The early college was succeeded in 1802 by Jefferson College, with James Foster listed as one of the original trustees. This institution of learning later incorporated with Washington College, and is now situated at Washington, Pennsylvania. But the original Jefferson College buildings at Canonsburg are still standing, and the old log college, where, history tells us, one hundred pioneer ministers received their training, is still preserved on what formerly was the campus of Jefferson College.

On Stephen's mother's side, the Claylands and Tomlinsons settled on the Eastern Shore of Maryland, and in Delaware, in the latter part of the seventeenth century. The Claylands were a huge and mighty clan. The founder of the family in America was the Reverend James Clayland who came from England about 1670. His great-granddaughter, Elizabeth Clayland, was the mother of Eliza C. Foster. Eliza was the child of her mother's second marriage; the first was to John Costin, by whom she had four daughters, Susannah, Hannah, Ann, and Sarah Costin. Ann Costin married Marmaduke Tilden, but the three other Costin girls all married Claylands. During the eighteenth century, Maryland was thickly populated with Claylands, almost all of whom had two or three sets of children. To add to the general confusion, the boys were mostly named James, John, and Thomas, and nearly all the girls named Elizabeth; and as nieces married their half uncles and stepsisters married stepbrothers, it is, as Eliza Foster herself said, "like trying to find out perpetual motion to delve into the Clayland clan." Dr. John M. Clayland, of Brooklyn, a descendant of the Reverend James Clayland, has been able to unscramble many different branches of the family and arrange them in an orderly fashion. Most of the clan were wealthy slaveholders who played a prominent part in social and political life during the Revolution. Eliza Clayland Foster tells us in her personal reminiscences that two of her uncles fell at the Battle of Brandywine, and another uncle, Colonel James Clayland, was praised by General Washington for gallant conduct in the same engagement.

After the death of John Costin, his widow moved to Delaware, and there married Joseph Tomlinson, who we understand was a saddle maker of Wilmington. Their daughter, Eliza Clayland Tomlinson, was born on January 21, 1788. The mother could not have lived long after that, for we find that on April 28, 1791, Joseph Tomlinson was married to a Miss Margaret Noel. The little Eliza went to live with her mother's family in Baltimore, and Joseph Tomlinson and his wife migrated to the state of Kentucky where Eliza's two half brothers, John and Joseph, were born and brought up. John became a physician in Augusta, Kentucky, and Joseph Tomlinson, Jr., gained distinction as a pioneer educator, and was president of Augusta College for many years. He occupied this position when his half sister, Eliza, visited Augusta with her two little children, Henrietta and Stephen Collins Foster, in the spring of 1833.

Eliza Tomlinson's girlhood days were spent largely with her mother's people in Baltimore, but while visiting her aunt in Philadelphia, she met William B. Foster, young Pittsburgh business traveler who had come over the mountains to buy and exchange goods in the great city of Philadelphia. Eliza's aunt (Joseph Tomlinson's sister, and daughter of John Tomlinson, farmer, of Delaware) was the wife of Oliver Evans, the famous early American inventor of steam engines. Morrison Foster wrote in the first penciled draft of his biography of Stephen C. Foster:

Mr. Evans lived on Race Street in the City of Philadelphia, and at the time Miss Tomlinson was there, he built his wonderful amphibious steam-boat. Miss Tomlinson saw him walk with great pride beside it as it moved out of his yard into the street and down to the Delaware River, where it entered the water and paddled around in the harbor of Philadelphia.

When Eliza Tomlinson met her future husband, he was already a partner in the firm of Denny and Beelen, of Pittsburgh. William B. Foster had attended the log college at Canonsburg (where his father, James Foster, was a trustee) until he was sixteen years old. Then he set out for himself to find his living in the promising town nineteen miles northward. When William rode into Pittsburgh, on April 20, 1796, he was a rather short, good-looking, blue-eyed boy, the typical independent son of a typical Scotch-Irish pioneer family. In Morrison Foster's penciled manuscript, he describes William B. Foster's early activities in Pittsburgh as follows:

He entered into business in the employ of Anthony Beelen and Major Ebenezer Denny, who were engaged in extensive general merchandising. Afterwards, he was admitted to partnership with Major Denny, and attended to the active part of the business. It was their custom at that time, the beginning of this century, to load flat boats with the products of the neighboring country, furs, peltries, whiskey, flour, etc., and float them down the Ohio and Mississippi rivers to New Orleans, where the goods were exchanged for sugar, coffee, etc. Mr. Foster went on these expeditions about twice a year. Sometimes he returned by land via Natchez, Nashville, Maysville and Wheeling to Pittsburgh, traveling with large parties strongly armed, for the Indians were hostile and dangerous. At other times, he took ship and sailed to New York. On one of these voyages, the vessel he was on was captured by pirates off the coast of Cuba, but was rescued by a Spanish man-of-war before the pirate crew could board her. At New York and Philadelphia, he bought goods for the store at Pittsburgh. These goods were transported across the mountains on the backs of horses in the earlier years of the business. Afterwards, large wagons were used, drawn by six horses. On each horse, (except the one on which the driver sat), a string of bells, attached to a bow above his collar, "discoursed most eloquent music" as the long line of wagons traversed the still forests of the mountains. The wagons were of the pattern used by the farmers east of the mountains, and were called Conestoga wagons.

William B. Foster and his nineteen-year-old bride were married in Chambersburg, Pennsylvania, on November 14, 1807, by the Reverend David Denny, and immediately proceeded on their four-teen-day wedding journey to Pittsburgh, traveling over the wintry mountain country, changing from stagecoach to horseback where the road, for many miles over rough country, had not yet been made wide enough for coaches or wagons. They arrived tired and worn on the evening of November 28 at the hospitable home of Major Ebenezer Denny. We do not know where the newly-married couple set up housekeeping in 1807, but in 1812 the house they were living in was one owned by William B. Foster on the northeast corner of Sixth Street and Cherry Alley, and was an "excellent two-story brick, well finished, on four full lots of ground." Besides his business with Major Denny and Mr. Beelen, William B. Foster was the proprietor of an "Iron Works" on Grant's Hill, listed in the directory of 1812 as "Steam Mill and Tilt Hammers." Mr. Foster sold this ironworks in January, 1812, to his friend, Magnus Murray.

William B. Foster invested in a varied line of enterprises in early Pittsburgh. About the time he sold the "Mill on the Hill," William B. Foster became one of the managers of the Pittsburgh and Greensburgh Turnpike Company, which operated a line of stages and wagons between Pittsburgh and Philadelphia. During the War of 1812, he offered his services as a volunteer commissary to the Pennsylvania Brigade, enduring the utmost hardships incident to a period of intensely cold and stormy weather at the outbreak of the war. In 1814, he was appointed a deputy commissary of purchases at Pittsburgh, and while acting in that capacity performed the additional duties of assistant or issuing commissary of the U. S. A.

What happened in Pittsburgh just before the Battle of New Orleans, is graphically described by Morrison Foster:

When the Army of the Northwest appealed to the Government for supplies to enable them to continue the contest, the answer was "a mournful echo from the vaults of an exhausted treasury." But my father with his own money and upon his own personal credit procured the necessary supplies.

When the British army, which had captured Washington and burned the Capitol, turned their vessels' prows southward for the capture of New Orleans, urgent orders came to Pittsburgh to send forward clothing, blankets, guns and ammunition to the relief of Jackson's army. But no money was sent with which to purchase them. Again my father extended his generous hand and himself procured the much-needed supplies.

He loaded the steamboat *Enterprise* (the fourth steamboat which ever turned a wheel on the Western rivers) and dispatched her from Pittsburgh on the 15th of December, 1814.

She was commanded by Capt. Henry M. Shreve, the pioneer boatman. Brave Shreve left Pittsburgh about dark of a winter night, and as the boat rounded to and straightened herself for the voyage, he called to my father on the wharf:

"I'll get there before the British, or sink this boat!"

He pushed on through the wilderness, amid the storm and floating ice, and reached New Orleans on the 5th of January, 1815, three days before the battle which saved Louisiana. Captain Shreve unloaded part of his cargo at the city, and ran down the river, passing the British batteries, to Fort Philip, returned again, and was engaged in the battle of the 8th of January, serving at the sixth gun of the American Batteries.*

October, November, and December, 1814, found the Pittsburgh commissary, William B. Foster, frantically trying to raise money to pay for the following supplies, with just $2,000 on hand in treasury notes to cover the bill:

> One Thousand Eighteen pound balls, and
> One Thousand Twelve pound balls, at $110 per ton.
> One Thousand 5½ inch shells at $150. per ton,
> 40 Tons of lead at 12½ cts. lb.
> One Thousand Camp Kettles,
> Two thousand Mess Pans,
> 500 Inft. coats.
> 500 Inft. wool overalls,
> 1000 pairs of Shoes,
> 500 of the lightest Blankets,
> 500 pairs of Gaithers,
> 500 Prw. Vests.

Several of the Pittsburgh manufacturers of army supplies refused to accept William B. Foster's official signature alone, as they had no confidence in the government's promise to pay, and insisted on receiving Foster's personal notes, which the distracted commissary immediately gave them. When Washington finally settled his claim after the war, it was $2,704.90 short; Congress refused to approve certain sums advanced, contending that Mr. Foster had paid for the goods with his own notes on his own responsibility, and that reimbursing him for losses sustained by reason of the depreciation of treasury notes would establish a dangerous precedent. Quoting from Morrison Foster:

Upon the hearing of the cause in the United States Court at Pittsburgh in 1823, the venerable Judge Walker (father of Hon. Robert J. Walker) in his charge to the jury, used these memorable words: "Terminate as this cause may, Mr. Foster has established for himself a character for zeal, patriotism, generosity and fidelity which cannot be forgotten, and has placed a laurel on his brow that will never fade." The jury without

* Morrison Foster, *Biography, Songs and Musical Compositions of Stephen C. Foster,* Pittsburgh, Percy F. Smith, 1896.

leaving the Court returned a verdict in favor of my father. That judgment still stands unpaid on the records of the United States Court at Pittsburgh.

In 1846, General John H. Eaton (secretary of war under Andrew Jackson) did his utmost to secure justice for William B. Foster, who was a personal friend, but his efforts were unavailing.

In 1821, Governor Heister of Pennsylvania appointed William B. Foster register (not "registrar" as they say today) and recorder of Allegheny County, an office which he held for three years. In 1825, he was elected to the Pennsylvania Legislature, or Assembly, at Harrisburg, where he remained until the fall of 1828. Although he was a zealous supporter of Andrew Jackson, William B. Foster was still listed in the Butler *Sentinel* for November 11, 1826, as a Federalist when he was elected in that month to the assembly from both Allegheny and Butler counties, as was his associate, Harmar Denny. At the same election, the Democrats elected John Brown and William Beatty to the assembly. James Buchanan, afterwards an ardent Democrat, went to Congress that year as a Federalist. Party divisions and names evidently had not yet become established in western Pennsylvania, and the assemblymen seem to have been elected mainly on their sympathies in regard to the proposed route of the new canal. In the Pittsburgh *Mercury* for July 19, 1826, published by John M. Snowden, William B. Foster's candidacy is advocated in the following terse announcement which shows no party affiliations:

> Communicated.—William B. Foster, of Pitt Township, will be supported at the approaching annual election, for a member of the State Legislature, by a number of
> VOTERS.
> *July 15, 1826*

Lawrenceville and the Young Folks at Home 1814-1832

THE White Cottage where Stephen Collins Foster was born on July 4, 1826, was built on a beautiful knoll on the farm which his father purchased from Alexander Hill on April 5, 1814. This farm of one hundred and twenty-one acres was a tract of land originally known as "Good Liquor," and was entered at the Patent Office of the Commonwealth of Pennsylvania on April 1, 1769, on special application No. 20, by Colonel George Croghan, who was a famous Indian trader and Indian agent of the Crown at Fort Pitt. Morrison Foster, who was born in the White Cottage on June 10, 1823, gives us the following description of his childhood home:

In 1814, my father established his residence upon a tract of land belonging to him on the Allegheny River, 2½ miles above Pittsburgh. Here, he built a beautiful white cottage, on Bullitt's Hill, a height commanding a view up and down the river for miles. It was on this same piece of land that George Washington was cast on the night of December 28, 1753, and nearly frozen, when he and his guide, Christopher Gist, were returning from Fort Venango. My father sold thirty acres of this tract to the Government, on which now stands the United States Arsenal. He also laid out a town there and called it Lawrenceville, in honor of Capt. James Lawrence, who was killed while gallantly fighting his ship, the *Chesapeake,* and whose last words, as he was carried below, were, "Don't give up the Ship." . . .

At the White Cottage, overlooking the village of Lawrenceville and the winding Allegheny, the family spent many happy years. Here hospitality and kindness prevailed. Being the only private residence outside

10

of town in that neighborhood where open house was kept, its generous board was free to all comers at all times.*

The White Cottage was built on Outlot No. 9 of William B. Foster's plan of Lawrenceville, in the midst of a splendid grove of forest trees. Back of the Foster property to the south spread the "Big Woods," owned by James O'Hara until his death in 1819, and afterwards by his son-in-law, Harmar Denny. The wide front lawn before the Foster homestead was sloped and terraced for about a hundred feet to the Philadelphia Pike (now Penn Avenue), and a graceful curving driveway led up to the house. The course of this old driveway can still be traced today where a semicircular footpath leads up to the front door of the large brick house that now stands upon the spot, known today as the "Stephen C. Foster Memorial Home." The four-acre plot selected by William B. Foster for his own homestead was well up around the bend of the Turnpike Road, and the house stood upon an elevation, commanding, as Morrison said, "a view up and down the river for miles." Although they called it a cottage, the Foster homestead was comfortably spacious. The main building measured fifty feet across the front, and contained four rooms on one floor with a center hall. It was painted white and finished with green shutters. A two-story wing of three or more rooms stretched to the east. Rising through the center of the house were the two main chimneys, and large fireplaces were built into the inside corners of each of the four rooms of the main part of the homestead. At a very early date, Pittsburgh people had abandoned wood hearth fires in favor of coal grates; coal was plentiful in that district, and much more efficacious in keeping their houses warm in the cold, damp Pittsburgh winters than wood alone. The Foster homestead also contained a basement "summer kitchen" and in the rear of the house were the usual bake oven, smokehouse, cow barns, horse stable, and hog-pens of a country place that was partly self-sustaining. Despite his various real estate and other activities, William B. Foster managed to keep up his farm, with outside help, and supplied a large number of Lawrenceville residents with milk from the good cows which he

* Morrison Foster, *Biography, Songs and Musical Compositions of Stephen C. Foster,* Pittsburgh, Percy F. Smith, 1896.

had purchased from Daniel Beltzhoover, a wealthy gentleman-farmer who lived a little farther east on the pike.

About seventy-five feet northeast of the White Cottage, a little back from the road, was located a wonderful spring which was such a well-known landmark of that locality that Robert Patterson, early Pittsburgh publisher, included it in a topographical map which he prepared in 1816, now filed in the National Archives, Washington. "Foster's Spring" was a favorite resting place for thirsty, weary travelers journeying afoot, on horseback, and in stagecoach or Conestoga wagon along the dusty turnpike road. The springhouse was built with three underground chambers of stone covered by a wooden superstructure. This wooden part was rebuilt about 1866, but the original underground stone chambers were still in good condition as late as 1901, just as they had been when little Morrison and Stephen Foster watched Lieve, the colored bound-girl, set the milk away. The top of the door was arched and of brick, and the sidewalls and ceilings were of stone. The stairway led down into the room where the spring bubbled up in a constant stream of ice-cold water. At the side of the stairs, the roof was supported by a pillar made of the trunk of a forked tree. A pipe ran from the springhouse to the roadside where the water gushed into a large horse trough, to overflow and run through a culvert under the road, "down the ravine" to meet the Two-mile Run, and thence to the Allegheny River. On a hot summer day, it was the custom of "Col. Billy Foster" to take his friends down to the springhouse for refreshment and conversation. There the gentlemen sat themselves on benches under the large oak tree, and argued the political questions of the day; discussions were prevented from becoming too heated by copious drafts of cool, sweet milk from the crocks on the springhouse floor.

The old springhouse is gone now, and the water has been diverted into the city sewer. The hard paving stones of Denny Street and Penn Avenue today cover the spot where once flourished lush green grass and woodbine in the pleasant little dell that surrounded "Foster's Spring."

The nearest neighbor to the west was the Scott family who also had been neighbors when the Foster family lived in the "brick house" downtown in Pittsburgh, prior to 1814. George Scott, Jr., purchased Outlot No. 8 from William B. Foster on July 20, 1816. Down below the Scotts, on the south side of the turnpike road, at the forks, stood the great tavern stables beside the Two-mile Run. They were built of brick and stone, and could accommodate from thirty to forty horses. On the opposite side of the turnpike was J. W. Hunter's tavern, "The Sign of Captain Lawrence," a well-known landmark even as late as 1875.

In recent years, a frame cottage standing at the foot of Bullitt's Hill, at 3414 Penn Avenue, down near the forks of the road, built on outlots 6 and 7 sometime during, or after the year 1828, by a carpenter named William Toman, frequently has been mistaken by uninformed residents of Lawrenceville, and even by some Foster relatives of a later generation, for the original White Cottage, possibly because of a slight similarity in the general layout of Mr. Toman's house to published pictures of the Foster homestead, and because these persons did not know that the Foster dwelling had been torn down and replaced with brick. In 1934, the legend that this ancient Toman house was the "birthplace of Stephen C. Foster" was accepted as a fact by a wealthy automobile manufacturer of Michigan, Henry Ford, who purchased the old cottage, and moved it "piece by piece," to an early American exhibition established at Dearborn, Michigan. But this cottage was not the birthplace of any of the Foster children; in fact, no member of the Foster family ever lived a day under its roof. The homestead in which Stephen C. Foster was born was erected by his father on the exact spot now occupied by the Stephen C. Foster Memorial Home, at 3600 Penn Avenue, Pittsburgh. In 1865, the last remaining portion of the original frame White Cottage was torn down by a subsequent owner, Andrew Kloman, who replaced it with brick; and so it stands today.

In April, 1914, one hundred years almost to the day after William B. Foster established his home in Lawrenceville, Mr. and Mrs. James H. Park of Pittsburgh purchased the brick homestead built by Malcolm Leech and Andrew Kloman on the foundations of the original White Cottage and presented it to the people of Pittsburgh to be maintained as a birthplace shrine in memory of the composer whose songs they loved. Acting for Mr. and Mrs. Park, John C. Slack, one of the ablest and most conscientious attorneys in the city of Pittsburgh, made a painstaking examination of the records before purchasing the historic mansion at 3600 Penn Avenue, (owned in 1914 by Mrs. Samuel McKee). These county records, and genuine recorded evidence left by members of the Foster family, prove beyond the shadow of a doubt that the birthplace shrine owned by the city of Pittsburgh is the authentic site of Stephen C. Foster's birthplace, the White Cottage. (See Appendix II.)

We believe that Henry Baldwin was the first of the Foster children born at the White Cottage, March 23, 1816. Four children of William and Eliza Foster were probably all born in the brick house in Pittsburgh, that stood at the corner of Sixth Street and Cherry Alley, the first home, we believe, of Stephen C. Foster's parents in Pittsburgh. The first child, named Ann Eliza, born on November 2, 1808, lived only until December 23. Charlotte Susanna Foster was born on December 14, 1809; and the second Ann Eliza Foster (who lived to a good old age) was born January 12, 1812. The first son, William Barclay Foster—his father spelled this "Barckly" in the old family Bible—was born on May 7, 1814. This little boy lived less than eleven months. He died on March 26, 1815, possibly in the new White Cottage in Lawrenceville. William Barclay Foster, Jr., the "Brother William" of these Chronicles, was older than these other children, and was born, we believe, about 1806. He was an adopted son, a motherless young relative of William B. Foster's, who was taken into the family soon after they moved to the White Cottage, and given the name of the baby William who died in 1815. He bore the name with honor and respect, and was a loving and devoted son and brother.

After Henry, the children born at the White Cottage were Henrietta Angelica, on September 14, 1818; Dunning McNair, born January 26, 1821, was named for Colonel Dunning McNair, Revolutionary officer and friend of William B. Foster's; Morrison Foster, born June 10, 1823; Stephen Collins Foster, born July 4, 1826; and James Clayland Foster, born February 3, 1829. "Little Jim" died the 19th of May, 1830, leaving Stephen the baby of the family. Henry Baldwin Foster was called after his father's close friend, Judge Henry Baldwin, a brilliant, eccentric lawyer of early Pittsburgh, who was appointed to the United States Supreme Court by President Andrew Jackson. An eternal bond of fealty does not always result when parents name their children for admired friends and business partners. It wasn't many years before Messrs. Foster, Baldwin, and Dunning McNair, Jr., were on speaking terms only when they met to sue each other in the courts, and what they said then can well be imagined.

II

A FEW YEARS before her sudden death in 1855, at the earnest solicitation of her children, Eliza Foster began a series of reminiscences recording her early married life in the "western country," and the outstanding events that marked its course. Seated by the bedside of her invalid husband, her work occupied Mrs. Foster for many hours of the day. When Morrison Foster set himself the task in 1860 of copying the story from the loose sheets left by his mother, many sections of this manuscript had been lost, destroyed, or divided amongst the other children. Many interesting narratives are started by Eliza Foster, but the reader too often does not learn the outcome for Morrison Foster is forced to make the notation: "Here a part of the manuscript is missing." Enough of it remains, however, to piece together a very vivid picture of her happy, and sometimes sorrowful experiences as a young wife in old Pittsburgh, and at the new White Cottage in Lawrenceville. If ever the lost portions of this manuscript come to light, we shall learn the complete story of what happened at the White Cottage on July 4, 1827, when little Stephen was just one year old. Eliza Foster tells us that a rousing party was held in Denny's woods on that day, just as on the day Stephen was born; that the ladies, including all the Collins family, foregathered at the White Cottage while the gentlemen cheered and made patriotic speeches in the grove—and then, Morrison notes—"the manuscript is incomplete!"

But, fortunately, we have several almost complete portions, and, from one of these, the following is taken.

ELIZA FOSTER'S FIRST EVENING IN PITTSBURGH

I love to court the shades long passed away,
The noble, hospitable, and the kind;
And raise the honored of another day,
For contemplation to the present mind.

Many a summer's sun has set upon her life's pathway since the writer of these annals wended her way, a young and joyous bride, accompanied by her gallant groom, over a rough and mountainous road, to reside in what was then called the far West. Not having the present advantages of canal, turnpike or railroad, the journey was slow and monotonous, and it was not until the fourteenth day [November 28, 1807] after staging in an uncomfortable coach, that she hailed with delight the dingy town of Pittsburgh, her future home, where every joy, and every sorrow of her heart since that bright period have been associated with the joys and sorrows of its people.

It was evening, when weary and faint with fatigue, the writer was conducted, or rather borne, into the hospitable mansion of her husband's partner, the benevolent Major Ebenezer Denny, a dwelling in the centre of the town, where she was kindly received and treated by the family. After resting and changing from traveling apparel to other garments, she was shown into an apartment below stairs where blazed in all its brilliancy, a coal fire, casting its light upon the face of beauty clothed in innocence, a sight refreshing to the mind of angels, and acceptable at the throne of God, where none can enter but the perfected through Grace, or those as sinless as that little child. Nancy Denny, at that time five years old, sat in her little rocking chair, casting upon me as I entered, her earnest blue eyes, whilst her tiny hands parted the yellow ringlets that clustered about her brow, and fell carelessly over her fair shoulders. The well-cleaned grating of the chimney-place, the light that blazed brightly from the fire, the vermillion hearth, the plain, rich furniture, the polished stand with lighted candles in candlesticks resembling burnished gold, made an evening scene that fell gratefully on my pleased sight. Upon a sofa lay the tall and military figure of the Major, a gentleman of the old school, easy and dignified in his bearing, a soldier who had served his country well under Washington at Yorktown, and Harmar, St. Clair and Wayne in the subsequent Indian campaigns.

Nancy leaped from her chair to pick up an orange thrown upon the carpet by her youngest brother. "Where did you get an orange, St. Clair, so late in the season?" demanded his Aunt.

"It was given to me for Nancy by Mary O'Hara."

"Sister," said Major Denny, "you should not let the children be troublesome to their neighbours; they have everything at home to make them happy. Consequently, they need no visiting."

When the evening meal was spread, the family circle consisted of the father, the Aunt, four sons, and an only daughter, the lovely little Nancy. Mrs. Denny, the daughter of Mr. Wilkins, (some squares from them) had died ere this, and the sole care of these charming children had devolved upon the amiable Aunt, now present.

"Father," said Harmar, the elder Master Denny, "William O'Hara has returned from his trip abroad; I wonder if he will marry Miss Carson."

"Molly is a charming creature," said Miss Denny, as she drew the tea and sent it about, "whoever marries her will be happy. She is not very beautiful, but she is gentle, and is always doing so much good. She thinks of everybody but herself."

"Aunt," said William, the second Master Denny, "I saw her going in to see old Mrs. Hadaway who has been so long an invalid; the wind was blowing her bonnet almost off, and the snow pelting into her face. She could not keep her cloak about her because her hands were full of something to nourish the old woman."

"That is like her," said the Aunt with a smile, as though such benevolence was familiar to herself and consequently met with her entire approbation.

"Betty, there is a rap," said the Major.

"The Wilkins's," said Betty.

Mary and Nancy Wilkins came smiling in from the cold frost of a November night, which heightened the roses on their cheeks and added brilliancy to their already bright faces.

"We came to tell you the news," said Nancy, "William O'Hara and Miss Carson are to be married at last, we have our invitations for Thursday. What a merry time we shall have of it! What parties, what gaiety! Mrs. General Butler will give a party, and so will Mamma, and all the rest of the people. Everybody is so rejoiced, for poor Molly's sake, she is so deserving."

"And William! Oh, is he not handsome!" said Mary, "They will be a perfect couple. But I must bid you good evening, I have everything to do."

The evening closed with a few moral observations from the Major, and we separated for the night.

The wedding of William O'Hara and Molly Carson did not take place until July 9, 1809, and their happiness together endured only two weeks. The young husband died very suddenly on July 24. Eliza Foster's description of William O'Hara's funeral gives us a picture of the simple frontier town and its neighborly customs, as yet unspoiled by urban affectations.

The borough could only boast of two double carriages ready for use. One was a large baronial coach that would hold nine persons, belonging to the O'Haras. The other one, a newer style belonging to the Collins's. I think there were other carriages, but like old pianos, they were out of use. I understand the Ormsbys and Wilkins's each had one, but they were reserved for travelling carriages. Be that as it may, the company in attendance that day all walked, except the mourners. The procession moved without pomp; not even a pall covered the coffin. The pride of these people did not lean to vain glory. In those days, strangers were few, consequently all knew the amount of wealth owned by every person. It was not necessary to impose external show upon the eye of the beholder to affect his senses with a false respect. Their frequent associations, kindnesses bestowed by the rich upon the poor, whose services they schooled themselves to value, mutual exchanging of benefits, pecuniary and otherwise, made confidence and friendship go hand in hand among them. There was but one usurer; too contemptible to be named in these pages. A few of his descendants live to reap the benefits of his extortions. Some of them have been visited with the just retribution of God's wrath. But, I should not bring him in with the people of whom I am now writing. He could not then be welcome even at a funeral such as that which left the house of O'Hara on the forenoon of that remembered day.

The instruments of music were closed, a covering was drawn upon their best furniture, and all gay things were put away for happier days. Parson Taylor preached his sermons with more solemnity, warning them of the shortness of life, therefore it would be better not to spend it too gaily; but as to meddling with their amusements, he was the last to interfere.

Why did this people hold the reins of custom in their hands and extend their influence to new comers? Because they were a consolidated, federal voice. The O'Haras, the Butlers, the Dennys, the Collins's, the

Nevilles, the Ormsbys, the Wilkins's, the Kirkpatricks, the Addisons, the Craigs, etc. were one voice in state affairs and gave the same tone to every opinion. The ignorant stranger that differed from them, after he had time to learn their code, need never appear in their presence. There was none to make them afraid. Cheerfulness and gaiety seem'd to be the order of the day, unless it was on some such sad occasion as had at this time drawn them together, when they deeply felt, because the grief of one was the sorrow of all.

With business men, there was none of that running to and fro with hollow cheek and sunken eye, there were no failures, no broken down families. All were gradually rising, the lawyers, the physicians, the merchants, the mechanics. The lawyers have been in the Cabinet and in the Senate, the physicians died rich, the merchants became large land-holders, and the mechanics retired to their country residences. The boot-maker became a rich man and a judge, and the cobbler has refused the hand of his pretty daughter in marriage with the son of the judge!

Parson Taylor mentioned above by Mrs. Foster, was the Reverend John Taylor, the first Episcopal minister of Pittsburgh. He had been educated at Trinity College, Dublin, and became minister of the Round Church, an octagon-shaped building erected in 1805 on the site of the present Trinity Church; Mr. Taylor served as pastor until 1818. In Judge J. W. F. White's recollections, he says, "Father Taylor, as he was affectionately called, had rather a hard time of it. The members of Trinity Church were not very wealthy then, or else not very willing to pay a good salary. For twelve years before he resigned, he was struggling with poverty and had to support himself by teaching school." Father Taylor was devoted to science and astronomy; he was also in great demand as a surveyor, and laid out many tracts of land for William B. Foster and his neighbors. Father Taylor's maps are still to be found in the archives of Allegheny County, among them William B. Foster's original plan of Lawrenceville, surveyed in 1814, and also a plan of the out-lots made in 1815-1816, showing the White Cottage drawn in on Outlot No. 9, on the spot where the Stephen C. Foster Memorial Home stands today.

Eliza Foster described Father Taylor as a "short, stout, stern, fair philosopher, like many of Erin's sons."

He was a welcome guest at the White Cottage, and it was from

Father Taylor that William, Jr., received his first instructions in the science of surveying land.

III

*T*HE deed for the land upon which the arsenal is located passed from William B. Foster to the government on April 29, 1814, for a consideration of $12,000. The price embraced thirty acres and the deed was acknowledged before Lazarus Stewart, then a justice of the peace in Pitt township. Mr. Stewart, afterwards sheriff, had the unpleasant duty of hanging John Tiernan, in 1818, for the murder of Patrick Campbell, a contractor on the Pittsburgh and Greensburg turnpike. Judge White says:

Tiernan was a laborer on the turnpike, living in a cabin on the hill this side of Turtle Creek, and Campbell boarded with him. At night, when Campbell was asleep, Tiernan killed him with an ax, robbed his body, and fled on Campbell's horse. A few days after, he appeared on the streets of Pittsburgh with the horse and was arrested. His execution at the foot of Boyd's Hill was an event which became an epoch in our history, from which witnesses in court, and others, would fix the date of occurrences, being so many years before or after the "hanging of John Tiernan."

After the government had received the property, Captain Abraham R. Woolley of the Ordnance Department was detailed to draw up plans and superintend the construction and equipment of the new garrison. Nathaniel Green Gunnegle, who, as a little boy in old Lawrenceville, went to school with William, Charlotte, and Ann Eliza Foster, recalls the following facts in a letter to Morrison Foster, dated August 8, 1883:

In the month of March, 1815, the news of the victory of New Orleans was received at the Old Garrison in Penn Street, Pittsburgh. The soldiers illuminated the Garrison with candles stuck into the holes in the blocks of wood in their cartridge boxes. These illuminated blocks were placed in the windows of the Barracks, or wherever they could be seen from Penn Street. Being a little fellow, I was delighted with being permitted to whittle the ends of the candles to fit the holes in these blocks. This is the last I remember of the Old Garrison. My next recollections are of Lawrenceville, or the New Garrison.

The times must have been 1816 or 1817, and I must have been seven or eight years old then. The old schoolhouse was located about ten feet from a deep ravine on the East, and about 30 feet from a fence separating the property of Abner Fisk on the south from the Graveyard. I went to school with Mr. Reed, Mr. Ray, Mr. Dolph—who was the Author of a primary grammar for young students, Mr. W. W. Fetterman, who later in life became eminent as an Attorney-at-Law, Mr. Johnson and Mr. John Garrison. Of my schoolmates, I remember that Wm. Foster sent three children; there were the children of Scott the painter, Henry and James Atkinson, Mary Ann and Fayette Winebiddle, children of Philip Winebiddle, three children of Peebles who kept the tavern at the sign of the Black Horse, two Roupe children and two from the Koontz family. All of these lived on or near the Greensburg Turnpike, as it was then called. (Now Penn Avenue.) The eight Bishop children and two Kings also attended. They lived on the banks of the Alleghany. I also remember the hanging of a man named John Tiernan on Boyd's Hill, when I was eight or nine years old.

When William B. Foster bought the farm of Alexander Hill in 1814, Mr. Hill was proprietor of the "Brick Tavern" which stood down beside the Two-mile Run, about a third of a mile southwest of the wooded elevation on which William B. Foster built his White Cottage, and on the opposite side of the turnpike. This historic old tavern can be found drawn in on Outlot No. 1 of the Lawrenceville Plan of Lots, on several early maps of Lawrenceville reproduced in Appendix II of these Chronicles. Mr. Hill moved out when he sold the farm to William B. Foster, and the following advertisement appears in the February 4, 1815, issue of the Pittsburgh *Gazette:*

TO RENT

AND POSSESSION GIVEN 1ST APRIL NEXT

That Well Known
Tavern Stand

formerly occupied by Alexander Hill, on the Philadelphia Road, 2 miles from Pittsburgh and adjoining the Village of Lawrenceville where the United States are erecting very extensive works. The subscriber has, during the last season, made considerable additions to the house and stables. The house has 5 large well finished rooms on the first floor, 7 chambers on the second floor, and 2 large rooms in the garret, well finished for servants lodging. There is a never failing fountain of the best water running in the yard, and an ice-house filled with ice. The stables (to which is attached a carriage house) are built of stone and brick, and will contain from 30 to 40 horses. A garden and six or eight acres of land may be had with the buildings. The Turnpike Road from Pittsburgh to this place being now completed renders the situation very advantageous for a Public House.

WILLIAM B. FOSTER.

January 25, 1815

The name given the tavern by William B. Foster, the new owner, was "The Sign of Captain Lawrence." The figure of the dying Lawrence with his arm raised in a commanding gesture, with the words "Don't give up the ship!" issuing from his mouth, were displayed on the sign, to greet the weary traveler from the East as he rode down the last hill on the outskirts of Pittsburgh. For a while J. W. Hunter was tavern-keeper. In 1821, Alexander Hill was back at the old stand; he held a mortgage against the property, and he and William B. Foster made an agreement which included the following clause:

It is further understood and agreed between Alexander Hill and William B. Foster that the said Alexander Hill is to have possession of the Brick Tavern, and with the ground attached to it as laid off in the plan of William B. Foster, and the said Hill paying a reasonable rent to said Foster until the mortgage of the aforesaid Hill becomes due.*

Some time later, John Sarber became landlord of "The Sign of Captain Lawrence," and he and his sons kept tavern there for many years. Mr. Sarber was highly respected in Lawrenceville; in 1831, he was senior warden of the Lawrenceville Masonic lodge. This lodge was organized in 1819 as Hamilton Lodge No. 173, and

*The advertisement and information regarding the "Brick Tavern" were kindly supplied by George A. Brown, of Dormont, Pennsylvania.

was constituted February 20, 1820, with the name of William B. Foster, Sr., as treasurer. William, Jr., was initiated in 1828, but his certificate of membership was not issued until September 19, 1831. By that time, he was filling the office of secretary, with Dunning McNair, worthy master; John Sarber, senior warden; and William Gillespie, junior warden. Unfortunately, the warrant of this lodge was vacated in 1837 for nonpayment of dues!

The little schoolhouse to which Mr. Gunnegle refers was built by private subscription on a plot of ground donated to the borough by William B. Foster, and primarily used as a burial ground for the residents of Lawrenceville, and all soldiers who died in that vicinity. Ann Eliza Foster relates the following sad anecdote concerning the old Washington Graveyard, as it was called:

What always invested the spot with peculiar interest to me has been that there, in 1819, was laid the body of my dear little school-fellow and bosom friend, Eliza Woolley, only daughter of Colonel Woolley. You have no doubt heard frequently of her sad death; how we, two little seven-year old children were at school in the old Two-mile Run house, and starting across the road, hand in hand, were thrown down by a run-away with a heavy carriage, from the wheels of which I was almost miraculously saved, while they passed over the body of my poor little comrade. This was in cherry time, as our temptation to cross was a tree on the opposite side laden with ripe fruit. The carriage held several gentlemen who had just been calling on Col. Woolley at the Arsenal. Time will never efface the sight which met my eyes as I arose, or the awe with which I saw her loved remains deposited in the old grave-yard. Her mother, Mrs. Woolley, died a few years afterwards at Fort Leavenworth, after making a special request that her body should be laid beside her darling child. I was present at this burial also, my childish fancy much struck by the remains having been brought such a distance.

Nathaniel Gunnegle also remembered this event.

I knew Major, (afterward Colonel) Woolley. He had a child buried in the Lawrenceville Burying Ground. After he was ordered to Council Bluffs, Madame Woolley died and was brot from Council Bluffs to Pittsburg in a metallic coffin charged with Jamaica Rum to preserve the body. It was brot in a "keel boat" and landed at the foot of Market Street, from whence the funeral proceeded to the Lawrenceville Burying-Ground and interred by the side of her child.

While life in those unsettled times in a new country but lately a savage wilderness was hard, and sometimes tragic, the people of Lawrenceville and Pittsburgh made their own good times; and parties, theatricals, and balls were the order of the day. Morrison Foster states in his biography of Stephen C. Foster that their father and mother kept open house, and its generous board was free to all comers at all times. The officers and ladies from the arsenal held rehearsals at the White Cottage for the theatrical performances which they gave to entertain the townsfolk, and many evenings were made enjoyable with "a little wine and a great deal of nonsense." Eliza Foster especially remembered that *The Heir-at-Law* was a favorite play. One of the pleasant summer pastimes was to organize a party upon the steamer *Shamrock*, on which they would sail gaily up the blue Allegheny, to disembark for a picnic, or "corn party" as they called it when the sweet corn was ripe, at Pine Creek on the beautiful farm belonging to General John Wilkins.

Some of the happy times experienced by the children are described in the following lines by Ann Eliza Foster, taken from a poem written many years after, called "My Three Worlds." These verses recall memories of her "First World."

What wealth of summer pastimes and of winter sports were ours,
What frolics in our wandering for Springtime's earliest flowers.
What gambols on the hillside where the old log schoolhouse stood,
What strolls along the river bank, what rambles in the wood.
What seats beside the limpid spring, sharing our basket's store,
While to our lips the leaf-made cup, its fragrant waters bore.
As our schoolmates in their idle pranks were scattered far around,
Drowning with noisy merriment the tiny cascade's sound.

That world was full of gladness, and a merry band was there
Which gathered to one evening hearth, and claimed one mother's care.
And the memory of the joyous days in which we reveled then
Has power still to waken up my heart to mirth again.
What boots it now from thoughts like these that memory turns aside
To tell, how in her youthful bloom, the gentle sister died, [Charlotte]
Who, with such sweet and queen-like grace, our restless spirits ruled,
And into something like her own, our ruder natures schooled.

Or how the oldest of us all, mid usefulness and worth, [William]

The White Cottage, the original Foster homestead, painted by a Mr. Miller in 1828 .

The steamboat *Enterprise* in 1815
From *Lloyd's Steamboat Directory and Disasters on the Western Waters*
(Cincinnati: James T. Lloyd & Co., 1856)

Obeyed the sudden, midnight call, which summoned him from earth.
Or, how the little one we led, (whose bearing bold and free,
Already shadowed forth a type of what his course would be;) [Dunning]
In the full vigour of his youth and flush of manhood's hour
Felt the Destroyer's withering touch, and sank beneath his power.

Or, further, how the infant boy, who filled the cradle then [Stephen]
Grew up to weave a magic spell of melody for men:
And when the world was fully waked to listen to his strain,
Yielded his life, and gift of song, to Him who gave, again.
These sorrows came in after years, for not a shadow fell
Upon our happy spirits then, their coming to foretell.

The sketches and incidents of her early life at the White Cottage
were set down by Eliza C. Foster for the benefit of her children
and were not intended for publication. It was solely a labor of love.
She read extensively the flowery style of fiction so popular in her
day, and believed her children would find her story more like a
novel if she adopted the romantic phrases of that period. Her writing
was rather small and cramped, and her spelling, like that of
many other ladies of her day, was very faulty. There are 178 pages
of this closely written manuscript, and it must have been a huge
task for Morrison to copy it all. As he was always a hard-working
young man, it meant many of his evenings were thus engaged; it
was a labor of love on his part as well as his mother's.

Reading between the lines, you will discern the sweet affectionate
personality of Eliza Foster. How she loved her friends! She found
no fault in any. The women were beautiful, talented, and virtuous;
the men, handsome, brave, and honorable. No unkind word is
directed against anyone more fortunate or wealthy.

Through all the pages, you will sense her longing, as an older
woman, to bring back to memory the dear home of her early married
life. The White Cottage bathed in moonlight! The scent of
roses, lilacs, and locust, and the fragrant flowers she called "pineys,"
that Mrs. James O'Hara had sent her, blooming "crimson and
bright scarlet" beside the "broad, long walk edged with boxwood"!
The dear little children who clustered around her in the evening,
waiting for the sound of horses' hoofs on the gravel outside telling

them that Father was home! They are all gone; but the memory of this household will never die as long as these pages are cherished by the descendants of gentle Eliza Clayland Foster.

MORNING AT THE WHITE COTTAGE [1818]

It was on a summer morning, early in the month of June, when a plain, square-bodied carriage turned slowly up a shady road two miles from Pittsburgh. The fresh breeze fanned the green foliage of the locust trees that grew along the white fence which surrounded the grounds belonging to a beautiful Cottage that stood upon an elevation, retired from view: for the road wound half circularly round the base of the hill.

The carriage contained four ladies, one an elderly lady, one about thirty; and the other two from fifteen to sixteen years old, and as lovely as I have ever seen girls at that age. [Miss Nancy Denny, Mrs. Foster, and Miss Denny's nieces, Nancy Denny, and Mary O'Hara.] Were they so beautiful, or was it the influence of the scene and the recollections that now crowd upon my mind softened by time? The full blown roses and scented clover, heavy with night dews, breathed their odours on the balmy air that was warming with the genial rays of the not-long-risen sun. The air was full of melody from the throats of warbling birds, and the blue eyes of those fair girls beamed with joy, while their light brown hair was gently moved by the winds that blew soft as zephyrs over the daisy clad hills. Their faces flushed with gladness when they beheld a little girl with sunny locks and swan-like neck, fair like themselves, but yet a child, peep through the fence, and with a delighted smile point across the hill towards the new Arsenal, where, for the first time, proudly floated upon the summer air, the striped and star-bespangled ensign of our happy land.

From the house, quickly and with buoyant step, there came one whose heart was gladder than the bird that flies toward heaven when he sings. Twenty-one summers had not yet bronzed his cheek, nor had sorrow dimmed his brilliant eye. [This youth was young Mr. Edward Muller, who was visiting in the Foster home, and was in love with Nancy Denny.] The sloping terraced grounds about the Cottage, dressed off with many a rose and dancing flower, laughed gaily on that sweet morning in the bright sunlight. I knew that a happy home awaited me, with breakfast table laid, and husband kind, and infant footsteps pressing the green sod. Was it these images, all blended with the sylph-like forms of the two young ladies who accompanied me that made them both so beautiful to me? Or is it that the memory of long-buried joyous hours comes o'er our spirits like a pleasant dream, and drapes the loved ones in such angelic shapes, as makes them seem indeed the favorites of a better world. . . . When fancy lends her wings to bear my memory back, it seems as if in some sweet dream my happy buoyant steps had been within Eden's walls.

EVENING AT THE WHITE COTTAGE

The sinking sun still fainter beamed upon the rich verdure of the rolling hills that threw their long shadows upon the valley, clothing in sombre hue the strong walls and Armory of the new Fortress, while the clear waters of the blue Alleghany seemed to grow green and cold. The rich roses that hung in clusters beside us drank in the evening dews, and the pale moon came forth and already gleamed afar off through the tall trees. The enchantment of the scene spoke in its own silent eloquence to my heart. It did not drape the future with sadness. It did not tell me that my sweet little Charlotte would be loaned to me but for a few more years, and then, in the warmth of her youth and budding genius, in the development of her moral worth, and the brightness of her beauty, when many an ardent friend looked upon her with rapture as a bright star of virtue, loveliness and accomplishments, that she should die, die unexpectedly, die far from home, far from that sweet spot where nature and art had combined so to beautify the scenes of her innocent childhood.

Many a better heart than mine has broken when a Charlotte died; then, Oh, forgive me, if I pause awhile at a strange time, when my bosom beat with hope and the air I breathed seemed mystic with a perfect happiness, for darkening the picture with my own woes.

The clear moonbeams serenely and brightly fell upon the scene. The large windows daily polished with whiting and buckskin, glistened like mirrors. The neat white country seat, with dark marble colored steps, and full blown roses blooming on the green sward, the white graveled terrace gently sloping off into the broad turf, the gay, handsome officers, the elegant light carriage in which were seated the lovely Nancy Denny, the scarcely less admired Miss Irwin, and the dignified William H. Denny, the brown grove, the distant Arsenal, the glassy river, and the rolling fields that divided it from the Cottage, composed a romantic scene which memory delights to recall.

Small wonder that Stephen's mother wrote so sorrowfully to William in 1832:

Although the vessels are broken which I hewed out to hold the sources of my earthly joys, the delightful cottage and the sound of the deep-toned instrument still comes dancing on in the arrear of memory, with pain and sorrow at thought of how it closed forever with the departure from this transitory stage of her we loved so dearly.

A letter from Ann Eliza, dated March 5, 1872, gives us another glimpse of old Lawrenceville.

My recollection goes back to the day on which Pa rode out with President Monroe, when he visited the Arsenal, when he must have been on the committee of reception—as, when I was carried into the parlor of Major Woolley, our man of all work having taken me to see the show, for the double purpose of stopping my crying after it (I was not more than three or four years old) and for his own gratification. Pa was sitting in the midst of the uniforms and officials by which His Excellency was surrounded. . . . [President Monroe's official inspection of the Arsenal was made in 1816; Ann Eliza was four years old.]

Then I remember so well the appearance of old John Darragh—so long Mayor—carrying an umbrella over La Fayette, during his broiling ride through the city, and how they both looked as if their "Too, too solid flesh would melt!"

This notable occasion was probably Mr. Darragh's last public appearance as official umbrella-bearer to an honored guest. General Lafayette visited Pittsburgh the last day of May, or first of June, 1825, and Mr. Darragh resigned his office on June 20 following; he was succeeded by John M. Snowden on June 28, 1825. There has been a tradition handed down in our family that when General Lafayette visited Pittsburgh, he stood as godfather when Morrison was baptized. Morrison and Henrietta were both baptized in Trinity Church on September 25, 1825, Henrietta aged seven and Morrison aged two. I can find no record that Lafayette revisited Pittsburgh in September, but it is quite possible that he held "little Mit" on his knee when he (Lafayette) visited the arsenal, in May or June, 1825, and probably during the conversation that took place, the noted visitor offered to stand sponsor for Morrison when he was baptized. Whether he actually did so or not, we do not know. The records show, however, that General Lafayette actually did "stand up" as godfather for little Gilbert Fetterman, grandson of Anthony Beelen, formerly a partner of Ebenezer Denny and William B. Foster.

IV

ELIZA FOSTER'S ambition for her daughters was that they should have the advantages of an education in the aristocratic tradition in which she herself had been brought up. No great effort was made in those days to prepare young girls to support themselves by any sort of work. If it became necessary for them to earn their own living, the only training they had for such a calamity was the music, dancing, or French they had learned from some unfortunate gentlewoman in like circumstances. Charlotte and Ann Eliza's early training in these branches was received from Mrs. Brevost, the daughter of a French gentleman who had lost his estates through his adherance to Bonaparte, and had been forced to bring his family to America. Mrs. Brevost had been educated in Paris and presented at the court of Louis XVI and Marie Antoinette. With her husband and daughter, she conducted a very select "Boarding and Day School for Young Ladies" on Second Street, between Market and Wood streets, and became so popular a teacher, and so eagerly sought after by the residents of Pittsburgh, that she was enabled to support her aged parents in comparative luxury. One of Charlotte's instructors in singing at Mrs. Brevost's was the remarkable William Evens, a well-known figure in the early musical life of Pittsburgh. Originally a plane-maker, he opened a school, in October, 1817, in his plane-shop, for the teaching of sacred anthems, choruses and hymns from the "works of the most celebrated modern composers." In 1826, Mr. Evens was teaching practically all the wind and bowed instruments, writing organ music, and conducting choruses and choirs all over the city. He copied by hand volume after volume of the works of the great masters, Bach, Haydn, Handel, and Beethoven, using gallons of homemade black ink in this labor of love, and turning out the most beautiful musical manuscripts you can imagine. Several volumes of this hand-copied music, as well as three or four scrapbooks personally compiled by William Evens on the musical activities of early Pittsburgh, are preserved in the Carnegie Library of Pittsburgh.

An advertisement of Mr. Evens', dated January 25, 1826, reads:

> Wm. Evens, teacher of the French Horn,
> Trumpet, Bugle, Serpent, Bassoon, Clarionet,
> German Flute, Hautboy, Violin,
> Violoncello, and Tenor Viol—
> at Six Dollars per Quarter.
> W. E. professes the Andante stile. Those
> who wish to play Concerto's or become
> Prestissimo Players need not apply.
> Tempo Gusto.

(In other words, no jazz!)

Other composers were not lacking in early Pittsburgh days. An illustration in this book shows the title page of the "Pittsburgh Quick Step," by Wm. Staunton, Jr., dedicated to Miss Lydia Collins.

The townsfolk's admiration of music and French arts and graces was not shared by one forceful character of those times, old Molly Murphy, who kept the tavern at the "Sign of General Butler" for many years after her husband, Patrick Murphy, died. Old Mrs. Murphy had a beautiful garden of flowers, and was visited frequently by Eliza Foster and her friends who came not only to buy bouquets for their tables but to enjoy the pungent conversation of the old lady. Mrs. Foster has left us a vivid picture of Molly Murphy in her reminiscences entitled "Sketches and Incidents."

Mrs. Molly Murphy was seventy-six years old. She was tall, very tall, with black, piercing, intelligent eyes, a roman nose, and an earnest searching expression of the whole countenance. She wore a dark loose wrapper, confined about the waist with a belt, and a large gypsey straw hat upon her head to shade her from the noon-day sun. For hot sun never drove her from her idol, where she almost lived. She bent her keen glance upon our party as though she had never seen one of us before. Her right hand held the handle of her light weeding hoe on which she leaned, and her left was placed to her side. Thus she continued to stand statue-like.

"Good morning, Mrs. Murphy," said Miss Denny and I.

"Good morning, Mammy Murphy," said Eliza Beelen.

"Your garden looks so sweet," said Nancy.

"How beautiful that arbor looks," said Mary.

Still she answered not. At that moment a little girl came up to her with a tattered frock upon her and a shabby bonnet, carrying on her arm an old basket.

"Will you please, Mrs. Murphy," said the girl, "to send mother some cold victuals; she is very sick."

"If she worked as hard as I do, she would not be so sick, nor need cold victuals," said Mrs. Murphy. "Here, take that to her," throwing her a piece of silver, which she took from a long purse, drawn from her pocket, full of change. "Always taking out and never putting into the bag is sure to make a beggar. Start away with you, and get yourself to work among your betters, and quit cantramping about the country for a bite to eat. Go to Mrs. Beelen, and ask her to take you to mind the baby; or there is little Mrs. Foster, she has babies, go to her and ask her to give you work."

"I don't like to," said the girl.

"You don't like to, and yet you are always running to me, you and the rest of the pack like you. By the life, I have need to work to keep up such a crew. Begone, and don't let me catch you here again for a month of Sundays! And there's old Joslin leaning over the gate looking ill enough! I thought the worms had got him by this time. God help him, I think the 'Jammys' are getting scarce, Joslin, when they let you roam about the country half naked and so starved looking. Take that, and tramp off to town and see if you can find any of them living yet."

"Who does he call 'Jammys', Mammy?" said Eliza Beelen.

"He means the old people of '76," said Mrs. Murphy, "who give him good old clothes and bits of money." [Possibly from "Jamais," making fun of the rich Pittsburghers and their French lessons. The "Paddys" probably got their nickname from the poor Irish, of whom there were many in Pittsburgh.]

"Who does he mean by 'Paddys'?"

"Anybody that refuses to give him something to eat or wear, or a bit of money to buy tobacco. All the spare money nowadays is given to that French woman to learn their daughters foreign airs, to make fortune hunters of them, and set themselves up to catch strangers. The old schools that taught them plain facts are thrown by for these new flummerys. She shall get none of my money. I'll keep it for yon poor thing that will never have a farthing if I don't give it to her. But I shall tell her mother to make a plain, honest body of her. Play the harp forsooth! Who in the name of common sense will you play the harp for here? Our young men care no more about the sound of a harp than if it was a brass kettle!"

"Well, but," said Mary O'Hara, "we don't want young men, we only learn these accomplishments for our own amusements. At least, I speak for myself," said she, looking cunningly at Nancy Denny.

"Pshaw!" said Mrs. Murphy, "your fathers expect you to marry some rich man of some great family, when you settle yourselves to their liking. But just as likely as not, you will run off with some strange fellow that they never heard of, because he plays on the guitar and sings songs, or writes rhymes, or some such nonsense, and only want you for your money all the time."

"I must fall far indeed below my mother," said Mary, "if I condescend to give myself to any such fellow. But I want some flowers for tomorrow evening. If I send a servant for them, will you gather me all you can spare?"

"Save some for me, too," said Eliza. "And, Mammy, save some for me, too," said Miss Porter.

"Why don't you speak, Nancy Denny? You want some, of course," said Mrs. Murphy.

"No," said her Aunt, "her father likes to have Nancy plain. He would not suffer her to put a rosebud in her hair if he knew it."

"Her father is quite right," said Mrs. Murphy, "Major Denny is a wise man!"

"Come," said Miss Denny, "we had better proceed," and without ceremony, we all stepped into the carriages and were soon moving rapidly towards town, leaving Mrs. Murphy rejoiced to be able to go on again with her favorite occupation.

Another tribute to the renowned character of Molly Murphy is found in the Honorable H. M. Breckenridge's *Recollections* of early Pittsburgh:

Before my time, Black Charles kept the first hotel in the place; when I can first remember, the Sign of General Butler, kept by Patrick Murphy, was the head tavern [Northeast corner of Third and Market]; and afterwards the Green Tree, on the Bank of the Monongahela, kept by William Morrow.

The General Butler was continued by Molly Murphy for some years after the death of Paddy. She was the friend of my boyhood and youth;

and although as rough a Christian as ever I knew, I verily believe that a better Christian heart—one more generous and benevolent, as well as sturdy and fearless—never beat in a Christian bosom.

Many an orphan—many a friendless one—many a wretched one, has shed, in secret, the tear of gratitude over the memory of Molly Murphy.

After Mrs. Brevost's a convent school was decided on as the next step for little Charlotte, and in the autumn of 1821, she and her father, with her friends, Ann and Mary Cassilly, set out for St. Joseph's Academy, "near Emmetsburgh" [Emmitsburg], Maryland. This convent school was founded by the saintly Elizabeth Seton whose memory is revered by devout American Catholics to this day.* Mother Seton died on January 4, 1821, and as Charlotte did not enter the school until the fall of that year, she probably never knew this good and beautiful nun. But there is a possibility that Charlotte's mother was well acquainted with Mother Seton, for when Eliza Foster lived in Baltimore, Mother Seton was conducting a parochial school in that city.

To go away to school "near Emmetsburgh" meant a long and arduous ride by stage across the mountains for little Charlotte, but in those days it was not considered too hard nor too long a journey on which to send a child to receive a proper education. In fact, in 1822, when Ann Eliza was only ten years old, her parents seriously thought of sending her to Troy, New York, where Mrs. Emma H. Willard conducted a "seminary for young ladies" which was famous even so far west as Pittsburgh. It was finally agreed that Ann Eliza was too timid and shy to go so far away from home.

Not long after reaching the convent, Charlotte received the following letter from her mother, dated Pittsburgh, November 2, 1821.

My loved Daughter,

Your letter of the 19 to your sister Ann Eliza now lies open before me, which we were all much delighted on receiving, as it convinced us of your good health and strength to walk so far in one afternoon.

I wish in all your letters you may be able to say in the usual child-like manner, I am well, even if you think proper to omit the next common sentence, and I hope you are the same. We save your letters

*Leonard Feeney, *Elizabeth Seton, An American Woman, Her Story,* New York, America Press, 1938.

in your little red morocco trunk because they are precious as the absent child is always the darling during their exile.

Last week I return'd from Greensburg, after a few days visit to our friends of that place. Your cousin Frances Foster is here now. Mrs. Cassilly and little Sarah came out to see us the other day; tell the girls they are all well.—

Your Father has been drawing a few tunes on the violin for your little brother and sister to dance this evening—they have not forgotten the danceing tunes you used to play on the pianno; Henry whistles and Henrietta sings them yet. Dunning begins to walk around a chair, he has six teeth and can say *dont.* I rode to town this afternoon but Pittsburg looks dirty and smoky, there is no pleasure in it. We have much more comfort here in this vicinity, our Arsenal neighbours are all well. I rode to town yesterday with Mrs. Talcott and Miss Day, they enquir'd about you.

Your little companions are all well; old Mr. Holmes [Mr. A. E. Holmes, a dancing teacher] has begun his one, two, three—four-jump-five, -again. I wish you would tell me in your next letter how your eyes are as I frequently think of them, and how you progress in music. Learn some handsome pieces of sacred music.—

Mr. Coopper is gone away from Lawrenceville and George Talcott and the two Days have gone to Cannonsburg college and Ann Eliza and Henry will go to Captain Morrow's school this winter. Little Peggy Hunter and Catherine Thaw are here making a great noise.

Give my love to Ann and Mary Cassilly, and let me prevail on you to be all obedience and devotion to the sisters who are your guardians and tutors, and all gratitude to those who may do you any kindness; you profess so little, they will not in so short an acquaintance be aware your heart is so affectionate, nor that you are a child of such never fail-ing truth. Therefore when your word is doubted in company with others, do not let it pain you too sensibly. I write thus because it is so common for children to fib, and sometimes the inocent suffer with the false.

God be with you, my love, and protect you from all evil, be patient and meek and lift your thoughts to Heaven, and rough paths will be-come smoothe to you, and confinement and disappointment will only seem the retirement of peace, and the cloister of happiness. The days of good children are guarded, and their pillows watch'd by night by the angels of Providence.

Your Father, Cousins and sister present their affectionate remembrance to you, and let me conjure you to think with tenderness on your anxious and devoted Mother,

Eliza C. Foster.

Little Charlotte, not quite twelve years old, and so far away from her home, could not conceal the ache in her heart when she replied to her mother's letter:

I rise early, and I sometimes fancy myself at home with sister Ann Eliza, skipping along the lane leading to the barnyard, and stopping to look at the growing apple tree that my dear good papa planted for me with his own hands. I think I see the green leaves quivering in the wind and shining in the bright sunlight; and the sweet blossoms with the bees humming about them; and the pretty blue birds and robins that hop about its branches in summer. Then I see Lieve passing along with her pails of frothing milk, on her way to the springhouse, and Ann Eliza and I run before her to see her strain and set it away, and she orders us out, fearing the damp will give us colds; then we run to read the new names on the big tree; and see you waving your handkerchief at us to come in to breakfast. The tears sometimes for a moment fill my eyes, but I brush them away, for everyone looks so sweetly and kindly on me here, that I drive from my mind the beauties of home and devote myself to taking pleasure out of what I find here.

Although this little letter shows evidence of being carefully prepared for the critical inspection of the sisters, the child's longing for home and mother shines through the innocent attempt at "fine writing." The very day after this letter was received from Charlotte, the cherished "big tree," carved by skillful Brother William with the names and initials of all the children, met with irreparable disaster. We shall allow Eliza Foster to describe the catastrophe in her own rare style:

The next morning, the moment Lieve rang the first bell, Mrs. Foster was up. She had nearly finished her toilet, and Mr. Foster was drawing on his wrapper.

"That chopping sounds very near the house," said Mrs. Foster.

"It is the echo," observed Mr. Foster, "the morning is so clear."

Mrs. Foster took it for granted it must be the echo, as she resolved when first she obtained such a prize as a kind husband she would never contradict him, & therefore proceeded to pin on her collar.

When Mr. Foster had prepared himself for breakfast, he walked onto the side porch. At the same instant, Mrs. Foster was startled by the sound of a terrific crash! The first thought that struck her was that some one had shot her husband, for he leaped into the room and reeled to a seat exclaiming, "That rascal has done the business!"

Mrs. Foster instantly ran out on the porch to look for the person who had done it, when behold, Jack Devlin, the Woodman, had cut down the great tree, the pride of all the countryside, and now stood contemplating his work. Yes, there lay the splendid tree that had flourished for ages in his majesty, sheltering with its giant arms the polished and the rude, prostrated never to rise again, hewn down by the hand of a stupid clown!

Surprise and indignation rendered Mr. Foster speechless, but he was soon roused to action by the sound of chopping again falling on his ear as Devlin calmly proceeded to make firewood of the monarch of the forest.

"Stop that ax, you stupid monster!" roared Mr. Foster, as he rushed to the terrace, "and never let me catch you on this ground again."

"Didn't you tell me to cut the tree down?" said Jack in alarm.

"Why, no, you fool! I told you that dead sycamore. But what business had you to go to work this morning without seeing me? Begone! and don't talk to me!"

Now, Mrs. Foster never liked to make matters worse than they were, and when she saw her husband trembling with anger, she chose rather to comment upon subjects near the heart.

"Look, love," exclaimed she, "how healthy and sweet our children are this morning. Ann Eliza, will you go with your papa to town and take your music lesson, dear?"

Breakfast being over, the family barouche was at the door, and Mr. Foster placed little Ann Eliza in it. Seizing the reins he dashed out at the gate, while Mrs. Foster looking after him prayed that he might forget the destruction of the favorite tree, as he rode into town.

Mrs. Foster immediately turned her attention to domestic arrangements, frequently interrupted by persons coming up from the Village and asking for Mr. Foster, to secure deeds for the lots they had purchased from him. Not only by these was Mrs. Foster's attention called away, but also in giving necessaries of life to new comers who daily came up from the Village of Lawrenceville to ask for assistance. Indeed, some came to that place to settle without any money, expecting not only to get their lots from Mr. Foster, but to be supported by him also, without recompense. Some there are, that by the blessing and favor of God are now living in affluence in the large City of Pittsburgh, who at that time had reason to bless and pray for William Foster, whose liberal hand always stretched forth to help the needy, and saved them from poverty and want!

Thus, Mrs. Foster found little time for leisure, for at her house as at Mr. Daniel Beltzhoover's, the people of Pittsburgh and its vicinity found open doors.

In the evening . . . Mrs. Foster walked down the ravine to the Arsenal to visit her friend Mrs. Woolley, with whom she spent the rest of the evening.

Mr. Foster called for her at an early hour. As they walked home, she found him quite cheerful, seeming to have forgotten the fallen tree.

But the mind of Mrs. Foster grew sad and as her foot pressed the dewy grass upon that calm starlight evening, shadowy thoughts mingled as it were with the fallen tree, gloomed through her imagination. The fate of the tree seemed to her ominous of some dark prospective, although there was nothing in her affairs to induce such fear. She entered her nursery, kissed all her children, and retired to her room, where falling upon her knees, she prostrated herself before the throne of Omnipotence, saying, "Lord, thy will be done; if these joys must pass away, nourish me with grace to bear it!"

Her tears fell fast, why, she knew not, for her cup of life's joys was full to the brim. Blessings ushered in upon her in one continual stream, and why should a careless woodman cutting down a favorite tree cast such sombre shadows over her future path?

V

ELIZA FOSTER'S premonition of trouble was destined to be fulfilled. Early in the year 1826, William B. Foster came to the end of his resources—he no longer could cover the notes held against him by the Bank of the United States; the bank foreclosed the mortgage on all of Mr. Foster's property designated as the "southern half" of the borough of Lawrenceville, namely the outlots. Foster was able to save several parcels located in the inlots near the arsenal, but the outlots all were lost, and with them, the beloved White Cottage. The Foster family remained there for almost two years longer, renting their old home from the bank. William B. Foster was not able to reclaim it before it was sold, together with the four acres on which it stood, to Malcolm Leech, a prosperous wholesale grocer of Pittsburgh, living on Seventh Avenue, who purchased several tracts of the foreclosed Foster property and established his home in Lawrenceville. Stephen probably was too young to be grieved at the loss of the White Cottage, but the regret of his parents and older brothers and sisters was deeply impressed upon his consciousness in later years. The story is told that after Henry B. Foster was married, and living in Lawrenceville about a mile from the old White Cottage, a sympathetic neighbor remembered seeing his lonely figure walking long blocks out of his way in order to pass the dearly remembered spot where he had spent his childhood.

The ungrudging help that Wm. B. Foster was receiving now from his oldest son served the family in good stead, for ready money was scarce, and the young girls growing up in the household longed for many pretty little trifles that their father could not buy them. Even when he was a very young boy, Brother William was his parents' faithful help and pillar of strength. He came to them at the age of eight or nine years, a neglected, motherless waif, and they made him one of their own. Writing of his brother, Morrison Foster says, "He put on the harness of industry and usefulness at the age of sixteen years and wore it continuously to the day of his death."

William started his engineering career "carrying a chain" for good Father Taylor on the latter's many surveying and map-making excursions around the Allegheny County countryside. When Wm. B. Foster was recorder of deeds in Pittsburgh during 1821, 1822, and 1823, young William assisted him in the office which at that time adjoined the courthouse on the west side of the Diamond. There in the evening, William and a youthful friend, Daniel Agnew, used to read and work by candlelight. Dan afterwards rose to be Chief Justice of the Pennsylvania Supreme Court. It was Daniel Agnew's grandfather, Richard Howell, Governor of New Jersey, who encamped on Colonel Dunning McNair's farm (now the borough of Wilkinsburg) with the New Jersey Blues sent out by

Washington to quell the Whiskey Insurrection. Veteran Revolutionary soldiers were a familiar sight to the young men in the recorder's office; the frontier was just west of Pittsburgh. In those days, "patriot" was a word with real meaning. William Bender Wilson, of the Pennsylvania Railroad, tells us in a sketch of the life of William B. Foster, Jr., in the *Pennsylvania Railroad Men's News* for August 1897:

On the 5th of April, 1826, Nathan S. Roberts, an experienced engineer from off the New York Canal, was appointed by the Board of Canal Commissioners to proceed to Pittsburgh and locate a line of canal from thence to the Kiskiminetas. Mr. Roberts began his operations April 19th on the Monongahela at the foot of Liberty street, in the city of Pittsburgh, and continued them a distance of seventeen miles up the east side of the Allegheny river, though the opposite side of the river was finally adopted as the location of the canal.

Passing through the property of the elder Foster, Mr. Roberts and his corps were invited to dinner. After dining and about to resume the survey, Mr. Roberts remarked that he was in need of more help, and pointing to William B. Foster, Jr. who was then past seventeen years of age, [William was somewhat older—possibly 19 or 20 years of age in April, 1826] said to the father, "Suppose you let your son go with us, Mr. Foster, and learn to be an engineer." The proposition was accepted, and the young man immediately entered the corps as axeman at a salary of one dollar per day. Promotion followed, and he was soon a rodman, and then a levelman. His quick action, judgment and high moral character advanced him in a short time to the position of Assistant Engineer. He remained with the work until it was completed. For a short time, he served as a Deputy Sheriff of Allegheny County under William Caven.

VI

FROM early childhood, Stephen Foster always was accustomed to music in the home of his parents and their friends, and it was probably as good as any the small town of Pittsburgh then afforded. Pianos were commoner than one would think, for some were brought over the mountains from the East by the arduous means of mule train and canalboat, and other pianos were manufactured right in the town. As early as 1815, and perhaps earlier, a piano-forte maker named Charles Rosenbaum had an establishment on the north side of Front Street, between Wood and Smithfield, where he manufactured square, upright, and even grand pianos on order, at prices of $250 and $300. We do not know if Stephen's mother bought a piano from Mr. Rosenbaum, or brought one with her from her old home in Wilmington, but the following extract from her reminiscences indicates that the Fosters had one as early as 1818. Mrs. Foster is describing an evening at home when some friends and neighbors had dropped in.

After spending at least a half hour in the nursery, I returned again to the parlour, leading Charlotte by the hand, who turned her attention to some pictures that were lying on the table.

"Come, Charlotte," said Mrs. Febiger, "before I ride, sing and play some of those favorite little airs of yours."

Charlotte lifted her soft blue eyes and looked sweetly at Mrs. Febiger. She did not whine, nor look affected, nor did she undertake to excuse herself by saying she had a cold, or other such reprehensible device, but walked modestly to the piano, and seating herself, sang *There's nothing true but heaven* in a manner that touched the feelings and moved the hearts of all present.

"It is alas the case," said Mrs. Woolley, "that we are continually de-ceived with the glitter of a delusive world. My dear little Charlotte, there is so much pathos in your song, do not leave the instrument until you have given us another."

Charlotte immediately complied, then rose, and slightly curtsying, with a gentle "Good night," left the room.

"How old is she, Mrs. Foster?" said Mrs. Febiger.

"Not quite nine years," I answered.

"She is much beyond her years in accomplishment," observed Mrs. Woolley.

Reference to a piano is also made by Mrs. Foster in her letter to Charlotte at St. Joseph's Academy, in 1821. In 1825, the family must have been without a piano, for Charlotte's father wrote to her, "Ann Eliza goes every day to Mrs. Malory's to practice on her piano—poor Mr. Malory is still in ill health. He says Ann Eliza plays and sings better than any person of her age he ever saw."

In 1828, when Stephen was two years old, kind Brother William surprised his sisters by purchasing them a brand new piano, "handsome and well-toned." William was doing well then in his new position as an engineer on the Pennsylvania Canal near Kiskiminetas, and was earning the fine salary of $3.50 a day. It is interesting to note that when his salary was raised to this sum, the boy's first thought was not for himself, but of his sisters' desire for a piano. The idea of getting a piano for any of his brothers to practice on did not occur then to the kind elder brother, nor to his mother or father. Music as a profession for a man, no matter how gifted he might be, had never been considered by any member of the family. Composers were regarded as far-off mighty geniuses on heights of glory never even dreamed of for one's own family. Copies of new songs by J. Hook, R. C. Spofforth, Th. H. Bayly, and Thomas Moore were loaned from one pioneer family to another, and handled with the reverence accorded volumes of Holy Writ. It was only by his own persistent efforts that Stephen acquired what knowledge he had of music though brought up in a family where skill in playing the piano and harp was regarded as the first requisite in a cultured young lady's education. Stephen's mother was amongst the first to recognize his unusual talent, and was anxious that he have a clarinet when William took him away to boarding school at Athens, Pennsylvania. The little boy who leaned against the piano whilst his sisters charmed their admiring family circle with "Come Rest in This Bosom," "Go, My Love," "Like the Gloom of Night Retiring," "Flow on, Thou Shining River," "I Have Loved Thee, Mary," "Home, Sweet Home," "I'd Be a Butterfly," and "Susan in the Valley" was probably of the same opinion as the relatives in Louisville, of whom Charlotte wrote with pleased surprise, "Would you believe it, they think I sing delightfully!" The girls must have been satisfactory performers, or their efforts would not have been patiently received by their father. In the scrapbook which he kept from 1825 for about twenty years, he has pasted the following clipping from an 1830 issue of Mr. Gales's *National Intelligencer*:

MESSRS. EDITORS: Music is, doubtless, a delightful accomplishment, it "hath charms to soothe the savage breast, soften dull rocks," and so forth; "the man who hath not music in his soul is fit for—" and so forth. All this I believe and acknowledge to be true. But, I would humbly submit to the young ladies of this precocious, intellectual and highly accomplished generation, that all the sounds which are produceable from a piano are not Music! Oh! is it not a torture to "sit with sad civility" and listen to that disease (excuse the bull) called a popular song? Why, the thing is more contagious than the cholera. Every amateur catches a popular tune; and one has to listen to it for the thousand and first time, varied only by the blunders and affectation of the player. Oh! parents! why will ye, in despite of Gall, and in contempt of Spurzheim, make your daughters learn music as a *mantrap,* whether they have the organ developed on their pericrania or not? Oh! Satan, what a sad blunderer you were to kill Job's daughters! Why did you not teach them to play on the piano, and sing "Come Rest in This Bosom!" Your business would have been done at once, you silly fiend. Job could not have stood it—he would have cursed and died. M.

William B. Foster, Sr., took frequent part himself in the family's evening concerts though his contributions were in a lighter vein and could hardly be listed among the classics. One of his ribald old tunes was about an agreeable milkmaid named Dorothy Draggletail; another that Morrison remembered hearing his father sing over and over, to the never-failing delight of all the children, was called "The Three Rogues." It went like this:

> In the good old Colony days
> When we were under the King,
> Three roguish chaps
> Fell into mishaps
> Because they could not sing.

> The first he was a miller,
> The second he was a weaver,
> And the third, he WERE
> A little tail-ER,
> Three roguish chaps together.

> The miller he stole corn,
> The weaver he stole yarn,
> And the little tail-OR
> Stole broadcloth FOR
> To keep these three rogues warm.

The miller got drown'd in his dam,
The weaver got hung in his yarn,
And the devil clapped his CLAW
On the little tail-AW
With the broadcloth under his arm!

VII

THE "bowery" dinner which was given in Foster's woods on July 4, 1826, was remembered perfectly by Ann Eliza, who was fourteen years old at the time. She writes:

The mention of the celebration of the Fourth of July brought forcebly to my mind the one which occurred in 1826 on the day of Stevy's birth, in the woods back of our house. I remember so well how we children were seated at the table and saw and heard all that went on, taken there for the purpose, as I now understand, of keeping the house quiet for our dear Mother. Stephen was born at 12:30 P.M. I also have a distinct recollection of the anxiety expressed by those in attendance at the house, lest the cannons of the national salute should deafen the little infant, not more than an hour or two old.

When the news reached the country of the death on the same day of Thomas Jefferson and John Adams, it created a great deal of speculation in the family connection regarding the future of the baby that had made its appearance at the same time these great men passed from the scene. One of the family's best loved relatives was cousin Susan Clayland (nee Kerr) who lived in Cincinnati and was the wife of Thomas Clayland, a cousin of Stephen's mother. This lively lady wrote to Charlotte soon after she heard that the new baby had arrived.

How does your Ma do, my dear Charlotte, and the little Hero, for I prophesy he will be one, being born on so great and eventful a day. You certainly ought to call him Jefferson or Adams, and no other name.

A few extracts from Susan's chatty letter may well be given here, as they reveal the place that parlor music held in the social life of the day:

Mr. Bosson, the bearer of this, is on his way to Boston, and expressed a wish to become acquainted with some ladies of Pittsburgh, as he intends spending a few days there. From our representations, he expects to find considerable worth and beauty among you, and you must, if you have it in your power while he is there, introduce him to the Collins's and some of the amiables of your Citty, not forgetting to exert your own powers, which in the musical line will delight him, as he is extravagantly fond of the piano. You will no doubt be pleased with the gentleman, as he is good-looking, respectable, polite and agreeable, qualities which are difficult to be found in one gentleman in a certain place not far distant from the junction of the rivers Monongahela and Allegheny; but that I said so, tell it not in Gath, publish it not in Askelon!

Thomas tells me Ann Eliza is as tall as you are, but I am a little incredulous; tell her to write to me, as a letter from her would give us pleasure, and if Mrs. F. would put in a line or two, it would be very acceptable; and for mercy's sake, do not you be as long as your Cousin Charlotte, who has not written to us yet.

. . . I understand there is great dessension among the gentlemen of Pittsburg concerning the canal. I am clear for the Pittsburg side, and am as much interested as if I was there.

There was indeed a great war on between the factions favoring different routes for the canal which was to connect the lake with the Ohio River; in August, 1828, the battle was still raging in the legislature. "The Pittsburgh side" (that is, the route from the mouth of the Kiskiminetas by the Allegheny, French Creek, Conneaut Lake, and Elk Creek, to Erie Harbor) finally won out over the route through Meadville and Waterford.

To go on with Cousin Susan's letter:

Mrs. Marshall returned from Pittsburgh not apparently much in love with it. I was at a party at her house the other evening, it was pleasant enough; there was no dancing fortunately for without it we were nearly baked, the evening was so excessively warm. It was a small party, there were plenty of *fellows* as Sarah calls them. They sometimes have three or four parties in one evening, and are well supplied with gentlemen at all of them. With some young ladies, Charlotte, this would be an inducement to visit this place, though I know it would not with you. I promise you when you come you have a beau every time you go in the street, for the gentlemen here are remarkably gallant; and generally fond of music. There is scarcely a young lady in this place that plays well on the piano, I have heard none except Miss Lea who does not reside here now. . . . Sarah sends her love to you, she has just gone out to take a ride with Miss Keys and Mr. Brackenridge. Mr. B. talks of going to Pitts. to live.

We are going to a little musical party tonight at a Mr. Kanoe's who himself exceeds everything I ever heard on the flute. I wish you were here to go with us, as you are such a lover of music.

Give my love to your mother and Father and Ann Eliza and kiss little *Jefferson Adams* for me. Thomas desires to be remembered to you all and joins me in the wish of soon seeing you in Cincinnati. Sarah says don't fall in love with Mr. B. as she has some notion of him herself, and does not wish to pull caps with you. Sarah is so much pleased here I will try and keep her all winter, with mother's permission and her own.

Answer this letter immediately, and tell me everything that is passing in black Pitt (some queer things going on there.) What has become of Henry Baldwin? *don't* blush, tis only a friendly enquiry. I don't see why you should be confused—it really makes me suspect that you are not indifferent to each other, as was reported before I left Pittsburgh— but I will say no more about it, because I can't—I have no more paper.

But, before Cousin Susan's letter was written, the little "hero" had already been named in memory of the son of Eliza Foster's girlhood friends whom she had known and loved in the old days on the Eastern Shore of Maryland. This was Mrs. Sarah Lowrey Collins, daughter of Colonel Stephen Lowrey, of Centreville, Maryland. Her husband was Thomas Collins, a very prosperous and prominent attorney of Pittsburgh. Like the Reverend John Taylor, Mr. Collins was born in Ireland, and was a graduate of Trinity College, Dublin. Eliza Foster was married and came to Pittsburgh in 1807, and her friend Sarah Lowrey was married and joined her in the "western country" the following year. When Stephen C. Foster was born in the White Cottage in Lawrenceville, the Collins's were residing downtown in a fine mansion on Penn Street, near Fourth. (They moved to their country place, "Whitehall," in Lawrenceville, in the spring of 1833.) The family consisted of four daughters, Valeria, Lydia, Margaret, and Sarah; an only son had died recently at the age of twelve years. The close friendship of their early days remained unbroken after the two young brides from Maryland established

their new homes in "black Pitt," and on the afternoon of July 4,
1826, shortly after half-past twelve a message was sent to Mrs. Collins by William B. Foster from the White Cottage, "The baby is
a boy, and is to be named for your son, Stephen Collins."

Stephen was baptized on April 22, 1827, in Trinity Episcopal
Church. He was a delicate child, if we can judge from the number
of anxious inquiries made by Charlotte and William when they
wrote home. When he was a year old, he was very ill with summer
complaint, and we have records of two cases of whooping cough
before he was seven, and another attack when he was about ten
years old. While it probably was not a true case of whooping cough
each time, the little fellow was evidently racked by coughing spells
severe enough to make his mother think he had it again. His father's
scrapbook contains a cure for whooping cough, with the word
"cure" encircled, which might have been the means of restoring
Stephen to health, but unfortunately was not efficacious in the
case of his baby brother, Jim. It is given below, and I leave it for
good physicians to decide whether the prescription was what cured
Stephen, or his mother's loving care.

20 grains salt of Tartar
10 grains of Cochineal
1 oz. refined sugar dissolved in 1
gill warm water.

1 Teaspoonful three times a day, for
a child 4 to 5 years old; and a
little every time the cough is
troublesome.

Many disastrous epidemics visited Pittsburgh, and the most fear-
some seem to have been cholera and "putrid sore throat" which,
in all probability, was what we call diphtheria today. Stephen's
mother was in continual demand by the neighbors of Lawrenceville,
for she was an excellent nurse, as the following letter indicates. It
is from little Ann Eliza to her sister Charlotte, who was then visiting
relatives in Meadville.

> The White Cottage, Pittsburgh July 29,
> 1825

Dear Sister,

You must be anxious by this time to hear the little news of our neighbourhood and family. There has been much alarm about the putrid
sore throat in the village, and Ma sent for the doctor and nursed Tom

[Tom Hunter] for two days, thinking he had it, but it turned out to be a toothache that swelled his jaw; so that alarm has subsided.

Mrs. Malary's infant has been at the point of death, and Ma sat up two or three nights with it. Mrs. Correy put little Frank out at Mammy Goshin's, where he died last Wednesday. Ma went to see Mrs. Correy and found her very friendly; she brought a Miss Billings up with her from Germantown; and left Emily in Philadelphia for a while.

I cannot tell you much about Pittsburgh for I have not seen it since you left me. Cousin Thomas [Clayland] has returned from Bedford, he says that Vally Collins is a great belle there, and much admired by Mr. Eaustace from the east, who is going to Saratoga Springs. Mrs. Collins is going after him, she sent up in great haste for Mr. Malary's carriage, but one of the horses was lame and it could not go.

I heard that Harry Hunter is dead. Oh, I forgot to tell you that Caroline Grace is gone to Saratoga Springs.

Law me, I forgot to tell you when I was talking about the neighbours, that Mrs. Churchill had a baby.

I have goten a new straw hat trimed with yellow ribands. Little Mitsh [Morrison] has worn out his hat, and every time Ma goes to town he says, Ma, na me new hat. While I am sitting here in the Hall writing he is pulling the carpet entirely off and thrown it on the front porch. Last Saterday Jim Read was standing in the yard and Eleck Foster was talking about the poor, and Mitsh said, That is not a good Jim Poe, meaning Jim Read. Anna Poe has gone to Philadelphia with the relation she met at Bedford to finish her education. I have just recovered from a very sick spell, but at present our family is very well.

Henry minds the pigs every day; he joins his love with the rest of the family to you. I have nothing else to say, but that I still remain,

Your affectionate Sister,

Ann E. Foster.

In 1825, "Mitsh" was still the baby of the family, and his little sayings and doings were of vital import to all the older members. His father called him his "little cotton picker," and writing to Charlotte a week later than Ann Eliza's letter, said, "Little Mitch is pulling down my wafers and paper."

"Tom," mentioned in Ann Eliza's letter, was Tom Hunter, a bound boy, who was born at the White Cottage on September 14, 1818, the same day as Henrietta Foster. His father was a soldier at the arsenal, and his mother was a servant at the White Cottage. Shortly before Tom was born, Private Hunter, in a fit of temper, one day threw his wife down the stairway, knocking her senseless. (We do not know whether this distressing incident occurred at the White Cottage or not.) Thinking he had killed her, Hunter rushed down to the Allegheny River and drowned himself. The deep spot from which his body was recovered was known thereafter as Hunter's Hole, and fearfully avoided by the children after dusk began to fall. Tom was brought up at the White Cottage, and was a devoted comrade and playmate of the little boys. He lived with the Fosters at intervals until his sixteenth year when he struck out for the great West and an unknown destiny.

VIII

IN the spring of 1828, William B. Foster was still in Harrisburg, having been re-elected to the Pennsylvania Assembly, and Brother William was in Kiskiminetas working on the canal with a surveying squad. The Grace family, cousins of Eliza Foster from Baltimore, had been living in Pittsburgh for several years, and their possession of a piano proved a great boon to Charlotte, in the pianoless state of her own home at that time. When the Graces returned to Baltimore, the following letter from Charlotte to William shows that she grieved not only for the loss of her cousin's company, but for Caroline's piano as well.

March 17, 1828

Dear Brother,

Ma receiv'd your letter telling of your safe arrival. I suppose you are anxious to hear how the children are. They have recovered. Stevy is not quite well, he is still very weak.

We had a smart shock of Earthquake on Sunday week between 11 and 12 o'clock. Not one of our family felt it. There were two shocks in close succession. Mr. Correy [Mr. Correy was the cashier of the Bank of the United States] thought some one was getting in to rob the bank, and got his pistol ready to fire it. Dr. Denny thought some person was under the bed and took his sword cane and push'd with it for the purpose of bringing the robber out, but all was silent. The next morning all who were disturb'd found the thief to be an Earthquake. I hope it is the last for nothing is so alarming.

Caroline Grace is still with us. I do not know what I shall do when she and the piano are gone. I do wish you could spare me enough to go to Cincinnati, but it is hard to ask you when I know you have sent so much to Pa. Ann Eliza was at home yesterday, she is quite well. When do you think you will be home again?

I suppose you have heard of the duel at Harrisburgh. I believe they did not fight but shook hands when they got to the ground.

Caroline came in just now and says Mary Herron tol'd her that Miss Johnston and Andrew Harris are to be married tomorrow morning at 9 oclock, that Mr. Herron is engaged to marry them. He has succeeded at last.

I have no more news to tell you.

Your affectionate Sister,
Charlotte S. Foster.

Caroline Grace was greatly attached to her Pittsburgh cousins, for when she reached Baltimore in April, she wrote to Charlotte:

You no doubt by this time wish to know something of her who so long shared in all your pleasures and pains. When I left your City, I felt as though I and happiness had shaken hands forever, and when the stage rolled from the door and those last friends (who were kind enough to stay with me to the last) had bid me farewell—Charlotte, my feelings can better be imagined than described. I had before suppressed my feelings to almost a suffocating degree, but the final word made a child of me.—Oh! how I long to see you all. I just imagine you and I sitting in our little room (I still call it ours), and then again I fancy myself sitting there alone, when all at once I see you and John coming arm in arm from Church, and again the report of a cannon draws us all to the door, when lo! and behold! it is the signal of the departure of the *Shamrock;* and then we see a sylph-like form clothed in white glide swiftly down the bank & lean in pensive melancholy against a post, while the boat passes, when with a convulsive sigh she—vanishes!

After this romantic flight of fancy (which leaves the reader in doubt as to which gave the "convulsive sigh," the *Shamrock* or the "sylph-like form," and entirely in the dark about which of the two "vanished"), little Caroline recovers her breath and has a word to say about the fashions, a subject of never-failing interest, even to the mourning heart.

Charlotte [her sister] has a most splendid pink gros de Naples bonnet; she and Eliza went out shopping today; unfortunately, Charlotte's bonnet was so large she got stuck fast in the door of a Milliner's shop. I have a light blue one, exactly like it. Tell Mrs. Correy the lady's here were large leghorn flats, the uglyest things she ever saw, with caps behind.—They also were trowsers—you know what a long confab you, Ann Eliza and I had on that subject. . . . Father says he would give anything to hear you play the Swiss Waltz again.

It is quite possible that the "John" to whom Caroline refers was young John Gormley, who was a frequent caller at the White Cottage. Charlotte Foster was still engrossed, however, with Henry Baldwin, Jr., and received a great deal of teasing from cousin Susan Clayland on that score.

While her sister and cousin Caroline Grace were engaged in more frivolous pursuits, Ann Eliza was diligently pursuing her studies at the Episcopal Institute, a boarding and day school conducted by the Reverend John H. Hopkins in his home on Western Avenue, Allegheny (now part of Pittsburgh). It was here Ann Eliza entered into a shy friendship with a young theological student who was destined to play the most important role in her future life. Edward Young Buchanan was one of Mr. Hopkins' most promising pupils. The minister was as devoted to Edward as to a son, and successfully directed the young man's inclinations and ambitions into the ministry of the Protestant Episcopal Church. The Buchanan family were originally from Mercersburg, where Edward was born, but they had lived in Allegheny some time before Edward went to study with Reverend John H. Hopkins. There were several Buchanan girls (Mrs. Henry, Mrs. Lane, and Mrs. Yates) and three sons, Edward Y., George (a delicate boy who died in the 1830's), and James I. Buchanan, President of the United States from 1857 to 1861.

The religious atmosphere of Mr. Hopkins' home made a great impression on naturally devout little Ann Eliza, as can be seen from

The Reverend Edward Young Buchanan and his wife, Ann Eliza Foster

Composition dedicated to the sister of Stephen Collins, after whom
Stephen Collins Foster was named; probably published in the late 1820's

the following letter which she sent to her father in Harrisburg. Some of the startling exhortations and pious admonitions which it contains sound as though they had been quoted directly from pulpit utterances of her pastor-teacher. At various times in their lives, William B. Foster's worried daughters, Ann Eliza and Henrietta, made attempts to snatch that cheerful and unperturbed brand from the burning, but we have no record that they made any serious impression on the amiable man. He went serenely on his way, loving his neighbor, and praising the Lord, always a churchgoer, but not a member for some reason of his own. Years after, Ann Eliza, who despite her deeply spiritual trend was blessed with a sense of humor and a sympathetic understanding of the motives of others, deplored the unctious tone of her youthful efforts to convert her family, and wrote to Morrison:

Although I found nothing in them [some early letters Morrison had desired to read] which I would have the least objection to your seeing, I confess to have taken such a disgust to the twaddle and egotism they contained, to say nothing of wretched writing, that I could not bring myself to the idea that any human being should see them, and so consigned them at once to the "devouring flames." It takes a long life to get all the nonsense out of us, & we are happy if we can get over the worst kind even then; & I should think there were not a great many persons who could look over the effusions of their early life with any satisfaction—at all events, if they have been no wiser or better than I have been!

The following gem escaped the "devouring flames," and we ask Ann Eliza's forgiveness for reproducing it now, but feel sure she would regard it with the same loving amusement felt by her father when he first perused it in his "lodging at Mr. Wilson's near the House of Representatives."

Pittsburgh, March 23rd 1828

Dear father,

I was very aggreeably surprised yesterday at receiving a letter from you, for I confess that I was growing a little impatient. I hope that the injury you received is not a serious one, but however trifling, do, dear father, be careful of it, for you know from what a slight cause the loss of your left hand proceeded. In this very instance, I have often thought that we have cause to be abundantly thankful that a Merciful Providence has preserved that hand that is of so much importance to you in the support of the family which has been lent you. As far as I can see back, we have been the especial care of our Maker, otherwise we never could have stood, for you know my dear father, that you have surmounted difficulties which beforehand it seemed impossible to overcome and I can ascribe it to no other cause than that of the Lord of Hosts watching over us and guarding us from all the perils that seemed to await us. Oh, what a dreary time it was when you (our only earthly supporter) were stretched on what all thought to be your bed of death. No one can imagine the feelings that took possession of even my heart though at that time at an age when sorrow is likely to make but a slight impression and when we are not very likely to weigh the future consequence of present miseries. To my imperfect view, the scene was full of darkness and despair. What then must have been the anguish of that dear Mother, who knew so well what our situation would be if you were taken away; with a large family of young children, none capable of alleviating the anxiety or relieving the burden except the two oldest. But God did not forsake us, He not only spared you, but also raised another protector in the person of our dear brother, and you can tell the bitterness of sorrow which we all experienced when sickness brought him low, and daily and hourly we expected to see him numbered with the dead.

There too was a hair-breadth escape, we were not yet to be left destitute, and our unthankful hearts contentedly ascribed it to the skill of the physician and thought no more of it. All that the Lord does is for some wise though unseen purpose, and we are not to suppose that all these manifold blessings were conferred on us merely for our gratification (though he indulges us in numberless pleasures and does not willingly afflict us.) And I hope that the day is at hand when his gracious design shall be divulged in seeing us all (the creatures of his bounty) joining to render him that praise which is due to him and that homage which He requires of us.

Ever since I can recollect, every coming year had a more formidable aspect than the preceeding one, and it seemed almost impossible to withstand the storm any longer, but all difficulties were cleared and at its end when we looked back we scarcely knew how we had passed over them. The Eye that rules the Universe was upon us and the strong arm that reaches through Eternity upheld us; and with such stays we could rest secure, though misery in its new & hideous forms was staring us in the face. [!]

Oh, father, unworthy as we are, there is still a Mediator for us above; the blessed attonement has been made for us and God only waits to be gracious. Jesus long since ascended to the throne of his Father after having with his own precious blood removed the stain that rested upon us, and no man comes to the Father but by him. There is unspeakable delight in the idea of owing our redemption to the mediation of the blessed son of God himself which cannot be uttered and I fear not deeply enough felt.

I fear dear father that my letter is growing rather tiresome, and if I were to say all that I wish to say, it would take up more time than I have at my disposal this afternoon, and more of your time than you can conveniently spare, and as I write every week there is no danger but that you will hear, and I write as much as could be expected.

I was very sorry to hear you say that the Legislature would not adjourn until the 15th of April, as I had every reason to expect that I would see you before that time. I will have to bid you good bye rather abruptly, dear father, for Ma has just sent Henry out to know if I would not come home to spend the night with them, and as Mr. Hopkins has given his consent, I intend accompanying him immediately; Henry is very well and so I presume are all the family, and lastly so is

Your affectionate daughter

Ann Eliza

Almost drowned in the flood of "highfalutin" theological phrases poured out by Reverend Hopkins' zealous young student, appear several interesting bits of information concerning the family affairs during Stephen's infancy. We learn that their father had lost his left hand, probably from blood poisoning, which occasioned a long and anxious siege of nursing. We know that the finances of the household ran very low after William B. Foster's loans to the government forced him to raise money frequently by the method which he himself described as "flying a kite." The loss of the White Cottage two months before Stephen was born was a terrible blow; furthermore, many persons who had bought Lawrenceville lots on a time payment plan, were not able to meet their notes when they fell due. Consequently, William B. Foster could not meet his own. Then, when Brother William was old enough to step into the breach with his help, he also was brought low by an almost fatal sickness. Theirs was like any other household where there is a large family of children, and their mother was harrassed by the usual cares that accompany financial worries and the struggle to keep them all well in an age when medical knowledge was so meagre. Each year brought more responsibilities though conditions were hardly as bad as Ann Eliza pictured with youthful and enthusiastic exaggeration, "misery in its new & hideous forms was staring us in the face"!

Poor little Ann Eliza! Just a little over a year after the foregoing letter was written, she experienced real grief, and her scene was really full of darkness and despair when she lost her adored older sister, Charlotte. It was soon no longer necessary for her to conjure up imaginary afflictions, for genuine ones became plentiful. At the age of fifty-three, she wrote to Morrison:

Her [Charlotte's] death was my first great sorrow, and my feelings have never entirely emerged from the shadow it cast upon them. I still dream of her at intervals. I am told she is not dead! I am taken to see her! She looks naturally at first, and I am in a transport of delight, but she soon changes and finally fades away & I wake up with the bitter feeling that it was all too true after all. Well, it cannot be very long before I shall really meet her where there will be no danger of disappointment.

IX

IN May, 1828, Charlotte set out on the *Waverley,* one of the favorite steamboats of the day, to visit her parents' friends and relatives in Cincinnati and Louisville. Young girls of 1828 did not travel unless accompanied by older people, and Charlotte was placed in care of Mr. and Mrs. Henry Baldwin. Mrs. Baldwin took delight in introducing her charming young friend to the people of Cincinnati, and attentions of the kindest sort were showered upon her. The happy girl wrote long, enthusiastic letters to her home folks, mentioning many names that will be familiar to readers of Cincinnati and Louisville.

Cincinnati May 29, 1828

My Dear Mother

Since I last wrote you we have been at several parties—one last week at Mrs. Benson's. She entertains company very handsomely and is an agreeable woman. We had strawberries in abundance, danced to the piano once or twice, the rest of the time promenading the room arm in arm with different beaux, it being very customary here. My gallant was Mr. Findley. On Saturday last, I spent the day with Ann Marshall, that is dined at Mr. Cassily's. Ann is very well married, the Dr. is highly respected. In the afternoon, I went with a small party to Longworth's garden; Miss Jones, Miss Currey, Miss Barker, Mrs. Davenport, Mrs. Currey, Mrs. Baldwin, Major Davenport, Mr. Burnet, Mr. Foster, Mr. Curry, and Mr. Lytle with me. It is a lovely spot, we seated ourselves around a table under a grove of impenetrable shade, and partook of strawberries and cream. Having saunter'd about until sunset, we return'd home to tea. After tea, we went to the museum, Mr. Lytle my attendant; the next day being Sunday, he call'd and escorted me to church. On Monday, I went to another canal party—we started directly after dinner and returned at bed time. Mr. and Mrs. Baldwin were along. The party consisted of about 30 persons, we had a band of music and danced. Mr. Findley was my gallant. I am a great deal with Mrs. Baldwin, we return all our calls together. I have dined at the hotell three or four times, and see her every day. She is delighted with Cincinnati and talks of going to Louisville. On Wednesday, we were at a party at Mrs. Kilgore's, she lives in one of the most beautiful situations I have seen. It is elevated and overlooks the Ohio, as you ascend to the house, there is an avenue of trees from the river to the top of the hill. It was one of the most beautiful moonlight nights, which made the place look still more romantic. There was no dancing; music, conversation and promenading were the amusements. Miss Curry and myself play'd and sang several songs and a duett together; she is a young lady from Virginia on a visit here who has one of the sweetest voices I ever heard. She and myself are very intimate. I see her every day. We are the only young ladies who play and sing of my acquaintance here. Mr. Lytle was my attendant. At about 11 oclock, we were handed to supper, and one of the most exquisit! Of course strawberries abounded. It reminded me of Mrs. Talcott's party, the table being quite as tastefully arranged. This evening Mrs. Baldwin and myself are invited to two different houses, and tomorrow there is to be another party to which I will go if the boat does not arrive. I look for it, but not very anxiously while Cincinnati is so attractive. The people are not willing to let me go—at least they flatter me by saying so. I would prefer going now before the weather grows too warm, hard as it is to tear myself away.

The greatest anoyance I have had since my arrival is that abomanable chip bonnet, which began before I left home. Being out in the wind, it is torn and out of shape every way. I must either wear my trav'ling bonnet, or get a new one when I get to Louisville. If Pa has return'd, perhaps you could send me some money to get it with. I am provoked that I did not get a silk one at first.

I suppose Mr. Biddle has not gone yet; when you see him tell him I wish he could hear Miss Curry sing "Ide be a Butterfly", it is a favourite song of his. She is not much larger than the insect itself and the song is appropos.

If Rebecka Dunholand wants to come here, now is the time. Mrs. Lea told me to tell you to tell her she will insure her a place in the family, either at Thomas Lea's or Mrs. Febigers. The wage is 1 dollar and 50 cents per week, and good girls very scarce. As I promis'd to let Miss Thomson the miliner know if there was any opening here for her, I feel it my duty to do so. The ladies I have asked think there is no encouragement here; they send to Philadelphia, and many make their own bonnets.

Yours affectionately,

Charlotte.

Charlotte knew and shared the family's enthusiasm on the subjects of canals and Andrew Jackson, and when writing to Brother William or "Pa," she was careful to mention the former and cheer them with news of the "ould Ginneral's" progress in the South. In a letter to her older brother written June 13, 1828, she says:

I spent two weeks in Cincinnati delightfully, it is the most beautiful city in the Western country. To me who had been accustomed to see houses look black, it appear'd to have been all built in a week. The country around is very pretty, I went 10 miles up the Canal and pass'd through several locks. I think on a long journey it would be tedious, I should prefer a Steamboat, although it is more dangerous. The Portland Canal digging here is wide enough to admit steamboats, but you hear enough of Canals where you are, I will change the subject, perhaps Politicks will do. In Cincinnati, it is the constant theme of conversation even among ladies. In this state, although it is Mr. Clay's, Mr. Baldwin was highly honored. In Cincinnati, they gave him a Jackson dinner at which Mr. Lytle who was secretary told me more than 6 hundred sat down. It was call'd a Jackson Tarrif dinner. Mr. B. made a long speech, I saw it in a Louisville paper yesterday. You have no idea of the great respect that was shown him.

Early in June, Charlotte tied the strings of her "abomanable chip bonnet" under her adorable chin, was escorted to the Cincinnati wharf by a host of loving friends and beaux, and under the chaperonage of one of Mrs. Baldwin's friends, a lady of unchallenged respectability, sailed away on the steamboat for Louisville, to be received there with open arms by her father's relatives, Joshua G. Barclay, his wife, Cousin Sally, and their little girls, Kitty and Mary. Soon after she arrived, the Rowan ladies, Ann, Josephine, and Eliza, daughters of Judge John Rowan of Bardstown, Kentucky, called upon her and urged her to make them a visit. "They claimed connection with Pa," Charlotte said. Although William B. Foster and Judge Rowan were related through their mothers' family, the Barclays, their two households had not been acquainted with each other before this time. Charlotte soon made friends on every hand, as the following letter to her mother shows.

Louisville, August 12, 1828

My dear Mother,

Since my last letter to Ann Eliza, I have been in the country. I believe I told her I was going, we returned this morning. Our party consisted of Miss Mary and Matilda Prather and myself. When we got to Mrs. Pearce's we found Mr. & Mrs. Paine there, a young and very sprightly lady. I have just proceeded this far in my letter when Cousin came in with one from Ann Eliza dated the 6th. It gave me great pleasure as I had been looking anxiously all day for one and shall sleep more soundly at night knowing you are all well. I received a letter from Brother William telling me of the Piano. You, my dear Mother, who know almost my thoughts on every subject, can imagine how delighted I was, not from merely selfish views which would be sufficient to delight me, but now my dear Sisters will have the advantage of learning and practising— it must have been a day of rejoicing when it was brought home. It is well I was not there, I should have behaved like a fool. Ann Eliza must practice a great deal. Although so many ladies learn to play, I have seen only two or three who you would like to hear; while I was at Mrs.

Pearce's they kept me playing constantly and singing. Miss Sarah Pearce plays very well on both the Piano and Harp, but does not sing. Since I have been there, she has been trying her best in the vocal way. The girls think Go, my Love and Like the Gloom of Night Retireing more beautifull than any they have ever heard, and would you believe it, they think I sing delightfully.

I think a Kentucky farmers life is very happy, those who are rich and have their negros and overseer as Mrs. Pearce has; when the gentlemen come from Town, they never think of returning, but have their horses and themselves provided for, sometimes they had more than a dozen to breakfast. Mr. Prather and Mr. Churchill came out almost every day, and Mr. Nicholas Grason and others; it reminded me of the happy times I used to spend in the country at home. Every one felt perfectly at their ease. Mrs. Pearce seems to have taken a fancy to me, she took me in her arms and hug'd me saying at the same time she did not know what made her love me so much. I think if I could be spoil'd I would have been, the girls every night bespoke who should sleep with me, and always express that warm affection that is easly distinguished from incincerity.

I mentioned in my last our intention of going to Bardstown, I shall go as soon as convenient for Mr. Barclay. The day before I went to Mrs. Pearce's the last time, Miss Louisa Bullitt, sister of Mrs. General Atkinson, came with her brother (Washington) and Captain Hopson to ask me to go to Bardstown with them. I was to go in a gig with her brother, and she with Capt. H. but I declined going; perhaps I was a little prudish on the subject, I did not like the idea of two young ladies and gentlemen traveling without a married person. Miss Bullitt might have gone as she had her brother, but I was a stranger, and *Prudence* said stay. I will perhaps go with Mr. Barclay this week or next.

There has been great excitement in the election, the Jackson candidates for the Legislature were elected, but it is very doubtful whether the Jackson candidate for Governor will be. All the counties have not been heard from yet, but from what we have heard, *Metcalf,* the Administration candidate is ahead, and the Jacksonites begin to despair of Barry, their man. I hope the luck will turn yet in favour of our cause. Mr. Grayson, who I mentioned above, was one elected to the Legislature; he is call'd a beaux, but *not as young as he used to be.* The young ladies were very anxious for his election, and they were gratifyed.

I must tell you Mrs. Pearce who has been so polite to me is a full cousin of Mr. W. Croghan now in Pittsburgh. She inquires very particu-

"Federal Hill" at Bardstown, "My Old Kentucky Home," and Judge John Rowan

"Cotton Plantation," by H. Lewis

From *Das Illustrirte Mississippithal,* von H. Lewis (Düsseldorf: Arnz & Comp. [1855-1857])

larly for all the O'Hara and Denny clan. If it could be any way accomplished, I should like Mr. Croghan to receive some polite attention
from Pa on account of the attention I have received from his relations
here. Ann Eliza says in her last he is to be confirmed, and I was greatly
surprised.

                    Adieu, my dear Mother,
                         Your affectionate daughter,
                                             Charlotte.

Charlotte hastened to write to Brother William on August 13,
1828, to express her gratitude for the new piano.

You can not imagine, my dear Brother, how delighted I was when
the agreeable news reach'd me you had bought a new Piano and one
so handsome and well-ton'd as Ann Eliza says it is, I am sure it will
hasten my return home, if we had not one I do not believe I would
have return'd before Spring, as it is if nothing hapens, I will return
this Fall. I am glad to hear you say your pay is increas'd, I can only
express my thanks to you by telling you it was one of the hapyest
moments of my life when I read your letter. I should have writen sooner
after receiving yours but have been in the Country more than a week
past at Mrs. Pearce's, she is a rich widdow who lives on a large Farm
and has her negros and Overseer with abundance of evrything good the
country affords. I spent a delightfull time there, there were two other
young ladies beside myself, the Misses Prathers, and Mrs. Pearce has
a daughter just 16 years of age who would suit your taste, she has jet
black eyes, dark hair, is very pretty and plays on the Piano delightfully
and the Harp a little and is rich to boot. . . . There is great excitement
at present about the election for Governor, the Jackson candidate Barry
I am fearfull will be beaten by Metcalf his opponent. All the counties
have not yet been heard from, Metcalf is ahead yet and without a
change in luck will be elected. The candidates for the Legislature
elected are Jacsonians.

When you write tell how the election is going on in our County. I
believe it does not come on untill Octr. but who are the candidates?
I have heard Judge Wilkins is one for Congress;—I want you to tell
me how it is with Pa's appointment, if he is to have a house built him in
Allegheny Town this Fall or not till Spring, and if he receives any pay
yet? These are questions I do not like to ask him but which would be
very satisfactory to me to know.

Adieu my dear Brother, write soon to me. . . . Your affectionate
                                   Sister, C. S. Foster.

In September, Charlotte's parents grew anxious about her health, for news had reached them that cholera and malaria were creeping up the river to Louisville. Many persons are still living who can recall the fury with which these plagues used to sweep the country in the sweltering days of August and September when the rivers were low and the wells went dry. They say that on one occasion cholera struck only one side of the road that passed through Bardstown, sparing the family at "Federal Hill," and all the relatives and neighbors they could crowd into the house who had fled from the "wrong side" of the road. Then there was the fearful danger that they might bury their loved ones too soon, and many harrowing tales were told of supposed victims of the disease regaining consciousness just as they were about to be lowered into their graves. Mrs. Edith W. Howry, of Louisville, who is a granddaughter of Ann Rowan's, informed me that her great-uncle, young Atkinson Hill Rowan, stood guard over one of his friends, and refused to allow his body to be taken to the burying ground, declaring that he was not dead; and that friend came back to life again to live many years, and bless the name of Hill Rowan.

And, alas, Charlotte's mother and father were prophetic in their fears for her safety though they could not foresee how truly justified those fears were. But Charlotte was eager to make her promised visit to "Federal Hill," and did not return to Pittsburgh until the middle of November.

Meantime, state and national elections waxed hot and furious, and William B. Foster, Sr., wrote his daughter on September 7, 1828:

You know I do not enter into the news of the town except a little in politics; tell our friends Barckley, that Kentucky has done her part nobly in her late vote for the Jackson ticket, far beyond what the Hero's friends here expected, and places the election of General Jackson beyond all doubt; tell them they need not fear Pennsylvania, if we do not give a majority of 25 thousand votes for the Jackson electors, I shall be more disappointed than I ever was in my life in an election; notwithstanding all the noise about great changes in favour of Adams. I have no doubt the Generl. will pass through Pittsburgh in January or February next, when I flatter myself with the expected pleasure of hearing you play to him *Hail to the Chief!*

Our election for members of Congress and representatives in the State Legislature grows warm; the contest between Wilkins and Stevenson will be a hard one, and the result somewhat uncertain. They are both Jacksonites. I have declined a re-election to the Legislature, in consequence of the arrangement made with the Board of Canal Commissioners.

Dear little Stephen was very unwell a few days ago, your mother took him out to Gillespies a week; the mosquitoes being very troublesome at our house. He is now quite well, as are all the family.—As the season of fever and ague has now arrived at Louisville, where it prevails, we wish you to embrace the first good opportunity of ascending the river as far as Cincinnati, the water being now too low to come all the way home. I am aware how sensibly you will feel the parting with so many dear friends and acquaintances as you have described to us at Louisville; you will, however, have the consolation to reflect that you are complying with the wishes of your anxious parents, whose will it has ever been your pleasure to perform. Your friends at Louisville may tell you there is no danger, but I do know few strangers remain there during the summer and fall without being attacked with the fever and ague.

The following is Charlotte's reply:

Federal Hill, Bardstown, Sept. 16, 1828

My dear Father,

Your letter in which you express a wish that I should leave Louisville was duly receiv'd. I left that place on Tuesday week last with Judge Rowan, and his daughter; I mentioned in my last to Ann Eliza my intention to come. They claim me as a relation and treat me as such. Judge Rowan insists upon my staying with his family until he goes to Washington City and he will be my escort home; but that I could not think of doing, although I am grateful for the invitation. He will go in November, and it is very probable I will return with him if the River is in order, it will be an excellent opportunity. There is another young lady going to Baltimore under his protection; we came up in the stage.

Bardstown is a beautifull vilige—its Catholick institutions deserve some celebrity, the Cathedral is the finest publick building I have seen, since our own Church. I have not yet visited the Nunery and Coledge, but intend to do so soon. I have two beaux who are ready for my commands, Mr. Rowan's sons; his family consists of four daughters, three sons, one married, and three grandchildren, and there are always visitors. They live in a plain, but farmerlike way, just in sight of town. I spend my time very pleasantly, he has an extensive library. If Sis Ann was here, she might have a feast of literature.

I never met a man so aggreeable to be a great man as Judge Rowan is. I sometimes listen to his conversation until I am lost, and fear to draw my breath lest I should lose a word. His family almost adore him, he is one of the kindest husbands and fathers. He enquired of me about Mr. James Ross—he says he learned his letters of him.

Mrs. Rowan is in a very afflicted state, they are aprehensive she will lose her sight. She has had sore eyes for six weeks and no alteration for the better. She is oblig'd to stay in a dark room constantly.

The evening before I left Louisville, I had a party given expressly for me by Mrs. Prather—I have written so frequently of their attention that you must be well acquainted with the family by this time. Indeed, people in this country are too kind to me, I am afraid I shall be spoil'd, but all the attentions they can bestow will never lessen my attachment for my friends at home, indeed my affection increases with my absence. It will be with the greatest regret I will leave Louisville. It is true this is the season of fever and ague, but I have not heard of any cases yet; where I am at present, there is no possible danger. Bardstown is said to be one of the healthyest places in the world.

I hope my dear Mother's health is again restored. Tell her she must not think too much of my *red head,* two is enough in the family. [William and Charlotte had red hair—Dunning's portrait also shows that his hair was red, but dark.]

How is dear little Stephen? I am uneasy about him. I suppose it is the summer complaint, and teathing. Do write now and tell me how he is. Kiss the dear little pets all for their affectionate Sister,

Charlotte S. Foster.

Stephen must have recovered entirely, for his mother does not mention him in her next letter to Charlotte. All the family, and their circle of friends, were engrossed at this time in preparations for the wedding of Vally Collins to Evan Rees Evans. Vally was the daughter of Mr. and Mrs. Thomas Collins, for whose son Stephen had been named, and was so dear to them all that Charlotte was moved to write as follows:

You tell me again we are to lose our dear Vally; ere this she is Mrs. *Evans.* I cannot realize it. I have had several crying spells about it when

I think of returning home and not finding her there to meet me, but if she is happy, I must be satisfy'd. Mr. E—— is certainly blest in having such a wife, as I am convinc'd she will make. I should like to have seen the *sweet bride*. God bless and protect her and grant her the happiness I think her deserving of.

My dear daughter,   Pittsburgh   October the 4th.

The gentleman who will hand you this letter is a Mr. Lilly, he is from Baltimore, he keeps a fancy store, and seems to be a very genteel man. Robert Grace clercks for him. It was Robert who introduced him to us.

I sent Ann Eliza's frock out to be iron'd for the weding today. I saw Emily Hurst this afternoon who had been at Miss Dicsons for her new dress for the occasion, but notwithstanding all this getting ready, poor Valleria is sick in bed.

Leave is lying in a Billious fever, and John Duncan is very ill.

Ann Eliza has been out riding this afternoon with her new beaux, George Holdship, who presented her with a print box tonight, worth about eight dollars.

Mr. Baldwin told Mr. Foster the other day you were the Belle of Louisville—now is the time to bring her home, said he, as much as to say, before her value is lesson'd.

Your Father is in great spirits about the election of Jackson. I am afraid he is too sanguine.

I will close my letter as Mr. Lilly will call presently for it.

Good night,
Your mother
Eliza C. Foster.

Miss Charlotte Foster,
A. & J. Barckley, Louisville, Ky.
Politeness of Mr. Lilly.

In another of her cheery epistles, cousin Susan Clayland (who now lived in Pittsburgh again) sent Charlotte the latest gossip of their little circle.

Saturday Nov. 8th. 1828

You will be surprised, my dear Charlotte, at recieveing a letter from me, though I ought not to call it a letter, for I have not time to write more than a few lines. Alfred Cochran starts tomorrow for Louisville, your ma has a few things to send with him, and thinks they will be more acceptable if accompanied by a note. Ann Eliza cannot write on account of her French lesson, which she is now taking in the parlour, and your ma is busily engaged sewing; therefore, I am commissioned (nothing loth) to be the channel of communication—now what shall I tell you? I really believe there is nothing worth relating. I believe they do say Lydia Collins has a new beau, Let. Phillip. I think he is a brother of Mr. Phillips of Louisville. Yes, we had sort of a ball the other night, a public ball, given by the dancing master, Mr. Bond. A great many of the young ladies were there, though I believe they did not enjoy themselves much. There is also a concert tonight. Ann E. is going with Charlotte Pettigrew.

You cannot even imagine how spruce Ann Eliza looks in a new suit which she wore today, a beautiful brown silk bonnet, and a Circassian dress of the same colour. She has made divers conquests since you went away, among the rest young Holdship, who has the wheels, you know.

I must hurry and run home and wash all the childrens' faces, and make myself look amiable, for I expect Mr. C. this evening. He has been absent three weeks, been to N. York, Baltimore and Philadelphia. All your family and friends are in perfect health and anxious for your return. Do not make so much havoc down there, if it were only for the many hearts report says you have slain, we must have you home. Be merciful and take compassion on some clever fellow—good ones are scarce here. Farewell, my dear Cousin, I am in a perfect flurry, therefore can write no more, only desire you to burn this scroll whenever read, if read it you can.

Susan Clayland.

In October, the family of Judge Rowan gathered on the steps of "Federal Hill" to bid good-by to their young relative. As more than a hundred years have passed since that farewell was said, I hope it will not be considered a betrayal of confidence to reveal that one of that group watched with a heavy heart as Charlotte stepped into the gig which cousin Joshua Barclay had driven down from Louisville.

Louisville, Octr. 12, 1828

My dear Mother,

On Wednesday last, I return'd home from Judge Rowan's where I spent three weeks very pleasantly. Cousin Joshua came for me. I left the girls all in tears, and I may have the vanity to think the young gentlemen were not a little griev'd at my departure. The family all urged me to remain but I could not be perswaded. Whilst at Federal Hill, I receivd a letter from Pa and one from Ann Eliza. I am sorry you and my dear Father have again begun to be uneasy about me. It is my intention to return home next month if the water will permit. I do not think a few weeks will make a material difference, my health was never better. As much as it is my inclination to remain here, if a good opportunity offer'd I would go to Cincinnati, but merely for this reason, it is Pa's wish. At present, I could not go were I ever so anxious, very few boats are runing and I do not know of any person going under whose protection I could go. You know, my dear Mother, I never deceive intentionally, and if I thought there was danger would tell you. I hope you and dear Father will not think me disobedient and obstinate, but forgive me for arguing the case with you.

Does Cornelius come to see Sis Ann now? She will be a very foolish girl if she slights him, I think him one of the finest little fellows in the world, you do not meet one among a thousand with a mind like his; as he always was a great favorite of mine, remember me to him.—

As for me, I believe I am to be an old maid, I am too hard to please, but is it not better to be one than marry without loving? I will tell you a secret about my late visit to Federal Hill. I tol'd you Mr. R. had two sons at home, the eldest is about 25, a Lawyer, very clever and generally considered handsome; now it must remain between you and I if I tell you he wish'd me to engage myself to him, but as usual I could not love him, and would not do him or myself the injustice to make promises I was not inclined to perform. You may conclude I was glad to get to Louisville again. I suppose he would think I might be glad to get the son of a Senator of the United States and so distinguish'd a man as John Rowan, but I cannot let considerations of this kind influence me when my happiness for life depends upon it. You have always posest my confidence and always shall. I think it a duty from children to parents, but I hope my dear mother will let what I have said go no further as it would appear like boasting in me.

Whilst I was in Bardstown I visited the nunery for the purpose of seeing Eliza Beelen—tell Mrs. Fetterman and Mrs. B——she is very well and appears perfectly happy. When I told her my name she recolected me and was delighted to see me.

Adieu, dear Ma, God bless you all and keep you in health, kiss the dear little chileys for their sister Charlotte and tell them she says they

must be good and mind what Ma and Pa tell them. Once more, Adieu,
                    Your affectionate child, Charlotte.

Young Cornelius Darragh, Charlotte's great favorite, who had
a liking for her more demure sister, Ann Eliza, truly possessed a
fine mind, for he graduated from the Western University of Pennsylvania, Pittsburgh, in 1826, at the age of seventeen, and at the time
Charlotte's letter was written, was studying for the bar to which
he was admitted on motion of George Seldon on November 3, 1829.
A suitor who "had the wheels" like George Holdship was at an advantage over the unfortunate swain who could only ask a young lady
to promenade with him when he wanted to get her away from her
family for a little while. But, since Cornelius was the son of former
Mayor John Darragh, doubtless he also had some wheels, perhaps
a high two-wheeled gig, dashing and dangerous. Considering that
Ann Eliza was such a "quiet little thing," she seemed not to have
lacked attention from some of the city's most desirable beaux.

Charlotte left for home in November on the *Waverley*. Her
mother was not well, little Stephen still ailing, and their good colored
Lieve lying in a "billious fever," so she was needed at home to relieve
the faithful Ann Eliza. But, in the meantime, she had found in a
few short weeks that if she could not give her heart to "handsome
Cousin John," there was a place she could bestow it without reserva-
tion, and on none other than "dignified Mr. William Prather,"
brother of her friends, Mary and Matilda Prather. From Charlotte
herself, we learn nothing about the personal characteristics of her
fiance. We know he made a special visit to Pittsburgh to see her
father and mother, but the date is not designated. We can be sure
that Charlotte loved him truly, for she had ample opportunities
to choose another for a husband had she wanted to. William Prather
was the son of Thomas Prather, one of Louisville's pioneer citizens,
who crossed the Wilderness Trail from Maryland and opened a
store in Louisville in 1794. His wife was Matilda Fontaine. They
lived in a beautiful home in the center of the town, bounded by
four streets, Third and Fourth, Walnut and Green. The present-
day Broadway in Louisville was originally known as Prather Street.
There were seven young people in the Prather family when Charlotte Foster knew and loved them—William and James, Matilda,

Mary Jane, Maria, Catherine, and Emmeline. (Some time after Charlotte died, William Prather married Penelope Pope, of Louisville.)

On November 30, 1828, cousin Joshua Barclay wrote to her that when he went to meet the *Waverley* on the steamer's return trip from Pittsburgh, in hopes of receiving a letter from his "other daughter Charlotte"—"Who do you think I overtook going there also? If you can't guess, it was Mr. Prather and Mr. Rowan making the same inquiries that I was, and that you can pretty near tell!"

Another note from Cousin Joshua to Charlotte, after she had returned home, contains little items of Louisville news which he knew would interest her, and also may interest Louisville readers today.

Louisville 14th Decr. 1828

Miss Charlotte S. Foster

Dear Cousin

Your little note with Books came safe to hand and I delivered them as you requested. About 2 weeks since Miss Garrard lost her Mother, which induces Mr. Ernest to provide for her—they are to be Married very soon, so says Mrs. Gwathmey, her sister, which is very good authority,—and on the last day of this month Miss Mary Ann Robertson is to be married to Mr. Anderson.

I was at a party last night at Mr. Silas Fields and Mr. Nicholas told me he was to start today for Pittsburg. I cant tell whether he was in ernest or not.

. . . Old Lady Wheeler is with us waiting an oppy. [sic] to visit her relatives at Wheeling and Wellsburgh.—I have got our Piano Fort tuned ready for you against you come home. Recollect you are not to be disapointed in our contemplated visit in Jany. with Mr. P. as I before stated.

I have nothing of importance to say to you now, but hope to have the pleasure of communicating any that may be verbally in the course of three weeks.

We are all in good health. My sweetheart joins in the purest of Love and sincere Affection for you *our oldest daughter* with a large proportion to the rest of your family.

Your Affect. Cousin,

J. G. Barclay.

Cousin Joshua made good his promise to visit Pittsburgh, and arrived late in January, 1829, alone. What a disappointment it must have been to Charlotte and Ann Eliza that the young Prather folks, William, Emmeline, and Mary Jane, who had planned to accompany Mr. Barclay on his trip to Pittsburgh, were prevented from coming by the death of a near relative.

The last little Foster, James Clayland, was born on February 3, 1829. The Foster family were getting along happily enough, as the first shock of losing the Lawrenceville home had worn off somewhat. William B. Foster had been appointed collector of tolls on the preceding August 10, 1828, on the Pittsburgh-Blairsville Canal, still under construction. Until the canal was completed, and the water let in, there were no tolls to collect, but before the water reached Pittsburgh, William B. Foster's letters show that he was very busy with preliminary work that kept him traveling frequently between Pittsburgh and Blairsville. The family had moved from the White Cottage to a house on Water Street, the location of which we do not know. William B. Foster still continued his dealings in Lawrenceville and other real estate.

Cousin Joshua returned to Louisville at the end of February, and took Ann Eliza back with him. As their mother and Baby Jim were both doing nicely, Charlotte soon followed her sister to Louisville, on the urgent insistence of her friend Matilda Prather, who was to be married to Samuel Smith Nicholas on May 19, and desired to have both Charlotte and Ann Eliza at the wedding.

Evidently, Charlotte believed that cousin John Rowan was recovered sufficiently from his recent infatuation, for the letters show that before the summer was over she and Ann Eliza had delightful visits at "Federal Hill." Ann Eliza was quite as popular as Charlotte, but she was shyer and more diffident than her sister. In writing to her father from Joshua Barclay's on June 22, 1829, Charlotte gives him some intimate details of their activities.

Ann Eliza is getting tired of company. There is not an evening without three or four, and sometimes half dozen beaux, and most of them come to see her, but there is not one I believe she likes as well as Cornelius, except our *Cousin John.*—he is one that few girls could be with and not admire. He is a young gentleman of the finest talents, and very attractive.—

Cousin Joshua has not returned yet, although we look for him soon. . . .

The celebrated Mr. E. Forrest of the American boards will be here tomorrow when the Theatre will be open.

Henry Clay Will be here next week and is to have a dinner given him.

Judge Rowan will leave for home on Sunday—he says they have a grudge at me for not coming up to Federal Hill; that it was as much as to say, I have been there once and that is enough. Since Ann Eliza came home, [from Bardstown] I have persuaded her to take an emetic—she was not sick, but complained of a headache. It relieved her. She is perfectly well, and very glad she took it as it was the means of her geting a splendid edition of *Byron's works;* Cousin Hill Rowan came up—I told him she was not well, and when he went to his boarding house, he sent a present to her of the above mentioned works.

Write often and tell us how you all are. Adieu, my dear Father. My love to dear Ma, and the little children. God bless you.

May and June passed very happily for the two girls, but in July, the dreaded cholera began to appear here and there. Ann Eliza returned home, as Baby Jim had the whooping cough, and little Stephen was not well. Charlotte remained for what she intended should be only a short time, in order to make her promised visit to Bardstown. In his numerous letters to her, urging her to return home while there were still some steamboats running, William B. Foster reported to her the progress of the canal. On June 11, 1829, he wrote:

The water in the Canal had reached within 4 miles of Allegheny town about ten days ago—when a breach took place 30 miles up. It is now nearly repaired, and we will look for the water here in a week.

On June 22, he wrote:

The water in the Canal reached Allegheny Town last night, and in a few days if no accident happens, boats will be passing from Blairsville to Pittsbg. a distance of 70 or 80 miles by water.

By the first week in August, 1829, Charlotte's father was actively engaged in the business of his new office as the collector of tolls on the canal.

Charlotte stayed with the Joshua G. Barclays until after the birth in the early part of July of Cousin Sally's baby girl, Georgianna; then, although she would much rather have returned home,

Charlotte proceeded to Bardstown. The following letter, dated July 24, was addressed to her from Sally Barclay in Louisville:

Are you not out of patience, my dear girl, about your Bundle! Ben Duke promised to come and get the articles you ordered him to take to you; I suppose, he forgot again, as I have not seen or heard from him since. I have not known of an opportunity in time to send them untill this morning. Mr. Rowan told me he would take anything to you I had to send; it is no trouble to him if you should not use them before you come home. I am glad the girls are coming home with you. I think Mrs. Rowan might spare one or both of them to stay with us whilst you are here.

I received an affectionate letter from A.E.F. this morning. I send one to you, I suppose from her. I wish she was with us again. I did not know how much I loved the little thing whilst she was here. She said, Don't let Mary forget me. Mary sais, I shant forget Miss Badness! If you write to her before you come down, tell her what Mary said.

I have no excuse to make for such a scrawl but my screaming babe, I don't know what to do with her, she is so cross.

My affectionate love to our relatives at F. Hill. Ask Cousin Wm. if he has forgotten me.

Be sure no one sees this but yourself; and don't forget you have a home in Louisville.

Friday eve. 24th. (July)   S. Barclay.

I must tell you Washington Bullitt sais Mrs. Bakewell took a violent fit of the Cholic and miscaried. It is true!

From Bardstown, Charlotte wrote to her mother and father that she would start for home immediately upon her return to Louisville if the boats were still running, and asked them if they thought it would be proper for her to travel on the same boat with William Prather and his sister, who were anxious to accompany her to Pittsburgh. So concerned were her parents about the danger of sickness in Kentucky that her father wrote urging Charlotte to come home by all means with the Prathers, that neither he nor mother could "see any impropriety in it."

But, when Charlotte reached Louisville, she found Cousin Sally's little daughter, Kitty, stricken with cholera—so, she stayed in Louisville to help the relatives who had grown so dear to her, and who now needed her greatly.

Ann Rowan in Bardstown wrote affectionate letters to "dear, dearest Charlotte" to cheer her; when Hill Rowan came up to town he sent her the following note, undated:

I send you by the boy Mrs. Caldwell's Scrap Book. She did me the kindness to say that it was entirely at the service of my friend, Miss Foster. I hope you will find entertainment in it—something to amuse, if not to make you laugh, not violently, for that w'd crack your pretty lips, which, by the way, I hope are better today. Have you any messages for Bardstown, as the old gentleman leaves tomorrow, or any commands for your friend and obedient cousin,

A.H.R.
[Atkinson Hill Rowan]

All through August and September, Charlotte was consumed with homesickness, which she had not seemed to feel the previous summer. Her letters reveal her eagerness to be home, but Cousin Sally was now seriously ill, and Charlotte could not leave her. The water in the Ohio rose, and with longing eyes, she watched the *Waverley*, the *Talisman* and the *Pennsylvania* steam up the river towards her dear Pittsburgh. In her last letter home, written August 12, 1829, she seems to have a premonition of parting.

Ann Eliza says you are all well, and I hope does not deceive me, for if I thought you for a moment were in need of my assistance at home, nothing would keep me from you. O, my dear, dear Mother, how much gratitude do I owe you; all mothers must claim a portion, but, you I am sure, deserve a greater share for the constant solisitude and study for our happiness. I have seen many mothers, but indeed I never yet have seen one like my own. God bless you all, and grant I may find you all well when we meet.

She wrote later, on September 4, to William, and at that time did not seem to feel any apprehension about her own health:

Yours of the 23d. I received yesterday, and with delight hear you say you will perhaps come down for me. I hope it will be in your power to do so. Since my letter, I have gone out very little. Mrs. Barclay's eldest daughter has been ill with bilious fever, and I have attended her. She is now quite well. I think this place has not been as healthy this summer as last. The weather has been extremely warm and we have had a great deal of rain. There is now a change, it is quite cool today, and we hope will continue so, for the health of this place depends on the weather. Mrs. Lane went up to Wheeling yesterday, and had it not been that I was fearfull I would not get all the way home by water, I should have gone with her. I shall not look for another opportunity untill I hear from you. I do not aprehend any danger of being sick, my health at present is very good.

But, on October 13, George W. Barclay, brother of Joshua G. Barclay, dispatched in haste two letters bearing the same message, one by steamboat and one by horseback, to William B. Foster.

Charlotte is very much indisposed, and I think you had better come to Louisville immediately. Mrs. Joshua G. Barclay has been and still is extremely ill, and from fatigue sitting up with her no doubt is the cause of Charlotte's indisposition.

Yr. Frnd.   G. M. Barclay.

Less than two hours after the letter was received, Ann Eliza was on her way to Louisville on the steamboat *Sylph*. Her mother feared to leave the two sick children, and it was agreed that Ann Eliza would be more useful than her father in caring for Charlotte if she still remained alive. During the terrible week of October 13, A. Hill Rowan wrote to Ann Eliza of every change in her sister's condition—letters that Ann Eliza did not see until her return from Louisville. The young girls of the Rowan family, Ann and Josephine, had come immediately to the assistance of cousin Sally Barclay when they learned of their adored Charlotte's grave illness, and were in constant attendance upon her. Every night, all night long, the brothers, John and Hill Rowan, kept watch in the hall downstairs in the Barclay home while the sick girl raved in delirium in the room above. Hill's letters, written by flickering candlelight, are blotted and tearstained, each one telling Ann Eliza, yet dreading to write the words, that Charlotte was dying.

Charlotte died at half past six o'clock on the morning of October 20, and by the time Ann Eliza reached Louisville, her remains had been laid in the family burying ground of their friends, the Bullitts. How heartbreaking the return journey must have been for the seventeen-year-old sister weighed down by the tragic news she was bearing to her mother and father!

The following description of Charlotte's last hours was written by Hill Rowan to Ann Eliza.

Fedl. Hill, Bardstown.
Novr. 19th, 1829.

I cherish the memory of Charlotte; and if one agony more could have been wrung out of my heart than that which her sad, sad fate inflicted, it would have been for that Sister and those parents who have sustained in her untimely death a bereavement so heavy and so lamentable. The truth is, I knew not, and I know not, *what* to write. I trust then that I will be pardoned the seeming forgetfulness, and I will I know be excused, my dear Cousin, the "sad recital" if I redeem that promise by a general tho imperfect account of her dear, dear Charlotte.

I have in former letters already told you that I believed her distemperature was superinduced by fever, anxiety of mind for Mrs. Barclay, and individual apprehensions of death from sickness in Louisville. I do not believe that there was any other cause, if there was, it was perhaps a deep melancholy, not perceivable when she was in health, and which could not be traced to any certain cause in sickness, as it indicated its seeming existence *alone* in the wild, plaintive and touchingly tender songs which she always sang; for she was generally cheerful, animated, vivacious & witty in her remarks, and in her deportment throughout. She preserved her complexional beauty, suavity and simplicity of manners, and except to a few whom I regret to say she could never tolerate, she was either bland & affable, urbane and polite, or gentle, affectionate and caressful, in the proportion which she loved them, for she was even to her friends, discriminating in her marks of attachment. In those moments that were not occupied with observations to her attendants, when her mind, wearied by the bewildering influences of surrounding objects, seemed to retire to her own bosom for refuge and relief, the spirit of her disease w'd catch the hue of kindred associations, and indicate its mild supremacy in a kindly assimilation of those objects most valued around, with those most cherished in health, and at such moments she was frequently the most perfect Ophelia in every particular I ever saw.

The night of the morning which she died (Oct. 20), I sat up and was frequently in her room. She was more tranquil, yet did not sleep, but seemed as attentive as at any time during her illness to the movements of her friends, occasionally speaking to them, and about an hour before day, when all were silent, she sang a song preserving with much melody

& great accuracy, every note, but her voice was then so thickened that she did not articulate sufficiently plain for the words to be heard, or for the song to be recognized. It soon however, became more distinct, and she called for Josephine. Josephine had sat up with her the whole of the three preceding nights, and perceiving that she was more calm had permitted herself to be prevailed upon to retire and rest. She was sent for and came, and Charlotte, taking a ring from her finger, gave it to her. Josephine asked her, successively, if she must give it to Miss Simpson, Miss Collins, or Mrs. Hopkins, (all of whom, as well as Mr. Hopkins, she spoke much of & frequently asked for) receiving no answer to either of these inquiries. She asked her if she must give it to Ann Eliza, and she immediately and with eagerness replied *Yes.* She then gave her some messages of an affecting character to her Father, Mother, yourself & sisters & brothers. They were prayers for blessings upon you all—after this she soon became flighty and talked much, and until within twenty minutes of her death, which took place at half after six o'clock in the morning, and never, never have I seen anyone die so easy, no convulsions, not the writhing of a feature—there she lay serene, placid & quiescent—all the innocence of her soul complexion't out in a countenance which seemed chastened by the tranquillity of a sweet sleep; so lovely, that could her last breath have been observed by her friends, they could not and would not have believed that her gentle spirit had flown.

Such, my dear cousin, were the last moments of the lovely & beloved Charlotte.

I have dwelt perhaps overlong on the sad story of Stephen Foster's oldest sister, but the story is as he certainly heard it told many times by his elders. He must often have read over Charlotte's last letter to her mother with its loving and tender messages to them all.

The sorrowful event was further impressed on his mind, when, in 1852, he and Morrison and Henry gazed again upon the face of their long-lost sister at the time her remains were moved from the Bullitt graveyard in Louisville to their last resting place in Allegheny Cemetery, Pittsburgh. According to Morrison, her features were not badly disfigured. After twenty-three years in her grave, there were still discernible traces of the beauty he had carried in his memory from childhood. The lovely red-gold hair, chief of her charms, lay upon her shoulders in thick clusters. One of the brothers, I do not know which, clipped a lock of this hair for their mother, and it lies beside me now, gleaming as brightly as it did when its lovely owner bent over harp or piano in the soft candle-light, more than a hundred years ago.

X

THAT Charlotte's death cast a mournful shadow over the household for years is evident from the tone of her mother's letters. Stephen's earliest recollections must have been associated with sadness and death. Not only was the grief for Charlotte, but for the baby James, whom his father describes as a "fair, sweet fellow," and who died on May 19, 1830, just seven months after Charlotte was taken from them. Before their deaths, the mother's handwriting is firm and clear—after them, it shows the effect of great shock, for the writing is small, cramped, and trembling. Her spelling, never very accurate, is so uncertain that it seems as though she were actually in a daze. In later years, her handwriting becomes clear and legible again, and misspelled words less frequent.

The only evidence we have that Stephen's father was also given to expressing his feelings in verse is a few lines inscribed in his scrapbook, written much in the style of Tom Moore:

CHARLOTTE S. FOSTER,

Lament by her Father.

Oh! had she but died in her own native city
    With sorrowing friends to weep o'er her;
Soft sympathy's tears would have soothed us in pity
    And in time we might cease to deplore her.
Yet on as we journey o'er time's rapid wave,
    Our hearts her blest image still keeping—
Fond mem'ry sad vigil shall keep by the grave,
    Where her dear sainted relics are sleeping.

Stephen's gentle mother was not the only one from whom his poetic fancy might have been acquired. William B. Foster's old scrapbook is full of sentimental verses pasted beside the columns of political news. Sad, wistful little bits they are mostly, and not the work of great geniuses, but they seem to have struck a responsive chord in his heart. From the character of most of the selections, one might think that Eliza Foster had preserved them were it not for the fact that a number of poems by Mrs. Lydia Huntley Sigourney are written out in full by William B. Foster himself. Another poem, "Where Can the Soul Find Rest," by Charles Mackey, or Mackay, shows the melancholy trend of his thoughts. The first verse is:

> Tell me, ye winged winds,
>   That round my pathway roar,
> Do ye not know some spot
>   Where mortals weep no more?
> Some lone and pleasant dell,
>   Some valley in the west,
> Where free from toil and pain
>   The weary soul may rest?
> The loud wind dwindled to a whisper low,
> And sighed for pity as it answered—"No!"

Many columns from the newspapers of October, 1837, are preserved describing the wreck of the steam packet *Home* off the South Carolina coast; nearly one hundred passengers were drowned, mostly women and children. The loss of the ship was ascribed to the intoxication of the captain, and as Stephen's father was then becoming absorbed in a local temperance movement, he doubtless saved these accounts for use in his speeches. The life of a politician of the 1820's and '30's was a very convivial one. Wherever two or three of them gathered together to settle knotty problems of the day, there was sure to be liquor flowing, and plenty of it. Eliza Foster spent many an anxious hour, for she was aware of every weakness of her impetuous and genial husband. For several years, she had good reason for her uneasiness, for he did not seem to realize what the end might be. But suddenly, in the year 1833, his splendid good sense asserted itself, and he not only signed the pledge of total abstinence, but threw himself heart and soul into a local movement formed by businessmen and workingmen who traveled about the neighboring towns holding temperance rallies. He and his fellow workers actually met opposition and resistance from some clergymen in villages near Pittsburgh who resented the invasion of what they considered their own realm, and declared the efforts of the crusaders were presumptuous and undesirable. One indignant divine held forth in his country newspaper thus:

Men who have hardly yet opened their eyes from the drunken doze of years, exalted to the rank of public teachers, to rebuke the Christian ministry and reform the church—men so obstinately perverse that, contrary to the instructions of their employers, they spend much time in reviling all who oppose them!

If William B. Foster needed any incentive to carry on the fight, this opposition would have done it, for he loved a battle, political or moral. In 1837, he was still working vigorously for the cause, conducting meetings in Butler and Allegheny counties. Just a few years before he died, Henrietta wrote to her father to praise him for the splendid example he had set for his children, and urging him to complete the good work by uniting with the church. But he retained his old independence of thought, and kept himself apart.

If Stephen, so like his father in many ways, had lived but a few years longer, what might not those years have shown of victory in his struggle with the enemy that sapped away his strength and genius!

XI

DURING the spring and summer of 1832, Dunning and his father remained in town, while Mrs. Foster, with Henrietta, Morrison, and Stephen took lodgings in Harmony, a small village on the Conoquenessing River in Butler County, that was considered very healthful. Henry, now sixteen years old, was sent to Bassenheim, a manual training institution at Zelienople, a mile from Harmony. His parents hoped the outdoor work would be beneficial to him because Henry was a delicate boy, and they feared consumption. Brother William was now assistant engineer of eastern canals, with headquarters at Jersey Shore in Lycoming County, and Ann Eliza was happy in Meadville, visiting at the home of Mrs. Yates, whose brother, Edward Young Buchanan, had replaced Cornelius in Ann Eliza's affections. But the faithful girl joined her mother in Harmony early in the summer, and set herself to teaching Henrietta and the little boys. On June 16, 1832, Ann Eliza sent a letter marked "favoured by Mr. Theodore Nevin" to her father in Pittsburgh.

. . . It is just one week to-day since I reached this place where I find myself very happy, and entirely contented to remain during the summer.

On my way home I spent a day or two with Mrs. Evans in Butler, as, owing to the indisposition of one of the passengers, we were obliged to stay all night at Georgetown, and by that means, lost our chance of the stage to Harmony. Mr E brought me from Butler in a dearborn. On arriving, I found all the family perfectly well, though the boys had just recovered from the sore throat. Ma has thought it best that they should cease going to school, as the weather is so intensely warm, and their walk was long. I employ myself by assembling them together every day—and putting them through the usual exercises, with which arrangement, they appear well pleased. We see Henry frequently in the evenings—and I have visited him once at Basenhiem. Mr and Mrs Williams were very kind and agreable. Yesterday afternoon I visited Mr Muller's, and took tea with Miss Caroline, who as you know, [is] the only member of the family left in this part of the country. Henry Muller is expected home this week.

We have been expecting to see you my dear father, for the last two or three days—when you do come, will you let me trouble you, to bring a few articles with you, which I shall want very much during my stay in the country. Now! if you will be so kind as to take that small *new looking* key—which I gave you in Meadville, it will let you into the beaureau, which stands in the little room to the left hand, in which you will find all I want. and first my parasol is in the top draw.—My pink calico wrapper, I think in the second draw—and if will trouble yourself to rumage among the books, I should be very glad to have "Plutarch's Lives," and the two first volumes, of "Hume's History [of England]" —these I wish partly for the children.

If I have not troubled you too much already—will you permit me to give you another commission—you remember the large Bible, which belongs to George Buchanan, it is packed in the large box of books. As it is not proble that he will ever return to Pittsburgh and I would wish that he should receive it before he leaves this world. Will you be so kind my dear father, as to give it into the hands of Dr Spear, and request him to forward it when he has an opportunity.

We would be very much pleased if Mrs Spear would come out and spend a short time here. I think she would pass it very agreably. If you could bring Charlotte Petigrew with you, it would be very pleasant.

For the present my dear Father I will bid you farewell, hoping to see you very soon. The blessing of God be with you

Your Affectionate daughter, Ann Eliza

If you do not come out this week we would be glad to hear from you by tomorrow's mail. Henry wishes to know when we may expect you.

The Mullers mentioned by Ann Eliza evidently were members of the family of Dr. Detmar Bassa Muller, a native of Germany, who had owned large tracts of land in Butler County at the turn of the century. In 1803, he sold six thousand acres to George Rapp and his associates, leaders of the Harmony Society. Here they established their first colony in this country and called their little settlement Harmony. About 1806, Dr. Muller laid out the town of Zelienople one mile southwest of Harmony, and later opened the Bassenheim manual training school. Mr. and Mrs. Williams appear to have been the proprietors in 1832.

Plutarch's *Lives* and Hume's *History* were a rather strong mental diet for infants such as Stephen, Mitty, and Henrietta were at that time. But, just the same, they undoubtedly absorbed quite a little learning from their zealous young instructor, probably much more than they ever would have at the village school. Dunning, aged eleven, escaped "Sissanny's" formidable course of study by working in Pittsburgh in the office with his father who said he kept him writing the most part of the day, as he was such a dependable little businessman. The rest of the family continued to live at Harmony where William B. Foster reported to Brother William, they were "all well and very happy," until October when their new house in Allegheny was ready.

It was from Harmony that William's mother sent him the first letter she had courage to write to him after the death of Charlotte and Baby Jim. It reveals the way she always poured out her heart to her foster son. Eliza Foster's letters to the other boys are full of motherly advice and counsel meant to strengthen them in good behavior and faith in God; but, to William, she gives neither advice nor instructions. She turns rather to him with all her own doubts and fears, always sure of his full understanding and sympathetic response.

My dear Son   Harmony   May the 14 1832

As I have written one letter to Ann Eliza the only time I have had a pen in my hand that I can recolect, for two years or more, in fact I felt fearful of making unpardonable mistakes, which prevented me from makeing the attempt when my inclination led me to communicate by letter with an absent friend.

Besides the very many perplexities of housekeeping, there was the weak and tremulous state I was left in after the death of your ever to be lamented sister Charlotte and equally interesting little brother James, that my body has only recovered strength, since my mind was restored to that tranquillity which a perfect reconciliation to the will of that omnicient power which regulates and rules, and although the vessels are all broken which I hew'd out to hold the sources of my earthly joys, and all my goneby hopes are nothing but a dream, the song of joy, the delightful cottage, and the sound of the deep-toned instrument still comes danceing on in the arrear of memory, with pain, and sorrow at thought of how it closed, with the departure from this transitory stage of her we loved so dearly—but now I have little to ask, all is well that God in his mercy sends me. I lead a quiet life—you are getting along— Ann Eliza is in Meadville and content, Henry likes the manual labour institution. Your Father is in Pittsburg, and the little children go to school with quite as happy faces as though the world had no thorns in it, and I confess there would be but few if we would all follow the Scriptures in which we would be made strong.

Write to me soon, and I will try to answer it.

Your affectionate mother,
Eliza C. Foster

I thought the mail would not close untill I could finish my letter but being late, I concluded rather hastily without saying anything about Stevan who has a drum and marches about after the old way with a feather in his hat, and a girdle about his waist, whistling old lang syne. He often asks why you dont come home. There still remains something perfectly original about him.

Dunning has writen several letters to you and he does not know but they are worthy of being answer'd, however he drives on; he means to write another soon. We should like to hear from you, as Pa may receive letters from you in Pittsburg without our knowing how you do out here.

That we may all be together again when it pleaseth God the unseen influence that directs our ways is the sincere prayer of one who proudly clames the name of Mother to the best of sons.

"Stevan" was not yet six, but his mother and his family had divined in him before this "something perfectly original." Morrison tells us that his younger brother's susceptibility to music was evident at a very early age. When Stephen was two years old, he would lay "Sissanny's" guitar on the parlor floor beside the square piano at the dear old White Cottage, and pick out harmonies on the strings of the tuneful instrument. He called it his "ittly pizani." One day in 1833, Stephen and his mother were in Smith & Mellor's Music Store at No. 9, Fifth Street, when Stephen accidentally took up a flageolet displayed on the counter. In a few minutes, he had so mastered its stops and sounds that he played "Hail, Columbia" in perfect time and accent. He had never before handled either a flageolet or flute. As soon as she could afford it, Eliza Foster made haste to get her boy a clarinet. Perhaps William Cumming Peters, who afterward published Stephen's first minstrel songs, was in the store that day and witnessed the little boy's performance. Mr. Peters was at that time in partnership with Messrs. W. D. Smith and John H. Mellor in their Pittsburgh music store.

W. C. Peters had been in Pittsburgh from 1825 to 1828 teaching music, and in 1829, opened a music store in Louisville, according to John Tasker Howard. He evidently returned to Pittsburgh very shortly, for on December 8, 1830, he inserted the following advertisement in a Pittsburgh paper:

NOTICE

The subscriber has removed his "Musical Repository" to No. 19 Market Street where he has for sale two splendid Piano Fortes from the manufactory of Loud & Brothers.

The subscriber will always keep a supply on hand, and will also furnish pianos on order. Old Pianos received in exchange at a fair price.

W. C. PETERS, *Professor of Music.*

In February, 1831, W. C. Peters announced a concert:

> Mr. Peters will give a concert on Wednesday evening
> next, the 16th inst. at Mr. Bond's Concert Hall, on Penn
> Street. Tickets may be obtained in the principal Book
> Stores.
>
> The qualifications of this gentleman as a musician are
> already too well known and admired to require com-
> ment from us.
>
> Mr. Burns is engaged to perform some Solos on the
> Kent Bugle, which alone would be a treat of no ordinary
> value.

In December, 1831, W. C. Peters' name appears in company with
W. D. Smith and John Mellor, offering new music and pianofortes
at No. 9, Fifth Street.

Morrison Foster tells us that William C. Peters was at one time
a music teacher in the Foster home, and, judging from Mr. Peters'
long stay in Pittsburgh, it is quite likely that he taught music to
all three of the young Foster sisters.

Stephen had his first experience in a schoolroom when he was
five years old. Morrison Foster has left us the following description
of his little brother's unconstrained behavior the first day he attended the dame school.

> Stephen was not a very methodical student. He early developed er-
> ratic symptoms which ill accorded with the discipline of the school
> room. The first experiment with him was made when he was about five
> years old. He was sent, along with the rest of us, to an infant school
> taught by Mrs. Harvey, an elderly lady, and her daughter, Mrs. Morgan.
> He was called up for his first lesson in the letters of the alphabet. He
> had not proceeded far in this mystery when his patience gave out, and
> with a yell like that of a Comanche Indian, he bounded bareheaded into
> the road, and never stopped running and yelling until he reached home,
> half a mile away.

The direct cause of Stephen's outburst might have been the
primer that Morrison and Stephen studied from in their childhood,
found preserved amongst Morrison's family treasures. This little
New England Primer was a school lexicon very popular in early

times, both before and after the Revolutionary War. The copy
from which the little Fosters learned their letters is a pamphlet
three and a half by four and a half inches, bound in green paper.
That it is of an edition printed after the Revolution is evidenced by
the couplets under *K* and *W*, "The British King Lost states thirteen," and "By Washington Great deeds were done." It contains
the other well-known alphabet jingles beginning with "In Adam's
fall, We sinned all," on through to "Zaccheus he, Did climb the tree,
His Lord to see." There is a warning at the end of one of the spelling
lessons which evidently did not scare Stephen the way the author
intended it should:

> He that loves God, his School, and his Book, will
> no doubt do well at last;
> But he that hates his School and Book, will live and
> die a slave, a fool, and a dunce!

Another lesson considered suitable for infant minds is a grisly
description of the burning of John Rogers. A woodcut shows Mrs.
Rogers and her nine children, "one at her breasts," lined up at the
stake, watching with bored expressions the fire that is consuming
their father. This is followed by a four-and-a-half page poem attributed to Mr. Rogers, and supposed to have been written a few
days before his execution, a dying man's bequest to his children.
The verses sound so much like the other pious rhymes in the primer
that one is led to suspect that the same hand penned them all. It
is hard to imagine a man condemned to be burned at the stake
composing lines like the following:

> Though here my body be adjudg'd
> In flaming fire to fry,
> My soul I trust will straight ascend
> To live with God on high.

This little book also contains the entire "shorter catechism" and
a list of "short and easy questions for children," of which the following are fair samples:

> *Who created you?*   God.
> *Of what was you made?* Of the dust of the earth.

The compiler of this remarkable primer was as reckless with English history as he was with English grammar, but nevertheless the book was widely used, and Stephen must later have resigned himself to his fate, for Morrison said they studied from it as long as they attended Mrs. Harvey's school.

XII

OPERATION of the Pittsburgh and Blairsville Canal was frequently interrupted by breaks and slides, and boats would be tied up with cargoes of freight for weeks at a time, while the water was shut off and the damaged bed or sides of the canal repaired. In the spring of 1832, while the water at Allegheny was cut off, William B. Foster and David Lynch were appointed by the Secretary of the Treasury to compile a manufacturing report of the western Pennsylvania judicial district preparatory to a revision of the tariff. The government seems to have been forehanded enough to get the work done first, then try to have its appropriations approved by Congress. The inconvenience this caused is commented upon by the collector of the tolls as he writes to his son, William B. Foster, Jr., on June 17, 1832:

Mr. Lynch has return'd from Washington without a Dollar of money; although the Secty. gave us the credit of having furnished the most satisfactory returns and report on the subject of Manufactures that he has recd. from any part of the U. States, we must wait for our pay until an appropriation can be made by Congress, which places me in a very disagreeable situation, having been constantly on expenses, generally traveling, and having made considerable advances to different of our assistants, makes me very hard run. I felt very unhappy, on account of Mr. Gamble, to whom I could not advance more than 30 Dollars.

On August 7, the money still had not come through:

Your letter by a stage passenger of 2d. inst. was recd. yesterday, and I had recd. one a few days previous from Mr. Gamble on the subject of the Tariff money. I am not surprised that he and you both may suppose that it has been received by us before this time, but the truth is, it has not yet reached us.—Congress did not make the appropriation until the last day of the Session, and of course at that particular period, the Officers and clerks in the different departments would be much engaged. On examining our documents, one of our Vouchers was found to be informal, and returned to us on Thursday last; a new one was of course made out and forwarded by us on Saturday, and now, as they have taken the business in hands, I have strong hopes of getting the needful on Tuesday next.

In the letter of August 7, William B. Foster informed William, Jr., that the Pittsburgh and Blairsville Canal was again in good order; there was a great deal of freight coming down, principally iron blooms, and salt. Mr. Foster's familiarity with all the shippers and their cargoes enabled him to secure bargains every now and then for himself in such commodities as salt and lime, which he bought in bulk, and exchanged with the farmers for wheat and meat, and for groceries at the store. The collector's office was a convenient place to gather early news and views, local and national, and at this time, all America's interest was centered on President Andrew Jackson and the United States Bank. William B. Foster's letter of August 7, to William continues:

Thanks be to Providence, Old Hickory has put his veto on that *villainous mammoth Bank* cal'd the United States, in which there has been more fraud, in favouritism, corruption and oppression than in any monied institution in the world. We are all veto men now, or nearly so; we have gained more than we lost by it, although we are immediately under the Guns of their *Corrupt Battery,* which keeps some poor devils quiet.

He soon found that collector of the tolls was not the ideal position he had hoped it would be. The "corrupt battery" under which he labored delayed his salary and that of his subordinates on every trifling technicality they could invent. While he was compelled to handle large sums of money in tolls collected, he was not permitted to pay the workmen with any of the money until an accounting had been forwarded to Harrisburg, and a voucher returned, which took two weeks if everything was found correct, and much longer if any items were questioned. This continual bickering kept him in a state of ferment and irritation; his men were always in arrears of wages, unless he paid them out of his own pocket which he was seldom in a position to do.

Owing to the scarcity of cash all over the country, it was the general practice for businessmen to pay their obligations with notes owed them by others. When a borrower and his bondsmen signed a note, they never knew who would present the note for payment when it fell due. If, after it passed through perhaps a dozen hands, it matured in the possession of someone who was willing to renew, or take someone else's note in payment, all well and good; but if the holder of the note was being pressed by his own creditors, and could not extend the term, the signers were in a very bad way. For a sale amounting to as little as $200, one might receive three or four notes drawn on as many different persons, each falling due on a different date. This medium of exchange required a great deal of careful bookkeeping, and a watchful eye on one's own liabilities. It is not strange that so many business failures resulted—many a man thought his notes were safe in the hands of friends, and woke to find the bank holding them all, and demanding payment.

Consequently, the years 1832 and 1833 were troublous years to Stephen's father, but, as his mother said, "The little children go to school with quite as happy faces as though the world had no thorns in it."

We do not know the exact location of the house the Fosters moved into in the fall of 1832, but we do know it was located in the general neighborhood of other houses they occupied in Allegheny, between what is now Ohio Street and the river, and not far from the Federal Street bridge. Allegheny was still a small village in 1832, and just a few squares north of the Allegheny River were farms and steep wooded hillsides. One happening the residents of the town could depend on each spring to relieve the monotony was being flooded out by the rampant waters of the Allegheny, the Monongahela, and the Ohio rivers. The rising that was known as "the great flood" occurred on February 10, 1832, when William B. Foster reported that "the water was 2 feet higher than was ever seen by any person now living. The water passed up St. Clair Street to the South Side of Liberty." During this flood, Smoky Island, or Killbuck Island (named for a single settler who lived there alone

Harmony May the 14 1832

My Dear Son

As I have written one letter to Ann.
Eliza the only time I have had a pen in my hand
that I can recolect. for too years or more. in fact
I felt fearfull of makeing unpardonable mitakes.
which prevented me from makeing the attempt when
my inclination led me to communicate by letter
with an asent freind.

Besides the very many perplexitys
of house keeping. there was the weak and tremulous
state I was left in, after the death of your ever to
be lamented sister Charlotte and equally interesting
little brother James, that my body has only recovered
strength, since my mind was restored to that
tranquility which a pifect reconciliation

Letter from Eliza C. Foster to her son William, May 14, 1832
(continued on following pages)

to the will of that omnicient power which regulates and rules. and although the vessels are all broken which I hewd out to hold the sources of my earthly joy, and all my gone by hopes are nothing but a dream, the song of joy. the delightfull cottage, and the sound of the deep toned instrument, still comes danceing on — in the arrear of memory. with pain, and sorrow, at thought of how it closed with the departure from this transatory stage of her we loved so dearly... but now I have little to ask. all is weell that God in his mercy sends me. I lead a quiet life — you are getting along. AnnEliza is in meadville and content. Henry likes the manual labour institution. Your Father is in Pittsburg. and the little Chilldren go to school. with quite as happy facees as though the world had no thorn's in it, and I confess there would be

but few if we would all follow the scriptures in which
we would be made strong. write to me soon and I
will try to answer it. your afectionate mother
                                        Eliza C. Foster.

I thought the mail would not close untill I could finish
my letter but being late I concluded rather hastily. without
saying any thing about Stevan who has a drum and marches
about after the old way with a feather in his hat and a
girdle about his waist whistling old lang syne. he often
asks why you dont come home, there still remains
something perfectly original about him.

                    During has writen several letters
to you and he does not know but that they are worthy
of being answerd however he drives on he means to write
another soon, we should like to hear from you. as Pa may

receive letters from you in Pittsburg without our knowing
how you do out here. that we may be all togeather again
when it pleaseth God the unseen influence that direts our ways
sincere prayr of one who proudly clames the name of Mother to
the best of sons ---

Mother

May 14 1832

Wyoming Pa
16 May
} Forwarded from
Lycoming Cleaverlay
22nd June

William B Foster jun.
Larys Creek P.O
Lycoming County

for many years), in the Ohio just below the point, was swept almost entirely away; only a sand bar remained. While one of these big floods was at its height, and when almost every conceivable kind of farm building and household article was being carried swiftly down stream, Stephen and Mit watched in breathless excitement their big brothers Henry and Dunning row out into the rushing water to rescue a beautiful shepherd dog; and not only the dog, but the dog's house, to the roof of which he had been desperately clinging for dear life. What a happy ending to that dog's fearful adventure to be received eagerly by the excited little boys, warmed and dried in Mother Foster's kitchen, and the inner dog renewed and fortified with juicy meat bones, bread and gravy!

Allegheny Town, 1833-1845

*A*S early as 1833, the building of railroads was beginning to threaten the existence of many lines of canals in the East. Stephen's father wrote to William with great concern that the Improvement Bill had passed through the Committee of the Whole in Senate, with the addition of an appropriation of $400,000 to make a double track of railroad from Columbia to Philadelphia. He wondered how this would affect the canal commissioners, but hoped that justice would be done, and that they would have nothing to fear.

This year was a memorable one for William and Eliza Foster, as Ann Eliza was married on April 9, 1833, to the Reverend Edward Y. Buchanan, who took her away to live in Meadville, Pennsylvania, where the young minister had his first charge.

Following is an extract from William B. Foster's letter to William dated April 10, 1833, and Ann Eliza's first letter to her mother from her new home.

April 10th 1833.

... As you will naturally expect, I have the satisfaction to inform you of the marriage of your dear Sister last evening, at half past six oclock; it took place in Christ's Church (Allegheny Town) in the presence of all our family, and a very respectable collection of friends and acquaintances. The ceremony was performed by Doctor Upfold, and was very interesting and impressive indeed. Dear Ann Eliza is gone from us, but it is a source of great consolation that she is under the protection of a most amiable and worthy man. They set out in a Carriage this morning to Greensburgh to visit Mr. Buchanan's mother and sister; they will return on Monday, remain a few days with us and set out on Friday week for their residence at Meadville.

—I should have written you sooner, but waited your answer to your sister's letter of invitation, on the rect. of which a few days ago, and finding you could not be here, she desired me to address a note of of leaf Tobacco, which he could have bought at 2½ cents, now he has to pay from 4½ to 5 cents.

His parents' fears for William's safety were not allayed until late in September when a letter from their son finally was received. His father replied on September 24, 1834, urging William to leave Kentucky just as soon as he could finish his work there.

Your kind letter of 22d. ult. was duly recd. which gives us the pleasing intelligence that a good Providence had thus far guarded your health. We all felt great solicitude about you, and are very happy to learn that you have determined to return home, if God spares you to fill your present engagement. I do trust that nothing will induce you to change your determination, for what is all this world to a man without health! Should you not find immediate employment as an Engineer in this country, you cannot want for good business enough.

Your Cousin Thomas Struthers was with us yesterday; you know he has married a daughter of Zachariah Eddy, of Warren [Pennsylvania] who is quite wealthy. Thomas is doing very well, he has an excellent practice as a lawyer & has lately made a fine speculation in land—bot. 25,000 acres lying in a body south of Broken Straw Creek, at 25 cents per acre, payable in eight years, with inst. Has already sold several tracts at from 1.25 to 1.50 per acre. He is extremely anxious that you should come up and join him in that, as well as a store in Warren; he says he will keep it open for you until you return & look for yourself. . . .

The prospects of the success of our ticket brightens daily; Bank or no-Bank is the question, and we will get many anti-Masonic votes. The Bankites are making extraordinary exertions, and all that money and lying can do, they will perform. Individual character, however, thus far has been respected, except the candidates for Congress.

II

IN December, 1834, William B. Foster decided to revive an old claim of upwards of $3000 against the company in which he had been an officer in 1815, which owned a stagecoach and wagon line running to Philadelphia. When the company broke up in 1818, and failed to the amount of perhaps $100,000, several of the officers

had diverted to their own use the amount of a bond posted by Mr.
Foster as collateral security contingent upon the settlement of his
accounts as agents of the company. This suit had been dragging
on since 1822, and Mr. Foster had already made two trips to Philadelphia to try to "push the business to a close." He became hopeful
once more that something would come of it, but it was years before
he was finally forced to settle for about two-thirds of the amount;
he said it had already cost him upwards of $500 in traveling ex-
penses. Each time he was put off, his hopeful letters evince that he
had perfect confidence that all would yet be well, and that the
money really would soon be forthcoming. All his life, Wm. B. Foster
was full of unbounded enthusiasm for every project he went into,
and his confidence in his fellow men was proof positive of his own
utter lack of guile. William B., Jr., was of a more cautious nature,
and could see the consequences of entering into business alliances
with untried strangers. He continually cautioned his father not
to be "too sanguine" about the future of certain enterprises, and
it generally turned out that William was right. William's letters
reveal that he disliked to throw too much cold water on the bright
hopes of his father, but he did not join in any premature rejoicing
regarding the old Pittsburgh and Greensburgh Turnpike Company.

The following extracts from a letter dated December 7, 1834,
show William B. Foster, Sr., in a very cheerful frame of mind,
brought about by promising business prospects, William's good
health, and the hope of having his son home soon again.

You may suppose we were all much pleased to learn that your usual
health was restored, and trust most confidently that no consideration
whatever, even double pay, will induce you to remain in that country
another season; what money can compensate for health and constitution
destroyed? We look for you towards the end of February.

We have removed to a three-story Brick House about 100 yards north
of the Allegheny Bridge, a very pleasant house. . . . [This house was
on the bank of the Allegheny River, on the Allegheny side; the other
had been on the bank of the Ohio.]

. . . Mr. Baldwin is expected here in a few days, when I expect to
make an amicable arrangement for his part by giving him time & perhaps deducting a part of the interest, etc. etc. I have also a plan in view

to raise about $1500 dollars on the credit of the coal lot, and with these two sources hope to aid you and Henry to establish a good store in Partnership. You will of course bring with you all the funds you can save.

Land in the vicinity of Town is rising in value and an excellent Turnpike Road will be finished by Christmas, which goes within 100 rods of our lot. It will command 4000 Dollars next summer I am confident.

. . . I wrote to Thomas Struthers and desired that he would write to you, perhaps when you return it may suit for us all to go to Warren & join him in a Store and Land trade—more of that when you arrive.

We are now very poor, but hope and good health keeps us up.

Your cousin, A. W. Foster, Jr. is married to a Miss Singer, formerly of Greensburgh—her father, a respectable mechanic, a chair maker.

We had a most pleasant party at Mrs. Collins's on Thursday evening last. Miss Sarah was married to Wilson McCandless. There were, I presume, near one hundred persons present and upwards of 30 carriages. Your Ma, Henrietta and myself went in a Barouch and pair, and did not get home until a half after 12 oclock. It was indeed a splendid entertainment. Sarah, you know, is the "last of the Mohegans."

The President's message has reached us, and is a most excellent document. I fear we shall have a war with France; be it so, "let Justice be done, if the Heavens should fall."

I think it probable that Mr. Jas. Buchanan will be U. S. Senator in place of W. Wilkins.

Your mother and all the family send much love to you—and may God preserve and protect you to return in safety is the sincere prayer of your affectionate father,

W. B. Foster.

W. B. Foster, Jr.
Long Falls P. O.
Davies County, Kentucky.

The election unfortunately did not fulfill Mr. Foster's sanguine expectations. Anti-Masonry had not yet died in Allegheny County, but helped to send the Whig candidate, Harmar Denny, to Congress, and gave Foster's Bankite opponent a place in the assembly. So, being out of politics for the time being, Foster devoted himself to buying and selling land, and planning to go into business with William when the latter's work in Kentucky was finished.

Early in January, 1835, Ann Eliza and little James left for Mercersburg to join Mr. Buchanan, whose family originally came from that town. They traveled by stagecoach in company with Dr. and Mrs. McDowell, Stephen's future parents-in-law, who also had many relatives living in Mercersburg. It must have been a very cold ride, for William B. Foster reported that the three rivers were frozen over so hard that the boys could skate across. Dunning, Morrison, and Stephen were going steadily to school at Mr. Stockton's academy, and Henry, now nearly nineteen, was employed at Hutchinson & Ledlie's warehouse. His father was greatly pleased with his earnestness, and predicted that Henry would make "quite a business man."

The big boys, however, were not above playing the tricks that most older brothers like to inflict on the younger ones. Morrison used to chuckle as he recalled an incident that occurred when he was about ten years old, and Stephen seven. The little boys had hung up their stockings on Christmas Eve, in anticipation of the simple toys and candy and oranges which they always received when they were "good"; especially, the oranges—they were regarded as the supreme treat. But this Christmas, Henry and Dunning told them they had been bad boys, and Kriss Kringle would leave them just what they deserved. On Christmas morning, little Stephy and Mitty came downstairs to find, instead of the usual presents, that Morrison's stocking was filled with ashes from the grate, and in Stephen's stocking nothing but Pa's whip from the horse stable. They went with loud lamentations to their mother who, suspecting the older boys, whispered to the little ones what she would do if she were they. Shouting with joy, Morrison carried his stocking upstairs and emptied the ashes onto Dunning's head as he lay slumbering, while Stephen belabored Henry with the horsewhip until the latter cried for mercy, and revealed the place where he and Dunning had hidden the presents they had sneaked out of the little fellows' stockings in the night. And, Morrison said, "Ma made Dunning take out all the bedclothes and shake the ashes out of them in the cold wintry air!"

William spent the winter and spring of 1835 in Rumsey, Muhlenberg County, Kentucky, and remained there until his contract ended in May. He experienced no difficulty in securing at once a position, in a climate where there was not so much "fever and ague," as assistant engineer on the Pennsylvania and Ohio Canal, with his headquarters at Youngstown, Ohio. The commissioners in Kentucky saw William leave with great regret, and a resolution was drawn up which shows in what high esteem the young engineer was held.

At a meeting of the Board of Commissioners for the Improvement of Green River at Rumsey on the 19th day of June, 1835.—

RESOLVED, that this Board most sincerely regret the departure of Wm. B. Foster, Esqr. from their service.—

They take great pleasure in bearing Testimony to the very satisfactory manner in which he has discharged his duties as Engineer.—His official conduct has been marked by firmness of purpose, and by sterling integrity.—He bears with him the most sincere wishes of every member of this Board for his health and prosperity.—

Resolved, that the Secretary hand Mr. Foster a copy of this Resolution.

A Copy.   Test.

DILLIS DYER,
Secrety.

William did not follow up the subject of a store in Warren, Pennsylvania, with cousin Thomas Struthers, because he preferred canalling, and an active partnership in any business would have necessitated his giving up the work he was better fitted for. But, prior to his removal to Youngstown, William and his father formed a partnership with a Mr. Hall, of Pittsburgh, in a general store located at 106 Market Street, with William providing a share of the capital and William B. Foster, Sr., assisting Mr. Hall in the store. William also invested in a large lot in Allegheny; about ninety feet faced on the East Common, directly below the Methodist Protestant Church. There were two old frame houses on the property, and, in 1843, William built a new brick house there.

Although the Bank of the United States had taken over all the southern half of William B. Foster's Lawrenceville holdings, including the homestead on Outlot No. 9, in May, 1826, there were a number of small inlots in the northern half of the property that still remained in his possession. In January, 1835, the borough of Lawrenceville, desiring a site for a public market, secured Lot No. 100, down near the arsenal, from William B. Foster, and also the rights to a public boat landing on the Allegheny River, still held by Mr. Foster. Malcolm Leech, who now resided in the White Cottage, was treasurer of the Lawrenceville council at this time, and the council's president was William Toman, who had recently erected a comfortable cottage on the two outlots 6 and 7, which he had secured from the United States Bank on January 8, 1828. (Many years afterwards, this little "Mansion House" of William Toman's, at the forks of the road, was frequently mistaken for the original Foster homestead.* As such, it was sold to Henry Ford in 1934.)

Eliza Foster's young folks were given to much gaiety and music these days. Henry was going out to "swarrys" as they called them, and gallanting charming young ladies home from church. Henrietta was sixteen years old, and quite a belle. She played the guitar very prettily, singing to her own accompaniments, and took pleasure in teaching her brother Stevie all the simple chords that his eager little hands could manage. About this time, the younger Foster boys, in company with boys of neighbor families, started their celebrated Thespian company, in which Morrison says Stephen was the "head-liner." Other members of the little troupe were the Robinsons, Cuddys, and Kellys. According to Morrison:

The Theatre was fitted up in a carriage house. All were stockholders except Stephen. He was regarded as a star performer, and was guaranteed a certain sum weekly. It was a very small sum, but it was sufficient to mark his superiority over the rest of the company. "Zip Coon," "Long-tailed Blue," "Coal-Black Rose" and "Jim Crow" were the only Ethiopian songs then known. His performance of these was so inimitable and true to nature, that, child as he was, he was greeted with uproarious applause, and called back again and again every night the company gave an entertainment, which was three times a week. They generally cleared enough to enable the whole party to buy tickets to the old Pittsburgh Theatre on Saturday nights, where they could be seen in the pit listening to the acting of Junius Brutus Booth, Augustus A.

*See Appendix II, pages 636 and 637, will of William Toman.

Pittsburgh Sept. 3. 1841

Dear William —

your very kind letter
to your mother of 23. Ult. covering a ten Dollar
Bank note, came duly to hand; as also Henry's
letter to her of 20th Ult. covering a like sum
of ten Dollars. for these kindness's you both
deserve and receive, our kind thanks and blessing.

The money came in good time, as we had
two weeks ago, scraped our little plunder
together, and your mother with Stephen and
myself Commenced house keeping in the
old place. Thomas and Henrietta with
their little ones, soon after joined us, and
we are now all together. Thomas pays
us one Dollar per day for boarding and
lodging his family, including a hired girl. —
they talk of returning to youngstown in a
week or two. I expect I shall be obliged to
go to Warren in a day or two in order to wind
up (if I can) his business there, they will re-
-main until my return. —

I regret extremely, that Stephen has not been
able to appreciate properly, your generous
exertions in his behalf, by availing himself
of the advantages of a College education, which
will cause him much regret before he arrives
at my age; and he will no doubt express
those regrets in much sorrow to you should
you both live; long after I shall be no more. —
He is at school, now, with Mr. Moody, a
first rate teacher of Mathematicks in Pittg,
and it is a source of much comfort to your
mother and myself that he does not appear to
have any evil propensities to indulge; he seeks
no associates, and his leisure hours are all
devoted to musick, for which he possesses a
strange talent. —

Letter from William B. Foster, Sr., to his son William, September 3, 1841
(continued on following page)

your determination to enroll yourself as a member of the Church of God, has given us all heart felt gratulations. — — The cause of temperance continues to flourish throughout our Western Country. We have a Washington total abstinence society in Allegheny, in which I am a member, with others numbering in all about 150 members, many of them reform'd. — — We meet every monday evening, and new members from 8 to 15 join us every meeting, — We receive many calls from different parts of the Country to send out members to address Conventions on the subject of temperance — I have attended, and address'd three — yesterday, six of us address'd in succession a Convention of upwards of one thousand persons assembled agreeably, to previous arrangements, at the church in which your Uncle James is an elder, eight miles South from Pittsburgh. — I was call'd on first to address them; and thought I done it pretty well Was followed by John B. Mahon Esq. in a thrilling appeal to the feelings of considerable length, then followed in succession four others, all of us acknowledging ourselves reform'd drunkards. — the people appeared well pleased and upwards of three hundred subscribed the teetotal pledge — Tell your dear brother Henry that his letter and money was duly received and the next letter will be written to him this is, as that will be, intended for you both, as you are together now — Thomas Wick, thinks he is better, but it is very little if any — I have not a word from Washington City yet — your mother and all the family join in much love to yourself and Henry

With your affectionate father —

W. B. Foster Jr.   Wm B. Foster

Addams, Edwin Forrest, Oxley, Conner, Logan, Proctor, William and John Sefton, Mrs. Drake and Mrs. Duff.

A contemporary minstrel song which Morrison does not mention above, but which he frequently sang for the amusement of his children, was another of those made famous by the great minstrel man, T. D. Rice, who immortalized "Jim Crow." The first verse of this classic goes something like this,

> As I was gwine down Shinbone Alley,
>   Long time ago,
> To get a bonnet for my Sally,
>   Long time ago.

These old songs each contain about twenty verses, but they all could easily be used up in an evening, because of the repeated and enthusiastic encores. "Jim Crow" must have been a great hit, with its ridiculous stanzas, especially adapted to singing by small boys.

> Dere's possum up a gum stump,
>   Coonie in de hollow,
> Wake snakes for June bugs,
>   Stole my half a dollar!

One can imagine slim little brown-eyed Stephen bringing down the house with a delightful line, "Wake snakes for June bugs," and finishing up the "w'eel about and turn about, and do jis so," to a thunder of rapturous applause!

"Long Tail Blue" lent itself well to juvenile comedy efforts. The last word in elegance in those days was a blue broadcloth coat cut off at the waistline in front, trimmed with a black velvet collar, and finished off with two swallowtails at the back. "Daddy" Rice, as he was called, captivated the country with this song, and little Stephen came a close second as he strutted the boards in the old carriage-house attired in Pa's best blue, with the tails sweeping up the chaff on the floor behind him.

It is not likely that the Jim Crow type of song won Stephen great approval from his mother; she certainly would have preferred "Come Rest in This Bosom"! But Eliza Foster was very indulgent, and Stephen seems always to have been allowed to express himself in his own way, and follow his own bent. His nature, like his mother's, ran to two extremes; the deeply melancholy side which beheld nothing but sadness in all the world; and on the other side, a sense of the ridiculous that was continually popping up when the occasion demanded a solemn and dignified demeanor.

Stephen carried his enjoyment of nonsense songs well into his own composing days. Compare the tomfoolery of "Shinbone Alley" and "Jim Crow" with some of his own early minstrel songs—"Dolcy Jones," "My Brudder Gum," "Angelina Baker," "Away Down South," and "Oh! Susanna." There must have been a grin on Steve's face when he set down the following beautiful lines in "Away Down South," reminiscent of Rice's "Long Time Ago":

> I went last night to see my Sally
> Two story house in Pigtail ally,
> Whar de skeeters buz, and de fleas dey bite,
> And de bull dogs howl and de tom cats fight.

And the "old hoss" which occasionally ambles into Stephen's plantation songs pricked up his ears to hear:

> Went one berry fine day
> To ride in a one-horse sleigh,
> Hollow'd to de old hoss comin' through de toll-gate,
> Hay! Brudder Gum!

Stephen later supplanted these amusing, but pointless doggerel songs with minstrel melodies which retained their humor, but told a sensible story in their three or four verses. "The Glendy Burk," "Camptown Races," and "Nelly Bly" are happy, light-hearted folk songs with a negro background as positive as a crap game. With a change of mood, but without abandoning the racial characteristics of the gayer songs, Stephen produced the plaintive and poignantly beautiful "Nelly Was a Lady."

III

AFTER William's removal to Youngstown in June or July of the year 1835, there was a great deal of traveling of the Foster family between Pittsburgh and the Ohio town. William B. Foster, Sr., grew interested in the prospect of Youngstown real estate, and both he and William invested in several lots in that young, growing city. William's land was a large tract adjoining the farm of Henry Wick, located in what is now practically the center of the business district—at the corner of Henrietta (named for Henrietta Foster) and Federal streets. Doubtless it was when he was negotiating his purchase that William became acquainted with Henry Wick's pretty, delicate daughter Mary, who drove all thoughts of Kentucky girls from his mind, if in fact he ever entertained any. And, as though Fate had a romantic purpose in influencing William to leave Kentucky just when he did, Mary Wick's younger brother, Thomas, fell in love with Henrietta Foster about the first time she came to Youngstown to visit her brother William.

Stephen's mother made frequent trips to visit Brother William, and Youngstown began to seem as much like home to the Foster children as Allegheny. The senior Foster disliked the confinement of the Market Street store, and was glad of an excuse to get out on the road, buying up merchandise as in the old days with Denny & Beelen, and casting his eye over the country for profitable land deals.

Henrietta and her father stayed in Youngstown the latter part of 1835 with Brother William, while their mother, with Kitty, the colored girl, kept house in Allegheny for Henry, Dunning, Stephen, and Morrison. But by the first of January, 1836, the mother took the two little boys to Youngstown, leaving "Canebrake Kitty" to look after the others.

In January, 1835, the Reverend Edward Y. Buchanan had accepted a call to St. John's Pequea Protestant Episcopal Church, in Chester County, Pennsylvania, and Christ Church, Leacock, a few miles distant in Lancaster County. St. John's Church is not situated in the town of Pequea (pronounced Peck-way)—this village is down along the Susquehanna River—but the church takes its name from the Pequea River and beautiful Pequea Valley. St. John's Church is on the old King's Highway, at Compass, Pennsylvania, and had been established for more than a hundred years when Edward Y. Buchanan took over the pastorate. The first church was built by a group of early settlers, who, according to R. Chester Ross, historian of St. John's Church, "as soon as they had provided log cabins for their families, turned their attention to the erecting of a church wherein they could worship Almighty God." The first page of their pioneer records, dated 1729, reads as follows:

We adventurers from those parts of His Majesty's dominions called England, Scotland and Ireland, transplanting ourselves and families into America, and taking up our first settlement in the township of Pequay, Lancaster county and in the township of Salisbury, Chester county, both in the province of Pennsylvania. We from a due sense of duty to God, finding no part of the universe agreeable to us without a place of public worship where we might perform Divine Adoration to the Great Creator of the universe after the form and manner of the Episcopal Church of England, and that for the good of our own immortal souls, as well as, those of our posterity. We therefore according to our small abilities did erect in the year of our Lord 1729 a wooden frame church of about 22 feet long and 20 feet broad upon a plot of ground containing about one acre.*

Mr. Ross tells us that in 1753, the wooden church was replaced by a stone church forty-eight feet long and twenty-nine feet broad. This stone church was the one in which Mr. Buchanan took up his duties in 1835, but the building which stands there today was erected while Mr. Buchanan was the rector in 1838.

Only a few miles distant from St. John's Pequea Episcopal Church, there flourished the Scotch-Irish Presbyterian congregations at Octorara and Donegal, which Ann Eliza's paternal ancestors, William Barclay and Alexander Foster, had helped to establish. Alexander Foster, and one of his sons, the Reverend William Foster, are buried in the churchyard of the Upper Octorara church which was founded in 1720, and is located in Chester County about one mile north of Parkesburg, Pennsylvania. William Barclay and his wife Mary are buried in the Middle Octorara churchyard, in Lancaster County, which was established in 1727 as a mission of the parent Upper Octorara church. The Lower Octorara church is still farther south, in Maryland. These fine old burying grounds are still kept in splendid condition by the present-day generation of Presbyterians. Although their ancient churches, and also the Episcopal churches of St. John's Pequea, All Saints at Paradise,

*R. Chester Ross, *Two Hundred Years of Church History: The History of St. John's Pequea Protestant Episcopal Church Located at Compass, Chester County, Pa.*, Intelligencer Printing Co., 1929.

and Christ Church, Leacock, were situated in wild, lonely places, even in early times that section of Pennsylvania and Maryland was a prosperous farming country.

In Mr. Ross's *History of St. John's Pequea Protestant Episcopal Church,* he tells us:

Mr. Buchanan occupied the property known as the Dr. Shippen farm, about one and one-half miles north of Cains. There were a number of acres of ground connected with it, but Mr. Buchanan did not farm the land. He called it "Grace Parsonage."

Mr. Foster made another futile trip to Washington in February, 1836, to press once more his claim against the United States government. On his way home, he stopped to see "Sissy Anny," and dear little James, and from Mr. Buchanan's parsonage wrote on March 2, 1836, to his wife in Youngstown:

As I intimated to William in my last letter from Washington, all my exertions fail'd in procuring my just dues from the Government, but as I had made the attempt, I determined to persevere to the last, and did everything that was expected, or required of me to set the equity of the claim in full view of the Committee; but all in vain. I found it useless to remain any longer.

About the same time, Henry and Dunning went on an excursion for Hutchinson & Ledlie to Tennessee and Kentucky, and Henry wrote his mother on March 10:

We have at length arrived here [Pittsburgh] after an absence of nearly 2 months, and have enjoyed excellent health during my absence. While at Nashville, the Bar Keeper & myself (for want of a better companion) [Henry knew his mother would ask, "Why with the bartender?"] Hired a Horse each and Rode out to the Hermitage which is a very neat Building, much the form of Mr. Avery's in Allegheny, surrounded by 1200 Acres of land & worked by 100 Negroes; from thence I procured a Hickory Staff for Pa and some Rose Roots from the garden for Etty.

A planter who lives close by where we stopped all night says he was well acquainted with Aunt Betsy & Mr. Morrison—Mr. Morrison has been dead about 2 years. [Aunt Betsy was William B. Foster's sister, Elizabeth.]

I procured some oranges while in Louisville which were intended for you. But finding no opportunity of sending them out, shall have to use some means to prevent them from spoiling, as a number have already.

I wish Etty would write soon and tell me how she employs herself and what kind of society you have.

Tell Mit & Stevy to be good boys and go to school regularly, and when they have time what kind of fellers they have for playmates and how they spend their time, will be thankfully recd. in a letter from either.

Give my best respects to Brother William. I will ever remember him for his kindness shown to us all.

In haste, yours affectionately,

Henry B. Foster

There are quite a number of mistakes in spelling and punctuation in this letter—Henry was just nineteen, which is a careless age. Brother William evidently went ruthlessly through it with a pencil, for the corrections are in his handwriting. Henry's next letter, which was directed to William, is a flawless example of penmanship, spelling, and punctation, fit for a copybook. Doubtless he received a sound scolding from his older brother for sending his mother a letter so poorly written.

The rose roots that Henry had procured with loving care from the "Hermitage" were intended for the garden of the new home in Youngstown that Henrietta was soon to preside over as the bride of Thomas Wick. At this time, Eliza Foster and the little boys were boarding in Youngstown at Mrs. Squires'. They had not given up the house in Allegheny, but evidently it was closed for the winter, for when Henrietta and her father returned to Pittsburgh from Youngstown in April, 1836, they stayed with Mrs. Foster's cousin, George Evans. From there, Henrietta wrote to her brother William on April 30, 1836, and her greatest longing seems to have been to see Mit and Stevy, though doubtless a sight of Thomas Wick also would have cheered her. The little boys were then alone at Mrs. Squires'; their mother had been called east to be with Ann Eliza, who was expecting her second child.

My dear Brother,

I have received your letter by Mr. Hall on yesterday evening and was very sorry to hear that you have such a cold. Pa is going home next week & he says that I may go with him. [Henrietta now called Youngstown "home"!] Do write to me soon and tell about the little boys. Oh! I do want to see them so badly, poor little fellows, they must be as lonely as I am. Sometimes I get so homesick (when I see any person from Youngstown) particularly, that I do not know what to do with myself. Mr. Hall gave me some money to get a pair of shoes and a belt and other little articles, which were three dollars. Mr. Mahon is as attentive as ever, only a little more so. He comes only once a day now—that is, he comes in the morning and stays all day. I am in a most awful pickle about it, for I am afraid to do or say anything to him on Cousin Jane's account, for she thinks so much of her *dear brother Will.*

I was at the theatre on Monday with Mr. and Mrs. King, La Tour de Vesle was played, Mrs. Pritchard making her first appearance as Margaret of Burgundy. She is a splendid actress, but that is all I can say of her. I went to Mrs. McClure's party on Friday night and was surprised to find a large company collected of the most fashionable people in the city, we danced and had an elegant supper. I went with the Miss Reynolds. Pa took me yesterday afternoon to see Major and Mrs. Herron from Fort Jessup. Dunning and Henry are very well now, but they have both been taking medicine for bad colds. (This side of the sheet is written a little better, as I have got a new pen.)

I wish it would be possible for you to have a partition put up in that large room. Do not forget the green blind.

The flowers are coming out. This is the first warm day we have had this spring. I have no more news to tell you. Oh, do write to me soon. I am going down street now and will write more when I come back. Give my love to all who may ask after me, either man, woman or child.

I have learned a beautiful new song since I saw you, My hopes have departed forever, is the name of it.

Tell Mitty that Dunning is going to get him the book he spoke of to me. Pa was here this morning, he looks very well indeed. I am very much obliged to you, my dear brother, for sending me those little nicknacks, which I mentioned to you; tell Mit to write to me very soon. Cousin Jane sends her love to you and Tom Wick. I shall try and be contented for another week, but indeed I cannot possibly stay longer, for Mrs. King is going up home today.

Your affectionate sister,

Henrietta.

"How lonely my guitar must be" wrote Henrietta in the margin of her letter.

It was a long, wearisome journey to Lancaster County, almost as far as Philadelphia, and it meant many changes from one type of conveyance to another; but in comparison to Eliza Foster's bridal journey of 1807, in 1836 it was one of ease and comfort. A writer of that year, describing the hardships of traveling in pioneer days, evidently thought the limit of dizzy speed had been reached in 1836, for he said:

In those early days, no daily stages rattled along stone roads at the rate of ten miles an hour—no commodious Conestoga wagon, even, creaked along the national road with its three tons of goods—no whizzing iron horse dragged his hundreds of passengers with frightful velocity among the mountains of Cumberland.

It was necessary for Eliza Foster to travel by stagecoach, canalboat and railroad to reach her daughter's home, but she willingly endured the tiresome discomforts of the first two means of travel, and braved the "frightful velocity" of the new railroad that Ann Eliza might have the comfort of her presence. The house in which the Buchanans lived was a mile from the nearest neighbor, and a half mile from the public road.

Mr. Buchanan's work in his new field kept him away from home many nights. Not only was he occupied with the management of the three churches that he served, but he was greatly in demand at Episcopal conferences and meetings, frequently held as far away as Philadelphia, Harrisburg, and Reading. Eliza Foster reached the Buchanan home in time for the arrival in May of Ann Eliza's little daughter, Charlotte, and after staying long enough to be sure the baby's mother was well on the road to recovery, Mrs. Foster set out to Philadelphia to visit girlhood friends and "kin" whom she had not seen since her marriage. To William, Jr., as usual, she relates her experiences.

Philadelphia   May the 28   [1836]

My Dear William

I know you have wonder'd what has become of me, I have been so long answering your very kind letter. I came to this city with Edward Buchanan last Tewesday week. I am at Mrs. Spencer's in fifth Street, an old acquaintance from the eastern shore of Maryland. Mrs. Wright her sister, who lives with her, was my early friend. Judge Baldwin and Mrs. Baldwin also Board here. They have been extreamly polite and kind to me, as also Govenor Finly who boards here. He hired a cariage, escorted me to see the mint in full operation. The French money had arived the night before from New York. I saw them weighing it, each Bullion of gold weighed ten thousand dollars, which I had in my hand but was too heavy to keep.

I expect to leave this for Pittsburgh on Teusday next, cousin Jesse Tomlinson has frank'd me a free passage. I hope and pray you are all in good health; as for the rest, I have so much confidence in my ever to be loved son, that I do not feel the least uneasy. At the same time, I will hasten home as soon as I can get company. Tell my dear Henrietta to keep herself in good heart, and keep peace with Mrs. Squire, if possible. Tell Morison and Stephen I know they are good boys, and look up to thear kind Elder Brother for countenance and protection, with submission.

I have nothing more to say at present, only to tell you how nesesary you are to my happiness. I am indeed your affectionate mother,

Eliza C. Foster.

IV

WILLIAM'S health improved greatly during the year he spent on the Pennsylvania and Ohio Canal, and in May, 1836, he ventured to return again to the state of Kentucky, taking the position of engineer in the vicinity of Tompkinsville, down in the Cumberland Mountains of Monroe County. His interest in Mary Wick, or "Dolly," as she was called affectionately by William's father, had now reached the point where the gentle girl felt it proper to take pen in hand and send a discreet reply to a letter from William. The young engineer did not know he was making history on the wilderness trails of the Kentucky country, and his letters, instead of telling very much of his own interesting experiences, are full of minute details of how mail shall be addressed to him to remote mountain post offices, so that he will lose no precious scrap of news from home. His latest letter must have given Mary more than the usual brief description of his way of living and working, and it pleased her a great deal, as shown in her letter of June 9, 1836:

Henrietta having left a blank in her letter, kindly invites me to fill it, and although to use your own words, "I have scarcely a half a dozen ideas," yet I feel that it will beguile a leisure moment to engage in the employment. The account you gave me of your itinerant cavalcade afforded me much pleasure, as I believe I can from that form a tolerably correct idea of your situation. Imagination pictures you moving along, followed by Assistants, Rodmen, Axmen, Wagons, &c.—all of which contribute to produce a confusion in your mind, well calculated to banish from it the idea of friends. I would be happy if those "sundry gentlemen" whom you mentioned would not again take it upon themselves to monopolize the time set apart for absent friends, especially if they have no other duty to perform than that of drinking a bottle of Champagne. You will discover from this that I advocate the cause of "total abstinence." And have you finally come to the conclusion that it is not the wealth of the Indies, or even a considerable part of it, that produces happiness? If so, I am truly gratified, and hope a lesson of experience will prove a benefit hereafter. For the present, nothing remains, but for you to make the best of your time, looking to Him in whose hands is all the power, to preserve you and protect you, and finally guide you to the presence of those who will be delighted to meet you. My health remains much the same. I spend some of my time practicing on the piano, some I devote to my friends, and some in performing domestic duties. Matilda and her husband are busily engaged in endeavoring to repair their old house for the reception of some bells from New Lisbon, who expect to spend some two or three weeks with them, and the consequence is I shall have to make a party for them. I wish you were here to participate in it. I could write on an hour to come in the same uninteresting manner, but fearing I shall weary your patience, I will bid you farewell, though not until I have sent the respects of my father and mother, and beg you to believe me your very sincere and faithful friend,

Mary A. Wick.

do write soon

Mary did not understand the steady William as well as his mother did, or she would have known it to be quite unnecessary to warn him against reckless companions who did not subscribe to the cause of "total abstinence." William was as reliable as the Rock of Gibraltar, but a young lady of 1836 would have been considered remiss indeed if she did not include a few moral reflections when writing

to her fiance, especially when the latter was far away from the refin-
ing influence of genteel female society. The touching little postscript "do write soon" reveals the true state of her feelings. Mary
spent much of her time with Henrietta, as the latter was alone now.
Mrs. Foster had returned to Pittsburgh in May, taking Stephen
and Morrison, and leaving Henrietta with Mrs. Squires, in whose
home they had been boarding. Stephen must have missed his sister
greatly, as well as Mary Wick, for there were plenty of home concerts when they were all together. Brother William had made such
a place for himself in the hearts of his Youngstown friends, that,
after he left for Kentucky in May, Henrietta wrote to her brother,
"Old Mr. McEuen goes about like a lost sheep. He has been in to
see me several times since you left, but we can hardly get him to
laugh."

Henrietta and Thomas Wick were married on October 20, 1836.
Thomas was kept busy in the general store managed by the three
Wick brothers, and therefore Henrietta was glad to have any of
her family stay with her. Stephen visited Henrietta frequently, and
was happy and contented, but of course he missed his lively brothers.
He was as enthusiastic as ever about the minstrel music in which
he excelled as a performer, and, in the earliest of the little fellow's
letters that has been preserved, he reminds his father that he had
promised to send him a "commic songster."

Youngstown   Jany 14th   1837

My Dear father

I wish you to send me a commic songster for you promised to. if I
had my pensyl I could rule my paper. or if I had the monye to by Black
ink   But if I had my whistle I would be so taken with it I donot think
I would write atall.   there has been a sleighing party this morning with
twenty or thirty cupple   Dr Bane got home last might and told us Henry
was coming out here   I wish Dunning would come with hin   tell them
bothh to try to cone for I should like to see them both most two much
to talk about.

I remane your loving son

Stephen C. Foster

Although little Stephen had trouble with his *n*'s and *m*'s, he
did very well with the more difficult words in his letter. It seems

likely that Morrison was with Stephen in Youngstown at this time, and both boys probably longed to see their brothers, Dunning, and Henry—"most two much to talk about." Dr. Bane, mentioned by Stephen, was married to Matilda Wick, Thomas Wick's sister.

Brother William delighted them all with a visit to Youngstown and Pittsburgh in February. He was anxious to close out his and his father's share of the business of Foster & Hall, for although the store had done well at first, the threat of coming hard times was reflected in the many failures all around them. The man who bought out their share of the store did not dare have his name published as a partner, on account of the numerous suits standing against him. This was not learned by William and his father until after the deal had been closed, and the Fosters mentioned that they intended to publish notice of the dissolution of partnership. Matters were finally adjusted by William who allowed them to use his name for two months longer until the new partner could collect money that was owed to him and pay off his threatening creditors.

Dunning, Morrison, and Stephen were all in school, and Henry was still traveling in Ohio and Kentucky for Hutchinson & Ledlie. Their father was rejoicing that William was now "cock of the walk" and commander in chief of his cavalcade in the woods, and that Mother was feeling better after a bad attack of rheumatism.

One of William's letters to his mother headed "Encampment No. 1, Barren County, Ky. May 14, 1837," contains a little more news of his travels than he generally gives.

On the 25th April, I left Frankfort and arrived at Bowling Green on the 27th. From the 27th of April until the 11th inst. I spent at that place in getting my tents and camp furniture prepared for about a three months' tour. I reached this place on the 12th and commenced my survey yesterday. This has been a dreary, wet Sunday and has confined us pretty closely to our tents; we are very fortunate in having good capacious and waterproof ones; so that we experience no other inconvenience from the rain than being obliged to keep under our canvass.— I have a company of twelve, with a waggon for baggage, and everything to render us as comfortable as it is possible to be in the woods, and in this way of living.—

In addition to the usual supplies, for subsistence, I am furnished with a medicine chest, so that in case of any sudden illness we have medicines at hand. I do not apprehend much use for the medicines as the country is perfectly dry & the stream along whose banks our survey will extend has rocky bluffs and mostly gravelly bottom, indicating pure water.

As we extend up the stream, I suppose we shall not be favorably situated for Post Offices, and I shall not be enabled to write very often; I shall not fail to do so as often as opportunity offers. I expect to finish this survey in about two or three months and will be engaged in the latter part of the season farther North in the State.

My health never was better and I do not anticipate evil—sufficient for the day is the evil thereof. Will you, my dear Mother, write to me; address "Bowling Green," Warren County, Ky. & tell me everything.— If you have any late news from Youngstown give it to me.—I am writing on a board set up on forks (wooden ones) in my tent, and cannot be very prolix, nor very nice about it.—Adieu, my good mother; may God bless & keep you until we meet again.   William

Ann Eliza, in her far-off home, with her many duties as a minister's wife and the mother of two babies, always found time to write long, loving letters to her mother, for with a growing family of her own, and surrounded by strangers, she missed her mother sadly. Ann Eliza had one woman to help her, and a person named John "hung about" and helped with the chores, but otherwise, she and the children, James and Charlotte, were much alone. Some of her homesickness is expressed in a letter to her mother, written in June, 1837:

It is generally thought, I believe, that as we grow older, our attachment to our parents and our first home weakens—but the case is widely different with me. Not a month or a week passes over my head, without leaving me more full of tender recollections of the home and friends of my childhood, and I think I am becoming every day more sensible of the kindness and affection of my parents towards me, and more grateful for it. In return now I strive to offer with sincerity my poor prayers to Almighty God in their behalf. I had indulged the hope that I should have got out to Pittsburg this summer, but taking all things into consideration, I think it most prudent for me to stay at home. When I know you are all well and doing well, I can content myself better. Should there be any serious sickness in the family, I would let nothing prevent me from going to your assistance. Tell Henry and Dunning they are both in debt to me a letter, and I shall be happy also to receive any communications which Mitty or Stevy may have to make, and will reply to them promptly. Give a great deal of love to my dear father and the boys. Write as soon and as often as you possibly can, and may the blessing of the Lord be with you always. Ever your affectionate daughter,

Ann Eliza.

From a short history of Allegheny published in the *Pittsburgh Leader* of January 8, 1888, we gain more information of the serious economic situation which developed all over the country in 1837, and which bears out the facts mentioned by William B. Foster, Sr., in letters of that year.

The borough [Allegheny] increased slowly until May, 1837, when the banks suspended specie payments, which caused a panic over the whole country. Mills, workshops, etc. of all kinds were shut down, money and change was so scarce that a system of swapping or trading had to be carried on. The borough council came to the relief of the people by an ordinance passed May 18, 1837, authorizing the issue of certificates of loan (commonly called scrip) in notes of three, two and one dollars, and for change fifty and twenty-five cents, all bearing interest at the rate of 2 per cent per annum. A committee of two councilmen with the burgess and treasurer were authorized to issue such amounts as the borough needed for the improvements and for change for the people, which was a great relief to them.

A popular song by the editor of *The Mountaineer*, sung to the tune of "The Long Tail Blue," was carefully preserved by Wm. B. Foster, and dated September 17, 1837. The entire piece is too long to quote here, but several verses will suffice to show the wheels within "De Balance Wheel"—burning issues of the day, long since forgotten.

Now SHINPLASTERS are "all the go!"

As all the people feel,

Because old Nick and our "old Joe" [*]

Have broke de BALANCE WHEEL.

Oh! de Balance Wheel!

De PAPER Balance Wheel!

De PEOPLE'S sick of Joe and Nick,

And curse de "BALANCE WHEEL."

*Nicholas Biddle, head of the United States Bank, and Governor Joseph Ritner, of Pennsylvania.

Brave JACKSON made a tarnal kick,
   Through patriotic zeal;
And he capsized the mighty Nick,
   And his great Balance Wheel.

De Whigs den all began to stare,
   And run about and squeal!
And axed old Josey to repair
   De broken Balance wheel.

The DEMOCRATS—(though fond of noise!)
   Are all as true as steel!
And out of "BENTON'S YELLOW BOYS"
   They'll make a Balance Wheel!
     A STEADY Balance Wheel,—
     A LASTING Balance Wheel,—
     We will be free,—and Equitey
     SHALL GUIDE THE BALANCE WHEEL!

Extracts from letters of June 6 and June 8, 1837, from William B. Foster, Sr., to his son, William, throw further light on the extent of the panic in Pittsburgh.

   . . . Since writing you on the 6th, I have seen Wm. Robinson, Jr. who inform'd me that he had brought with him from Youngstown a package of money for you; and had, agreeably to his instructions, delivered it to the cashier of the Bank of Pittsburgh. I call'd on Mr. Snyder, who inform'd me he had rec'd. the money (I think 480 Dollars); but as it was in such notes as they did not receive on deposit, he had not placed it to your credit, but should hold it subject to your order. You will forward an order immediately on the rect. of this, for that money, either to Mr. Fisk or myself.—Our court will meet on Monday the 19th inst. when I will be ordered to pay over the money in my hands from the administration of Duncan's estate, and which we used to pay Stephens the 1st. of May. We must get your money changed by some means, either for specie, (which is out of the question) U. S. Bank or Pittsburgh Bank notes. . . .

   . . . Another failure yesterday; Fundenburgh the hardware folks, shut up. Sam'l P. has fail'd and made an assignment; so goes the thousand dollar pair of horses! Koneky and Joseph Amores are shut up by the sheriff, and God only knows how many more will share the same fate.

Such times you never saw, and the worst, much the worst is to come. The Banks all refuse Specie, and nothing but shinplasters for change. You are well out of merchandising. They must owe, I presume, from 15 to 18 thousand Dollars; but Sam is good enough. . . .

And on July 16, he writes:

The Bank of Pittsburgh after some time agreed to place your rag money to Mr. Fisk's credit, so that all that concern came out right. Our country is in a terrible state of depression; the silk stocking gentry are damning Jackson for killing their savior God Moloch, but the countryman, when he looks at a *shin plaster* for 25 cts. to take the price of a quart of cherries, damns all Banks and hurrahs for Jackson.—I'll tell you a good joke—your brother informs me that young Whittlesey of Ohio, (his father you know a great Bank member of Congress) sent Warren Bank notes to Pittsburgh to pay a debt, and it would not be received; he damn'd all Banks and proclaim'd for Jackson on the spot!

Though harder times threatened, and fortunes were being wiped out on every hand, Stephen's mother found cause for thankfulness for all her blessings. Her children, her friends, her church, and her Allegheny home more than compensated for luxury displayed by some more affluent neighbors.

June 16, 1837

My dear William [Jr.]

I would have written to you some days before this, only that I waited to hear from Youngstown before I would write. I received a letter yesterday from Henrietta in which she says "I wrote to brother William, and Mary wrote to him." In my letter, she also says she (Mary) is a great deal there, but as for the place itself, there is not the slightest new occurence in the town or its vicinity.

I received a letter from your sister Ann Eliza in which she also mentions haveing written to you and taxing you with an intention of takeing a help mate, which is very laudable. Henry is yet absent, but your Father is very domestick, and I am much better fixed than I expected to be by this time, and I pray that God, through the sangtifying influence of the spirit and being directed by the doctrine of the mediator, the meek and lowly Jesus, may keep me in grace, that I may dayly number up my blessings with thankfullness for the present and gratitude for the past, knowing that I have ever been an unprofitable wife and a careless Mother. In the midst of all this, the Lord has been always remembering me in Mercy. My tears fall fast and heavy, my dear William, while I write these lines with deep repentence for my life of thoughtlessness.

Stephen has recovered from the whooping cough, and going to school with Morison to Mr. Todd. Duning is still at the old place. There has been several failures, but Hutcheson and Ledly I believe is like to stand. Pittsburg looks very dull as to business in Market Street, but yet one would not suppose business to be going down when they see the elegant coaches with silver trapings on the splendid Horses by which they are drawn, and to hear of ladies copeing for the hiest pric'd and most accomplish'd drivers; but for my part I am truly thankfull that I have shoes to put on my feet without haveing earned them by the swet of my brow, and that my ancles are again strong enough to enable me to step my way on a pleasant Sunday down the Hill and over the bridge to Trinity Church, and think myself most happy that if their is none to court me, their is none to trouble me. . . . While the whole community is disputing about Theoligy, which is right, the High church or low church, the three decrees or no decrees, the Episcopal methedist or the radical methedist, if the whispers of a benign deity decend upon my affections with the gentle voice of a reconcil'd Father soothing away the thick darkness which will shade the mind when points of doctrine is discust, the preacher whose words drop to this purpose chases the mists of uncirtainty from the mind, and it is therefore comfortable to hear him; but these new lights, as they are call'd, seem always to have some political question in view. . . .

Now, we have had a great preacher here from Philadelphia trying to establish what is cal'd the low Church, and half of Doctor Upfold's Congregation has run mad after him, leaveing their own parson to preach to emty pews. Service was held in Doctor Heron's meeting house, because Doctor Upfold did not invite Doctor Ting to preach in Trinity, and said he did not acknolege the Parish of St. Andrews over which Doctor Ting came to preach. . . .

Pa has made a beautifull little garden, and rises early every morning to dress and weed it. It has served him for a hobby. Our next door neighbours are boath excellent and pleasant, so that I do not miss little Mrs. Thorn in Youngstown. We go through a little gate to bake in their oven.

There has been a great many of my old acquantences to see me. Mrs. Evans has not got a beaux for her sister yet. Sarah Evans has been a trip to Philadelphia without her Husband—this is quer!

I have nothing more to tell you that you would take the trouble to read, therefore give me leave to beg that you will take very particular

care of your health, not for my sake, or your own sake, but for the sake
of one who I have no doubt lives but for you alone.

I am, my Dear Son, with many a fond rememberence of your moral
virtues,

Your truly affectionate Mother,

Eliza C. Foster.

Though greatly concerned about her imagined spiritual short-
comings, Eliza Foster could pass serenely from the sublime to the
mundane in a most lovably human way. Her preoccupation with
otherworldly things did not prevent her from taking a lively interest
in Sarah Evans' trip to Philadelphia without Mr. Evans. This was
"quer," and that's that. Mrs. Foster made quite a number of trips
to Philadelphia without her husband, but she had a daughter to
look after who was intent on raising a large family, and Sarah
Evans evidently had no such excuse for her goings on! One likes
to picture that peaceful household on the East Common: Pa working away in his garden, glad to be released from the vexations of
the store and the cares of disheartened business friends; Mrs. Foster and "the girl" trotting through the back gate with pans full
of freshly raised bread dough to pop into Mrs. Pentland's outside
bake oven, and stopping to chat with her neighbor over the latest bit
of news of the town; Stephen and Morrison living the average,
happy life of the small town boy. Perhaps it was this summer (1837)
that they had one of the biggest adventures of their lives. At any
rate, this happened while they were attending school at Mr. Stockton's academy. Morrison relates:

There was some elevated ground at the corner then, but it has been
dug away since to make room for the railroad tracks. On the bluff overlooking the low ground near the academy, some other boys and I began
digging a hole in the ground one day. I don't know what made us
do it. Perhaps it was just a boyish inspiration to dig a hole. Perhaps
we had heard that some Indians were buried there. Anyhow, I have
forgotten just what it was, but all the same, we dug up the remains
of six or seven Indian chiefs. They must have been powerfully big
men, judging from the size of the bones. We also found in the grave
a tomahawk and a lot of arrow-heads, beads and pottery. What became
of them? Now, really I don't know. I have an idea they were turned over
to the Western University of Pennsylvania, and if they have not been

lost sight of long ago, they may still be found somewhere in one of the spare rooms at the University.

V

EARLY in July, 1837, Henrietta sent word that she would soon need her mother's care, so, accompanied by "little Stephen" (as they still called him), Mrs. Foster and Dunning took stage to Youngstown. The latter saw his mother safely to Henrietta's, and left Stephen in Poland, Ohio, about six miles south of Youngstown at the farm of uncle John Struthers. Dunning returned to Pittsburgh, and the three boys and their father and a "good girl" were left at home. The term of Kitty, the bound girl, had evidently expired, for there is no further mention of her.

On July 16, 1837, William B. Foster wrote to tell William, Jr., of his mother's departure, and the latest news regarding their firm's dissolution of partnership.

I think you are unnecessarily uneasy respecting your business with Sam and Hall. It is out of their power to make you liable for a dollar of debt, so long as Sam is worth one, and he, you know, is amply able for all, if they were mean enough to even let suit be brought against you. Hall has not changed his friendly course in the least, he came over and drank tea with us on Sunday evening last. I advise you to write to him, not touching your old business, but some account of the country and your progress in Kentucky.—I have the copy of the notice of dissolution of partnership in safety.—I shall shortly make another pilgrimage to Erie on the old business.

The "old business" at Erie was old indeed. It concerned sheriff's sale of a tract of land owned by one of the directors of the defunct stagecoach company. Wm. B. Foster knew it would be necessary for him to be right on the ground to enter his claim if he wished to receive any consideration. He left home July 20 and remained about a week at Youngstown, during which time Henrietta's first child, Mary Baldwin Wick, was born July 28. He made great plans to be carried out if he should receive even a thousand dollars from the sale. The first of these was that Dunning should be sent to a school for civil engineers at Georgetown, Kentucky, and Henry, who was now out of a position at Hutchinson & Ledlie's, on account of the hard times, should be set up in a business of his own. But there were several claims ahead of Foster's, and this trip and many more were made to Erie without result. Dunning was not sent to college, but his father was able to help Henry in 1838 to go into partnership with A. Skinner in a general store at Warren, Pennsylvania, and by that time Hutchinson & Ledlie were a little more prosperous, and took Dunning on in Henry's old place.

Mr. Foster returned home from Erie by way of Youngstown, and brought with him Stephen and his mother, who had been with Henrietta about six weeks. William's fiancée, Mary Wick, and her sister, Mrs. Bane, accompanied them to Allegheny, and while they were there, there occurred the most astounding event of their lives, with the possible exception of their first sight of a locomotive; in the latter part of August, 1837, Clayton made a "splendid ascension" in his balloon from the East Common of Allegheny, "within twenty roods of our door!"

It was [Mr. Foster wrote to William] the most beautiful sight I ever saw. I send you this morning's newspaper containing an account of it. He landed near Johnstown, and return'd yesterday [September 4] by the canal, Balloon and all, safe and sound. He goes up again on Monday next.

It must have been a happy week for gentle little Mary Wick in the sunshine of her beloved William's family; what a satisfaction it must have been to choose her wedding clothes in a town that was a metropolis in comparison to quiet, little Youngstown. And then to see the great Clayton make a balloon ascension practically in their own front yard! That event provided a topic of conversation among the Foster boys and around the family supper table for many days to come. So great was the interest, that William's mother held off writing him a note of thanks for a twenty-dollar bill he had sent her, "untill after the next Balloon ascension!"

Strange to say, in his letter to his oldest son, dated September 5, 1837, William's cheerful-hearted father allows a slight tone of doubt to creep into his expectations.

. . . My business at Erie is not yet closed. The property was sold while

I was there for 5000 Dollars, but proceeds not yet divided. I still hope
to get over 1000 Dollars, but, with my luck, all things are uncertain. . . .

Small wonder that he thought Fate was against him—there were
few, however, in that disastrous year of 1837 who did not believe
their luck could be anything but bad. But William B. Foster, Jr.,
was not dwelling much on business reverses. He was making haste
to finish his work in Kentucky, to be free to have a few short weeks
which his instinct told him were all he was fated to share with the
sweet girl who was slowly but surely fading before his eyes. Perhaps
to Henrietta he owed the precious few days which a warning from
her gained for him. She wrote to him on September 7, 1837, from
Youngstown, Ohio.

My dear brother,

As it has been a long time since I heard from you, I think it is time I
should write and find out whether you are living or not; but I hope
we shall soon see you here, as you have been gone five months.—
Mary has been to Pittsburgh for a week, but got home on Friday last.
She does not look so well lately, poor little dear. She got her wedding
dress and a great many little nice things when she was in town. I think
you had better come as soon as you can, for if you were here, it seems to
me she would be better. I only judge of her health by her looks. I have
call'd my little babe for her; she is a sweet little creature (at least I
think so) she has very deep blue eyes and black hair. She will be six
weeks old tomorrow. I will not have time to write much as my little
Mary is beginning to wake up, for I take care of her myself altogether,
and she has been asleep for some time. I have to rock her with my foot
while I write.—
I do not want you to be alarmed about Mary, for she may be no worse
than when you left, and perhaps it is only my imagination, and I don't
want you to be uneasy, but still I thought it would be best to tell you
what I think about her, so that you can manage your affairs accordingly,
although I know that you will come as soon as you can. She was bridesmaid for Mrs. Reno . . . who was married about four or five weeks ago,
and has gone to Beaver to live.
Do write to me soon, my dear brother, for I have not heard from you
so long that I am getting uneasy for fear you are sick. I wrote a long
letter to Sissy Anny the other day, the first time I have written to her
for more than six months.

Henry Wick and his wife and children have gone traveling, so you may know I am pretty lonely now, as she was the only one I cared much about of the brothers' wives, and little (or *your*) Mary is so busy now that I do not see a great deal of her. When she is here she talks all the time about you; she says *It will not be long till you come now.*

Thomas is going to move the store down to Dennick's old stand in a week or two, as he and Lemuel have bought a furnace out in Franklin, Pa. Dennick will take his store with him.

Thomas sends his love to you and believe me to be your sincerely affectionate sister,

Henrietta.

This letter is directed to William at Frankfort, Kentucky, and readdressed from there to Bardstown. William had his headquarters in the latter place for about a month. Although he does not mention doing so, surely in that time, he must have made a call on his father's kinsman, Judge Rowan, and made himself known to the cousins in whose hearts his sister Charlotte had held so strong a place.

Nelson County, Ky. Sept. 29, 1837

My dear Father,

On Sunday evening last, I recd. yours of the 5th inst.—it had been sent from Bowling Green to Bardstown in this county, where I had directed the Post Master to forward until the end of this month.—I am now about ten miles above Bardstown, on the Beach Fork of Salt River, and have two or three days work more to complete the survey of this fork.— I have finished the Rolling fork, and have yet the main Salt River from the mouth up about 80 miles to examine. Should the weather prove favorable, we shall get through with that, in all October, so that by the middle of November, I shall be able to leave Frankfort for home. It will keep me very busy to make up my reports in two weeks & they must be ready before the meeting of the Legislature, which takes place on the 1st. Decr. Major W. is a Senator, reelected, last August, and I shall have opportunities of seeing him during the winter, if not before.

I think my business arrangements will be such as to require me to take Steam Boat at Louisville, and in that case should have no opportunity of seeing him before I go home.—If, however, I should be able to go through Lexington and take boat at Maysville, shall see him on my way.—

I wrote to you on the 10th. giving my opinion in relation to Georgetown College, &c. and also telling you that I had been slightly ill with ague & fever. It now gives me pleasure to say that I feel quite well, not having had any symptoms of it since the first attack.

The weather has been remarkably pleasant since I have been on my present survey, until yesterday and today, we are detained in camp by rain.—I do not stay much in camp, but procure lodgings in farm houses. I am now at a comfortable Farmer's house, who is remarkably kind and hospitable.—Indeed, I find no difficulty in getting the best the country affords, and as this is an old settled part of the state, we have all the comforts, at least, of life.—I learn by a letter from Mr. Reno that he has been compelled to leave the Crosscut Canal; this I am sorry to hear; it appears to be a dangerous experiment, this thing of taking a wife. Between you & I, the Principal Engineer is a *mighty* mean man.

I wish you to call, (or get Henry to do it) at Caleb Lee's, and select suitable cloth & have a suit of clothes made for me, the same to be used *upon an extraordinary occasion* soon after I get home—Of the fineness, color, etc. I am not particular, I want them *good* & *plain*. Also, get him to make me an overcoat of fashionable shape & color, not exceeding in price about $40.—You will please have the clothes sent over home & keep until I come.—Please to acknowledge the rect. of this, so that I may know when I get to Frankfort that the clothes will be ready for me, otherwise I would provide them before I left Frankfort.

With much love to dear Mother and brothers, I remain

Your affectionate son,
William.

P.S. Address in future "Frankfort, Ky."

Brief mention is made now and then in William B. Foster's records of his brother, Alexander Foster, who practiced law in Pittsburgh in the 1830's and occasionally attended to legal matters for William B. Foster. He later moved to Harrison County, Ohio, where he died in 1845. But the families of the two brothers seem not to have been very intimate, as nothing ever is said of visits being made back and forth between the two households.

The following letter to his son William from William B. Foster, Sr., mentioning "the Major" and "Mr. Fisk," refers to some still unsettled, troubling problem connected with the Lawrenceville property.

Pittsburgh, Octr. 11, 1837

Dear William,

Your two letters, one dated 10th and the other the 29th Septr. have been rec'd. and be assured it gives us great pleasure to learn that you have quite recovered from your indisposition. I saw Mr. Welsh here five or six days ago, who inform'd me that he had recently seen you in good health.—I perceive by your last letter that you had not then heard of the death of our worthy friend Mr. Fisk. A letter from your mother written a few days after his death gave you the information. You need not speak to the Major respecting the claim against Mr. Fisk, for that died with himself. They never can recover one cent from his estate, and they are well served. When I was at Lexington in June, 1836, Major W. desired that I would on my return here, make certain propositions to Mr. Fisk, and if he should accede to them, to write him, and he would authorize me to close with him. Fisk agreed to do all I asked, of which I inform'd W. by writing him three letters, the rect. of which he never acknowledged, by which they have lost Six Thousand, and myself one thousand Dollars. The Major at Lexington is pretty deeply in for his brother, & I dont pity him, he behaved rascally towards me.—You may tell him if you meet with him, that he and his brother have lost six thousand Dollars by his neglecting to answer my letters.

The letter inclosed in yours of the 10th. was immediately forwarded to Youngstown, where matters go on very well, and have no doubt you will be anxiously looked for before you arrive.—

Mr. Henry Wick and wife left us this morning for home, from New York and Philada. they remain'd in our house two nights and one day.— I brought Henrietta and the babe in, and they remain'd with us ten days. Thomas came for them & took them home a week ago—the old man is very kind to them.—

Your clothes from Caleb Lee will be ready before you arrive; a most beautiful suit, black coat & Pants and *white vest*. Lee says he will make you a black sattin vest also, which you may take or not as you please. Blue overcoat; they are costly, but the best in Pittsb'g.

The election over on yesterday; and we are defeated, Horse, Foot and Dragoons! The combined enemy, Whigs and Anti-Masons will beat us in this county from 7 to 800 votes, and I have no doubt it will be so all over the State. Van Burenism is done in Pa. Thank fortune I was not in the field this time.

In my next, will tell you something about my Erie business, etc. Friends all well—and the family join with me in much love to you.

Your affectionate father,

Wm. B. Foster.

Mary's affliction, which was consumption, ran its accustomed treacherous course, of relapse and counterfeit recovery. In October, she alarmed her anxious friends by a very severe sick spell which lasted about ten days, but from which she emerged in such seeming good health and spirits that all were encouraged to believe she was better than she had been in years. It seemed as though love and hope kept her up until her dear William joined her in the early part of December. Their period of happiness was short lived. We do not know whether she left her father's home for even a week after her wedding. She was not able to accompany William back to Kentucky, and the young man who had planned to return so happily with his bride, set out for Frankfort alone about the first of January. Almost before he had time to realize that he was married, a letter from Mary's brother, Lemuel Wick, informed William that his young wife had died on January 8, 1838.

Calm and composed, her tranquil spirit patiently awaited its last moment of time on earth. The family were called up to witness her last moments at 4 o'clock A.M., from which time she appeared more natural in mind and countenance than for months past. She was fully apprised of her immediate dissolution, & observed she would soon be in her own house, & desired that her God would make easy her passage from this world to the world of Spirits, which was the case, and may we unitedly be thankful. This day she was interred in the burying place on the hill, beside my older sister.

So ended the first romance of generous, tender-hearted Brother William. The future dealt more kindly with him, but it is doubtful if the memory of the blighted hopes of his youth was ever erased from his steadfast and devoted mind.

VI

IN March, 1838, when Stephen was nearly twelve years old, the Foster family, with the exception of Brother William, was reunited again in the pleasant home situated in Allegheny on a rise of ground above the Allegheny River. Before the house was a wide green common where cows grazed peacefully; it was a pleasant walk down the common, over the little bridge that crossed the canal, and down Anderson Street, to the river. We have Eliza Foster's word for it that the river was blue in the summer in those days, but one never sees it blue now. When it is not a slaty gray, it flows a slippery stream of dirty yellow between its shop-infested banks. But in 1838, Allegheny was still a country town; busy Ohio Street was then a pleasant road that shortly merged into the Butler Turnpike.

This spring the rivers had broken up very gently, and the Allegheny ice was clearing out without any flood or damage. Henry Foster, who was becoming quite a beau, regretted the passing of the snow, which took with it all hope of any more "delightful sleighing." But he was rejoicing with brotherly affection in the arrival of Mr. Buchanan and dear "Sisey Aney, with two of the finest looking children you would meet with anywhere," James and Charlotte; and then, Henrietta with baby Mary Wick came in, and as Father Foster said, they had a pretty smart family for a while.

Mr. Foster was still trying hard to recover something from the wreckage of 1837, but progress was slow along that line. He was earning enough to keep going by buying and selling for others, and acting in the capacity of solicitor for people having business to be attended to in other counties and states. These trips took him frequently into Ohio and Kentucky, but it was not a business that could be depended upon to furnish much income. Only Morrison and Stephen were now in school; Henry had taken a position with a grocery warehouse, and Dunning had Henry's old position with Hutchinson & Ledlie. Considering how little advanced schooling these boys secured, the general knowledge which they displayed, and the creditable success which they attained in life is remarkable. The handwriting of each of these young men is of the cultured class, not the painful and self-conscious efforts of the half-educated. Although William, Jr., attended Canonsburg Academy for a short time, as did his father before him, none of them completed what in the present day would be equivalent to a high school course. Morrison liked to recall how their mother and father set them long tasks of writing in the evenings, copying page after page of fine-printed classics, especially Shakespeare, Walter Scott, and Byron, and hearing them recite from memory as much of it as they could. In preceding pages we have mentioned some of the advanced texts from which Ann Eliza instructed Morrison and little Stephen.

To this patient teaching at home, augmented by constant encouragement to love the best in music and poetry, can be attributed their ability to appreciate good literature and art as intelligently as, and perhaps better than, many who had enjoyed the advantages of college and university training.

At this time, the spring of 1838, William, Jr., was making an effort to secure an appointment again in Pennsylvania. He was deeply attached to the many friends he had made in Kentucky, but the state was having a hard time to find money for improvements, and as the climate never had agreed with him, he was anxious to make a change. He was depressed in spirits after Mary's death and, following the example of his mother, sought strength and comfort by ordering his life along strict religious lines. Rather surprisingly, Henry, now twenty-two, and the most pleasure-loving of the Foster boys, had left the more liberal atmosphere of the Episcopal church and joined with the Presbyterians in whose church he became a most zealous worker. William did not go to this extreme, but he found satisfaction in devoting his spare time to Bible study, and attending services wherever a church was to be found in the Kentucky hills. He continued to interest himself in his father's and brothers' business affairs; in fact, the men of this family consulted each other on practically every move they made, and over a period of twenty years, not a discordant note, nor word of criticism one of the other, appear in their correspondence. The father's difficulties in collecting from the old stagecoach company became part of the daily routine, and there are few of his letters to William, Jr., that do not contain some reference to the struggle.

April 16, 1838—After I wrote you last, M. and myself had several conversations respecting the judgment, by which I found there was no use to urge the payment of the whole amount, as he honestly assured me if I did so, he would be compell'd to resort to the law for the benefit of insolvent debtors, and more than probable he would do so in any event; of this I felt pretty well convinced, when I found that he had been detain'd here after his family had started for Louisville, by the sheriff, on two cases, for large sums. He got bail for his appearance in May, and left for Louisville about six days ago.—

Under these circumstances, my course was to make the best arrangement I could, and to accept of any reasonable proposal which he would make, which was; to make arrangements to pay about the amount of the judgment without interest, say $350 dollars, as follows—to pay two debts of mine amounting together to about $127, the balance of accounts in his favour between us, $70, small notes and due bills which he gave me on different persons here, $85—and to send me from Louisville (which he will obtain through his brother-in-law there) sugar and coffee to amount of $68 in full.—He promised to send the groceries shortly after his arrival in Louisville.—"Better take half a loaf than no bread.—"

Mr. Buchanan and family started home about ten days ago, by the Canal. I feel anxious to know how your agent has succeeded in getting funds for the public improvements. Inform me as soon as you can.

I would not mention M's. circumstances in Kentucky; it might injure him, and could do us no good.

Our friends at Youngstown I believe are all well.—Dennick call'd to see us on this day week, on his way from the furnace to Youngstown.—

When you write again, address your letters to Allegheny Town, near Pittsb'g.

The family are all well and join in love to you, with your

Affectionate father,

Wm. B. Foster, Jr. Engineer,
Frankfort, Kentucky.

Wm. B. Foster.

Henry Foster was an earnest, dependable boy, and to him Brother William entrusted the task of having a suitable head- and footstone prepared for Mary's grave. Henry saw to it that they were neatly inscribed, and then hired a team of horses and hauled the stones to Youngstown where he had them installed over the remains of the young wife who had been dear to them all. He seemed to take great pride in attending to all William's commissions, hoping to please the kind older brother of whom he was so proud.

Allegheny Town, April 21st. 1838

Dear Brother,

Your kind letter of the 7th and 9th inst. came to hand yesterday, inclosing a 50 Dollar Note, for which you will accept our thanks. It came in good time; indeed, we are like many of our neighbours, pretty hard run, but we will not complain. Pa desires me to inform you that Cornelius Darragh, who returned from Harrisburgh a few days ago, told him day before yesterday that he had while in the Senate received a letter from Mr. Jas. Harris, requesting him to speak to the Canal Commissioners for a place for you. Mr. D. did so, and the Commiss'ers told him they would give you charge of the Allegheny feeder, that is you know, from Kittanning to Freeport.—Pa thanked Mr. Darragh very cordially for his kind interference, and told him he supposed that at the time you wrote to Mr. Harris you did not expect that Kentucky would be able to raise the necessary funds to carry on her improvements, but as they had done so, he presumed you would remain. Nothing was said about your pay here. Pa requests you to write to Mr. Darragh immediately to thank him, etc.

The portraits are here, and both excellent likenesses. Your request respecting them shall be attended to, as well as all your concerns intrusted to me. Mr. Hall has attended to the rents and paid Stevens. Since you wrote, we suppose you have received a letter from Ma, and one from Pa. He desires your attention to his, as he is afraid he may lose all his claim.—We received a letter from Sisey Aney a few days since, and were pleased to learn she had a very pleasant passage in the canal boat, there being but few passengers who were all quite agreeable.

Thomas Wick and his Brothers have sold out their stock of goods to Calvin Wick. Tom expects to turn his attention to Farming for the summer, and will commence business again perhaps next Fall or Spring.

We all enjoy good health, and lament to hear of your being unable to procure the same blessing, but hope, dear Brother, that you will accept our sympathies during your toil and fatigue. The family with myself join in love to you, hoping that ere this, you have recovered from your late attack of fever & ague. Will write you again in a few days.

Your affectionate Brother,

Henry B. Foster.

By the middle of May, 1838, Stephen, Morrison, and Dunning were the only boys left at home, for Henry started out bravely for himself in business in Warren, Pennsylvania. His father, of course, was intensely interested in the venture and wrote most hopefully of Henry's prospects to Brother William, then stationed at Brashear, Kentucky.

Allegheny Town   May 13th, 1838

Dear son,

Your letter of the 30th ult. and 2d. inst. was brought us by Mr. Snyder on this day week; he spent some time with us, and in the evening went to church with Henry. He appears to be indeed a man every way worthy of your friendship. He remain'd in town four days, not in good health; Henry or myself call'd on him every day and I accompanied him to the Boat.—

I have rec'd a letter from M. since he went to Ky. in which he speaks doubtingly; evidently in very low spirits, says the Staging has been a losing business in Kentucky, etc.

Henry has entered into partnership with a Mr. Skinner of Warren, Pa. who has been down, and they laid in and forwarded a very handsome assortment of goods, as well as provisions. Mr. S. started with them in a steam Boat a few days ago, and was fortunate as to get up all the way with the Boat to Warren. Mr. Skinner is a nephew of Mr. Tanner, is quite a business man, and comes highly recomended by Thomas Struthers; he has been in business there several years past on his own acct. and now intends to add the lumbering to the merchandizing trade—of course it will require two partners, as one must be a great part of the time from home. Henry will go up in the first Boat, perhaps tomorrow or next day.—I hope they may do well.—I will go up in a week or ten days and remain some time, to open their partnership Books, etc., a business to which you know Henry is a Stranger; and trust in Providence they may produce a better balance sheet than did the Books which I opened at Lowell.

Dunning is still with Hutchinson & Ledlie at 400 Dolls. per annum.—

On the subject of engineering here, I have not heard much said since I wrote you; old Davy Leech a few days ago enquired where you were, said he wish'd very much they would place you on the Kittanning feeder, etc.

We are very happy to learn as well from your letters as Mr. Snyder, that you have with you good Assistant Engineers, and hope you will be able to preserve your health.

Elizabeth Mahon is married to McCally the carpet merchant.

You will most likely hear next from me at Warren; I will write you from thence, after being there a few days.

The family all join in love to you with your affectionate father,

W. B. Foster.

[Postscript by Henry]

Dr. Brother,

I have delayed writing you until now for the purpose of giving you an act. of my prospects for going into business at Warren, but perceiving

Pa has said all that is necessary, shall make no farther comment on the subject at present, but hope by the time I get fairly established, to give one which will be entirely satisfactory. Had intended to visit you and consult on the subject before making an agreement, but receiving a letter from you stating that you intended soon to leave Frankfort for the headwaters of the Ky. River, thought it would be almost impossible to find you; & after visiting Warren for a week & the prospect for business appearing so flattering there, concluded to risk it, & hope by industry & economy to succeed. My partner, Mr. Skinner, is highly esteemed by all, & as long as he has any goods on hand which will answer the purpose, will purchase from no other. He is a member of the Presbyterian Church and as fine a business man as I ever met with. We found no difficulty in getting all the goods we wanted here on time, but Mr. S. thinks best to go East for goods hereafter, although goods taken from this place pay from 30 to 40 pr. ct. on an average.

I was much pleased with Mr. Snyder your friend.

As the time has arrived for my attending Sabbath School, will say no more at present, but in haste remain,

Your affect. Brother,

Henry B. Foster.

William B. Foster, Sr., was no stranger to Warren or its citizens. It is easy for strangers to confuse Warren, Pennsylvania, with Warren, Ohio, especially as the latter city is not far from Poland, Ohio, original settling place of John Struthers, who married William B. Foster's oldest sister, Mary. Between Poland, and Youngstown, Ohio, there is a little town called Struthers, named for John Struthers. But, Warren, Pennsylvania, located about 120 miles northeast of Pittsburgh, on the Allegheny River, was the town selected by John Struthers' son, Thomas Struthers, in which to found his home and make a comfortable fortune. Another town called Struthers, located a few miles east of Warren, Pennsylvania, doubtless was named in honor of Thomas Struthers. There was considerable business connection between Pittsburgh and Warren, Pennsylvania, in the 1830's, and 1840's, because of the great amount of lumber shipped down the river from Warren. Sherman Day, in his *Historical Collections of Pennsylvania,* published in 1843, says:

... at the breaking up of the ice in the spring, and during the subsequent floods, the town, and the whole country above, on the Conewango and Allegheny, is alive with the bustle of preparation among the lumber men. Large rafts are continually coming down the Allegheny, and smaller ones down the Conewango, and rounding in at Warren to be coupled into rafts of immense area, 60 or 70 feet wide, and from 250 to 300 feet long, in which shape they pursue their course to Pittsburg and Cincinnati. Large boats, too, or "broad-horns," as they are called, from the width of their oars, form part of the fleet.

These rafts, like immense floating islands, form at once the vehicle and the temporary residence of several families on their way down the river. Old and young, from the gray-haired pioneer of sixty down to the boy of twelve years, are interested in their departure, and compose the crews to navigate them. There is not probably a boy of twelve years old living on any stream in Warren co. who has not made his voyage to Cincinnati, perhaps to "Orleans."

It was perhaps only chance that decided that William B. Foster, Sr., should settle in Pittsburgh instead of Warren, Pennsylvania. I am indebted to William Galbraith-Smith, a descendant of John Struthers, for the information that William B. Foster was granted a patent on June 9, 1807, through the governor's office in Harrisburg, for four lots in the town of Warren, for which he paid thirteen dollars. This was the summer before he was married to Eliza C. Tomlinson. Mr. Smith states:

Nothing seems to have been done with these lots until 1819, when a dispute arose concerning their ownership. It seems that Zachariah Eddy [a pioneer settler of Warren County, and father of Mrs. Thomas Struthers] bought the same lots in Franklin. It was found that Wm. B. Foster had the prior title, and the matter was amicably settled between Foster and Eddy. Redmond Grace, of Baltimore [a relative of Eliza C. Foster] bought these lots on September 1, 1820, for $150.

Henry's father went to Warren, as he had promised, to help his son get started, and wrote William from there on June 12, 1838:

I arrived here about six days ago, found Henry in good health, and much pleased with his business, which has far exceeded my most sanguine expectations. They opened their store on the 8th of May, and on the 8th of June inst. had sold two thousand Dollars worth, and of that sum had received $1200 in cash.—

Mr. Skinner has just return'd from Buffalo, with an additional sup-

William B. Foster, Jr. (Brother William)

"Cairo, Mouth of the Ohio," by H. Lewis

From *Das Illustrirte Mississippithal,* von H. Lewis (Düsseldorf: Arnz & Comp. [1855-1857])

ply of goods, which they are selling very fast. He is a first rate business man, and the best salesman I ever saw behind a counter. He has the perfect confidence of the people, and knows every man that is perfectly safe to trust.— Henry thinks of nothing but his business, his Sunday School and church, in all of these Mr. S. joins with him, being a member of the same (Presbyterian) church, and principle of the Sunday School.

Henry Wick has lost his interesting little son Homer. He died a few days before I left home. I feel pity from my heart for his dear amiable mother; she is a lovely woman and must feel most sensibly such a bereavement.

Although the firm of Skinner & Foster had seemed to start out very auspiciously, it was not long before all concerned realized that it was not possible to place the same reliance on promissory notes as on cash. Wm. B. Foster reveals their first setback to William, Jr., on June 20, 1838.

They have both been a little disappointed in making up the amount they wished to begin with.—Mr. Skinner not being able to make collections as he expected, and in consequence of John's situation being a little doubtful, they could not use his indorsement for Henry for 500 Dollars.—M. also disappointed us, in addition to what he owed me, he took Henry's notes for 300 Dollars at 4 to 6 months, promised to indorse them and procure Groceries at Louisville for the whole, and send them up in time to go with the other goods; but in true M. style, he has done nothing but write a long rigmarole of stuff about the difference in exchange, hard times, etc. etc. Fortunately, Henry found a friend here who supplied them with a beginning in groceries.—Judge Baldwin, who you know is indebted to me about 2500 Dollars, was here in May attending court. He told me that his salary was yet pledged for two or three years, to save his indorsers in Bank from total ruin; but if he lived, that myself and family would be remembered, and if Henry went down this Fall to buy goods, that he would give him as much credit with the merchants as he might want!

One cannot help but admire the remarkable ingenuity with which the Judge settled with his creditors.

As usual, William had not been carried away by what his father considered "flattering prospects." Respectfully, he cautions his enthusiastic parent in a letter from Frankfort, dated July 9, 1838.

Dear Father and Mother,

I recd. on the 4th July at Irvine, on my way down the Kentucky River, Father's letter with a Postscript by Henry dated at Warren 12 June.

I was gratified to learn by it that the prospect for business is good at Warren, but I know so well Father's sanguine temperament on such matters, that I, in my own mind, make allowances, and if they only do a fair & safe business, I should have all my calculations realized.— Perhaps my unfortunate mercantile operations may make me rather skeptical and timid.—I would have them not led away with a flattering prospect at first, but conduct as if the appearances were not so favorable.

I was in hopes of remaining in Frankfort some days after I returned from the heads of the Kentucky, but I have just been one day here and barely time to settle with my hands, when I have to start to the upper Cumberland, and but for the circumstance that I persuaded Mr. Welch to wait until after dinner before we set out, I should not have had a moment to write to anyone.—I reached here on Friday night and found all my friends well.—Yesterday had a pleasant sermon & a fine congregation for our Church.

I might have written on yesterday, you would suppose, but I have to say in reply to that, that I am convinced of the impropriety of even letter writing on the Lord's day, and that if my health & mind are spared to me, I intend henceforth to devote at least the seventh day to the service of my Creator.

Mr. Stroughton & wife (the young gentleman) are here, and he informed me that he saw Ma a few days since, and that all were well.— I got through my labors on the Kentucky sooner than I expected, and shall have to ride about 100 miles.—The weather is now excessively warm and I anticipate a very disagreeable ride. My health is pretty good, but I am not strong & fleshly as usual.

It depends on the stage of water in the Cumberland River how long I may be absent from here; if it is too high for our operations, I shall return in 10 days or two weeks, but if it is low enough to work, we shall be longer absent, but cannot tell how long.—When I get leisure will write again; until then, accept this hasty scrawl—dinner is almost ready & I must close.

Your affectionate son,

William.

P.S. I heard a few weeks ago from Thomas & Henrietta—all well.

In the midst of their material problems, the Foster family were grieved, but nonetheless spiritually uplifted, on receiving news of the strange death of Father John Taylor, their good old friend and religious adviser of early days. On August 10, 1838, at the age of eighty-three, Father Taylor was killed by a bolt of lightning which entered through the window and struck him while he lay sleeping one night in the home of his daughter at Shenango, near Greenville, Pennsylvania. In the terrific electrical storm that followed, no other person or thing was touched by the lightning. As a friend writing of the event said: "It seemed as though the hand of God had reached down from Heaven for the express purpose of taking this saintly man painlessly, gloriously and swiftly home to his eternal reward!"

Fortunately for Henry and Mr. Skinner, they were able to close out their business in August, without serious loss to either. Henry's father was greatly disappointed in the outcome of the venture, but seemed to be resigned to the inevitable when he reported to William on August 18, 1838. Mr. Skinner, after making ineffectual attempts to collect money on the notes in his hands, could only put in about two hundred and fifty dollars, and as Henry had not been able to raise enough to buy the entire stock of new groceries:

. . . we found it prudent to close up the business with Mr. Skinner. We regret the necessity, but concluded it was the safest plan for all, rather than make a large debt for a winter's supply.—Mr. Skinner took the remainder of the goods on hand (a small amount) and all debts due the firm, and engages to pay all, and has given Henry his Bond with his uncle Tanner as security to secure him against all claims. He also gave Tanner as indorser on the notes for the amount which Henry had put in the business, with interest from the date, which will answer to buy goods equal to cash. He allow'd Henry $100 per month for the time they were in partnership, amounting to about 270 Dollars. Skinner's proposition is very honorable, and I am sorry he is disappointed.

Henry is now looking round for a new start. He can pay for about 1000 Dollars worth of goods with his notes, and if he could command eight or ten hundred more, I would advise that he continue on his own account at Warren. It is the best situation that I know of, especially as he has made many friends and acquaintances there, and it is a cheap place to do business.

Hall and McElvy would give goods at cost for amount of McElvy's note, which would be enough to commence this fall on, as he is now entirely clear of debt for goods bought.—If you should think it advisable to let Henry have that note, I wish you to write immediately; and he will not determine until I shall hear from you.

You are under a mistake about the Judge's note; it is drawn "for value received," but the Judge promises (Mr. Hall informs me) every week or ten days, most solemnly, to pay the amt. or give his negotiable note payable in Bank.

As to the election of Porter, I consider it certain, and do most sincerely hope I may not be disappointed. It would aid you and I both.

The Republican Party were never more united in Pennsya. on an election than they are at present; the Wolfites and Muhlenburgers go hand in hand.—Ritner has to contend against 12,300 votes, the joint majority against him at the last election; he will lose at least 1500 negro votes which he received at the last election, it being determined by the Supreme Court that they are not entitled to vote. He has to carry the Bank of the United States, with anti-masonry, abolitionism and all other abominations that a miserable tool of aristocracy can be loaded with. There is no such thing as getting a cash bet out of any Ritner man here on the result of the election.

Write me soon—all well and join in much love to you, with

Your affectionate father

W. B. Foster.

W. B. Foster, Jr. Engineer,
Rumsey, Ky.

Although William had every confidence in Henry's good intentions, he did not believe his younger brother possessed enough experience to justify the risking of the McKelvy note in an enterprise undertaken by Henry alone. He felt that a few years more spent in gaining experience in someone else's store would be better in the long run for Henry than plunging into debt to start a business of his own. He wrote his father accordingly, and the older man realized that William's decision was a sensible one. He admits as much in his next letter.

Allegheny Town, Octr. 20th. 1838

Dear William,

Yours of the 1st. inst. was received five days ago. The newspapers which I have sent you will shew the state of the votes for Governor, and confirms the election of Porter by a majority of about 9000 votes; thus is anti-masonry and abolitionism prostrate for a number of years in the Keystone State.—It is impossible to tell who will form the new Board of Canal Commissioners, but I have no doubt you will have an offer to return here again.

After I had written to you on the subject of McKelvy's note, I made some enquiries on the subject of Prices of dry goods, and was fully satisfied that I would not make the arrangement which I suggested, and had you sent the note, I would not have used it.—Henry has not yet commenced business, but I expect he will shortly. Thomas Wick is about to commence a grocery and produce store in Youngstown. We expect him in next week to buy goods.

Your sister Ann Eliza has added to their little flock another daughter, [Annie] about four weeks ago, and all well at last accounts.

I trust the election of Porter will remove from you every idea of purchasing property and settling on Green River, where you cannot expect to pass a summer without sickness. I remember well your young companion Miles, the son of Mrs. Mitchell, whose premature summons to another, and we trust a better, world, is well calculated to produce serious reflections in your mind. To this I must add another, who I believe was a school-fellow of yours, Banton Miltenberger, died on this day week, after an illness of two weeks, of bilious fever. He, too, has left a young wife and three little ones to the protection of Heaven, and an ungrateful world.

Hall & McKelvey have dissolved partnership, and quit business here. Hall takes the goods on hand up the Allegheny River, and joins his brother-in-law, Mr. Porterfield, in an Iron Furnace.

I shall apply, with good prospects of success for my old office, or at least the Recorder's office. It is worth about 1200 Dollars per ann.—

We are all in good health; the little boys go to school constantly.

Your mother and brothers join in love to you with

Your affectionate father,

Wm. B. Foster.

The Porterites barbecued an ox, a sheep, and a Hog on the sand bar opposite town in the Monongahela on Wednesday last!! The river is rising, small boats are preparing to start—the bar is now covered.

While the older boys and their father were absorbed in business affairs and politics, Morrison, aged fifteen, and twelve-year-old

Stephen, "the little boys," continued their routine of school and play and home. If Stephen had secured his "whistle," which he probably did, we can be sure all of his leisure hours were not spent on the playground, but many were taken up with sweet pipings on the little flute, probably a tin one. Gay minstrel tunes, and melancholy songs like "Home, Sweet Home," and gospel hymns to please his mother must have been practiced over and over until they satisfied the precise ear of young Stephen Foster. In some way, Stephen prepared himself to produce in 1841, his youthful, melodious composition, "The Tioga Waltz."

During the last half of 1838, all the family were anxious about Mother, who, their father said in a letter to William, was "so delicate at times she was hardly able to step about." Eliza Foster could not muster up strength this time to cross the mountains to help Ann Eliza, whose second little daughter, Ann Elizabeth Speer Buchanan, was born on September 23, 1838.

The cornerstone of Mr. Buchanan's new church had been laid a few months before the arrival of the baby, and Ann Eliza's letters home reveal how great her pride was in Mr. Buchanan's success in his new parish. The bishop of Pennsylvania, the Right Reverend Henry U. Onderdonk, laid the cornerstone for the new building on June 21, 1838, and on the following Christmas Day, the Pequea church was ready for "divine services." The new building measured forty by fifty-five feet and was really commodious in comparison to the two preceding ones. According to Mr. Ross, historian of St. John's,

The old stone church had been erected of local lime stone. It was torn down and hauled away by Robert Baldwin, Sr., the stones were burned into lime, and applied to the soil. The new building was erected from stones hauled from the hills east of Compass. They are a beautiful mountain stone, very hard and will last indefinitely. The pyramidal steps in the front are of Pennsylvania brown stone, and were hauled from Falls of French Creek, by two teams furnished by Thomas G. Henderson. It required two days to make a trip and the drivers stopped for the night at Plow Tavern on the Conestoga Pike.

Henrietta found time to write her own family news to Brother William occasionally. There was always a close bond between William and his younger sister; not only on account of their natural affection, but because of the tie created by their mutual connection to the Wick family. Thomas frequently sought advice from his brother-in-law; in fact, Henrietta was always easier in her mind in regard to Thomas' business ventures if he first consulted Brother William.

Youngstown, Sunday Oct. 21, 1838

My dear brother,

Although it has been a long time since I received your letter and have never written to you this summer, you must not think that I have forgotten you. I have been going to write to you every week for two months, but something always happened to prevent it. I have never written a word to Ann Eliza since last Spring. Do, my dear brother, write to me soon, for we are all very anxious to hear from you.

Little Mary is beginning to walk alone, and I think she is more troublesome than ever, for she is in all manner of mischief. She is not quite so fat as she was when you were here in the winter, but she is very well, so it does not make any difference about the loss of fat.

I received a letter from Ma a few days ago in which she mention'd that Sister Ann Eliza had another little daughter. You have not seen her since before she had her first child, and now she has three.

Poor old Mother Wick talks a great deal about you—she says you promised to write to her and she would give anything to hear from you. She says that you are the same to her as the rest of her children. I told her this morning that I intended to write to you today. Oh, well, said she, do tell him to write to me, for he don't know how I love him.

Thomas is going to Pittsburgh in a week or ten days to buy groceries. We are living in the house where John Squires lived. Thomas is going to move the old shoemaker shop back of the house and make a kitchen & bedroom of it, and I think it is a good deal better than to have rent to pay for a larger house.

Do write soon; there is no news here but the marriage of Johnston Wick & Emeline Griffith, & Judge Wick to Miss Mary Linn of Poland. My pen is so bad that I cannot write any more. Believe me to remain your ever affectionate sister,

Henrietta.

Here comes Thomas, he will finish my letter.

Dear Brother,

As Henrietta has finished, I will say a few words to you—I saw old Mr. McEuen this morning, he told me that he had heard from you and that you intended making us a visit this winter. I was glad to hear it I assure you, and I hope you will make your arrangements so as to make us a long visit, if you do not stay altogether; but as Porter is elected Governor of Pennsylvania, I am in hopes you will have a loud call from there, and then we will have you a little nearer us than we have you now. I am going into business this time by myself, and I think I will do better than to be ruled by *brothers*.

Henrietta mention'd something about our house being small, but when you come, we will have a spare room for you and we want you to come straight to our house and stay with us all the time that Mother will let you be from her, as she will want you to spend a greater part of your time there.

I must stop as Henrietta has got a fine Wild Duck roasted and dinner is ready. I wish you were here to partake. No more, but ever I remain,

Truly yours,

Wm. B. Foster, Jr. T. L. Wick.

Engineer, Rumsey, Ky.

How completely commerce in those days depended on the rise and fall of the rivers can be learned from frequent references to the stages of the water. Keelboats loaded with freight were still plying their trade between the river towns and managed to navigate when the rivers were so low that steamboats could not run. Of the three rivers, the Allegheny was the shallowest, so the towns along its course that depended on steamboat delivery for their goods watched the water anxiously. The canal system of western Pennsylvania had added greatly to the prosperity of the country, enabling the people to bring out the iron ore which abounded in Venango and Crawford counties. William's father knew his son would be interested in the fortunes of his former partner, Mr. Hall, and always mentioned the latest news regarding him.

Octr. 24th, 1838.—Mr. Hall has quit business here, and has the remainder of their goods packed up to send up the Alleghany River as soon as the water rises. He has gone into partnership with his brother-in-law, Mr. Porterfield, in an iron furnace near Scrubgrass; and says they have a large quantity of Pig Metal to bring down as soon as the water will admit, which is now rising slowly; the river was never known to have been so low as this Fall. . . .

Our Court is now in session, and Uncle Alexr. [Foster] says he will get my judgment against M. revived; if so, I think I can sell it here by making some discounts. There is, I believe, money coming to him; he sold stages and horses before he went to Louisville. . . .

The New Constitution having been carried by a majority of 5 or 6 thousand votes, cuts me out of my expected office of Recorder, the people having to elect them; the Anties will continue to rule the roost in this County, but the election of Porter is enough for three years. . . .

In the fall of 1838, Brother William is the only one who reports having attended any social affairs though, with the possible exception of Stephen, he of all the family was most averse to gatherings of strangers. When surrounded by his friends, William was of a kindly, sociable disposition; in a large company, he could not overcome his shyness. He complained to his mother of his inability to "get to know people" yet he seems to have got on wonderfully well with everyone he met in his work.

Frankfort, Ky. Nov. 27, 1838

As I have just completed writing my reports, and have a leisure hour, I concluded I could not employ it better than in writing to my dear Mother, whose last kind letter has been so long without an answer.

I have been at this place a little more than two weeks, after a tolerably laborious season's work, having been engaged in the field since the first of May, with the exception of a few short intermissions.

But I have to thank a kind providence for having preserved me in health. Although the season has been unusually sickly, particularly during the months of August & September, I never enjoyed better health in my life than in those months, & indeed ever since, with the exception of occasionally slight colds, which you know I am subject to.

On my way up to this place, happening to meet with Dunning McNair on the street of Louisville, I was prevailed on by him to spend a day there, which I accordingly did, and dined at his house with a small social party, composed chiefly of his relatives. [This Dunning McNair was the son of William B. Foster's old friend, Colonel Dunning McNair of early White Cottage days. The elder McNair died May 15, 1825.] Maria & her husband, Margaret & her husband, Miss Caroline Kerr,

Mrs. & Miss McNair, the widow & daughter of the late Geo. McNair of Missouri, & myself were the guests. They inquired very affectionately for you and indeed all of the family.—Maria and Margaret desired me when writing to give their love to you.

I also called to see our kinfolks, Mr. Barclay & family.—They were all in good health and manifested great kindness & hospitality.—Their daughter Georgiana, who must have been quite a child when you saw her, is an interesting little girl, and for one of her age performs remarkably well on the piano. [Note: This little girl was the baby born shortly before Charlotte died.] My business requiring my presence in Frankfort, I was compelled to make my visit at their house merely a morning call, but had to promise a longer one when next I journey that way.

I wrote some days ago to Father, saying that I was in hopes of making such arrangements as would enable me to return to Pennsylvania, during the winter, and if I can accomplish my views in that respect, I think I shall wander no more from my native state, but make it my home so long as a home is necessary in this passing world.

On next Monday, the Legislature of Kentucky will commence their session, and the people are already beginning their preparations for the gaieties of the winter, as they always calculate upon a season of amusement during the sitting of their law-makers.—My situation, during the last session was such that I could not, if I had desired, have participated in any of their amusements, and unless I change my mind, I shall pursue the same course during the approaching session.

I must tell you of a fine *venison dinner* which I assisted in the honors of today.—It was given by Col. Davidson, the State Treasurer, and attended by the Governor & Secretary, with sundry others of the most respectable gentlemen of the place, in all about twenty. The venison was well cooked and the accompaniments were diversified and pleasant to the taste, the servants numerous & attentive, and take it all in all, I am glad I had the honor of an invite, although I must say that just at this present moment, I should feel better if I had staid at home.

I am in hopes to be able to leave here by the early part of January, and to continue my journey as far east as Lancaster County in the course of the winter. I have not heard from there for a long time, except what Pa wrote in his last letter.

I am still boarding in a private house, and have to walk a quarter of a mile to the office, which is just about exercise enough to be comfortable & promotive of health. It is probable I shall have to set out in the course of two or three days on a little tour, to be absent two or three weeks.—I will, Providence permitting, be back before Christmas at farthest.

With my love to Father & brothers,

I remain, your affectionate son,

William.

VII

IN the winter of 1838-1839, William got together his credentials and recommendations and forwarded them to the Pennsylvania canal commissioners. These papers were all returned to him later and show the high regard in which the young engineer was held by his superiors and associates. In March, 1839, he made a visit to Pittsburgh, there to await word of his appointment or rejection. William was very anxious to return to Pennsylvania, and his exertions to reach Harrisburg before it was too late are described in detail in the following letters. They offer a graphic account of what a race against time meant in 1839, and make one wonder why it took a letter thirty or more days to be delivered the same distance that could be traveled in less than ten days by steamboat and stagecoach. Probably the sorting of mail at transfer points was a serious and laborious task requiring much time and cogitation for some of the rural postmasters.

Alleghenytown, Mch. 25, 1839

Dear William,

On Monday after you left us, which was the 11th inst., a letter came from Harrisburgh address'd to you, which I did not hesitate to open, and found it was from D. Mitchell, Jr., informing you of your appointment as principle Engineer on the North Branch line of Canal, and also stating that he had written you the day previous, (say on the 5th.) and address'd to Frankfort; knowing that his letter would reach you before any that I could then write, I omitted to address you, but did instantly, on the same day, write to Mr. Mitchell, acknowledging the rect. of his to you of the 6th. and gave him a short statement of facts as follows.—That shortly after you had certain information of the election of Govr. Porter, you had written to me requesting that as soon as the new Board of Canal Commissioners were appointed, I would inform them that in consequence of annual indisposition in Ky. you were desirous to return and enter the service of your native State as a principle engineer—that as soon as I learn'd who composed the Board, early in Febry. I had so written them, and stated you would be at my house before the 1st. of March, and if they had any communication to make to you, they would address you to my care at this place; that you came accordingly, and remain'd until the 7th, when, not hearing anything from the Board, you as well as myself, had concluded that those engineers who had been ordered to examine the damage on the several lines, were considered as the permanent engineers, knowing certainly that to be the case on the Erie extension.

In accordance with your promise to the Board of Internal Improvement in Kentucky, that if you were not appointed in Pennsya. you would be at Bowling Green on the 17th. inst. to commence the survey of a turnpike road, which would probably occupy your time two months, you left me on the 7th, and I presumed on the day I was writing, (the 11th), you were in Frankfort, and would proceed on the next to Louisville, thence to Bowling Green, and I presumed his letter of the 5th to you at Frankfort would not reach you until at Bowling Green. This letter I address'd, "D. Mitchell, Jr. Esqr., Engineer, in his absence to the Board of Canal Commissioners, Harrisburgh," so that they were early inform'd of all the circumstances. I have not heard a word from them since.

I have had communications with Thomas Struthers on the subject we talk'd of; and will write fully again.—I would have written you sooner, but waited to hear from you, expecting a letter from Louisville. —It gratifies me to see your name published in all our newspapers as being appointed a principle engineer, without the aid of our Neighbour!

You must judge of the future course to pursue, but I would rather you would return, at all events after you survey the road; this, I confess, is an interested wish, believing that we might live together and be mutually beneficial to each other.—In the meantime, I will collect all the information I can in relation to business; thus far I am strengthened in my views up the river.—

We are all well and join in love, with

> your affectionate father,
>
> Wm. B. Foster.

While William was in Pittsburgh, he and his father had discussed the idea of investing his, William's, savings in a profitable business, under the management of a good partner, to be conducted by this partner until William left the employ of the state. Wm. B. Foster, Sr., had been strongly in favor of uncle John Struthers' son, Thomas, of Warren, Pennsylvania, who he felt sure would have enough capital to match what William could put in; this was the "up river" business occasionally mentioned. Unfortunately, neither Henry nor he was in a position to enter into business with William in an equal capacity.

The above letter was postmarked at Pittsburgh on March 25, reached Frankfort, Kentucky, April 13 (nineteen days later), was forwarded from there to Towanda, Pennsylvania, where it was received on April 28, or fifteen days later, and from thence sent on to Tunkhannock, Luzerne County, where it was not postmarked—a total of more than thirty-four days on the road. Not a very good record for the post office, for the distance could have been covered in considerably less than ten days by William, according to his own calculations. In fact, he left Pittsburgh on March 7 and reached Frankfort on the tenth; he was at Portsmouth, Ohio, on March 30, and expected to reach Harrisburg on April 3.

The next letter from William, Jr., written on board the *Fulton,* indicates that the boat must have been steaming along the Ohio in true river-racing style, for the quivering and throbbing of the engine communicated itself from William's hand to the paper, and at first glance, the letter looks very much like a seismographic chart.

> On board Steam Boat, "Fulton," above Portsmouth,
> Ohio, March 30th, 1839. (Saturday 2 oclock P.M.)

Dear Father,

I have been so continually on the move since I left home, that I have not had a suitable moment to write you, & should not do it now, but know that you will feel some anxiety as to my whereabouts. As I expected, I reached Frankfort on the 10th. inst. and left on the 11th for Hopkinsville, with directions for the P.M. at Frankfort to forward my letters to Bowling Green.—I returned to B. Green on the 20th. and found several letters from different friends on the subject of my appt. in Penna. Among them was one from my friend, David Mitchell, Jr. who had carried with him some papers in support of my application, to the board.—He stated that the only objection to my appt. was the length of time that would in all probability elapse before I could be at Harrisburgh, and that he pledged himself to the board that by the 18th of this month (his letter being dated 3d. and one from Mr. Packer dated 2d. inst.) I would be there. As their letters were not received until the 21st. it may be possible that before I can reach Harrisburgh, some hungry hanger-on about the capital may supersede me.

I wrote to Mr. Packer dated 22d. inst. accepting, & saying that I would be in Harrisburg on or before the 5th. Apl., which I shall accomplish with ease; without an accident.—To save time, I shall take stage at Wheeling & go by Bedford & Chambersburgh, & expect to reach Wheeling on Monday morning in time for the stage, so that it is probable I shall get to Harrisburgh on the 3d. proximo.—

At 1 oclock (an hour ago) I parted company with brother Dunning at Portsmouth. The Troy was lying at the wharf putting out freight & we stopped a half an hour or so.—He was quite well. Brother Dunning said you had written to me, but I have not recd. any letter from you.

Please to see Judge Dallas, & say to him that I recd. a letter from him, apprising me of my appt. a few moments before I started, and that I will write him, very soon after my arrival at Harrisburgh.—

I write while the boat is under way & doubt whether you can decipher the scrawl.—If I am superseded in consequence of not getting on in time, I will probably be at Pittsbg. in two or three weeks; I will however write you all from Harrisbg.

I remain yours affecty.

Wm. B. Foster, Jr.

This letter bears the postmark of Washington, Pennsylvania, April 2, showing that William left the boat at Wheeling where he took a stage which passed through Washington, only twenty-seven miles south of Pittsburgh. There he dropped off his letter, hoping it would be delivered in Pittsburgh within the next day or so. A contemporary history says of Washington: "Three great thoroughfares —the National road, the Glades road, and the Pittsburgh and Washington turnpike—intersect each other here, and bring an immense amount of travel daily. Stages on the National road are rattling through the town at almost every hour." Such being the case, where was William's letter between April 2 and April 13? That is a mystery that will never be cleared up.

From Henry to his Brother William:

Allegheny, April 13th, 1839.

My Dear Brother,

I now write you in the language of our father, who sits beside me, and dictates this letter.

We regret exceedingly that *we have not received a line* from you since you left us, which is now more than a month.

I called (that is, Pa) yesterday on Mr. Clark, President of the Canal Commissioners, who is on his way to Erie, and he informed me that the line you are destined for is the second best in the State, and that they had not yet heard from you, but had determined to keep it for you, having appointed a principal assistant Engineer to take charge of the line until they could hear from you; and he assured me that it would be kept for you until they had received your acceptance or refusal of the appointment. I thanked him kindly for the confidence they had placed in you. He informs me that he will return here in six or seven days, and we do hope that in the meantime, we shall receive a letter from you. At all events, my dear son, you will accept the appointment, as it is complimentary and you can resign when you think proper.

Now for business—shortly after you left us, I wrote a few lines to Thomas Struthers at Warren in which I mentioned your ideas of business, in return for which I have received a very kind and flattering letter from which I copy the following extract.—

"I should be very glad indeed to enter into business with Cousin William as I have the most exalted opinion of his correct moral habits and business qualifications—but it is not in my power of joining him in business on so large a scale as he would seem to desire to engage in. I am only just beginning to see a glimmering of light through the dark gloom which has been hanging over my prospects for a year or two past, and am not yet entirely on *terra firma*."

By accident, I met on the street a few days ago an old friend (and once one of your bosses) John Horner, who hailed me to ask my advice whether he would go into the Pork or Lumber business. He was very candid and after a few remarks on the subject of business, he told me that he wished to sell one of his houses in Market St. for the purpose of paying his debts, which amounted to about 4 Thousand Dollars. He was offered Twelve Thousand, but asked fourteen, & believed he would take twelve and get clear of debt, which would leave him a capital of 8 Thousand Dollars to commence business with. I recommended the Lumber business, and mentioned you as a partner. He instantly said,

"If William can have the same confidence in me that I have in him, there is no man on earth that I would rather have for a partner."

I told him you could put in six Thousand dollars.

N.B. John Horner owns the corner store of Third and Market St. for which Baily pays him eight hundred dollars a year, exclusive of what he proposes to sell.

All Well.   Yours affect.

Henry B. Foster.

This letter from Henry was postmarked at Allegheny on April 14, and reached Frankfort, Kentucky, on April 20. From there it was forwarded to "Towanda, via Williamsport," reached Towanda, April 30, and was sent on to Tunkhannock, Pennsylvania, where it was not postmarked. This was a little less than half the time required for Wm. B. Foster's letter of March 25 to reach William, Jr., but still it makes one wonder at the slowness of the mail in comparison with the very creditable speed of the stagecoaches.

After receiving the disappointing news from Thomas Struthers, who was his choice of a partner, William did not pursue the matter of investing in a mercantile business, for his new position demanded all his time and energy. Following his race across the country, he plunged immediately into his new work, and by April 22 was writing to his father in regard to an assistant.

Towanda, Bradford County, Pa.
April 22d. 1839

Dear Father,

I have been so much engaged since I reached the North Branch that it has been impossible for me to write a line to anyone excepting on immediate and urgent business, and even now I am occupying time that should be bestowed elsewhere.—

I have a remeasurement & estimate to make on over ninety miles of canal, the greater portion of which has been worked over, and it will keep me busily engaged for two weeks at least.

I wrote on the 8th of this month, from Williamsport, to Mr. J. W. Butler, offering him a situation as an Assistant Engineer on this line, & requested him, if he accepted the Appointment, to repair to this place immediately & if he declined, to write me to that effect without delay.—Sufficient time has now elapsed for my letter to have reached

William B. Foster, Sr., painted by William Cogswell, of Pittsburgh, in 1840, and his wife Eliza, painted by a Mr. Clifford, of Pittsburgh, the same year

Dunning McNair Foster, painted by William Cogswell,
of Pittsburgh, 1840

Pittsburgh, and for Mr. Butler to have gotten here or to have written to me declining.—I am in great need of the services of an additional assistant, and having so much to do, have at a considerable sacrifice of my own comfort thus far kept the place vacant, although I have numerous applications, and could fill it at any moment by persons waiting here for it.

It may be possible that my letters have miscarried although it is not very probable, as I wrote to both Mr. Butler and Judge Dallas.—Will you be so good as to see Judge Dallas on the subject and say to him that by the 8th of May, I must fill the place, if Mr. B. does not arrive by that time.

I have hardly time to say more than that I am in tolerable health, though a good deal worn down with my journey here, and the severe duty performed since my arrival.

With much love to Ma, and all, I am

Yours affectionately,

Wm. B. Foster, Jr.

P.S. Please call at the Advocate office & have my paper sent to "Tunkhannock, Luzerne Co. Pa."

From Wm. B. Foster, Sr., to his son:

Alleghenytown, April 30th. 1839

Dear William,

Your letters of 30th. ult. on board the Steam Boat, and that of 22d. inst. have been received.—

Mr. Dallas informs me that John Butler was inform'd of his appointment by you, and left this place about the same time for Washington City, where he had the offer of a job of some sort, and where he would determine which he would accept of. His friends here all recommended that he should go direct to you. He regrets that you have been put to any inconvenience on acct. of John's indecision at once; says he surely must be with you before this time, or inform'd that he would not go.

I received a letter shortly after your appointment, from F. R. Shunk, Secty. of the Commonwealth, desiring me to intercede with you for the appointment of a young man of Harrisburg by name of Jacobs, son of an old friend of mine, who has been dead some years. The young man is supporting a widowed mother and a sister. I suppose you have seen him since you were at Harrisburgh. I should like to oblige Mr. Shunk, it is well to have a friend at court. You must be the judge.

We are all well; I will write you more at length, and respecting the up River business in a few days. The family join in much love to you, with your

Affectionate father,

W. B. Foster.

William's meeting with Dunning on March 30, at Portsmouth, Ohio, was occasioned by one of Dunning's collecting trips to the South for Hutchinson & Ledlie. It was not until a year later (1840) that the younger brother began his career as a "river man." Steamboating must have appealed to him strongly, because he never left the river during his life, except for the short seasons he spent in the office of Irwin & Foster in Cincinnati, and when he went to the Mexican War. Dunning was self-reliant and resourceful, like William, but unlike William, he was fond of social life. He was considered the best looking of the Foster boys, taller than the rest, and well proportioned. His hair and eyes were red brown, and his skin as fresh and ruddy as a child's. One of his enthusiastic lady admirers declared he was "the handsomest man in Pittsburgh." He was quite impartial in his attentions, however, and as he grew older, his interest, with one exception, never seemed to center on any woman except his mother, whose comfort and well-being were always uppermost in his mind. Dunning was now only eighteen, but he was entirely self-supporting, and so well equipped to manage his own affairs successfully, that his parents' minds were entirely at ease with respect to him.

VIII

AS was their frequent custom, during the summer of 1839, the Fosters rented their Allegheny house, and went to Poland to stay during the hot weather. The boys loved to be at Uncle Struthers', and it was near Youngstown and Henrietta. At the sale in Erie of the property belonging to the old stagecoach company, Mr. Foster had been successful in securing a portion of what was owed to him, and, after reaching Poland, he began hunting enthusiastically for a good farm. William also was interested in the project, and told his father he would invest a large part of his own money, if his father would live on the farm and improve it. While William's father often was overconfident, he had an uncanny sense of property values, and an ability to pick out spots where future business would center. William was frequently cautioning the older man not to be "too sanguine"; still, he seemed to feel confidence in his father's land instinct which had served the latter so well when he first came to undeveloped and untried Pittsburgh. Wm. B. Foster managed to impress upon his sons the value of keeping personal accounts. He kept an accurate account of all housekeeping expenses and was a careful buyer of household supplies, purchasing in large quantities when goods could be procured more cheaply that way. Stephen's talent for bookkeeping was undoubtedly acquired from his father. Mitty's early account books are an amusing mixture of business and personal expenses, classical quotations, poetry, steamboat races, Scripture references, and election bets. The habit acquired in boyhood remained with him through life. When the Fosters lost money, they had the doubtful satisfaction of knowing where it went. One of Mitty's entries is for one dollar to a steamboat acquaintance, who lost his life by drowning shortly after. Mitty accounts for this money, "at the bottom of the Ohio River."

Uncle Struthers seemed to be very glad to have his relatives, in fact, he borrowed money to fix up his old house that it might be comfortable and pleasant for "Brother W. B. Foster & consort." In July, Mr. Foster and Uncle Struthers put in an enjoyable two weeks driving around the neighborhood of Youngstown and New Castle, looking over farms, stepping off fields, calculating wheat and corn crops, and, in fancy, building gristmills and uncovering rich coal and lime deposits. The canal running through this section was the line which William had helped to make; therefore, he was familiar with the lay of the land, and knew the farmers his father mentioned. The latter sent William two hand-drawn maps, one of lands owned by William Hays and Benjamin Darlington, lying in the V or forks, where the Mahoning and Shenango rivers unite to form the Beaver; the other, a sketch of the Shiel farm. He enlivens his descriptions with some rural scandal.

Poland, Ohio, July 26th. 1839

Dear William,

We have not heard from you since Henry return'd from Harrisburgh, but knowing the additional duty laid on you by the act of the Legislature, I can well see that you can have but little time to devote to anything but your professional duties.

Henry informs us that you had express'd a wish that a good farm could be selected, that you would purchase it as a resting place for your mother and myself as well as such of the boys as might feel inclined to stick by us, and a comfortable retreat for yourself when you might wish to retire from your present occupation; with this object in view, I have explored the country along the canal and river from Youngstown to near the mouth of Beaver, and will proceed to give you some description of the best farms which I have found for sale.

The above rough sketch shews you a beautiful farm which lies on the Beaver River about 1½ miles below the junction of the canals, and which I suppose you may remember as the Adams farm, joining that formerly Doctr. Pollock's above; with a good two-story Brick House, and Kitchen on it, stands about 100 yards from the canal.

This farm came into possession of an Irish sea captain by name of Shiel about two years ago, who has resided there since. He left his family in Ireland, and took a tenant into his house, with whom he lived; but, unfortunately became too intimate with the tenant's wife, which came to his knowledge. In consequence of that, Shiel's Barn full of grain was burnt by the Husband and some of his friends, who were indicted in the court at Beaver; and two, besides the Husband, were found guilty by the jury, but have not yet been sentenced by the court. The friends say that if they are sent to the Penitentiary, that Shiel will be murdered.—Shiel has been indicted for adultery, and held to bail of 1000 Dollars.—I mention all these facts to shew you the reason why S. wishes to sell. Young John Struthers rented the place 1st. of April last, and he is now residing on it at 400 Dollars rent per annum. Since renting, Shiel's family came in from Ireland and are living on a farm in the Neighborhood.—

This place contains 209 acres strict measure, and is said by many to be the best on the river from Youngstown to Beaver, excepting perhaps Hays' & Darlington's in the forks. There appears to be great abundance of Limestone and coal on it, & from the partial opening of the Coal Pitt, I would judge it equal in depth to the strata at Pittsburgh. The Limestone lies a few rods above the coal, and presents a face of six to eight feet thick. An easy road can be made down to the canal. Would not lime pay well at the Lake, by taking it by Canal? It is known that Waggons returning from Youngstown take lime to the lake.

The Canal Commissioners have ordered Mr. Dodge to have the whole line of canal finished by the 1st. of Nov. in order that people may rely on the navigation for their spring business. Dodge says it shall be done—a daily line of freight and passenger Boats continue to run to Warren, and many passengers come this way from Pittsbg. to Buffalo.—

Darlington has advertised his land for sale. His agent told me he ask'd 50 Dollars pr. acre for the South Side, & 40 for that on the North, 1/3d. in hand, and balance on interest as long as the purchaser pleases. You could buy the South Side without selling at Alleghenytown.

The assist. engineer at the aqueduct told me yesterday he would put the level to the mill seat on the river, and write me in a few days— you know if you could get the waste water from the canal it would make an excellent site for a Mill!

The price of the above farm (Shiel's) is 40 Dollars per acre, 6000 in cash, the balance in one or two years, with inst. There is an excellent spring of water near the House, and several others on the place. The fences will require some repairs, and a barn must be built. It is most desirable property. There is about 135 acres cleared in cultivation. John Struthers has given out a part of the Bottom land on Shares. He is to get half the corn in the heap, after husking. He expects to get 25 bushls. per acre, for his share. I find this is the mode of renting in that neighborhood; the tenant finds all seed, and delivers half to the owner, Wheat in the Shock, Corn in the Heap, and Hay in the stack or barn, from which I make the following calculation, & which will hold good on any other farm that I will describe to you.

				(half)		
60 acres in Corn——50 bushls. per acre.	3000 Bush.	1500 at	50 cts.	$750
20 do. in Wheat—20 do. do.	400	200	$1	200
20 do Oats 40 do.	800	400	.30	120
2 do. potatoes 200 do.	400	200	.25	50
20 do. meadow 2 Tons do.	40	20	$6	120

$ 1240

13 acres for self, for pasture lot, orchard, garden, etc.

The more I examine the subject, I confess I like it, but if you purchase a farm let it be one of the first quality; it will pay well.

Mother joins in love, with your affectionate father

                       Wm. B. Foster.

A supplementary letter, written the same day, giving news of the family, shows that the only boy who was at all likely to be at home was little Stephen! William B. Foster had been brought up a farmer boy, but he was now nearly sixty years old, and had only his right hand. Eliza Foster had never lived on a farm. It would have been necessary to hire almost all of their labor, or depend on putting the farm out on shares every year. The statistics compiled by Mr. Foster were very attractive, but a cold analysis undoubtedly compelled him to admit that although it is easy to figure bumper crops from 102 acres (with 20 acres in meadow) it is quite a job to plow that much land. Such a farm would have proved to be anything but a "resting place." It would have been delightful for his grandchildren if William B. Foster had bought this farm and kept it for them, for these valuable acres lie directly south of the wealthy city of New Castle, Pennsylvania, but it was well for "mother and myself" that the project was abandoned.

His other letter of July 26, 1839, is as follows:

Dear William,

I wrote today and address'd you at Tunkhannock, and gave you a description of a good farm for sale, and will now give you an account of some others. [He then describes several places in detail, in the vicinity of Shiel's farm.]

I wrote you before we left Allegheny, and told you our plan. We are still in Poland, that is your mother and myself. Uncle Struthers has not yet got his House in Order, but will in a week or two, when we will go there. We have excellent board & lodging here for 2 Dollars each per week.—

Henry is in Youngstown at Mr. Reno's; he is in treaty with the company who owns the packet line of Boats for the occupancy of a new Ware House which is being built at Doctor Manning's basin in Youngstown, and to do the company's business there; I think he will get it. Clarks of Bridgewater, Sanky of New Castle and others are the owners of the line.

Morrison and Stephen board at Mr. Reno's, going to free school at 1.50 per week for boarding. Morrison is to go into the warehouse of Wrenshall & Co., cotton factory, at Pittsbg. on the 1st. of Septer. Mr. McCormick, one of the partners, took a great fancy for him.

Mr. Stephens was paid the interest due up to the 1st of July.—The

House we left is rented at the rate (I think) of 175 Dollars per ann. from 1st. July to 1st. of April next—Our expenses are very trifling, except the boarding—wear our old clothes, etc.

I was very happy to learn by the Newspapers that you and your canal commissioners came off with flying colours before the committee of the Legislature. I hope you and Mr. Harris will conduct your business amicably.—Present to him my kind regards.

Thomas Wick and Henrietta are living very happily, and your mother is quite contented in hopes of shortly being placed in a home for life, where we can render you service, and cost you little.

Dunning is still at his labours with Hutchison & Ledlie. He made a long tour collecting for them in Tennessee this Spring.

Write, and direct to me at Poland, Ohio.

Your mother desires to be affectionately remembered to you. She says you must excuse her for not writing to you; her eyes are weak, and fingers stiff.

Your very affectionate father,

William B. Foster, Junr.   Wm. B. Foster.
Principle Engineer
Towanda, Bradford County, Pennsya.

From the foregoing, it can be seen that investment in a large farm would have been extremely hazardous, and further consideration seems to have convinced both William and his father of the futility of such a plan.

Uncle Struthers, of Poland, Ohio, was one of the old fighting pioneers. He was born in 1759 and, according to the history of Warren County, Ohio, served as captain of a company of mounted rangers during the Revolutionary War, and in the border warfare which opened up western Pennsylvania and Ohio to settlers. He knew the great Cornplanter, chief of the Seneca Indians, when the latter was in his prime. Morrison Foster has left us the following description of his uncle:

John Struthers . . . had been a surveyor, hunter and Indian fighter in the first settlement of the country, and . . . now, past eighty years old, was very fond of Stephen and always pleased to welcome him to his log house in the Northwest territory. Old Uncle Struthers had dogs and rifles, and himself would lead the hunt at night for 'coons, oppossums, and such like nocturnal game. It was tame work to the old pioneer, who had been used to bears, panthers and hostile Indians. These hunts and the stories of adventure told by his aged relative, of course gave great pleasure to Stephen, and kindled the flame of his vivid fancy. One cold day, he was missed from the house, and was hunted for everywhere outside. At last, his uncle discovered him sitting up to his neck in a pile of chaff, watching the movements of the chickens and other barnyard animals—"just thinking," as he briefly explained. The old gentleman always prophesied that Stephen, who even then displayed great originality and musical talent, would be something famous if he lived to be a man.

Uncle John and Aunt Mary Foster Struthers had in their time quite a fine large family. William Galbraith-Smith, formerly of Warren, Pennsylvania (now living in Cleveland, Ohio), a descendant of their daughter, Matilda, tells me that a son, Ebenezer, born in 1801, was the first white child born in the township that is now the town of Poland, Ohio, but which was a savage wilderness when John Struthers settled there in his log homestead on October 19, 1799. Another son, Lieutenant Alexander Struthers, served in the War of 1812 and died in Detroit in 1813. Two young daughters, Emma and Drusilla, were drowned in the Mahoning River in 1826. Matilda Struthers married Abraham Morrison Galbraith. In 1839, Thomas Struthers was prominent in business in Warren, Pennsylvania. John Struthers, Jr., lived on a farm not far from his father. Aunt Mary Foster Struthers died in Poland, Ohio, in 1819. It is possible that Uncle Struthers' daughter, Mrs. Galbraith, kept house for her father in Poland when the Foster family visited them in the summer of 1839.

While Morrison and Stephen boarded with Mr. Reno, in Youngstown, they were under Henrietta's watchful eye, and Eliza Foster enjoyed a much needed rest at Uncle Struthers'. In September, Stephen was back on his uncle's farm and Mitty started out in the world for himself. Henrietta still refers to her youngest brother as "little Stephy," although Stephen was thirteen years old on July 4, 1839.

Youngstown, Sept. 29, 1839

My dear brother, [William]

We received your very affectionate letter of the 12 of this month, more than a week ago, and were truly glad to hear that your health had so improved since you returned to Pennsylvania. I am in hopes you will not be troubled with that *vile* fever and ague any more.

Thomas has just taken the Buggy and horse down to Uncle's for Ma. She has not been up to see us for some time, and we thought she must be very lonely there now, with no one but little Stephy, as Pa is in Pittsburgh, having gone there to get Mitty fix'd at Mr. McCormack's. I have not heard from them since they left here, but believe Henry intends running on a Steam Boat.

Do, dear brother, write to me as often as you can. I really thought before we got your last letter that you never intended to write to us again; if it is only a few lines, still it is a satisfaction to hear from you.

Mary Manning is to be married this week, and I am told will have a very large wedding. Judge Wick's health is still declining. I am afraid he will not live many months. His wife gave birth to a fine son about three weeks ago. Poor woman, her prospect is very dull, but not so much so, either, as it might be, as Judge will leave her enough to support herself comfortably without doing anything, as she had before she was married to sew for a living.

Father Wick's health is very poor. He has lost his appetite entirely and looks more like a walking skeleton than anything else. I have tried to think of all the news I could, but my stock is rather limited.—I think the Population of Youngstown will have increased amazingly by the time you visit it again.

Little Mary still continues very healthy. She talks like a jay bird, her tongue is never still. She can say Unky Villy quite plain, at least I think so, for being with her all the time, I can understand her better than anyone else.

If Thomas gets home in time, he will write a few lines in this, but he started since afternoon church and I expect it will be pretty late before he gets back. It is after four o'clock now, and it is five long miles to Uncle's. Stephen enjoys himself finely at Uncle Struthers. He never appears to have the least inclination to leave there, and don't seem to feel at all lonely. Uncle just lets him do as he pleases with the horses and cattle, which makes him the greatest man on the ground.

I received a letter from Sister Ann Eliza ten days or two weeks ago. She said they were all well. I suppose she will not be out here till next Spring. I wish she could come this fall, but wishes are vain. You must not disappoint us this time, for I shall prepare and look for you, and it will be too bad to serve me as you did last Spring. It is nearly two years since you were here. Be sure and write to me whenever you can get a moment to spare, and believe me to remain your sincerely affectionate

Sister Henrietta.

Morrison did not at first enter the employ of Mr. McCormick, but went into the office of Cadwallader Evans, who was a cousin of Eliza Foster, and married to Jane Mahon. There was no doubt of Mitty's success from the start, for he was faithful, hard working, and intelligent. But he was only sixteen, and his father and mother could not help being anxious about him, for it was the first time he had been away from home. After taking Mitty to Pittsburgh, his father stayed on for about six weeks, attending to the sale of some land in Wilkins and Plum townships, and on the Nine-mile Run. He wrote to William on October 23, 1839:

I have got Morrison, I think, in a good place, with Cadwalader Evans at the Steam Mill in his office—Mr. Evans will teach him to be an accountant, and also Mathematics, as far as he knows himself; he will also, if Morrison likes it, instruct him in mechanics. He says he won't have him bound; if he does not wish to stay and be useful without an indenture, he is not worth having. You know they have no son, and are very kind to Mitty, who appears to be quite happy. Mr. E. told me yesterday that he was a very smart boy, but I don't think he has found him out yet—Mitty is as steady in his office as an old man.

Cadwallader and George Evans were sons of the inventor, Oliver Evans and Sarah Tomlinson Evans, Eliza Foster's aunt. Another brother, Oliver Evans, Jr., died in 1838. Cadwallader Evans lived on the south side of Pittsburgh in a beautiful house set amidst spacious grounds. The Evans brothers were the proprietors of several prosperous industries in Pittsburgh, including a steam flour mill, a large foundry, and a "Steam Engine Factory" which manufactured engines on the plan invented by Oliver Evans.

The young people of the two families were George Muhlenberg Evans and Oliver Ormsby Evans, sons of George Evans, and Sarah, Ann, and Mary, daughters of Cadwallader Evans. (Annie Evans is said to have been the inspiration of Stephen's song "Gentle Annie," composed in 1856.) When Wm. B. Foster mentioned "your Aunt Evans" in a letter to Morrison, he evidently meant Mrs. Cadwallader Evans, in whose home Morrison was staying. She really was Cousin Jane, but quite often a man is a little hazy about the exact relationships in his wife's family. Eliza Foster's Aunt Sarah, mother of George and Cadwallader Evans, died in 1816.

The office where Morrison started his business career was at No. 10 Water Street. Amongst the number of clever devices manufactured by Cadwallader Evans was a patent safety guard to be attached to steam boilers to prevent explosions. In Mr. Evans' current newspaper advertisements, he appeals to the feelings of the nervous traveler in the following manner:

The traveling community are respectfully requested before they make a choice of a boat, to reflect a moment, and see whether it wouldn't be to their advantage and security to choose a Safety Guard boat, in preference to one not so guarded against explosion.

Then follows in large type, a list of steamboats equipped with Evans' safety guards. It was undoubtedly to the advantage of steamboat owners to see that the names of their boats appeared in Cadwallader Evans' approved list.

IX

IN the late fall of 1839, Mr. and Mrs. Foster and Stephen moved in from Uncle Struthers' farm in Poland to Youngstown, and commenced boarding at Mr. Richards' near Henrietta and Thomas. Henrietta proved that she knew what she was talking about when she predicted to William an increase in the population of Youngstown before he visited there again—her second little daughter, Matilda Eliza, was born shortly before Christmas. Brother William arrived in Youngstown at Christmas time, driving his own two-horse sleigh. At a family conference, it was decided that "little Stephy," the last fledgling, should leave the shelter of his mother's wings, and return to Towanda with Brother William. It was hard for Stephen's mother and father to have him go so far away, but William had offered to pay his younger brother's expenses and would (as William B. Foster wrote to his son Morrison on January 12, 1840) "put him to school at the academy in Towanda where William's office and headquarters are. I think it is an excellent chance for the dear little fellow to get education."

William and Stephen started from Youngstown in William's sleigh on January 14, and reached Pittsburgh the following day. When they arrived in Pittsburgh, Morrison, in accordance with instructions received from his father, took Stephen out to Aunt Evans' to spend the night, while William remained in town.

I need not tell you, [wrote his father to Morrison on January 12, 1840,] to be kind and affectionate to him; the gun which you bought for him, I will take in when I go to town & give it to you—you can buy some little trifle for a keepsake and give it to Stephen. Tell Dunning to do so also.

Morrison mentions his little brother's trip in his biography:

The distance traveled was over three hundred miles, but the sleighing was good, and, of course, it was a jolly journey for the little boy, especially as Brother William was a man of great personal popularity, and had many friends and acquaintances everywhere along the road.

When they reached Harrisburg, the eventful excursion was made memorable to Stephen, for William took him to the House of Representatives and introduced him to their father's old friend, Governor Porter; they finished off the evening with a fine concert. Stephen's attachment to music was already understood and encouraged by his family. After he left Youngstown, his mother asked Morrison especially for little details of Stephen's stay in Pittsburgh, inquiring if he had a clarinet, and most important to her anxious heart, "Was he well wrapt up when he started?" Kind Aunt Evans without doubt made certain that they had plenty of blankets and hot bricks in the sleigh when they left her house.

While the mother and father waited anxiously to hear from their oldest and youngest speeding over the Pennsylvania mountains behind the cheerful sleigh bells, they were not unmindful of the welfare of their sixteen-year-old Morrison, who, left much to his own devices, displayed some boyish weaknesses that alarmed his parents. In the same letter of January 12, 1840, which contained instructions regarding Stephen, Mitty's father admonished him earnestly.

You cannot imagine how very anxious your mother and myself are respecting your health; pray do, my dear son, try to control your appetite, and don't eat so much meat and strong food. Above all, let me entreat of you, not to be led out after night to those eating houses, where Oysters and all manner of food is gormandized, and the system loaded with bile, by which disease and death soon follow.—You cannot soon forget the state of your system when I last arrived at Pittsburgh; and owing entirely to an unrestrained indulgence of your appetite. An interposition of kind Providence sent me at the critical moment to be, I hope, instrumental in saving you from an untimely grave. How thankful ought we all to be for your timely rescue & preservation. Pray do remember these things!!!

You will be punctual in attendance at a place of public worship every Sunday; and I could wish that you and Dunning would go together. Tell him this is my wish.—

William refuses to have anything to do with mercantile business here, with Thomas Wick or anyone else. I wish you to not mention the subject to him in any way.

You will feel yourself abundantly rewarded by devoting all your time when not employed for Mr. Evans, in reading and writing. God has been pleased to bestow upon you a mind superior to most boys of your age, and how ungrateful would it be on your part to suffer it to languish and dwindle into apathy and uselessness for want of cultivation by a little exertion now, before you are call'd out to act your part as a Christian man, and a good & useful citizen.

Your Ma, and all the family join in much love to your Aunt Evans and her family—as well as to yourself.

May God preserve and direct you in all things is the sincere prayer of an affectionate father,

Wm. B. Foster.

Not only the physical but the spiritual well-being of their absent boys was of paramount importance; while letters to Stephen have not been preserved, we can be sure the same loving instructions were sent him, to give him courage to live every day the way his mother hoped and prayed he would. Eliza Foster knew her boys—she knew what they needed in order to be "always strong." They felt no impatience at what some children might consider "preachy" letters. Morrison preserved them in his own secret strongbox until his dying day. No one would have presumed to touch them. He read them to his own children with tears in his eyes, tears for the long-ago, faraway mother he had loved so dearly. To quote his own words, "Ah! what a mother was that! Her precepts were listened to by her children with the reverence due to oracular utterances, and were never unheeded."

Youngstown January the 20 1840

My Dear Morison,

Feeling that I am in debt to you a letter, I will at least write a few lines to enquire after your health, and especially to enquire if William gave you any money, if not tell me your real wants, and as far as lies in my power I will alleviate them.

Nurse your mind to love your mother and obey her wishes, and she assures you, dear son, that while Providence provides anything for her, she will share with you. I feel a very great desire to see you, but I must have patience, trusting that everything will turn out for your bennifit at last.

But I wish you to remember, my darling, that no advantages can profit you very long unless the grace of God is with you in your out goings and in comings. It is simply that still, small voice which says to your soul, Beware, tuch not nor handle not the unclean thing. You must be in the habit of lifting your thoughts up to him whose dwelling place is above this scene of darke and deep depravity. I tell you, you will commit sins that will shame your face by and by, if you do not day by day ask of that spirit that can alone protect you from the power of your own evil immaginations. It were in vain for me to tell you to be virtuous unless I put you on a plan to walk abroad in the strength of true virtue, namely the grace of the inward mind which is taught you in the New Testiment. Everything else you can get up to walk by, saying to yourself, I will do no harm, I will be industrios, I will obey those who have the rule over me, I will be Honest, I will keep the moral law, I will be Honnourable with my friend, I will obey my parents, and surely after all this, I shall be a great man.—Now, all these resolutions, if your mind and body were strong enogh to keep them, would do, but here comes, like a thief upon you when you are without arms, this snare and that temtation and the other conspiricy, laid in the desires and immaginations of your own heart; and there is none to deliver you, because you will not want deliverence at the time. Every Frend that wants to snatch you from distrucktion will be as a medlar in your eyes, and away go all your fine immages of a good boy and a great man.—But keep yourself well arm'd with the influence of the holy Spirit and you will be always strong.

Give my love to Duning and tell him I should like to hear from him if he can get that much time, and be sure to write to me yourself without delay. We are all well here. Tell me little particulars about Stephen while with you. Did he get a Clearionett? And did you see him when he started, was he well wrapt up?

Love to cousin Jane and family. I am, my dear son, your ever affectionate

mother, Eliza C. Foster.

Two days after the departure of William and Stephen for Pittsburgh, William B. Foster, Sr., also undertook to go on a wintry journey, for the purpose best described by himself in a letter to William, Jr.

Youngstown, Ohio, Jany. 27th. 1840

Dear William,

Thursday morning after you left us, Thomas Wick and myself set out with his Horses and Sleigh to Warren in Pennsylvania, with the view of ascertaining what encouragement he could have for removing his store and family there for a permanent establishment. We made the journey in two days, 100 miles, remain'd there two, and return'd home in two more; he was much encouraged by Thomas Struthers, Mr. Falkner and others to go out immediately.—Skinner had lately bought a double saw mill on the river above, and had removed the remainder of his store there, and commenced the lumber trade. The store house which he had occupied was empty, the best stand in town; you remember it on the bank of the river belonging to Tanner. Thomas made a conditional bargain for it, and immediately on his return here, obtain'd his father's approbation; packed up his goods, loaded up two sleds with them, and rigged up a large sled with carpeting round it, in which he placed himself and family; his clerk, Wm. Clayland, drove, and in two days after our return, he was under way for Warren.—They took only a few trunks of clothing with them, left the House and furniture here just as it was. Their furniture we are packing, and if the sledding remains good, will send one or two loads, the balance by canal and Steam Boats via Pittsbg. when the navigation opens.

I never saw the roads better; snow four feet deep from Franklin to Warren, the road well beaten by heavy sleds carrying flour and pork to Warren.

Your mother has been so completely overwhelm'd in business since this new turn in affairs, that she desires me to say to you that you must excuse her for not writing now, and accept this from me instead of that promised by her.

There is a good opening now at Warren for a new establishment and I think Thomas will do well. Skinner has made money. Thomas Struthers had rec'd Skinner and Tanner's note from you, says it is perfectly secure, and you may rest assured he will keep it so. There are no judgments against them, and Skinner promises to pay in the Spring when he runs lumber.

We received a letter this morning from Morrison, which informs us of your doings at Pittsburgh, and your departure. Surely Stephen must feel grateful to you for your brotherly kindness to him at Pittsburgh, and will I trust exert himself by carefully pursuing your advice and instructions, and returning to you kindness for kindness. You will please to shew him this letter, and tell him I will write to him after we hear from you, which we now daily expect.

We expect Thomas reached Warren yesterday, and we shall look for the return of the sleds on Wednesday night.—

Your mother and Henry joins in love to yourself and Stephen, with your

ever affectionate father,

W. B. Foster.

Thomas Wick's prospects for making a very good living in Warren seem to have been bright. An advertisement which appeared in the Warren *Democrat* (published by Henrietta's cousin, Thomas Struthers) in February, 1840, shows that Thomas Wick had laid in a remarkably large stock of merchandise.

NEW STORE

The subscriber has just opened in the Store Room lately occupied by A. Skinner, on [W]ater Street, in the Borough of Warren, a general assortment of

WINTER AND SPRING GOODS,

consisting in part of

CLOTHES,	CASIMERS,
SATINETTS,	MERINOES,
SHAWLS, &	HANDKERCHIEFS,

An extensive stock of

BRITISH AND AMERICAN PRINTS,

CHECKS,	TICKINGS,
DRILLINGS,	CAMBRICKS,
BOOK, JACKENETT and other	MUSLINS,
BOBENETTS, FOOTINGS,	LACES,
EDGINGS,	SILKS, &c.

A fine assortment of Ladies' Kid and Morocco Slips, and Gentlemen's   SHOES & BOOTS

MEN AND BOY'S CAPS,

CROCKERY,	LOOKING-GLASSES,
GROCERIES,	LIQUORS

LEATHER, &c. &c.

All of which will be sold on the lowest terms for cash, or on approved credit at short date.

Warren, Feb. 10, 1840   T. L. WICK.

William Galbraith-Smith, whom we have mentioned before, states that Thomas Wick continued to advertise extensively all of that year, and also well into the spring of 1841; then Thomas was forced to close his business on account of the failure of his health. The store was taken over by another merchant in February, 1841, but evidently the publisher of the paper had not yet filled the space.

The removal of Henrietta and Thomas to Warren left the mother and father for the first time with none of their children "by them." They did not leave Youngstown until April, as the boys in Pittsburgh were being well taken care of. Eliza Foster kept in communication with all of her children, which meant a great deal of letter writing for the fingers already becoming cramped and stiff. The following is to Morrison.

[Youngstown, Ohio]   Febuary the 7th, 1840

My Dear Son,

I know you are looking for a letter from me by this time, and am sorry to disappoint you as to funds, having none to spare at this time, but keep up heart, I will send you some bye and bye.

You ask me what your Father is doing; he has been assisting me in packing up and sending off their things on sleds, one reason for their going in the winter. We heard that they ariv'd there safe and comfortable and well, and Thomas thinks he will sell more goods in Warren than in Youngstown, as Henry and Hugh Wick was doing the heaviest business, because of the largest capitol.

Henry thinks he will leave this place on Monday next, but when your Father and myself will go to Pittsburgh I cannot now inform you. We are very happy here, having a pleasent room and good boarding and a kind family in that of Mr. Richerds.

Paul Wick is in the Colnel's store, and William Cleland is gone with Thomas, and I feel quite contended about Stephen, beleiving that William will take good care of him. He took him to see the Govenor and house of representatives and to a fine concert in Haresburg.

I receiv'd a letter from Ann Eliza some few days since, they are all quite well in that quarter.

You did not tell me how cousin Jane and her children are. Do everything Cadwallader and she may ask of you, unless it should be something that would lower you as a gentlemen, but that charecter I know they would desire to support for you as much as anyone, and of course will not ask you to do anything that will make you apear cheep, when you are smart enough to ern your bread without it. Never the less, be respectfull to them, and do not be idle or noisey, and be perticulary carefull as to change.

I think you improve in your writing, you have only to take pains, and I thank my dear son very much that he has not suffer'd the vagaries of a frivolous world to divert you entirely from your duty to your Mother. Your letters are truly acceptable to me, in so much that they apprize me of your affection for me, and I am not one who is dull to the vallue of the return of tenderness in a child. My love to Duning and tell him if he does not write soon, I shall conclude soon that he declines any farther acquaintence with me. I have nothing more to say at preasant, only that I remain your truly affectionate   Mother. P. S. You will accept for yourself and Dunning, much love from Henry and your affectionate father,   W. B. Foster.

Although she does not say so, does the above not contain a gentle reproach to Dunning, who is suffering the vagaries of a frivolous world to divert him from his duty to his mother? It was not for long, however, that Dunning was remiss in writing to his mother. In a few years' time, he put aside his boyish carelessness, and became a thoughtful and faithful correspondent.

X

WILLIAM B. FOSTER, SR., gave no hint to William of the inward dissatisfaction which attended his present state of unaccustomed idleness, but Eliza Foster was concerned about his restlessness; she feared that being much longer without a settled business to occupy his mind would change his buoyant and hopeful nature to one of pessimism and irascibility. Therefore, she welcomed his revived interest in politics. Although Wm. B. Foster was a Democrat, he took his stand with the Whigs against Martin Van Buren in that great and exciting campaign, "the revolution of 1840." The prospect of once more entering a contest where the fight was hot and public feeling ran high against the "scoundrels", was like the smell of powder to an old war horse. As he sailed into the fray, his despondency dropped away from him, and Mrs. Foster wrote happily to Morrison, "Richerd is himself again in all his glory!" In the spring, his interests were centered chiefly on the doings at Harrisburg, because his son William's future prospects depended mainly on the sum the legislature was willing to set aside for improvements.

Youngstown, O. March 24th. 1840

Dear William,

By your mother's last letter, you were inform'd of our intention to return to Pittsburgh about this time. The canal here was fill'd with water yesterday, and we shall look for the arrival in two or three days of a packet Boat, when we will depart for Pittsburgh. It is said here that a Boat will leave Ackron on the 1st of April to pass through to Beaver, perhaps to Philada.—

I have been anxiously examining my Harrisburgh papers as they came to hand, to find something like a Bill, to authorize a hope that the State improvements would progress to completion; and I assure you I was delighted with the Bill reported by the Committee of internal improvement. Under the embarrass'd state of the financial concerns of the Commth. I thought it a very judicious plan to save the credit of the State, as well as that of the Banks, and to relieve the people at the same time.

My paper of the 16th, which I did not receive until this morning, informs me that the bill is attack'd from different quarters; but I still hope that the sober second thought of the Legislature, by leaving out the destructives in both parties, will be able to pass the bill or something like it. To be sure, its passage would give a death blow to the Banks in Ohio.—But Pennsya. must look out for herself. To compel the Banks to resume instantly would certainly ruin the improvements, by stopping all work on them. It would destroy the Banks, as well as the people generally. I certainly never would set fire to my Barn to get clear of the rats; I would much prefer to put in commission a few experienced cats, to watch their movements, *and expunge* them, in detail, as they might be found cutting high capers.

An adjourn'd court I believe will sit in Pittsburgh early in April, when I hope to get our land business settled.

We think it time to receive another letter from Stephen. I hope he is attentive to his studies. Give much love to him from his mother and myself, tell him his old Uncle Struthers looks to him to become a very great man. He says he is confident that he is possess'd of superior talents for one of his age. I hope Stevy will not disappoint the fond hopes of so good an old man.

By letters from Thomas Struthers and Thomas Wick, we are encouraged to hope that Thomas Wick will do well at Warren.

Henry expected to go into a ware house at the Canal Basin in Pittsbg. about this time.—Dunning is still on a Steam Boat as clerk, and Morrison remains at Mr. Evans'. They are all well and continue good boys in high estimation, which is a great comfort to us all.—

We are both very well, your mother is quite composed and resign'd to her destiny, and I still look forward to the time when we can have a permanent situation where we may "totter down the Hill together" in peace and quietness, and "sleep together at the foot," and be forgotten by all the world except our dear children.

Robert Taylor and Louisa Woodbridge are to be married tonight.

Accept much love from your mother and your affectionate father,

Wm. B. Foster.

Wm. B. Foster's wish that he and his wife might "totter down the Hill together, and sleep together at the foot," was granted; for when the time came for them to join their daughter Charlotte, they were not long parted; only six months after his wife's sudden death in 1855, William Foster was laid to rest beside her. Baby James was buried in Trinity churchyard, but the five other boys sleep in the Allegheny Cemetery with their mother and father, never to be parted again.

The following letter to William, dated April 27, 1840, indicates that there had been no improvement in the mail service, and shows the general undependability of the post office before the railroads crossed the mountains of Pennsylvania. Poor little Stephen must have felt greatly depressed when he received his father's letter "scolding him pretty smartly" for not writing. Doubtless, he was homesick enough already, and such a letter could not have improved his drooping spirits.

Pittsburgh April 27th. 1840

Dear William,

I wrote to Stephen on the 18th inst. and scolded him pretty smartly for not having written to us more frequently, but he is not quite so much to blame as I then thought, for on the evening of that day, (the 18th) I rec'd a letter from him which was dated on the 27th of March, and must have been 21 days on the way. I wish you to tell him of this; I presume letters would come with more certainty by the way of Harrisburgh, if you have a daily mail from there to your place.

The prospects for an appropriation to your line of Canal, I fear, are dull; but George Darsy told me on Saturday that he had not a doubt that an appropriation would be made to your line and the Erie Extension, soon after the meeting of the Legislature. I cannot imagine how the Democratic members of the house are to account to the people for their gross misconduct. There never has been a legislative body so entirely destitute of every principle which ought to govern honest men.

It is, I think, five or six weeks since we had a letter from you, perhaps one may have been lost in the mountains on its way hither. Clayton is here preparing a large Baloon to cross the mountains in. He proposes to carry letters and newspapers with great despatch; he will start on Friday or Saturday next; it is not likely he will go as far as Towanda.

We are all very well. Your mother and brothers join in love to you and Stephen with

Your affectionate father
Wm. B. Foster.

Wm. B. Foster, Jr.
State Engineer,
Towanda, Bradford County, Pa.

What a stir Clayton and his balloon made in Pittsburgh, that they are mentioned so frequently! The prospect of air mail between Pittsburgh and Harrisburg evidently was considered a near possibility. But just what advantage it might have had over the stage-coach on days when the wind was blowing in the wrong direction is not brought out in the correspondence.

As the tenant had left, the Fosters were back in the Allegheny house where Mother and Father stayed with the boys until August. The country was slowly climbing out of the depression following the panic of 1837, but real money was still hard to find. Mr. Foster was busy making secure his title to land in Wilkins and Plum townships, and taking care of some of William's affairs. He finally settled for William with the buyer of his son's share in the old firm of Foster & Hall, by accepting in lieu of cash:

... either 180 acres of first rate land in Trumbull County, Ohio about 20 or thirty miles northwest from Youngstown, unimproved, at 2000 Dollars; to pay the difference when you please, say about 400 Dollars on interest, or stock in the upper [Mechanic Street] Bridge at par for the amt. of your debt. You may take your choice. The bridge stock at present is below par, it may become good property, but the Bridge may be swept off.—I give you this information that you may act according to your own judgment; let what will happen, I shall keep a sharp lookout, and advise you accordingly.

William decided to run the risk of the bridge being swept away, for he chose the stock, the certificate for which reads,

> THIS IS TO CERTIFY, that William B. Foster, Jr. is entitled to twenty-nine Shares of the Capital Stock of the Company for erecting a Bridge over the Allegheny River, opposite Northern Liberties, Pittsburgh.

It is signed by J. H. Shoenberger, president, and G. E. Warren, secretary, June 16, 1840. These early bridges were all toll bridges, and as travel was increasing every day, it is possible that the stock proved a good investment for William. Toll charges on several of the Allegheny River bridges were not abolished for many years; some descendants of the original investors received dividends as late as 1920.

During the summer of 1840, William sent for Henry, offering him a position in the engineers' office at Towanda. Henry hastened to accept, and joined William and Stephen in July. While she probably missed her children greatly, Eliza Foster was in a very happy frame of mind when she wrote the following letter to William.

Youngstown August 7th, 1840

My dear Son,

I received your very welcome letter of the 28, the morning before we left Pittsburgh; I was highly grattified with its contents, independent of the 20 dollars you were so generous to enclose.

As to Stephen, I leave everything regarding the future for him to your own Judgement. West Point or the Navy, I have no choice; you are not only his brother but his Father; and I trust all his feellings will assend to you as his patron.

Henry speaks of your conduct toward him in the most exalted terms, as far exceding his expecttations; he is quite happy and full of hope that he will be able to stand the fatigue.

We came down to stay at uncle Strouthers untill the tenth of September, when your Father's business that you have been already aprize'd of will call him back to old Pitt.

You mention Miss Louisa McNair. Maria told me that she had engage'd herself to a young gentleman of family in Louisville, but from the time she travell'd with you, she commenced slighting him, and finally broke with him, which made a great war with the friends of both parties, and somehow or other got into the newspapers; but in the midst of it, her mother came and took her home to Orleans, and the excitement died away, but in all probability she will not return to Louisville where he has so many friends.

Duning and Augustus Anshutes have purchased and loaded a keel boat and have been seven days under way to Louisville.

Morison is place'd for too years with Mr. McCormack, as clerck, and messenger, boarding and washing found, and 100 dollars a year. He was applied for, and is highly pleased, having a fine little Poney to ride on when he is sent out. He has no lamp lighting, shuting up, ware house cleaning, or anything to abuse his clothes, and is treated with much respect, as he performs his duties promtly and well.

So that I am begining to think that we are all together a favour'd family, and must not forget to give God the praise, instead of attributing any merit to ourselves, for if his spirit had departed from amoungest us we would have long ago been a prey to the devouring enemy; but blessed be his holly name, who has given us the victory, that we are not sunk in vice and curruption, as many a fair family has been who call'd themselfs higher born and better bred.

The same monotiny is portray'd in the movements of every one here. Father Wick sits in his own front door exactly as he use'd to do, and Doctor Maning rides along the street with precisely the same benevolent aspect as in other times. There is no house building, but several vacant. I saw Mrs. Bane yesterday, who is as friendly as ever, as well as the Doctor. The old lady is not quite well.

Give much love to my dear boy Stephen and endeavour to realize a full share of anxious solicitude for your welfare and hapiness existing in the breast of your affectionate Mother,

Eliza C. Foster.

Your Father desires to be affectionately remember'd to you.

She does not say so, of course, but is there not just a little touch of motherly satisfaction in Eliza Foster's telling William the story of the faithless Miss McNair, who had never been the same to her Louisville suitor after traveling with William. We do not know whether the momentous journey was made by stagecoach or canal, but passengers traveling either way generally became very well acquainted by the time they parted. William would have been horrified at the thought of being even the innocent cause of a broken engagement, but far be it from his mother to be surprised at the young lady's disaffection.

The business which called her husband back to "old Pitt" was still indirectly the same old stagecoach lawsuit, but this time principally against the cashier of a Pittsburgh bank who had collected some of the claim in Erie County for Wm. B. Foster, and some other suitors, and then calmly removed himself to Mobile, Alabama, without troubling to hand over any money to any of his clients. He had been traced to Philadelphia, and Mr. Foster, armed with an attachment, proceeded there with his lawyer, James Dunlop. Mrs. Foster accompanied them on the canal packet boat from Pittsburgh to Harrisburg where they changed to the railroad, and from there were "hurled with frightful velocity" to Philadelphia. Mother Foster left the "cars" at Kinzer's Station, and took stage to Pequea to visit Ann Eliza while the gentlemen wrestled with the courts at Philadelphia. A letter which his mother wrote to Morrison from "Picqua" reveals that she is none too sanguine about the outcome, but her fear of failure was not entirely borne out by results, for Mr. Foster eventually succeeded in recovering $2000 or $2500 from the slippery cashier. We do not know whether the others who had claims against him obtained any redress or not.

Poor young Mitty had evidently been feeling very low in his mind and wrote his mother of some slight he had received, or thought was meant for him, from one of his more affluent companions. Eliza Foster knew that youth's heartaches are not imaginary ones, and gave him the loving advice and help he needed.

Picqua   October 7   1840

My dear Morison,

I received your letter today and was much pleas'd that you attended to my request in wrighting to me so promptly, and giving me every minute circumstance in relation to those with whoom we have had the most to do.

I am sorry for poor George Evans. I hope you aford him all the consolation you can. Nevertheless, take good care of your own health for the sake of your poor Mother, who loves you very much and could ill bear to have anything happen you. And should the loss of your health take place through your own intemperence either in eating, drinking, over exercise, or neglect of early rest, we cannot charge providence with his neglegting you, especially when you are thus warn'd, a benefit for which you can raise your thoughts in gratitude to God; that he has in mercy left you a mother to direct your steps; when present, with her advise, and when absent with her letters. When you do any thing wrong, you need not fear to communicate the worst to me, for my chideings shall be gentle as the rains of summer, that your confidence may revive, and your eye brighten when the tear has been wipe'd away that my kind reproof may call fourth.

Your Father is still in the Citty, and this is the eleventh day since he went on; Mr. Dunlop is also there. They surely must be doing some good, but alas, I fear it is like everything else, not to be depended on.

I receiv'd accounts from Warren they are all well; your sister Ann Eliza and her charming children are also quite well.

I wrote to Duning a day or too since, but give my love to him, and tell him not to hunt too much, lest he be taken sick in some of his excursions.

There has been no lack of visitors here since I arived. Mr. Buchanan has two neices staying here, the Miss Lane's. I do not know how long they will make their visit. They are young and lively, something in the stile of Mary Evans.

Now, my dear son, be content with your humble lot, and bear yourself with dignity, as one feeling the weight of his own merit. Avoid huge talkers who have a contempt for religion and poor persons. Regard not the boasting nor the coldness of those who can neither tuch your body or your soul, or health or virtue, or reputation. Lose not your patience for a slight, for if they can neither hurt your body nor your soul, which makes the whole man, you are none the worse. Your levity is corected by your not being too well off, and your actions are govern'd by your not being able to draw too freely of the draft of plenty, which can only create a fever of which we are sure to die.

Adieu, my dear son, you need not write again untill you receive a second letter from me. I am, my dear boy, now as ever, your truly affectionate Mother,

Eliza C. Foster.

Morrison Foster,
Care of McCormick & Brackenridge,
Pittsburgh, Pa.

Although the Philadelphia trip did not result in a definite set-

tlement of the case, a promise was obtained, with which the suitors
had to be satisfied for the time being, and William B. Foster returned to Pittsburgh to engage with enthusiasm in the strenuous
campaign for "Tippecanoe and Tyler, too." Mr. Foster opposed
Van Buren on the grounds that in 1835 he had caused the defeat
of Governor Wolff of Pennsylvania whom he greatly admired.
William Henry Harrison's majority in Pennsylvania was 343 votes,
and William's father wrote to his son on November 8, 1840:

The result of the election in favour of Harrison being only confirmed
today beyond a doubt, we will have a tremendious illumination tomorrow night. I take to myself a goodly share of the credit of giving the vote
of Pennsya. to Harrison.

Your mother has not yet return'd from Mr. Buchanan's, but I shall
look for her the last of next week.

With much love to Henry and Stephen, and my silent preyers for
your health and happiness.

The election returns were coming through much faster than they
did during the Jackson-Clay contest. Communication had been
hastened to such a degree that the election held October 30 was
confirmed by November 8. "Tremendious" illuminations were
burning all over the country, now that the silk-stocking gentry were
"down, never to rise again." The battle even entered the sacred
precincts of the post office, and Mr. Foster was convinced that the
reason he had not received his newspapers from Towanda was
because a certain, "unprincipled caitiff" of the opposition had held
them back. Knowing the temper of the times, he was probably right
in his suspicions!

Pittsburgh, Nov. 16, 1840

Dear William,

As I wrote you on the 7th or 8th inst. would not write so soon, but
feared you would think it strange that I did not acknowledge the rect.
of your kind letter dated the 24th ult., but the truth is, it was not
delivered to me until Friday last, the 13th. inst. It bears the Post Mark
at Towanda 1st. of November, two days after the election, and I have
no doubt it was supposed by the miserable faction about the Post Office
here that it contain'd the accurate returns of Bradford County, and
perhaps others of the northern counties, which were the last to reach

us here and detain'd. I do not believe that Mr. Moorhead would do such a thing, but he is seldom about the office, having large contracts with the state in making improvements; and that other miserable unprincipled caitiff is still living in the house and has free access to the office. He is base enough to damn a whole administration with himself. Thank fortune, he is down never to rise again.

You appear to think there will be no appropriation to the Canals during the approaching session of the legislature. You need not fear that. Will Erie, Mercer, Beaver and Allegheny Counties permit their members to abandon the Erie extension? and will your Northern Whigs agree to abandon the North Branch? No fears of it.

And if they agree to appoint by the Legislature, or elect by the people, the Canal Commissioners, you may depend I can now send such an overwhelming demand from the Whigs here for your retention that they dare not overlook your reappointment. Some of them say I have been mainly instrumental in carrying the state for Harrison, and some of the Loco's say I took five hundred votes from them; be it so.

Dunning return'd from St. Louis last night in good health and spirits.

Your mother arrived on Saturday; well, except a severe cold. She had pleasant weather and agreeable company.—Your kind heart would not let you forget to send her some money, for which you have as usual our kind thanks. I had sent her some also, but there is none of it misapplied by her.

You shall hear of the Wilkins township land shortly; it is "right side up", no mistake.

Your mother joins in love to you, to Henry and Stephen, with your affectionate father,

Wm. B. Foster.

Decr. 1, 1840.

Dear William,

Your letter of 23d. came duly to hand on Sunday 29th. ult. It appears that you have fallen into a misapprehension of my letter of the 16th. respecting the detention at the Post Office here of your letter to me of 24th. October.—that letter, you will observe, bears the post mark at Towanda 1st. Nover. and was not delivered to me until the 13th. whereas, I ought to have rec'd it on Saturday, the 7th, the day we were most anxious to get certain intelligence from the northern Counties, and when bets were running high, and I at the office every day. Your letters always reach me in from 5 to 7 days. See your last, dated and postmark'd on the 23d. came in on the 29th.—I never attached any blame to Mr. Moorhead, but the other is capable of any mean and rascally act.—

I send you today the Pittsburgh Manufacturer of Saturday last, by which you will perceive the temper of the destructives in this quarter towards Governor Porter. I have attached also a scrap containing the most infamous abuse of the Governor, from the New York Evening Post, as also proceedings in Bedford County. Which all go to shew that the faction with Van Buren at their head had long since determined on his destruction if possible. I also send you the Saturday Evening Visitor of 1st. of August, which contains the first card of the *Straightouts* here, and an article over the signature of "An original Jackson Man," which was written by myself, and will I think give me some slight claims to the character of a prophet. The card was also written by me, and in the proceedings at our organization, the following resolution was unanimously adopted;

"Resolved, that as Pennsylvanians, it is our duty, as it is our pride, to stand by and support our noble minded Governor, who so firmly stood by the Commonwealth, when party madness was about to spread ruin from the centre to its circumference."

From all this, you may see how favourably he was held by those Democrats who abandoned Van Buren.—

The friends of Governor Porter will not let him withdraw now, and the *Barn Burners* will get up perhaps, Muhlenburgh; the Whigs will have either Harmar Denny or Walter Forward, either of which if elected will go to their death for you and myself.

I regret very much that the Governor rode through the country electioneering for Van, who is the head Devil against him.

I cannot doubt but your purchase of wild land will turn out advantageous. Would it not be prudent to select some 200 acres of the best and contract for clearing and fencing about 30 acres of it during the present winter, say ten acres for meadow and 20 for plough land. I would make no building until next summer, but in selecting a site for a house, pray leave two or three acres of the native forest standing, from which I would not have a bush or a shrub cut down. The land would sell much better by having the improvements on it.

Your mother says she had intended to write you today, but as I am writing she will defer it a week or ten days—for your continued kindness to your brothers, you have our grateful thanks. Heaven will reward you if we cannot.

A letter from Henrietta, rec'd. yesterday, says that Thomas is in delicate health, strong symptoms of the same disease which carried off your dear Mary. I fear he is not to be with us many years.

Give much love to the boys when you see them, and accept for yourself our best wishes for health and happiness.

You will hear in the next letter something about the Wilkinsburgh land, from

Your affectionate father,

Wm. B. Foster.

We are boarding at Mrs. Paul's, a widow lady, no boarders but ourselves, and are very comfortable.—The editorial in the Manufacturer respecting Governor Porter, you may rely on it, is all lies. Just so, they boasted about Muhlenbergh, and he only got 375 votes in the county!

The home of the "widow lady," Mrs. Paul, was then on Second Street, north of Smithfield near the bustling, pleasant steamboat wharves along the Monongahela River. Mrs. Paul seems to have been one of Eliza C. Foster's close friends, and it is interesting to know that she was the grandmother of Anne Paul, who married the celebrated composer, Ethelbert Nevin, in 1888.

XI

WHILE his brothers were pursuing their careers as businessmen, and his father was absorbed in politics, what of "little Stephen" in his new and unfamiliar surroundings? William first entered Stephen in the academy at Towanda where William had his headquarters, but we have no letters of Stephen's telling how he liked the school, or anything about his personal experiences in his new life. Reminiscences of one of Stephen's old schoolmates, William Wallace Kingsbury, give us a glimpse of Stephen's activities, and show that Stephen was in Towanda in wild strawberry time, which is generally the month of June. But Mr. Kingsbury does not state whether it was the summer of 1840, or 1841. We do know that in the fall of 1840, Stephen was no longer attending school in Towanda, but was a student in the academy at Athens, eighteen miles north of Towanda. Then, in the spring of 1841, we find him in Towanda again. Quoting William Wallace Kingsbury:

Well do I remember the inimitable Stephen C. Foster. He was my special friend and companion; being a year older than myself and considerably larger, he used to defend me in my boyhood antagonisms with belligerent schoolmates. We often played truant together, rambling by shady streams or gathering wild strawberries in the meadows or pastures, removed from the sound of the old academy bell. One mutual luxury, in which we jointly indulged in those excursions without leave, was in going barefoot and wading pools of running water that meandered through Mercur's farm and down Mix's Run, in the village of my nativity. Foster wore a fine quality of hose, and I remember how it shocked me to see him cast them away, when soiled by perspiration or muddy water. His was a nature generous to a fault, with a soul attuned to harmony. His love of music was an all-absorbing passion, and his execution on the flute was the very genius of melody, and gave rise to those flights of inspired pathos, which have charmed the English-speaking world with their excellence from cabin to palace. Genial, well remembered friend, how proud I have been in the thought that it was my good fortune to have been the boyhood comrade of a character, commanding such world-wide fame as you have established in the hearts of a song-loving people.*

Perhaps it was for the sake of stricter discipline and perhaps because Athens offered greater advantages to a student of Stephen's temperament, that Brother William transferred him to Athens.

Going away to school with William was a great adventure; seen in the rosy distance, it all seemed very exciting and romantic. But when his entrance to the academy at Athens was an accomplished fact, when he was settled down in the autumn of 1841 with a strange family in a strange little village, and the routine of the schoolroom in Athens proved to be as onerous as it was in Towanda or Pittsburgh, much of the romantic charm of his adventure vanished for Stephen Foster. He was probably consumed with homesickness the whole time he was away from Pittsburgh, but he stuck to it for almost eighteen months, because he realized that he was expected to be properly grateful and appreciative of Brother William's

*A. H. Kingsbury, "The Old Towanda Academy," Bradford County Historical Society, *Annual* (No. 4), Towanda, Pennsylvania, 1910.

generosity. No going home is mentioned in 1840, and unless he accompanied Brother William to Pequea in January, 1841, at which time William made a short visit to Ann Eliza, Stephen had no glimpse of any of his home folks except Henry and William in over a year.

It was the custom for the students of Athens Academy to board with the townspeople instead of living in dormitories, and Stephen was placed in a private home where there were several small children. Nervous and high-strung as he was, it was impossible for the temperamental boy to study in the general living room of the Herricks'. This trying situation made him write to Brother William on November 9, 1840, making an urgent appeal for a fire in his own room.

Dear Brother,

As Mr. Mitchell is going to start for Towanda today, I thought I would write you a line concerning my studies as he says you will not be here for more than a week.

My Philosophy Grammar & Arithmetic not being enough to keep me going I would ask your permision to Study either Latin or Book keeping.

I have no place to study in the evenings as the little ones at Mr. Herricks keep such a crying and talking that it's imposible to read. There is a good fire place in my room and if you will just say the word I will have a fire in it at nights and learn something. When you come dont forget my waistcoat at the tailors. there are several little articles which I need though I have no room to mention them. I must stop writing as I am very cold. Your affectionate Brother

Stephen

William ordered the fire for his little brother, and thereafter the Herrick family were regaled nightly by the strains of Stephen's lonely clarinet in the chamber overhead.

Although he kept to himself a great deal, Stephen was in demand at school entertainments for his musical and poetical accomplishments. Athens was unlike the general run of country colleges where musical talent is generally scarce; the fact that among two hundred students, they were able to find three who could play the flute is rather unusual. That Stephen wrote harmonizing parts for the two or three students who accompanied him in his own composition, "The Tioga Waltz," shows that in composition he was well advanced for a fourteen-year-old boy. Morrison Foster believed that "The Tioga Waltz" was composed for four flutes, but John A. Perkins, a fellow student of Stephen's at Athens Academy, writing in 1897, said that only two flutists performed with Stephen on April 1, 1841, when "The Tioga Waltz" was played with great success at the school exhibition in the old Presbyterian Church at Athens, and these boys were James H. Forbes and William F. Warner.* Stephen probably wrote his waltz in four parts, three flutes and piano.

Although the Fosters laid no plans to educate their sons along musical lines, as they did their daughters, Stephen received every encouragement at home after his musical talent became evident. Even with his natural ability, Stephen could not have composed "The Tioga Waltz" at the age of fourteen if he had not had some training, nor have arranged readable parts for other musicians, as young as he. Morrison has told us that Stephen's poetic gift seemed more pronounced at first than his musical talent, and the family expected that he might excel as a writer. Stephen's mother and sisters delighted in writing poetry, particularly of a religious or sentimental nature. A number of appealing poems written by Eliza C. Foster and Ann Eliza, but never published, have been preserved, as have also published and unpublished poems composed by Henrietta during and after the Civil War. All the records that have come down to us show that Stephen's home environment was admirably suited to a boy who wanted to "gang his own gait," and, when he persistently clung to the study of music, there is no evidence to show that his family disapproved; in fact, quite the contrary. His father said that although Stephen would not stick at school, it was a source of satisfaction to Stephen's mother and himself that he indulged in no "evil propensities," and his leisure hours were "all devoted to musick, for which he possesses a strange talent." Following his own bent as he did, his compositions are the natural outpouring of his spirit, unspoiled by hampering restrictions. If he produced no great symphony, he surpassed that by laying the founda-

*R. M. Welles, "The Old Athens Academy," Bradford County Historical Society, *Annual* (No. 5), Towanda, Pennsylvania, 1911.

tions for a deathless symphony that will enrich the music of America for all time.

Athens Academy possessed a creditable music department, but Stephen's letter of November 9, 1841, does not indicate that he was taking any musical subjects. His practicing and composing seem to have been diversions of his own choosing; he was fortunate in having for friends several fellow students who were musically inclined, notably amongst them seventeen-year-old Frances Welles, who lived with her widowed mother in "The Stone House" one and a half miles below the academy, on a large estate for which her ancestors had taken out the first Pennsylvania patent in that locality. A number of the young people of the Welles family attended the academy, and Stephen found them very congenial. An account of Stephen's acquaintance with this interesting family has been prepared by a relative, the late Jessie Welles Murray, of Athens, in which she states that Frances Welles was an accomplished musician from childhood, and Stephen's talents secured him a warm welcome in their domestic circle. To Frances, it is said, Stephen dedicated his "Tioga Waltz," named in honor of her pleasant home, the Tioga Point farm. Miss Murray says, "This lovely spot, where the Chemung River flows into the Susquehanna, circled by purple hills, was once the site of the Indian town, Te-a-o-ga, the meaning of which—*at the meeting,* or *the place between*—renders the English word *Point* superfluous."* It is reasonable to believe that Stephen, with his two friends James H. Forbes and William F. Warner, practiced "The Tioga Waltz" in Frances Welles' parlor, with Frances playing the piano accompaniment for the three young musicians. Frances left college, soon after the exhibition, to be married on April 17, 1841, to Major Charles Beebe Stuart, a construction engineer on the new Erie Railroad.

Stephen loved to study, but did not love school. He learned quickly, but did not enjoy pursuing any subject along the line laid out by a teacher. He was already well read in history and literature when he went to Athens, for study of these branches of learning was stressed at Mr. Stockton's academy. William B. Foster had collected a good library, and reading aloud in the evening was always

*Jessie Welles Murray, "Stephen C. Foster's School Days at the Athens Academy," *Foster Hall Bulletin* No. 11, Indianapolis, February, 1935.

the custom in the Foster family circle. Stephen's fellow student, John A. Perkins, whom we have mentioned before, remembered that Stephen, at Athens Academy, "showed some of the genius he displayed in later years."

I can see him [wrote Mr. Perkins] speaking "Lord Ullins' Daughter," as though it was yesterday; at the close he would fold his arms, throw back his head and tragically exclaim, "My daughter, oh, my daughter!"

This stirring classic Stephen and Morrison learned at Mr. Stockton's under Mr. Caldwell, the teacher of elocution. Another of their favorites was the noble old declamation from "The Tragedy of the Douglas," beginning with the lines:

> My name is Norval:
> On the Grampian Hills, my father tends his flock.

While Stephen was at Athens, his progress and his conduct were apparently entirely satisfactory to his parents and Brother William. Their correspondence contains no reference to anything unusual in his steady course. The affairs of their other children occupied a great part of their thoughts. The continued ill-health of Thomas Wick caused them much anxiety; something of a happier nature, regarding William, was of loving concern to his parents at the beginning of 1841.

Pittsburgh, Feby. 13th, 1841

Dear William—

You will think me quite remiss in not having replied to your letter of the 15th ult. written at Tunkhannock. I must have left home a few days before your letter reach'd this place.— I went to Erie induced to believe that my suit would be tried at an adjourn'd court in that county in January; but owing to the neglect of my attorney in not giving the proper notice, we could not get the suit tried, and must wait until the first week in April, when I believe they must try the cause.

From Erie, I return'd by way of Youngstown, and as I had no pressing business here, I delayed a week at Uncle Struthers, and the village, and only reach'd home yesterday.—

I set out this morning to obtain the information you desire respecting the small Steam Engine. There is but one manufactory in town which makes Engines of so small a description, Messrs. E. & F. Faber. They have no patterns to make a three-horse power, but they have on hand several of four horse-power; the price of one of those is 400 Dollars, one half cash, the other half in six months with a satisfactory reference in the city. They put the Engine together and place it on its blocks here; so that the purchaser will have nothing to do but build his walls and set it on, put up the pipes and set it to work. They will warrant its performance. All fixtures go with the Engine.—

Old Mr. Wick is quite deaf, you must speak very loud to make him hear. Thomas is here with his family. He is under the care of Doctr. Spear; it is thought by some that he is better, but I confess I have my doubts as to his recovery, but this I don't let him know.—When he became so ill at Warren as to induce his Physicians there to recommend him to quit business, he wrote and requested me to go up to help him to wind up his business, and I am glad I did so. I induced him to sell out his stock of goods at 400 Dollars less than he was offered for them by doubtful characters, to men whose character and capacity is undoubted, Judge Eldred and Abijah Morison, the Sheriff of the County. He has their joint Notes for about 2500 Dollars, and other good notes and accounts for about the same sum.

Your mother desires me to say that she will write you a long letter in a few days; and I may as well add that the *little secret* which you communicated to her receives her, as it does my, most unqualified approbation!! Depend upon it, my son, there can be no happiness in this world without a confidential bosom friend in whose confiding breast you can safely deposit the most secret impulses of your whole heart and soul— Your own good judgment is a sufficient guarantee of the value of the young lady who is willing to venture her happiness in this world, and perhaps, the next, with you and your fate.

I fear the blowing up of the Banks will destroy our hopes for an appropriation of the State improvements, unless the Legislature should unite and put forth their strength in some judicious financial operation to save the Commonwealth.

Your mother informs me she received Twenty Dollars from you during my absence, for which you have our thanks; and she joins me in love to you with

Your affectionate father,

Wm. B. Foster.

Dunning has gone on a steam boat in the Mississippi trade at 75 Dollars per month and found.

The "little secret" William had confided to his mother was that he was growing extremely fond of a certain young lady, Miss Over-

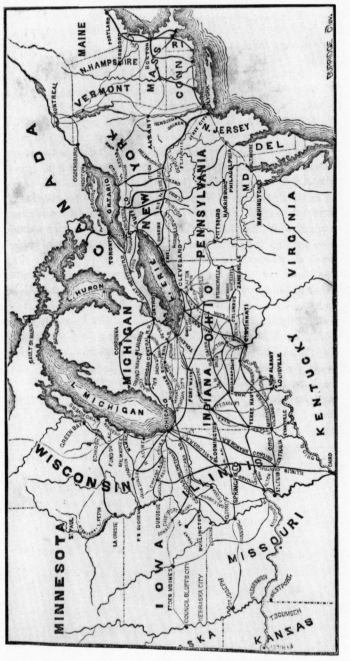

"Map of the New York and Erie Railroad"
From *Lloyd's Steamboat Directory and Disasters on the Western Waters*
(Cincinnati: James T. Lloyd & Co., 1856)

Jefferson College at Canonsburg, 1840

ton, but he feared that she was too young to care for an old widower of thirty-three. There were two Overton families where William was a frequent visitor, one living in Towanda, the other near Athens. Mary Overton, of Towanda, married James Macfarlane, assistant engineer under William at the North Branch Canal from 1837 to 1841. The late Judge James Macfarlane, of Woodland Road, Pittsburgh, their son, told me that his sister, Mrs. Mary C. Angle, had often heard their mother say that William Foster had shown attention to another Mary Overton, only her name was Mary Ann Overton; and she lived near Athens and "had a great many beaux!" That her youth, or her beaux, should be any hindrance to Mary Ann's marrying a fine man like William was unthinkable, of course, to William's mother. She lovingly reassures him in a letter dated February 24, 1841:

As you are a good son, you will I know be a kind husband, and it is time you should settle upon a rest for your mind. I have heard nothing of Miss Overton from any source but your own letter to me. I like her name, and as to her age, that is altogether your affair; for my own part, the younger she is, if I should ever be so happy as to see her, I would like her better on that account, because she would be likely to treat me as one who had more experience in small matters.

I have not heard from Duning since he left, which has been three weeks. Morison is a good boy, obedient to his parents, honest and diligent in his business, and respectfull to his employers—they like him very much.

William's next letter from his mother reveals her in an exalted frame of mind, grateful for her many blessings; a state of peace doubtless arrived at after she had shed many tears over an amazing slight received from an old friend, we know not her name, whose prosperity had evidently gone to her head. It was a sad blow to unsuspecting Eliza Foster to have her friendly greetings returned with coldness, but after taking her trouble to the Throne of Grace, she emerged as serene and smiling as ever.

                                    Pittsburg, March the 24th 1841
My dear Son,
The day is fine and everything around me wears an air of comfort, and I sit down to write to you, not only with a greatfull heart, but with an enthusiasm of soul which has to pass from my bosom to the

paper that I now endorse, while addressing my ever constant son.

I have been contemplating God's mercies to me for some time. I have been lashed with many stripes, it is true, but now I am ready to cry out with joy: "How good art thou, Oh my God, in every act of thy kind Providence; thou hast raised sons to comfort me, and hast not taken thy spirit from me and left me ungracious, unthankfull, a prey to discontent, fault finding, murmering, envying those who have gone past me, seeking revenge of the ungreatfull, and all passions that would break down my own soul, but would never reach them." On the day in which I close up my accounts in this sad world, what matter is it to me that she who is now rich in gold and lands, passes me with a cold smile, if I welcomed to my home and cheared her when she was neeedy? For that I shall not be called to an account, but she will. The ox knoweth his owner, and so does the lamb the shepperds fold. She will never let go these things that she worships without a hard fought battle with her fatal conquerer, while I trust that having no Idles to part with, neither golden calves, nor emerald goddesses, I may in the strength of grace, be able to resign myself into the hands of my creator whenever the purposes are full for which I have been made; and I will not say, God grant that it may be soon or late, for he knows exactly when it is the right time, only let me lose my affections from the objects about me, which I cannot do unless I occasionaly meet with some chastisment, for which I have learned to be thankfull.

Having written to you so recently I have nothing to tell you that can awaken the slightest curiosity. Everything is exactly as it was when I wrote to you last, for which I have to wonder, as we are a family subject to changes. Not that it is always our own faults, but that a change comes oe'r the spirit of the dream of those with whoom we have to do.

There are many of the Lazeroni returning from Washington Citty disapointed. Brutis had his friends, and Cesor had his friends, but Jupetor Ammon swepet them all!

Mrs. Paul will move to a neat brick house between Wood and Smithfield and can make you comfortable, if you like to stop with her while you stay in Pittsburg, which will add very much to my pleasure. I did not know in my last how we should be located. Duning has left again for Louisville, but will be here by the time you come. All well, your ever affectionate Mother,

Eliza C. Foster.

P. S. Poor little Stephen, how is he? I think of him very much of late.

Here is the first intimation that all was not well with Stephen. By this time, his homesickness must have been consuming him; his letters revealed his unhappiness to his mother, or she would not have referred to him as "poor little Stephen." In Towanda, William and Henry, being personable, eligible young gentlemen, had found no trouble in making places for themselves in the social and church life of the little town. Henry had returned to the Episcopal fold, and he and William were actively taking part in the new Towanda Episcopal Church by singing in the choir.

The following letter, undated, addressed to Brother William from Stephen, was written in Towanda, evidently while the little student from Athens was on a visit to his two older brothers.

Towanda   Thursday

My Dear Brother.

As you wish to have me go to Athens for fear I will not learn enough in this place, I will tell you what my ideas were on the subject.

Mr. Vosberry is a very good mathematition, and as he has quit keeping school, he is going to ocupy a private room in the house of Mr. Elwell.

Mr. Kettle will be here tomorrow and will stop at Bartlett & Fords. he will have a room there but will not be in it in the day time as his paint room will be at another house. Mr Ford says he will board me and give me as good a room as I wish for $2.00 per week.

If you will let me board here (while you stay) and room with Kettle I will promise not to be seen out of doors between the hours of nine & twelve A. M. and one & four P.M. Which hours I will attribute to study, such as you please to put me into. I will also promise not to pay any attention to my music untill after eight Oclock in the evening after which time Mr. Kettle will probably be in the room as he cannot paint after dark. I dont se how I could have a better chance for study. & the above price is as cheap as I could live in Athens that lonesome place —I can go over to recite in the forenoon at about 10 oclock and in the afternoon at 4—do please consent—Your affectionate & grateful brother—

Stephen

Please pay Mr. D Mitchell $3.00 which I borrowed from him to pay for pumps, subscription &c. for the exhibition. I allso owe Mr. Vandercook a very small amount.

Dont pay Mr. Herrick for fire in my room as I have not had any since you payed him last—

Brother William.

This letter bears no date nor postmark and is addressed on the reverse side simply to "Brother William," possibly for personal delivery by Henry. It was written some time after April 1, 1841, the date of the "exhibition" which Stephen mentions. Stephen was probably staying with Henry at Brother William's rooms in Towanda while William was out "on the line." The thought of going back to Athens was unbearable to the lonely boy, so he laid before William his plan to study with Mr. Vosberry in Towanda. Perhaps Frances Welles' marriage and departure from school had something to do with Stephen's reluctance to return to Athens Academy. "Bartlett & Ford" mentioned in his letter were the proprietors of the Clairmont Hotel in Towanda. Mr. Vandercook was a teacher in the Towanda Academy. We can be almost sure that William yielded to his young brother's plea, and allowed him to study the remainder of the term in Towanda with Mr. Vosberry, for letters to William from his mother and father always send love to Henry and Stephen.

William's work took him frequently to Harrisburg. A letter from his father dated March 30, 1841, is addressed to William in care of James Gamble, at the House of Representatives, Harrisburg. The elder Foster expresses no uneasiness in regard to Stephen, and does not mention him separately, merely including him in the message of "love to you and the boys."

Pittsburgh, March 30th, 1841

Dear William,

Your letter of the 18th inst. came duly to hand, as did that to your mother; the letter enclosed for Thomas Wick was forwarded to him at Youngstown, they having left this place on the 4th of March. I cannot permit myself to doubt but Thomas will accede to your offer.

My claim at Erie is still undetermined; the cause will be tried next week, and I must start for that place in a day or two. My attorneys still encourage me.

The great scarcity of money and the heavy exchange against the West is producing much distress here; and it is almost impossible to sell real property. I have offered the land in this county for 10 Dollars per acre, but little more than half of what it would have brought three years ago. A carpenter of this city is going to look at it when I return from Erie. There is about two hundred dollars to pay to clear it out and complete the title. I think I will sell it.

Since the election, on the recommendation of Walter Forward, Esq., I have not applied for any office under the General Government; he still told me that something would turn up for me. Two days ago, Mr. Forward received the appointment of first Controller of the Treasury; salary, $3500 per annum—12 or 15 clerks in the office, and he assures me that I shall in future make one of them, at least $1000 per ann. and added that it was unnecessary for me to hawk about a petition on the subject. I cannot doubt his sincerity, and as soon as he gets fairly into the harness, and gets his clerks ranked and sized, he will write me. I don't know how we are to get off and pay expenses to Washington, but "sufficient for the day is the evil thereof." I am pretty good at financiering and with an office in view, I will put forth all my genius to go ahead.

The Governor is placed in a most disagreeable predicament—if he signs the Bank Bill just pass'd, I believe our Straightouts would mostly support him, but he will lose some of the Destructives or Barnburners; if he vetos the Bill, he will lose most of the Straightouts, so that I fear the fate of that Bill will produce so much excitement in our Legislature that they will break up in a *row*, and make no appropriation.

Dunning is still on the river; he is absent at present, went to Louisville.

Your mother and Morrison join in love to you and the boys with

Your affectionate father,

Wm. B. Foster.

The two next letters, dated April 22 and April 28, 1841, were addressed to William at Towanda, and, as they were not forwarded, show that William had returned to his Towanda headquarters and his brothers Stephen and Henry.

April 22d.—I made my third trip to Erie, and strange to say, in consequence of the rascally neglect of my attorneys, in not giving the opposite counsel the necessary notice, the trial was put off until next term of the Court.—My counsel tried to get an adjourn'd Court in May, but fail'd, so that the next term will not be held until 1st. week in Septr.

next.—Thus it fares with men who are compell'd to seek justice in our courts of law, but I will not give it up. I have already paid out in cash about 200 dollars in pursuing it, and will sell my last shirt if necessary to bring it to a close. Nothing can, I think, prevent me from recovering; the amt. is uncertain, but cannot be less than 8 or ten hundred Dollars after paying counsel, etc.

. . . I don't wish Henry to return here; as soon as he is out of employment on the Canal, I will take him with me to Washington, and get a foothold for him there, which may be permanent. In case I should live or die, he can help his mother.—I don't wish you to say anything about us going to Washington, unless to Henry, for I am so accustomed to disappointments that I calculate on nothing favourable with certainty.

The person whom I expected to look at the Wilkins Township land has not been able yet to do so, in consequence of sickness in his family. His children are ill with the scarlet fever.

We will go through Towanda, this you may depend on.—On my way from Erie, I came through Youngstown. Thomas is no better, nor is he worse. Old Mr. Wick is failing fast, and Judge Todd is dead.

. . . Your brother Dunning is on a long voyage on board the Steamboat Maine up the Illinois River. . . .

April 28th. . . . I have heard nothing from Mr. Forward yet.—I send you the newspapers of yesterday which contains an account of a destructive fire in Allegheny Town. It commenced in the frame part of the Tavern house formerly occupied by old Mr. Lightner and since by his son-in-law, Mr. Dehaven; the brick part of it was saved, but the whole row of frames on that side of the street up to the corner house, was consumed; the corner being brick, was saved.—If the rain had not been falling in torrents the whole time of the fire, it is agreed on all hands that nothing could have prevented the fire from communicating with the buildings on the opposite side of the street, as the wind set gently in that direction. It was only by extraordinary exertions, by covering the buildings with carpets & blankets, they were saved, and if the fire had crossed the street, nothing could have stop'd its progress until it had consumed the whole to the East Common, which would have included your houses.—The Engines could not be one-fourth supplied with water.

The main object of this letter is to advise that you write to Mr. Stevens to procure an insurance on your two houses, to amount of $2000 or 2500 dollars. Better buy a lock for the stable before the horse shall be stolen. . . .

In the middle of May, William's father started on one of those expeditions which he so thoroughly enjoyed, this time to Louisville and Lexington in the interest of James Dunlop, who was his attorney. As he had heard nothing definite yet from Mr. Forward about the Washington appointment, these missions as agent were very welcome, as they helped considerably to replenish the family exchequer. While he was away, Eliza Foster went to Youngstown to look after little Mary and Lidie, while Henrietta came to Pittsburgh with her sick young husband to consult their doctor and settle some of Thomas' business affairs.

Dear William,

Pittsburgh, June 11th, 1841

Your letter of the 28th ult. did not reach me until yesterday afternoon.

I return'd from my tour in Kentucky on Sunday last, being absent just three weeks, and had a warm time of it, but succeeded in performing the objects of my mission, to my own satisfaction as well as that of Mr. Dunlop, who is much pleased.

The day before I left for Kenty. Mr. Forward arrived here from Washington. I had a short interview with him; he continues to give me the strongest assurance of his determination to aid me whenever an opportunity may offer, but says that there will be but few removals for two or three months; so that I must be content to wait the moving of the waters.—

When I return'd, I found Thomas Wick and Henrietta here, where they had been about ten days, your mother keeping their house and children at Youngstown in the meantime. They return'd home on Monday last—he is very weak in body, easily excited and very nervous....

... Old Mr. Ross has given me a power of attorney to go into Butler County, to settle and compromise a number of land claims there. I will go to Butler in a few days where I may be detain'd a week perhaps. After my return here, I think I will go out to Ohio, and with your mother take lodgings with old Uncle Struthers during the warm months, and wait the result of circumstances.—

... I am happy to learn that you will be in employment for some months yet, and hope you will be able to keep Henry employ'd also. If I should hear anything from Mr. Forward before you come out, will write you immediately. When you come, you must be sure to visit Youngstown. Thomas and Henrietta both spoke of you in the kindest terms and charged me to desire you to visit them.

The earth and crops are burning up here for want of rain; had none for four weeks; and it is now so warm, and being desirous to finish my letter before the mail closes, the perspiration is running into my eyes so that I can scarcely see what I am doing.

Dunning is gone to St. Louis on the Steamboat Maine.—Morrison is quite well.

With love to Henry & Stephen,

I remain your affectionate father,

Wm. B. Foster.

The proposed visit to Uncle Struthers' did not ensue, for Stephen and William arrived in Pittsburgh the early part of July. Although his parents were still at Mrs. Paul's, Stephen knew they did not expect to stay much longer, and the hope of actually being at home again with Ma and Pa was too much for him. When it came time for William to return to Towanda, the boy was obdurate—he would not, could not go back with him. If he must be sent to college, let it be some place nearer home, from whence he could come quickly if he had a few days' vacation. It is not hard to believe that Jefferson College, situated at Canonsburg, Pennsylvania, was suggested by Stephen himself; his father attended school there when it was still a little log college and James Foster, Stephen's grandfather, was one of the original trustees when Jefferson College was incorporated in 1802. Brother William is believed to have gone to school there for a short time, and probably all the family were favorably inclined to humor Stephen's desire. So, shortly after William had started back to Towanda, Wm. B. Foster, Sr., and his youngest son set out for Canonsburg and arrived there on July 20, 1841. Morrison said that Stephen "entered Jefferson College." Stephen did little more than "enter," for he stayed only seven days. I do not believe that Morrison, busy young man that he was, realized just how short a time his little brother lingered in the ancestral halls of learning. Stephen started in very bravely, however, with a firm resolve to endure school again, and wrote a fairly cheerful letter about it to Brother William.

My Dear Brother　　　　　　　　　　Canonsburg　　　Saturday

I arrived here on last Tuesday, and found among the quantity of Students of this institution, several of my old acquaintances.

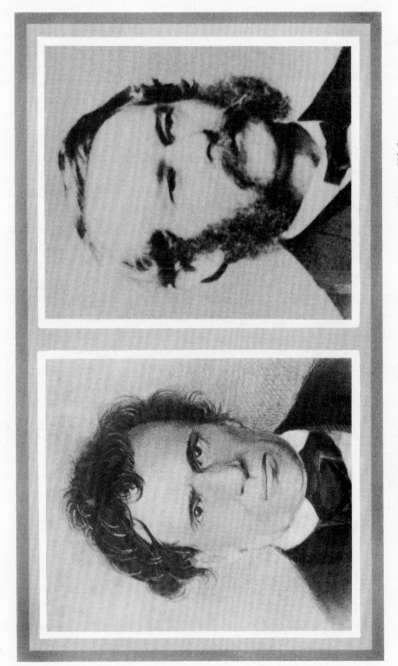

Henry Kleber

Augustus A. Addams

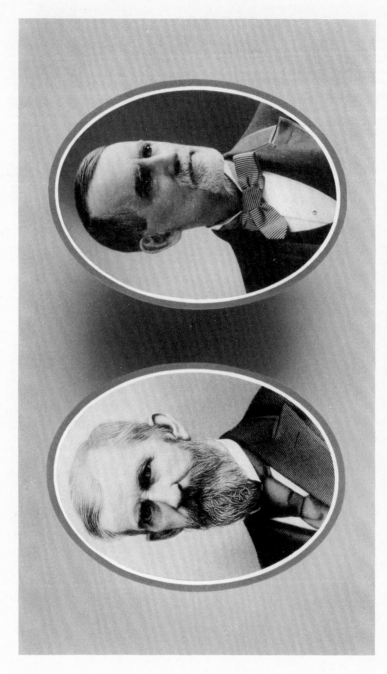

Robert Peebles Nevin, friend of Stephen Foster, and John Desmond Scully, Stephen's brother-in-law and close friend

This is a very pretty situation where I board as it is on an elivation of about four hundred feet. We have about two hundred and thirty students here at the present time, and a library of about 1500 volumes.

Pa left this on Wednesday last and is now at Warren I believe.

The tuition instead of being $5.00 amounts to $12.50 and boarding $2.00 per week.

Pa paid my tuition bill in advance, as is customary at this place. Their is several other bills which I have not paid as I have not the means. Such as 2 or $3.00 for joining one of the literary societies, as all of the studens belong to them I was requested to join one and put it of for a couple of weeks, for as Pa has not much more than the means of geting along I thought I would write you this letter that you might considder over the matter. I will also have to pay boarding bill at the end of every month which will amount to $8.50 that is at the end of four weeks and a half which generally makes a month, and if you see fit to send me a little of the rino. once in a while I will insure you their is no inducements here to make me spend any money unnecesarily. I will allso have to pay about $1.25 per week for washing as I have to keep myself very clean here.

I would inform you in the mean time I need another summer coat or two, and especially for Sunday

The Ohio river is very low and falling gradually. The boats have ceased runing.

As I have made out a mideling long letter and am clear out of information (news) I would only say, wishing you a safe journey home and through life, and that I may some day be fit to render thanks to you for your unceasing kindness to me. I remain your ever grateful and affectionate brother

Stephen.

To Wm. B. Foster Jr. July 1841

Wm B. Foster Esq
    State en'r
  Towanda
Bradford County Pa.
July 24th 1841

Stephen's mother must have been much surprised to see her boy come wandering into Mrs. Paul's just a week after she had kissed him good-by, but knowing him as she did, she could not be very severe with him. After all, why should he be forced to stay in a place that was so distasteful to him when there were good teachers in Pittsburgh, and, as she said to William, "I shall be almost too lonely without one child with me, for if I should be ill, I would be in a bad way."

Stephen's explanations to Brother William reveal a decidedly guilty conscience. He grasps at every straw that will serve as an excuse for leaving Canonsburg without telling William the true reason—just plain homesickness. To be so near home, and still not at home—to say good-by with welcome relief to Towanda and Athens, "that lonesome place," after months of sick longing for home—to experience the dear familiar presence of mother and father and have those loving arms around him again; then, within a month, to find himself surrounded by strangers as before, with the same hateful school routine to follow, was more than he could endure, particularly in the blistering heat of a Washington County summer. Added to this was the worry over small fees for this and that, which in all colleges, then as now, are always levied on the student after he believes everything has been paid. Stephen had little spending money, and it was small wonder that the disheartened boy seized upon the flimsiest excuses for leaving. Jefferson College undoubtedly was as agreeable a place as any school to which he could have gone. His friends Davy and Algernon Bell and Robert Nevin, who were then in attendance there, would have helped him make it bearable if he had stayed; Robert would have joined Stephen gladly in any musical efforts. But Stephen regarded with aversion any place where he was tied down to hours and rules. It was very easy to imagine that the "disiness" in his head was caused by an alarming "over flow of the blood" and how opportune it was that Samuel Montgomery wanted company to Pittsburgh! It would not have been kind to allow Sam to make the tiresome journey alone! With Ma and Pa planning to move to Allegheny, and money so scarce, it was much less expensive for Stephen to live at home where Brother William could pay his board. Dunning was away weeks at a time, and Morrison was at home only in the evenings. A strong fifteen-year-old was absolutely needed to help Pa tack down stair carpet and move heavy furniture! As to the future, the very far, far future, the life of a midshipman with all its romantic glamour was just what he fancied. It was a fascinating subject for conversation; in the meantime, Stephen was home again!

Very aptly do you close your letter, little Stephen: "We are all well, and in good spirits"!

Pittsburgh   August 28th 41

My Dear Brother.

I suppose you are surprised and probably displeased at me for not being more punctual in writing to you every fortnight, as you wished to have me do. I will therefore proceed to make my best excuses.

When I wrote to you from Canonsburg I did not tell you whether I liked the place or not (if I remember aright) but now I will take the liberty of telling you that I became more disgusted with the place as long as I stayed in it. It is not a good time to begin college in the middle of the Session as I could not get into any class for three or four days after I went there, and when I did get started into a recitation it was in irregular hours.

If I had went as a regular student, I might have been examined and got along very easily, but going as I did, just to stay a session or two, I suppose they did not care much whether I was attended to or not. Besides when I had been there but five days I took sick (from a disiness in my head occasioned by an over flow of the blood,) and was confined to bed for two days.*

In the night of of the second day of my Sickness, my nose took to bleeding which made me feel better the next morning.

It so happened that one of the students was coming in to town that day (Samuel Mongomery of Pittsburg) and I concluded I would come in with him, as he asked me to.

When I left Canonsburg your letter had not arrived. So that I wrote to Mr. Mercur (brother to the Mercurs in Towanda) to forward it on as soon as it arrived, but nevertheless, I did not receive it untill about two weeks after won [you] wrote it. Although you told me not to wate for your letters when I wrote, still I expected it every day so that I was put of beyond the regular time.

When I did get it, we were just preparing to move over here which kept me buisy for two or three days, and as soon as we got partly mooved I commenced going to School to Mr. Moody—So that I never got a fair chance to write untill today.

*When ever I would go to raise up out of bed I would become so dizy that I could scarcely see.

I hope you will pardon me for writing to you so extensively on the money subject. But at the same time I will let you know that a boy comes out mighty thin in Canonsburg without some of it in his pocket.

Pa had not told me that he would furnish me with as much money as I needed, or I would not have troubled you on that subject.

As were were all talking over different subjects the other evening among others the subject of the Navy was talked of. Now to be a Midshipman is just what I fancy.

Pa is away in Washington County at a temperance meeting and will return this evening I think.

With these few lines I will bring to a close by stating that we are all well and in good spirits. Hopeing that you will ever be blessed with the same qualities I remain your ever affectionate and justly dutiful brother

Stephen.

I will try hereafter to come up to the mark in the letter writing line.—

His mother also makes excuses for Stephen's presence at home, but as she has him safe by her, her real concern is William himself; his affair with Miss Overton is causing her great anxiety, for William had confided to her that he was doubtful of the outcome.

Pittsburg   August the 12-14th.

My Dear William,

I received your kind letter informing me of your finding all things at Towanda to your satisfaction; which gave me much pleasure, besides that I felt grattified at finding that I was so early your consideration after a fatiguing jurney.

Mrs. Paul has removed to Pen Street, where every thing is very delightfull, a fine house pleasantly arranged, good table and a respectable neighbourhood, but all this cannot be afforded, therefore I think we will go into your house on Monday. I can get a house for one hundred and fifty in town where Duning and Morrison could board with us, but your Father seems afraid to attempt it.

In relation to your own affairs, I am quite anxious, continue to apprize me of them as they progress, no eye has seen your last letter but myself, nor has any one became aquainted with its contents, nor shall they. Pa continues as you left him; whilest he is so, I will not thwart his plans, believing them to be wiser than my own. Indeed I am but a dependent being in every respect, being too timmid to contradict one so cute as your Father, for if I made a devided house and led off to something of my own invention, he would be sure to overthrow it all, so that I will ever and annon train my self into the first great necessary lesson of resignation, and raise my thoughts morning and evening to Jehovah for my daily bread, and to forgive me my trespasses as I forgive those who tresspass against me.

Stephen will not stay at Cannonsburg—he says he has lost conseat of himself because he was once in his life a great fool, and that was when he did not go back with brother William. He begs me to ask you to say that he must board with Ma and go to day skool; indeed, if I am in Allegheny Town I shall be almost too lonely without one child with me, for if I should be ill, I would be in a bad way.

Thomas and Henrietta will return to Youngstown shortly—he is much better of having come up here. Duning and Morison are quite well. I trust both Henry and yourself keep well during the hot weather.

May God the infinite and alwise director of your best life, guard and keep you in grace, that you may sit easy as a prince upon his throne, in whatever new sittuation you may think proper to place yourself. A man can allways sit easy when he is performing a perfect duty, therefore as you are one among the few that can feel concious of being a son in every acceptation of that truly noble title, I have no doubt but as a husband you will not lack in that first of all gifts, the capability of making a wife happy. May you be prosper'd or not prosper'd in this, only as it suits the plans of providence for your ultimate good, which pray'r I know you will fully join me in.

I am my dear son with much affection, your ever devoted and ever more than loving mother,

Eliza C. Foster.

After they were settled "across the bridge, and up the Hill" in William's house on East Common, as a few paragraphs from one of Eliza's letters to her son reveal, William's love affair terminated.

Pittsburg or rather Alegany City.
September the 16, 1841

We have been fairly settled down into housekeeping, having a good girl, which enables me to keep clean and comfortable; as I study nothing but our comfort, what little we have I take great pleasure in attending to it. I was quite pleased with the contents of your last letter in relation to the subdued state of your mind; surmounting all considerations with resignation to God's will alone, a trial he may be puting you through to save your soul, which is infinitly more precious to you than all the tender ties this world can posibly afford.—I will now close my dear William, having nothing more worth putting on paper. Give much love to Henry—and be assured yourself that a large share of the warmest feelings of an affectionate heart glows for a son altogether worthy of its highest confidence, which I trust will continue to be reciprocated by him, and duly received by his ever faithfull, Mother.

Stephen's mother and father were undoubtedly very proud of him when he brought "The Tioga Waltz" home from Athens. It must have been performed at home an endless number of times, with Stephen taking the lead on the clarinet, and Henrietta, or Susan Pentland, or even Morrison at the piano, for the latter could play chords in the key of C well enough to follow Stephen's graceful melody. There are eight different phrases in the little waltz, and the fact that Morrison was able to reproduce it completely from memory when he was seventy-three years old proves that he had heard it played repeatedly in his youth. Morrison had a true ear for melodies, but no musical inventiveness.

The Fosters realized that Stephen was a talented boy, but we can be thankful that they took their precocious child pretty much as a matter-of-course. If they had rushed him off to a conservatory as soon as he brought home "The Tioga Waltz" we can be reasonably sure that his instructors would have frowned on his predilection to "nigger minstrels" and strangled all his bent towards what have turned out to be American folk songs at their finest. While he eventually might have produced what are called major compositions, we never would have heard "Oh! Susanna," "Nelly Bly," "Old Uncle Ned," nor "Camptown Races," and probably not "Swanee River," "My Old Kentucky Home," nor "Old Black Joe." Would any so-called major work have been worth the sacrifice?

Stephen was now hard at work with Mr. Moody, and Morrison says "during this part of his life he studied French and German, and became proficient in both under the instruction of Captain Jean Herbst, a Belgian gentleman, who came to reside in Pittsburgh."

A few years later, Henry Kleber, a popular concert pianist and composer of great merit himself, was one of Stephen's teachers.

Stephen had that one thing essential to the successful pursuit of a study of music, plenty of time to himself. He was not forced to spend long hours at distasteful subjects, nor was he tied to a schoolroom. His father simply said, "He is a good boy, but I cannot get him to stick at school." That seemed to end the matter so far as school was concerned. Today, a truant officer would have been hot on his heels, and Stephen would have been dragged away from his self-appointed tasks, to the study of civics, and the construction of lopsided basswood whatnots.

XII

NOT long after returning to the Allegheny house, the Fosters had a "right smart family" again when Thomas Wick, Henrietta, the two children, and a hired girl came to stay. They were all very happy in Allegheny amongst the old neighbors and associations and William B. Foster, Sr., entered once more into the temperance cause with his old enthusiasm.

Pittsburgh, Sept. 3d. 1841

Dear William—

Your very kind letter to your mother of the 23d. ult. covering a ten Dollar Bank Note, came duly to hand, as also Henry's letter to her of 20th ult. covering a like sum of ten Dollars. For these kindness's you both deserve and receive our kind thanks and blessings.

The money came in good time, as we had two weeks ago, scraped our little plunder together, and your mother with Stephen and myself commenced house keeping in the old place. Thomas and Henrietta with their little ones, soon after joined us, and we are now all together. Thomas pays us one Dollar per day for boarding and lodging his family, including a hired girl—they talk of returning to Youngstown in a week or two; I expect I shall be obliged to go to Warren in a day or two, in order to wind up (if I can) his business there. They will remain until my return.

I regret extremely that Stephen has not been able to appreciate properly your generous exertions in his behalf, by availing himself of the advantage of a college education, which will cause him much regret before he arrives at my age; and he will no doubt express those regrets in much sorrow to you should you both live, long after I shall be no more.

He is at school, now, with Mr. Moody, a first rate teacher of mathematics in Pittsbg, and it is a source of much comfort to your mother and myself, that he does not appear to have any evil propensities to indulge; he seeks no associates; and his leisure hours are all devoted to musick, for which he possesses a strange talent.

The cause of temperence continues to flourish throughout our Western Country.—We have a Washington total abstinance society in Allegheny, in which I am a member, with others numbering in all about 150 members. We receive many calls from different parts of the country to send our members to address conventions on the subject of temperence. Yesterday, six of us addressed in succession a convention of upwards of one thousand persons assembled agreeably to previous arrangements, at the church [Bethel Presbyterian] in which your Uncle James Foster is an elder, eight miles south from Pittsburgh. [This was James Barclay Foster, Wm. B. Foster's older brother.] I was call'd on first to address them, and thought I did it pretty well; was followed by John D. Mahon, Esqr. in a thrilling appeal to the feelings of considerable length. The people appear'd well pleased, and upwards of three hundred subscribed the tetotal pledge.—Tell your dear brother Henry that his letter and money was duly received.

I have not a word from Washington City yet. Your mother and all the family join in much love to yourself and Henry, with your affectionate father,

Wm. B. Foster.

The fall and winter of 1841-1842 were perhaps the happiest the Foster family as a whole had spent for many years. All the children were well, and doing well; and except for their anxiety about Thomas Wick, nothing marred their resumption of the cheerful social life and church activities of the neighborhood. Morrison had but a short walk to his work in the morning. Mr. McCormick's Hope Factory was located in Allegheny along the river at the point where the aqueduct of the canal crossed the river a few blocks north of the Hand Street bridge. The Hope Warehouse was on Water Street, Pittsburgh. In those days, Allegheny was considered a new select residential section, and many wealthy Pittsburghers had established summer homes there. The Foster residence was a modest one in comparison with the palatial houses belonging to General William Robinson and Charles Avery in the immediate neighborhood. Mit's walk to work was a pleasant one, along the Common to Anderson Street, over the little bridge that crossed the canal, and then along Lacock Street several blocks to the Hope Factory.

At William's request and expense, his father had sat, in 1840, for his portrait to William Cogswell, a Pittsburgh artist with unusual ability, who also painted a portrait of William Henry Harrison when the President-elect visited Pittsburgh in February, 1841. Dunning was now at home more frequently, having left the river for a forwarding and commission business. It was Dunning who boxed his father's portrait and sent it on October 23, 1841, to William, by "D. Leech & Company Line Canal Packet," with the comment: "You will at once be struck with the correct likeness it bears of Father. I think it is as good a one as I ever saw."

At the same time, Mr. Cogswell had painted a portrait of Dunning. These two beautiful pictures are now owned by Morrison's son, William B. Foster, of Pittsburgh, as is also one of "Mother" painted by Mr. Clifford of Pittsburgh in 1840. (The portraits of Mother and Father may be found facing page 158; Dunning's facing page 159.)

In October, 1841, Eliza Foster makes pleasant comment to her son William on some interesting weddings, and pokes a little fun at the unusual gallantries of one of the bridegrooms.

Mrs. Fetterman's protegee, Mr. Vandike, is about to marry her intimate friend, Miss Grant. I saw them rideing out together yesterday, they reminded me of Nancy Denny and Edward Muller. The wedding of Miss Irwin and Sam Black has created quite a sensation, there has been so maney parties for them. For odity's sake, he effects to be so very attentive to his wife that should any of his croney's wish to have a word with him in company, he shakes his head and says he has no time, that he has to mind Mrs. Black, that she may wish to walk out of the room, or want her hankerchief picked up, and no one will do it for her now unless he does.

Doctor Day came over for me in a too-horse carriage and invited me to go over to the Monnongahalah House to call on Mrs. Talcott who was there but one day, having heard of the death of her father on her arival at this place. They came from Washington and hurried on to Albany, her Paternal home. Captain and Mrs. Harding have been here to see me. They are on a visit to Pittsburgh at this time. It affords me much pleasure to see these old friends.

After living several years in an unsettled state, it was a great relief to William B. Foster, Sr., to have two salaried positions in view, one in Washington, and the other, Mayor of Allegheny. As frequently happens in such cases, he received both appointments. The office of mayor, to which he was elected in January, 1842, was much more to Eliza Foster's liking than the Washington position, which would have taken the parents so far away from Henrietta and the trouble their daughter was facing. "Poor Etty," lamented her mother, "no rest for the soul of her foot! She is equally the object of our solicitude and our pity."

Wm. B. Foster's next letter to William, Jr., was very long and contained more than the usual amount of news.

Pittsburgh Oct. 1st. 1841

Dear William

Your kind letter of 23d ult. addressed to your mother, and enclosing a ten Dollar Bank Note was rec'd this morning for which you have our thanks.

Thomas Wick and Henrietta left us on the 10th ult. and are at present living with old Mr. Wick. Tell Henry that his mother wrote to him as soon after she got the house a little regulated as she could, perhaps about the 15th or 16th ult. She hopes he rec'd her letter shortly after you wrote on the 23—I received a short letter from Mr. Forward dated 11th Sept. after his promotion, from which I give you the following extract. "Do not be impatient you are not forgotten, I trust that your claims will yet be considered. If they are not, it shall not be my fault"—In addition to the above, I call'd on W. W. Irwin, Esq. who only got home day before yesterday and to whom I had written on the subject; he says: I may rest satisfied that he has the word of both the President and Mr. Forward that I shall be provided for.

The temperence cause goes on gloriously. I went out last week with two other delegates from our society to the congregation of the Rev'd. Mr. Kerr in Butler county 20 miles from Pittsbg where we addres'd an assemblage of about one Hundred persons; after which 77 of the number signed the tetotal pledge and organized a temperence society. Two other delegates had gone before us to the town of Butler, where they held two meetings, and out of the 850 the whole population of the town, upwards of 500 signed the pledge. The country is alive to the good cause, it is now in the right hands, the drunkards themselves have turned on the enemy and are looking anxiously and confidantly with the aid of Almighty God for a complete victory.

Mr. Gamble called to see us yesterday; unfortunately your mother and myself were both in Pittsburg but I met him at the Bridge on my way home.

We have got a new Episcopal Church finished in very neat style, it is erected on the same lot on which the old house which Mr. Buchanan occupied stands and is quite convenient to us. Our Pastor, a Mr. Woodward is a most agreeable man and a first rate preacher, he called on me a few days ago and asked me to accept of the office of vestry man. Said they wanted a capable person to act as treasurer for the Church!! And I was yesterday call'd on by a very respectable citizen to know if he might announce my name as a candidate for the office of Mayor of Allegheny City. The election takes place in January next. Like old Hickory, I replied that I did not seek, nor refuse office.

My Portrait is finished and box'd up. I will send it to Harrisburgh shortly in the care of some acquaintance, to Mr. Wilson, as the others were sent. Mr. Gamble does not go that far by canal.

Our election campaign goes on quietly here; there appears little doubt of the reelection of Gov. Porter. I shall do all I can for him and I know some of my most influential Straightout friends will do likewise. With Banks for Governor and Stevens in the Legislature, we might confidantly look out for another Buckshot War and we think it better to reserve our fire and keep our powder dry for a more righteous purpose. A war with Great Britain seems inevitable.

Tell Henry not to write on a newspaper again. The last he sent us the 22d ult we had to pay letter postage for; if we had not, it would have been returned to your Post Office where he would have paid five dollars for a Breach of the Post Office Law. They examine newspapers here.

Let Henry see this letter and tell him to accept with yourself our wishes and prayers for the health and happiness of both.

Your affectionate father

Wm. B. Foster

Although interested in his new affairs, William's father was not neglecting to follow up his old claim against the stagecoach company, and incidentally, the still unremitting cashier. The rebuffs, postponements, and setbacks he received in pursuing this claim would have discouraged a less doughty spirit, but he stuck to it until he accomplished his purpose, or a portion of it.

11th Oct. 1841. [To William]. . . . In my last letter, I believe I did not mention my Erie business to you.—By the carelessness of my attorneys at Erie, the cause could not be tried at the last district court in that County, the 1st. week in Jany. last; the Court then adjourn'd to meet on the 1st week in Sept. ult., but by the influence of the lawyers, the judge adjourn'd it still farther to the 3d. week in November, thus you may say, holding but one court in 11 months; and for this, the State is paying a Judge two Thousand Dollars per ann.—and suitors are perplexed and disappointed. I feel pretty confident of getting a hearing and favorable result in November.—

Since I wrote you last, I have seen John Dickey, Esq., former Senator from Beaver County; he told me he was on his way home from Washington City where he had been soliciting the office of Auditor in the Treasury Department. Said he could not get it, that Capt. Tyler would not remove the Locofocos to make room for him. But, said he, you will be provided for. I have it from Mr. Forward that the first vacancy in his department is to be fill'd by "my friend, Wm. B. Foster, of Pittsburgh." Thus am I cheered on my way in well doing.

Judge Wilkins dined on his visit east with *Capting* Tyler, and says he does not believe he will sign any U. States Bank Bill next winter. Our Bankites here have got the *Botts* and the Elections in Maryland and elsewhere will not bring them any relief. I think our election in this county will be a slim affair.

A friend of mine here wishes to get a Book, "Long's Rail Road Manual;" it is not to be had here. If you can get it, send it to me. He will pay all expenses and feel thankful.

Stephen informs me he wrote you not long since, & yr. mother two or three days ago, to Henry. They join in love to yourself and Henry . . .

XIII

S Dunning was frequently away from home on business for his firm, and Morrison left for his work early in the morning, Eliza Foster and her youngest child were left at home together all day, a situation that undoubtedly satisfied Stephen completely.

He was deep in his music and mathematics, to which he was now more attentive. His classes with Mr. Moody must have been short ones, and he spent many a peaceful moment lying on the hearthrug stroking and playing with the little stranger cat, while his mother rocked comfortably and read him bits of news from the Pittsburgh *Chronicle,* and the *Daily American.*

With her heart very thankful, Eliza Foster takes up her pen to paint for Brother William a word picture of the little family circle.

Aleganey City, October 18, 1841

Dear Son,

Thinking you would be crowded with letters from home, your father writing and Stephen, I defer'd answering your last kind letter acknoledging the receipt of ten dollars untill now, Pa having written to you immediately. He left this for Erie on Thursday last. I expect him back on Monday.

Stephen and I have the house to ourselves and lonely enough it is, so much so that it has induced a very pretty (girl, you think I am about to say, no, they like gay places where there is some stir on foot,) tortoise-shell collour'd cat to take up her boarding and lodging with us. Business is rather dull for her in this establishment, therefore she lies about the fire, taking possession of the middle of the hearth rug. She will not be look'd upon as a loaffer until she gets her beautifull fir singed, for notwithstanding there is no mice in the premises, she looks slick and nice, for Stephen gives her all the little bits he is permited to gather for the sake of her company, to the no small robbing of Emiline, a half-grown girl, who he has taken in his head shall never suffer herself to look at him, no how you can fix it.

He is not so much devoted to musick as he was; other studies seem to be elevated in his opinion. He reads a great deal, and fools about not attall.

If you give up settling in Towanda, I have a charming girl here for you, Ann Eliza Anderson. Every time I see her, I think how happy she would make you, I know of none who will compare with her.

. . . Everything around our neighbourhood looks natural and perfectly harmonizes with the very pleasant association of home. The Robinsons have been to see us, looking as cherrily as they could to welcome us back.

. . . The new Christ Church takes up the most of our attention at this time, as it is now completely under way; fine Preacher, fine musick, fine stoves, plenty of room, and people flocking. Mr. Woodward, our minister is indeed an indefaticable person, and is the agent in the hands of the Lord to make every thing prosper that he finds to do.

. . . There is a belle boarding at Mrs. Paul's, the daughter of Major Plymton, she goes to all the parties, and the young gentlemen say that the rest of the boarders never can go to bed untill she goes home, because she takes all the bed clothes to make her bishops. She wars a bonnet which looks precisely like a piece of rag carpet. She is all the go, so that she may wear what ever she pleases.

. . . What will I tell you about myself; a haknied stale story. You know what I am doing very well at this season, turning old clothes into new ones, looking after the baking and the cooking, and brushing about the house, and sometimes taking a comfortable rest in a rocking chair, by a pleasant coal-fire to read the Cronicle in the forenoon, and the daily American at four o'clock in the afternoon, going to bed at nine o'clock that I may rise at six to have breakfast for Morison who is off to his business the moment it is over. We have ever and anon a quiet and peacible and temperate house, exactly such a one as I have always been longing for.

Oh, my dear William, I trust we shall all see a happy day at one smileing board, all in health and good spirits, and Pa the hapiest of us all. Tell dear Henry I will write to him very soon. He does not write to me, why does he not? I am not happy when I am long without communicating with them.

I will not forget to say to you that with the blessing of heaven, and kind children, we are not in need and are all well. My dear son William in particular who has set them all so excellent an example, on whom I pray that the choicest blessings of an indulgent heaven may continually be power'd and that his last hour may be comforted with a rested conscience and a smiling Savior.

Love to dear Henry, and write to me soon. I anticipate much pleasure by being in possesion of your minature which you have in store for me, and thank you for believing that I shall prize it.

I am my Dear son, your very affectionate mother. Stephen requests with Pa that I will give their love to Henry and yourself.

Eliza C. Foster.

Dunning was now only twenty, but he took an active interest in politics. His letter of October 23, to Brother William, concerning the shipping of their father's portrait, is written in a beautiful flowing hand, so like Stephen's handwriting that at first glance, one might easily confuse them. The young men's interest in all that engrossed their father must have been a source of great pleasure and satisfaction to the earnest man.

Dunning says:

. . . "Captain Tyler" has been making some splendid appointments out this way. I mean that of the appointment of John H. Peebles as Consul to Campeatchy! I suppose you know him. He is the son of old Bob Peebles.

We had a tight time here in our last election. The Whigs,—alias Antimasons,—alias Harrison Democrats, beat us in the election of Senator *"One Vote."* But we slipped in three members of the lower house very neatly on them, and elected all the county officers with the exception of Treasurer, who was beaten Five Votes.

We are expecting the Ship "Lawrence" which we sent out to old Westmoreland at the last Governor's Election. She is advertised to leave Greensburgh on Tuesday at Half Past Eight oclock A.M. and will be received here on Wednesday by a large procession of Democrats as a tribute of honor for their glorious triumph in Allegheny County.

As Ma wrote to you the other day, I suppose she has given you all the news of any interest, and being called away on business for the House, I will close with my best wishes for your welfare and happiness. I remain,

Your brother, Dunning.

William B. Foster endured a generous share of winter traveling in November and December of 1841. In November, he made a trip to Erie to find that his suit had been postponed again; but this time he said:

I am as well pleased that the trial of my suit was put off, at the request of the Defendt. He pays the costs, and we are now in possession of all their testimony, it being documentary—I feel confident I can blow all its prominent points *sky high!*

On his return to Pittsburgh on November 21, he found a letter from Controller of the Treasury Walter Forward. Fortunately, the Judge had not been required to "go to his death" for his friend; without making this supreme sacrifice, he had secured a position for Wm. B. Foster, and desired him to come to Washington at once. "Salary 1000 dollars, perhaps more!" Hastily, William's father wrote his son on November 22, 1841:

I must now make arrangements to be off in two or three days if possible. —As the trial of my cause at Erie is put off until the first Monday in Jany., I will go to Washington & take my post, and wish Henry to meet me there and perform the duties, untill I can return and attend to my suit, and then take your mother with me; I must then stop at Harrisburgh to get the interposition of the Legislature in a final settlement with the Commonwealth. You will most likely be there at that time.

On November 30, he was in Washington, and to William he suggests:

I have thought that if you have your Barouch and two Horses, that if you would bring them down to Harrisbg. with you that I would go that way and take them out to bring your mother over the mountains. I fear the journey by stage in January would fatigue her exceedingly. I could go any time after Henry would be here a few days, but must be at Pittsbg. before Christmas Day.

A stagecoach or carriage journey across the Allegheny Mountains in winter would not have been dreamed of by Eliza Foster had she been only on pleasure bent, but Ann Eliza had recently had another baby, born on July 10, 1841, and she longed to see her mother, for she had been very weak and ill since the baby's birth. Eliza Foster decided it was best to go when she could have company, being timid about making the arduous journey alone in the wintertime. Henrietta was expecting another baby in the spring, but she had the help of Thomas' mother and sister, and several very kind sisters-in-law. Ann Eliza had recently removed to Paradise, in Lancaster County, where Mr. Buchanan had established a new church, All Saints, on July 31, 1841. He continued to serve St. John's Pequea Church and Christ Church, Leacock, besides conducting many missionary services in out-of-the-way places, in country schoolhouses and barns. The new home at Paradise was about eight miles from Lancaster. Thomas Wick's health was no better, but he had had no recent turn for the worse, so Eliza Foster decided to travel "to the Eastward" with her husband, make a few visits to friends and relatives and repair to Ann Eliza's in April, 1842.

In his letter of November 30, Mr. Foster had the following to report to William from Washington:

I arrived here today at 12 oclock, and have just been to see Mr. Forward, who received me very cordially, and asked me to dine with him today—tomorrow he says he will put me into office. If Henry should not have left when you receive this letter, tell him to come on as soon as he pleases; tell him when he arrives at Washington to come to Fuller's hotel, on the Pennsylvania Avenue, and near the Treasury Office. He can get a Hack to bring him there with his baggage for 25 cents—from the railroad Depot.

Two weeks later he started for Pittsburgh. William brought his horses and barouche down to Harrisburg, where he met his father, and the two trailed back over the hills, reaching Pittsburgh in time to spend Christmas with their family. Poor Henry! Holding the fort in Washington, he was the only boy absent from home that Christmas Day. Probably the state of his mind accounts for his first impressions. The nation's capital occupied quite a low place in his estimation compared with friendly and sociable Towanda.

Washington City, Decr. 20th, 1841.

Dear Brother, [William]

Pa left this on the 15th inst. for Pittsh. I found him when I arrived here busily engaged in the Treasury building, writing. After the usual salutations, he accompanied me to Fuller's Tavern and had my baggage removed to his boarding house—which I found to be a very Comfortable one, situated on Pennsylvania Avenue between 10 & 11 Streets, and kept by an elderly Gentleman by the name of King, who has a very agreeable family & ten boarders, among whom is General Stokely, member of Congress from Steubenville, Ohio, price of board per week $4, as low as any respectable boarding house in the Citty. (Mr. & Mrs. Pettigrew boarded here for some time.) Some of the members of Congress pay as high as $14 per week.—

Now, I don't consider this any great scratch of a place after all. There is one thing certain that it contains about as many fools as any place I ever was in. It appears as if Government was the whole and only Support of the Place, and yet the members of the most dependent families carry their heads so high that you could scarcely touch them with a ten-foot pole.—

We keep Bank Hours at the Treasury working from nine in the morning untill three in the afternoon, Really! The building is a magnificent one, built of solid stone four stories high with Thirty Three

Tremendous columns in front. There are four clerks in the room I write in, two of whom are old Gentlemen with nine & ten in family and receiving the same salary as Pa, ($1000). We are all engaged at the same business which is very simple, recording certificates of land sales and making out patents, which I can do as well as any of them.—I dine at three o'clock (it being the fashionable hour throughout the City) after which I generally take a stroll out to see the fassions, up to the Capitol, down to the steam boat landing, out to Georgetown or round the President's House.

The position and costume of the Statue of Washington is not generally admired, he being in a sitting position, with his right arm from his elbow to his fore finger pointing up, his left extending straight out in front of his body, in the hand of which is his Sword & belt. The only covering he has on is a loose robe wrapt round the lower part of his body and legs, one corner of which extends up over his right arm & hangs down. It is much larger than life, and is about twenty feet from the floor, a beautiful specimen of art, and very imposing.

As Congress adjourns before I get through my labours at the Treasury, I have not had an opportunity of seeing or hearing any of its members yet. There being nothing of importance, I care very little about it.

I suppose you have seen accounts of the House of Representatives having elected Moffett, the great Kentucky Methodist preacher their chaplain.

I could do nothing with Towanda money after leaving Williamsport & concluded to give it to Pa to take out to Pitt with him & should he be unable to get it off there, to let you have it when he sees you at Harrisburgh, for which you can let him have Western paper, or something that will pass, should it be convenient.

Pa traveled from York to this place with Mary Ann [Overton]. She spoke to him first and enquired if he was our father. I have not seen or heard anything of her since I arrived. Tell E.P. & M.O. [Emily Piatt and Mary Overton?] I have not forgotten them & say to the Miss G's [Goodwin] there is no scarcity of sugar here. Respects to Piatt & Mitchell & believe me ever your

affect. Broth.

Henry

in haste   would like to hear from you soon.

If Henry's money was issued on the Towanda bank, he was fortunate if he succeeded in disposing of it, for this bank failed disastrously in 1842, "causing severe commercial distress, and the suspension of the public works," including the North Branch Canal on which William was engaged.

Henry's description of the statue of Washington unmistakably applies to the heroic statue by Horatio Greenough which is now on exhibition in the Smithsonian Institution.

When his claim was presented at the January session of the Erie court, William B. Foster secured a portion of his judgment from the runaway cashier. He paid several debts and made over the remainder to William, from whom he had received some advances of money for traveling expenses, etc. On his return to Allegheny, he was elected mayor on January 25, and to the relief of his wife, he decided to accept this position, and let Henry stay on in his place in Washington. Early in February, William and his mother started east, the latter with a lighter heart, knowing there would be no breaking up of the pleasant home on the East Common. The family, consisting of Father, Morrison, Stephen, and occasionally Dunning, were left in care of a colored woman, named Catharine Russell. Although Stephen's father had mentioned to William the possibility of Stephen joining William again and attending school at Athens, Stephen did not accompany his mother and brother back to the East. He was studious, both at home and with Mr. Moody, and helped his father in the office which was fitted up in the back parlor of the Allegheny house. As he was not idle and caused his parents no anxiety on that score, they did not insist that he go back to college where he never seemed able to adjust himself.

Morrison and Stephen were contented together, and Stephen accompanied his older brother almost everywhere he went. They read the same books and magazines, enjoyed concerts and the theater, and held mutual likes and dislikes of certain ways and people. They must have done a great deal of reading to help put in the cold spring evenings while their mother was away. They read *The Mysteries of Udolpho,* and the wordy, but very exciting historical romances of George Paine Rainsford James, *Henry Masterton,* and *The Adventures of John Marston Hall.* Morrison's account books show that he spent most of his salary, after his board was paid to Mother, for books and theater tickets.

What she had intended to be solely an errand of duty, with a few pleasant but quiet visits to old friends, turned into a tour of triumph for unassuming Eliza Foster. Household cares and domestic problems vanished, as she moved from one scene of festivity to another. Her letters reveal that she entered whole-heartedly into every entertainment provided for her, and her naturally happy nature glowed in the warmth of her friends' hospitality. She and her son William drove in the barouche from Pittsburgh to Harrisburg. It must have been a great pull for the horses over the mountains, through Greensburg and Chambersburg, for that is the route William usually took. But though the ride was long and cold, the memory of her son's kindly companionship and tender consideration, lingered long in the grateful heart of Eliza Foster. They rested a night at Harrisburg, then boarded the cars of the new railroad for Washington. Henry was overjoyed to see them, and, as an old resident, took great pride in showing them the sights of the capital. The three Fosters went one evening to the theater to see "Mr. Hill" in a comedy, and also attended a levee at the President's. William left in a few days for Towanda; and with Eliza settled comfortably at Squire King's with Henry, her thoughts flew to her other boys so far away. She remembered Morrison's shabby hat, and having plenty of money in her pocket (both Pa and William had not wanted her to be "scimped" while visiting) she slipped five dollars in a letter to him unbeknownst to the others; mothers of large families have been known to do such things before. Apologetically, she says:

... I would be glad that you would not mention to anyone the having received the hatte or the money; but write to me as soon as possible everything that has transpired since I left you; have you been anywhere and how are you content? Has Mary Gallagher come home? Is all right with Pa & Stephen?

Although this was February 16, the weather was not "winterry" enough to keep the eager visitor indoors during the promenading hours!

... William is gone and Henry and I have it all by ourselves; we take a walk up the Pensylvania Avenue every afternoon to see the fashons. Arch Street in Philadelphia is nothing to it. I have been once at the

Capitol and at one levee. On Sunday the day was so wet I did not go to church. I saw Harmar Denney at the Presidents, he is now at New York. He and I had quite a long conversation about Miss Croghan. John Butler was there.

Tell the Evanses that black velvit spencers with short sleeves and white thin scirts for the evening is the latest trick, and small parisols in a cold winterry day with clocks and muffs. I saw at least one hundred on the Avenue the day I went to the Capitol.

Good night, my dear son, take care of your precious health. I will write to you shortly again a letter that you can shew to the rest. Remember that I am your own affectionate Mother,

Eliza C. Foster.

Writing to William and his father on March 11 and 12, 1842, Eliza Foster gives them a graphic account of her doings in Baltimore and Washington. One can picture her, a bright little lady with expressive brown eyes like Stephen's, sailing grandly around the East Room on the arms of her "Sennitors," paying her respects to President Tyler (whom she mentions so casually that you would not think he was giving the party!) exchanging merry repartee with her gallant admirers, and in general having the time of her life.

Baltimore, March the 11, 1841
[Should be 1842]

Dear Husband,

I received your letter of the 6th last evening, whilest siting in Mrs. Gwin's parlour, in company with herself, two daughters very pretty, and one not very pretty. She keeps a boarding house in Charles Street, Mr. Gwin having been dead five years. She does not look half as well as I do with all her past beauty. She has one son, a spoiled chap, studying law but not yet practicing. Thomas Tilden, who always attends to me, came for me at ten oclock, so that this morning after looking over Bennet's Herald, and the Clipper, in each of which I see Thomas E. Tilden has a very handsome appointment, he is nominated by the Sennet as a special agent for the postmaster department. [Eliza became hopelessly involved in this sentence, so she sensibly abandoned it, and went on to something else.]

John Blake has also received an apointment, but I cannot define it. Yesterday, I was at his house, he looks badly having lost one of his eyes, but he is as merry as ever, and would hug and kiss me in the presence of his wife and daughters, and Mr. Jacobs who was galanting me; at whose house I had spent the previous evening, night, and that day up to four oclock, when I was engaged to Mrs. Gwin and call'd at Mr. Blake's on my way to Charles Street.

On Monday last, Miss Tilden, and myself (the daughter of Charles Tilden, deceaced, who is a ward of Thomas Tilden and lives with him) started in a hack to Eutaw Street, too long a walk for me, where Blakes, Beaches, Jacobses, Emerys and a host of Estern Shore people resided. We were invited to Mrs. Beaches, where we spent the evening, the night and the next day untill five oclock, at which time Miss Ann Blake, Miss Tilden and Mrs. Tilden went to Mrs. Jacobses. Mr. Beach is a gentleman, but in bad health. Mrs. Beach is about my size; with a very pretty daughter who plays and sings to the pianno charmingly.

Mr. Beach and I had a great time making out the Cronicles of the Clayland family; so that we are all diving into it like a man trying to find out perpetual motion. Robert Wright, Mrs. Beaches son (by Gustavus Wright, a man of great wealth in Rio, South America) says he will be here this summer; that they must have things in a train to identify the descendents of Thomas Clayland, and Susannah Seth; for he has made up his mind to go to England and ferret it out. It seems that Mr. Kemble in New York, lern'd through a Lord Gage who came to New York, and lerning that Mrs. Kemble was a Miss Seth, said, that there was an ancient West Riding Castlelated (meaning with a Castle on it) estate, on the borders of Durhum, the lawfull heirs of which estate are somewhere in America. The last rightfull owner being an ancient maiden whose sister died in Queen Ann County, Eastern shore of Maryland, having fled from her family with William Seth, her Father's steward. It seems by her papers that there was no communication with her family untill her father and mother were dead, at which time she wrote to them that her only daughter Susan had maried Thommas Clayland, and beg'd that her offspring should be thought of when she should be no more. The old maid above mention'd being the last heiress, died, the estate being entail'd. These letters were written to a friend in whose possession they are, who sent this agent to inquire after the Claylands.

I wrote to you once from Haresburg and once from Washington **Tuesday Thomas Tilden will go with me. Mrs. Skinner wrote to me at Washington, and Amanda her daughter wrote to Thomas Tilden to accompany me.

I am, my dear husband, with much affection, still yours

Eliza Clayland Foster.

Between the asterisks a portion of the above letter is burned away. The following note is in Morrison's handwriting:

Note—This letter written by my mother to my father in 1842 was snatched from the flames in a general burning up of old papers by me after the deaths of my father and mother in 1855. Seeing my mother's handwriting, as the letter burst open by the heat, I could not bear to let it burn, & I grasped and rescued it, but not without the loss of a part of it.

My mother's mother's maiden name was Eliza Clayland, and she was the oldest descendant (in line of succession) of Thomas Clayland and Susannah Seth.

Morrison Foster.

The vision of the "Castlelated estate" danced entrancingly before the eyes of Susannah Seth's descendants for many years, but the writer has never heard whether any of them succeeded in establishing their claims or not; there are few families in America who have not been beguiled by such a dream.

Additional details of Eliza Clayland Foster's relationships to the different people she met in Baltimore are set down in a letter she wrote to Henrietta on March 5, 1842. In the portion of her letter reproduced below, a little editing of Eliza's punctuation was necessary, in order to untangle the Claylands. When she wrote to her daughter, Eliza just let her pen forge right ahead, with few stops for breath.

. . . I came to this place [Baltimore] on Wednesday last. Mr. Thomas Tilden, my Nephew, came to Washington after me. I wrote to him from that place that I intended visiting his family: he immediately wrote to me enquiring when he should come. I apointed the day—according to promise he came, he haveing written notes to all our relations that I would be here at such a time. Accordingly, they have been pouring in to see me. In the first place, Mr and Mrs Beech and Miss Beech, Mrs Beech being my sisters daughter, formerly the wife of Gustavous Wright, who was son to the Ex Governor of Maryland at whose house in this Citty I have promised next week. Her daughter, about seventeen, sings and plays in pervect stile; she is also very prity and extreamly intellagent. Her two Eldest sons, the Wrights, are immencely wealthy in Rio, South America. Mr and Mrs Jacobs, she also being of the Clayland family, came to see me. They live delightfully here. I have also to stay

with them. [Also] Mr. John Blake, wife and daughter—(Caroline Clayland, his former wife, was the mother of Ann Hopper Blake, the
daughter)—[and] Mrs. Emory, a Widow, formerly Mary Hopper, my
Eastern shore companion when young. How often, she remarked, have
you and I been row'd in a boat upon the river at Blakeford, by the
three young Blakes, and held our aprons to catch the big may duke
cheries whilest they pluckt them from the trees. Oh, said John, do you
remember the beautifull little Ponneys we three boys rode at that time.
Phil and I used to lick Bill like thunder because he would ware his hair
curl'd over his shoulder and look'd so much ha[n]dsomer than us. Phill
was a runtty little chub, and I lick'd my chops so much with my tungue,
that I always kept my mouth and chin soar. Law, Pa, said Ann his
daughter, you must have been a fright! No wonder the girls thought
the most of Uncle William. Well, said John . . . poor Phill and Bill are
gone to Davies locker long ago, and heres Moll and you and I, Eliza,
still rowing the boat of life, sometimes merry and sometimes sad I
guess with each of us. . . .

The following letter from Eliza Foster is addressed to William
in Towanda.

Baltimore March 12, 1842

My dearly loved son

I received your letter shortly before I left Washington, but have been
so engag'd ever since that I could not take time to be particular in
giving you all the news. Shortly after you left, General Patten and his
lady call'd to see me, and nothing would do them but that we must
change our boarding, accordingly she recommended Mrs. Van Cobles
where she boarded when she was Mrs. Gay for the same board, a much
better house and a thousand times more cheerfull. They went twice to
the Sennet Chamber with me, and twice to the court, and to one levee,
another sort of an affair from the one we were at. Having been introduced to General Erwin and his lady by Patten, and the Bumforts
having e'er this call'd, and Henry and I having spent the evening at
Calarama* we found them all in the dressing room. Young Bumfort
asked me to take his arm, offering the other to young Mrs. Bumfort,
his brother's wife, a New York lady then absent from her husband.
Henry, taking the hint, offer'd Miss Ruth Bumfort and Miss Twigs, her
companion, his arms, while General Erwin and General Patten ex-

*"Kalorama" was the Washington home of Thomas Barlow, of Allegheny, a relative of
Joel Barlow who had been minister to France and was connected to the Bumforts.

chang'd their wives, each takeing some other lady on the arm. We were anounced "Erwin, Patten, Bumforts, and suit!" having fallen upon that plan when we fix'd off in the ante-room.

After paying respects to the president, we took a prominade twice round the east room, then seated ourselves on divans, Mrs. Erwin, Mrs. Patten, Mrs. Bumfort and Mrs. Twigs belonging to the Bumfort party.

While sitting, General Patten came forward with the Honourable Mr. Russel of Bedford, and introduc'd him to me, who said he had the pleasure of knowing me when young and when he was a student at law, and felt the pang of being in love with me, but so unfortunate as to be two young to tell me of it. I said, and you never knew it was reciprocated, but I was two modest to let you know it! The rest of the party was much ammused at my answer as they herd all that was said.

In the after part of the evening, the gentlemen thickened so fast, that one lady promanaded with too gentlemen in which case I had General Erwin and the Honourable Mr. Russel, after which I promanaded one round with Judge Baldwin and the Honourable Walter Forward. We met Mr. William Robenson and Mr. McCandless of our place walking with old Mrs. Beach, Mrs. Erwin and Mrs. Walker's mother, Henry and Mr. George, another Bumfort with Miss Twigs. The lady leans on the arm of each gentleman—thus fashon makes itself out of circumstances.

Mr. Baldwin introduced me to Mr. Webster and his lady and others, and I was near bursting into a laugh when he said, wife of the Honourable Major Foster of the West! After we pass'd on, he observed, Forward, we must be even with these people-glancing at me with a kind of a half grave smirk, Forward answering with the same look, Oh, yes.

Sennitor Walker, his wife, W. W. Erwin, his wife and the Beaches all call'd on me, and invited me to spend the evening, where I met with several persons among them Madam Jarome Bonnaparte. General and Mr. Erwin call'd on me and the Honourable James Buchanan.

Now, for Baltimore—Mr. Thomas Tilden came up for me to Washington, and conducted me to his house, where I now am, having been call'd on by all my kin from Dan to Bershebah, and spending at least a day and a night with each of them. Meanwhile, letters from Mrs. Skinner, one to me at Washington and one from her daughter Amanda to Mr. Tilden, expressed the warmest desire to have me make them a visit, saying she would meet us at the Royal Oke in her double carriage to conduct us to Wood Lawn, her place, which place is a sort of a Palace in the midst of seven hundred acres of rich wheat land, with two hundred and fifty negroes on it. Her daughters are all musicians, so that I expect to have a pleasant visit. Mr. Tilden and I are going over on Tuesday. In her letter to me she very ernestly invited my two sons to visit them at any time they thought fit.

There are three charming young ladies who are connected to me here, neither of them have any money, but they are very kind to me, and are agreeable acquaintances for any young gentlemen. Yesterday, I took a ride to see the symmitry, a spot which reminded me of the ancient Elesian fields, the trees, the monuments, the vaults, the small enclosures, and here and there a solitary tomb; one inscribed to my beloved sister, and another to my mother were the particular and plaintive epitaphs that struck me with a pleasing sadness as I rode through the holy ground.

I must close, my dear William for want of room, but not for want of matter to fill my paper with. I cannot well write to you again untill I return from the Eastern Shore, when I will give you a concise description of the Skinners.

Your afectionate Mother,

Eliza C. Foster.

Meanwhile, at home, everything went along smoothly, but rather dully for William B. Foster and the boys. Stephen was still a problem, and his father fretted because he would not attend school. He understood his son very well, however, and did not attempt to drive him though he felt it was not right to leave the boy so entirely to his own devices. He brought up the subject to William on March 14:

I wish, if you could make a target bearer of Stephen, and find employmt. for him, that you would take him through the summer.—He is uncommonly studious at home, but dislikes going to school; he says there is too much confusion in the school. I dislike to urge him, so long as he discovers no evil or idle propensities. He says he would like to be in brother William's sunshine.

On March 30 he still had Stephen on his mind:

I wrote you on the subject of Stephen, and expect to hear from you soon. He is a very good boy, but I cannot get him to stick at school. He reads a good deal, and writes some in the office with me.

Writing to his daughter Henrietta on April 9, 1842, Wm. B.

Foster tells her of a thoughtful little gift Stephen had left for her on his last visit to Youngstown:

... Stephen bought you 50 cents worth of Flower Seeds; and Dunning informed me he had put them in one of the drawers of your little Bureau, or Dressing stand, I suppose you have found them before this time—they are in good time to plant now. . . .

William B. Foster had reason to worry about his sons. He saw no prospect of being able to leave them so well off that they need not earn their own livings, and he had a father's natural dread lest any of his children be forced out into the world unprepared to take care of himself. Although Stephen displayed a strange talent for music, and applied himself mightily to the study of it, it did not necessarily follow that the problem of his future was solved. That was the day when every young amateur who wrote a sonnet to his lady's eyebrow, had it published and dedicated it to the object of his affections. Glance through any old volume of bound sheet music of the 1830's and on, and you will find them by the score. It was the day of serenading parties, of sweet twanging under windows and in trellised arbors. Young gentlemen, hoping they would be asked to perform, lugged their guitars with them when they went calling. Stephen's parents had felt constrained to sit "with sad civility" and listen to many musical outpourings from the swains who called on their daughters. Consider how venomously a present-day father regards the young man who comes tripping in to see his daughter, armed with a saxophone and a "torch song." William Foster shuddered at the prospect of one of his sons becoming such a one! Even Eliza Foster reveals her distaste for young gentlemen of the sort, in a conversation previously recorded from her reminiscences. (See page 32.)

"Pshaw!" said Mrs. Murphy, "your fathers expect you to marry some rich man of some great family, when you settle yourselves to their liking. But just as likely as not, you will run off with some strange fellow that they never heard of, because he plays on the guitar and sings songs, or writes rhymes, or some such nonsense, and only wants you for your money all the time."

"I must fall far indeed below my mother," said Mary, "if I condescend to give myself to any such fellow."

His anxiety for the future accounts in great measure for William Foster's various attempts to establish himself and his sons in mercantile undertakings for which they were temperamentally unfitted, none more so than the elder Foster himself. He had been successful with Denny and Beelen because life on the western rivers in the early days of barge and keelboat was full of glamour and adventure. The demand for the goods he carried was so great that to dispose of them required little application of trading methods. Politics was his real field. William, Jr., was probably best satisfied with his calling, for he was pioneering on the canals and railroads where the charm of the wilderness still remained.

Some biographers have believed that Stephen was the only visionary in a family of hardheaded and successful businessmen. Their children know better than this. Hardheaded they certainly were not; and, while they were mildly successful in a financial way because they applied intelligence to all their undertakings, no matter how distasteful, their hearts were never centered in commercial life. Morrison started out bravely, and steadily pursued his business affairs, but his real passion was always the theater. Henry was much the same, but found an outlet for some of his dramatic urge in the church. Dunning's great love was the river. None of the brothers, nor their father, could drive a close bargain for himself though ready enough to fight for someone else when he could haggle like a Yankee peddler.

Settled in his office as mayor, William B. Foster found an outlet for some of his repressed crusader spirit in the "temperance cause." A wave of temperance rallies was sweeping the country about that time. The duties of his new office were light, and consisted largely in hearing cases of disorderly conduct and drunkenness which distressed him mightily. His early life on the frontier had probably been rough enough, for the keelboat traffic of the Ohio and Mississippi was notorious for wild and lawless living, but that was all long in the past; the peace and dignity of his own domestic life had made him almost forget the "depravity of poor human nature" so abruptly brought to his attention in his little court of justice. Police court characters were no different then than they are now, judging from the newspaper clippings which he preserved in his scrapbook. Even the reporters of the early papers wrote up the news in the same facetious vein as they do today, finding merely amusing the disposition of the poor old sots brought up for sentence. Here is a fair example:

LOAFERS' CORNER—WATCH HOUSE REPORT
Monday Oct. 11 [1842]

Mrs. Catherine M'Cune complained of Adam and Daniel Thorn for getting drunk and kicking up a spree at her house; they acknowledged the corn, and Dan paid their fines & costs, $3.50—Mrs. M., was therefore sent up to Mt. Airy, charged with keeping a "disorderly and ill-governed house" in Fourth Street, in said City, yesterday, the 10th of October inst. and for divers weeks previously. Hugh Bateman took charge of her. Oh! Hannah!

Another duty of the Mayor was witnessing deeds and contracts, such as a notary public or justice of the peace takes care of today. He wrote to his son William on March 30, 1842.

... My office affords me about business enough to keep me from desponding, but is painful in many respects, to witness as I must do, the awful depravity of poor human nature, in many cases of female intoxication & prostitution is truly lamentable.

March 14. ... Our temperance cause is prosperous.—I think I have redeemed one miserable drunkard, our first acquaintance being a commitment by me, to the jail of the County 24 hours for drunkenness and abuse of his family. After he came out, he call'd on me and sign'd the pledge, and has remain'd since (about two weeks) a sober, decent man, for which I am receiving the thanks and prayers of a wife and three daughters.

Wm. B. Foster does not give any more news of the drunkard's progress, but even the most sanguine might fear that two weeks' sobriety is not enough to guarantee a complete redemption! It is to be hoped the Mayor's kindly efforts were not in vain.

March 30. ... The boys and myself get along very quietly, but we are wretchedly lonesome without Mother—the days are getting very long and the evenings very dreary without her company, but as she is there, I wish her to see all her friends. I have not heard from her for two weeks, and do not know whereabouts she is, she last wrote us from Baltimore.

Here is Eliza Foster as her son Morrison remembered her:

Ah, what a mother was that! Handsome, brilliant, and admired, she was the soul of purity, truth and Christian virtue. Her example shone upon her household as a continual light from heaven. No unkind word ever passed between any members of that family, for strife was repelled and anger washed away by the pure stream of love that emanated from her presence. Her precepts were listened to by her children with the reverence due to oracular utterances, and were never unheeded. Whilst she was a devout Christian, she had no method in her teachings, no rules for daily or hourly observance. An unquestioning faith in the Redeemer, and charity in all things, was her rule. She was very fond of entertaining her children with historical facts or recitations from the works of the best authors, which her wonderfully retentive memory enabled her to draw on to any extent. Mother's room was the favorite spot to all the household. It was here that all assembled in the evenings, and gathering round her chair or couch, would listen with rapt attention to her words of wisdom and instruction.

Her discourses abounded in illustrations of the goodness of God and the necessity for our recognizing the fact that dependence on Him alone constitutes the happiness of mankind. Sometimes she would say, almost abruptly, "And now, my children, kneel down here around me and let us pray to our Heavenly Father."

And there on the floor around that blessed mother, her children, old and young, threw themselves and listened to her beautiful, touching prayers in their behalf. Rising, her face resumed its sweet, sunny aspect, and everything went on as though it was the most natural thing in the world to fall down and worship God at any time.

Her death, which occurred in January, 1855, created a void in the household, which, as beautifully expressed in one of Stephen's songs, "could never be filled."

No wonder they were wretchedly lonely, and the days seemed long and the evenings very dreary when that mother was away.

One important event did occur to break the monotony, the visit of Charles Dickens to Pittsburgh, during his triumphal tour of the United States. Morrison made a call on Boz on March 30, 1842, and Stephen and his father went to see him the next day. Morrison recalled Dickens as a very pleasant gentleman wearing an ornate flowered weskit with a large bunch of seals dangling from his watch chain. The famous traveler wrote a particularly ungrateful account of his experiences in the new, crude country, his observations being strangely shallow and superficial for so thorough a student of human behavior. Naturally, these articles infuriated those Americans who had outdone themselves entertaining the celebrated Englishman; but their anger was short lived. Who could hold a grudge against the creator of the inimitable Pickwick, pathetic little Nell, and Wilkins Micawber, Esq.? The elocutionary lady who let down her back hair and recited "The Blood Drinker's Burial," has more than compensated us for the few slurs Charles Dickens cast in our direction.

Both Dickens and Washington Irving attended a levee at the President's while Henry and his mother were visiting the Skinners on the Eastern Shore in March, causing Henry to bemoan the fact that they had missed this party, "the best one of all."

Henry's first slighting estimate of Washington changed after he had attended a number of friendly social gatherings, and made the acquaintance of certain agreeable young ladies. When he and his mother visited "Wood Lawn," the Skinner plantation on the Eastern Shore, he met four more charming girls, who "played delightfully on the piano," and evidently made things very pleasant for their young second cousin. Henry wrote Brother William about it on March 25, 1842.

Selina and I got up quite a flirtation and there is no knowing where it may end, as both of us manifested strong symtums of attachment for each other.

. . . Hill left this some time since, and was playing in Baltimore when I was there on my way to Mrs. Skinner's. I remained two days in Baltimore with Thomas Tilden, the place Ma has been for some time previous to her departure for Wood Lawn. I moved my quarters from Squire King's some time since to Mrs. Von Coble's on 4½ Street, near the City Hall, a much more pleasant house at the same rate per week for boarding. Young Biddle Roberts, son of E. I. Roberts, Esqr. of Pitth. who is going to school here, rooms with me & is a very agreeable companion, being both smart and witty.

About a week after you left, the President had another Levee which by far surpassed the one you attended, as he had the East Room thrown open and splendidly illuminated by five large Chandeliers, attended by a large concourse of People & a fine band of Music. Gen. Patton & I hired a hack between us, and took Ma & Mrs. Patton. We met there Mr. Wm. Robinson, Mr. Irwin, McCandless & Marks. There has been one during my absence which was attended by Chas. Dickens & Washington Irving, so I missed the best one of all. Ma & I spent a delightful afternoon at Mr. Bumford's, who has a very agreeable family. Miss Ruth is just the girl for you, or anybody else, if they can get her. She is about Etty's age and quite pretty and accomplished. Through them, I became acquainted with a Miss Twigs at the Levee, who is another very pretty little girl, so you will perceive I have the foundation for a pleasant and agreeable society.

April 24, 1842.—Mr. Clay took his leave of Washington City this afternoon and I understand it was quite an imposing sight, all the members of the Senate and several from the House being present. They all took off their hats and held down their heads.

They have just passed the Appropriation Bill in the lower house & I suppose it will be several weeks getting through the Senate. The Steam Ships Missouri & Mississippi are down at the Navy Yard and are to be visited by Congress on Saturday. I have not seen them yet, excepting as they came up the river from the Treasury Building.

I received a very affectionate letter from Selina and wrote her a very friendly one in answer. I do not know as yet what course to pursue until I hear what Pa thinks about it. What say you, brother? Had I better go the whole figure?

Although he felt strong "symtums" of attachment for Selina, Henry was not quite deaf and blind to the attractions of Miss Twigs and Miss Bumfort. Henry liked people—he made friends readily, and enjoyed society as greatly as Stephen disliked it. Henry was very much like his father, impetuous and friendly, and frequently disappointed in people whom he had vastly overrated. The witty and amusing Biddle Roberts, afterwards General Roberts of the Union Army, proved steadfast. Henry was fortunate in having him for his roommate.

Eliza Foster stayed on at "Wood Lawn" until the first of April when she and cousin Betsey Skinner journeyed to Baltimore together, taking the little steamboat from the "Double Mill" on the Eastern Shore to Baltimore. We learn from the *Life and Times of*

Frederick Douglass (1893), that the plantation of his master, Colonel Edward Lloyd, adjoined that of the Skinners', and their isolation from the rest of the world was complete. Mr. Douglass, famed negro orator and abolitionist, and friend of Abraham Lincoln, says:

Whether with a view of guarding against the escape of its secrets, I know not, but it is a fact, that every leaf and grain of the products of this plantation and those of the neighboring farms belonging to Col. Lloyd were transported to Baltimore by his own vessels, every man and boy on board of which, except the captain, were owned by him as his property. In return, everything brought to the plantation came through the same channel. To make this isolation more apparent, it may be stated that the estates adjoining Col. Lloyd's were owned and occupied by friends of his who were as deeply interested as himself in maintaining the slave system in all its rigor. These were the Tilgmans, the Goldboroughs, the Lockermanns, the Pacas, the Skinners, Gibsons, and others of lesser affluence and standing.

Mrs. Eliza Clayland Skinner, of "Wood Lawn," Talbot County, Maryland, was a cousin (though not a first cousin) of Eliza Clayland Foster. Her maiden name was Goldsborough and her mother was a Clayland. Unlike the Lloyds, the Skinners did not own a steamboat of their own, for Mrs. Skinner mentioned that Tuesday and Friday were "steamboat days"; there was a public carrier running to Baltimore twice a week. The steamboat also brought the mail; Tuesday and Friday were "mail days" when the Skinners went for letters at the nearest post office, Royal Oak.

Eliza Foster's own description of the household and customs of "Wood Lawn" is contained in a letter to her daughter Henrietta.

Baltimore April the 9 1842

My Dear Daughter,

I return'd to this place on Wednesday last in company with Mrs. Skinner, we crossed from Talbot County on a beautifull calm day, when their was at least four Hundred white sail skiming over the clear blue bay, beneath an unclouded sky, while the bright sun, reflected his rayes upon the elegant mansions along the extensive Eastern shore of Maryland, the land of my ancestors, whose bodies are moulderd with the dust of their feilds, and whose tombs compose the portico's of their palaces. when we had cross'd the bay we pass'd the gay English Frigate, War Spite, lying off in Anapalis rodes, not being able to get into the

Patasaco, which is the Baltimore river. she brought Lord Ashberton
the special British minister.

On Sunday last Mrs. Skinner and I rode to the place setled by my
great Grandfather, one hundred and forty years ago. Mr. Skinner purchased it to save the trees but the old stone mansion which was built
at a great expence in those days became entirely untenantable and finally
a rendavieu for fishermen, who lived upon the fruit and stole the live
stock from his farms, and it was not untill his patience was worn out,
that he had it all pull'd down to build houses for his overseers.

Mrs. Skinner is a widow, her Mother was a Miss Clayland she owns
one Thousand acres of land, too hundred and fifty negroes, and stock
innumerable, and considerable monney in safe banks. she says she will
always have a home and will be always prepared for every decendent
of her race when ever they may chose to come to it. As the stemer that
Mr. Tilden and I cross'd in made shore, I was releived from anxiety,
on nearing the strand, as to how I would get to the house which was six
miles from the landing, by a very agreable sight, her gigs her double
Cariage her cart and an out rider. Mr. Tilden got into the gig with her
younggest daughter who has a broken back. after joyfully meeting me
on the marjin of the river she place'd me in her Cariage where were
seated on the front seat, too very beautifull young ladies her daughters
Ammanda, and Ellen; the cart was of course for my baggage. when I
arived at her house, I found in her Elegantly furnish'd parlour, her
eldest daughter Salina who was left at home to receive us. a very gentle
charming accomplished and altogether interesting young lady. after
tea they all play'd and sang delightfully; they said they were overjoyed
to see me they had heard their mother talk so much about and Ellen
a merry creature took off her mother singing the songs for them that I
usd'd to sing, and ending with a sigh and saying poor Eliza, I wonder if
ever I shall see her again, *this side the grave,* but Caroline exclaim'd,
now Ellen, Ma dident put this side the grave to it. thus they kept me
on the laugh from the first evening untill the last which was three weeks
at which time I could scarcely get away. We walked we rode and we
sail'd, and eat fresh roasted oyesters around the kitchen fire the last
thing at night. we went on Sundays to Miles river, and St. Micheals
churches as they are Episcopaliens. we took long rides to Easton, Ben-
noni Beverly and Sethland, and also visited Mrs. Skinner neighbouring
farms, Ashby, Clifton, Royston Iland, and Shrewsbery.

There is a fixed Arastocracy of young gentlemen whoose great grand-
fathers own'd the land they are now in posesion of they visited Mrs.

Skinner whilest I was there, they are the highest youthes I ever heard of Loyd Tilman brought Mrs. Skinner one dozen fine linnen shirts, saying to her, Miss Liza, I want you to keep my shirts for me till I call for them. Hemsley is going to hunt up a wife, and is going the rounds hunting clothes he got Mury Loyds pants and Tilman Goldburoughs hat and watch, and Tom Emorys vest and my coat, but I dont want that he shall find my shirts, but before Mrs. Skinner could get them out of his hands there commenced a skuffle and Loyd Hemsley cram'd one of them in his big coat pockett saying now Mrs Skinner I came here first for one of your daughters so just let me go to my room and get dress'd up for the evening, to see if I cant make an impression keep them there shirts Miss Liza safe for I intend to come round as soon as these chaps get some new clothes that I can aford to go a wife hunting. Well said Mrs Skinner you needent come here if thats your business you are not a going to get one here to kill off with these sort of setlings down. now Miss Liza you needent to [letter torn here] for we are only going to stay four days. after staying three days, one of them said Miss Liza we will give you one day rest and pounce upon them at Spearwood or plankemen, and finish out the week here well I dont care much so that you dont come here whilst I am away. there is five of them they wear each others clothes. they would as leave take poison as tuch any bodys clothes beneath them, and nobody would dare tuch theirs. and they will never let one get any better off than the other   the ones that has no wife is eat up out and out by the rest. they carry off his horses carrages his clothes and any thing they want, and seem to have a sort of way about it that no one understands, but themselves. Mrs. Skinner has just come in from shoping, with little green handle knives and forks for Mary Wick and the Buchanans. I leave here for Paridice on Monday write and direct your letter to that place. give all the [letter torn here] from me to Thomas and remember me as your afectionate mother,

E. C. Foster

Eliza Foster describes the goings on of the gay young bloods of Talbot County with no little amazement, and certainly not with complete approval. It is not hard to imagine what she would have had to say if the Foster boys had started a like swapping of good linen shirts and Sunday-go-to-meeting clothes with their jolly companions.

Ironical indeed are the tricks Fate plays on many fatuous innocents who like to consider themselves representing irrevocably a nation's "fixed Arastocracy." The sole and only distinction that may be claimed today for the name of one of the most patrician of Mrs. Skinner's five playful young guests, who would "as leave take poison" as put on the pantaloons of a social inferior even in fun, is that its owner is said to have been the father of Frederick Douglass.

Despite the fine time she was having, and the attentions showered upon her, Eliza Foster was beginning to tire. When she reached Ann Eliza's home in Paradise, she was quite worn out by steamboat, canal, railroad, and stagecoach travel, and longed "again to be settled at home." Ann Eliza's little boy, Edward Young Buchanan, Jr., was born near the middle of April, just about the time that his baby cousin, Thomas Wick, Jr., arrived in Youngstown. Early in May, William, Jr., planned to make another trip to Pittsburgh, and traveled down to Paradise in hopes of being able to take his mother home with him. She explains to William her reasons for remaining a while longer with Ann Eliza:

"Paridice" May the 6 1842

My dear son,

I have not heard whether or no you went to Pittsburg—I thought I could not go far wrong writing to you and directing to Northumberland. Everything here is precisely as you left, only that your sister has been retarded in the recovery of her strength by the illness of the baby; it is now better; the weather is clearing up and she is able for too days now to keep off of her bed. I proposed to her on Monday last to let me start today, but she did not seem reconciled to let me leave her yet; therefore I cannot now say when I shall start for home.

We missed you very much the day you left, and I for one felt quite low spirited about passing over the comfortable and safe oppertunity of traveling with you, so careful a conductor, and one who at once placed me in the position of independence as a traveller; beside the pleasure of your kind and affectionate society, which no motive but the one by which I was induced would have temted me to forego, as I daily think of the journey from Pittsburg to Haresburg and thence to Washington City with the greatest pleasure; and I asure you that my reluctance at parting with you was only over-ballanced by the strong feeling of a seeming necessity. I long again to be settled at home.

Mr. Buchanan appears to think a great deal of you—he spoke of you in the highest terms at dinner the day you left, and said he wished you could come oftener, and stay longer. I received a letter a few days since from Pa—he says that Duning intends to come over home to board when I return; I am glad of that, I shall be able to tell you how his love matter comes on—I have not heard a word since.

I also received a letter from Henry; he is quite taken with the people at Calarama—he says he never saw a young lady that Brother William would like to have for a wife as well as he would like Ruth Bumford. He was up there one evening in company with some of Lord Ashberton's suit, and ladies accordingly; he boards now quite near the Treasury Department.

As soon as you get time I wish you would drop me a line. Edwin Lightner, rector of St. James Church at Muncy, with his bride, the daughter of Judge Ellis of that place, and a Miss Jeffries of Lancaster, spent the day here yesterday.

I am, my dear son, with much sincerety, your very affectionate Mother,

Eliza C. Foster.

She wrote him again on May 18:

I now write you a few lines only to say to you that as your sister and her family is getting much better, I shall leave this for home on Tuesday next. Mr. Buchanan left this yesterday for Philadelphia and will return on Monday. I wrote one letter to you directed to Northumberland (by the bye, I have made it a long word, but I write with difficulty, having been sick since you left; my eyes are still very sore). . . . I had hoped to hear from you, but I suppose I shall not now hear untill I cross the mountains. I expect my travel will be lonely indeed, but that will not be your fault.

(For a long time it was the custom to omit the noun when speaking of *this place,* or *this city;* often editors of early American documents insert *place* or *town* in brackets, indicating that they believe the writer omitted it by mistake. It was not a mistake—the word *this* was used as we now say, "I shall leave *here* tomorrow.")

XIV

ECAUSE of the failure of the Towanda bank, and the curtailment of public works in Bradford County, William was uncertain about retaining his position in the spring of 1842. The State Board of Canal Commissioners decided to employ but three engineers on the North Branch Canal. William's friends in the legislature, and in Harrisburg, Wilkes-Barre, Pittsburgh, and Towanda rallied to his cause, and sent letters and petitions to the commissioners urging that he be retained. Some Northern men resented the fact that William, a Westerner, was given preference on the North Branch, but a large number of Towanda and Wilkes-Barre partisans maintained that he was now a Northern man, because he was a resident of Towanda, and had bought wild lands in Bradford, Lycoming, and Juniata counties, besides being eminently qualified for the work. When William first went to the North Branch in 1839, he found it necessary to correct measurements on a good many miles of the canal—corrections which were bitterly contested by the old contractors. They took the matter to the legislature, and William was ordered to go over the measurements again, with the result that his calculations were found to be correct. It was a victory for William, but caused no end of hard feeling in some places.

Amongst the petitions sent the canal commissioners asking that he be retained was one from the Democratic members of the House and Senate, reading as follows:

Harrisburg January, 1842

To His Excellency
     David R. Porter—Governor—
          and, To the Canal Commissioners of Penna.

The undersigned Senators and Representatives of Pennsylvania, take pleasure in bringing to your particular notice, William B. Foster, Jr. Esqr., the present engineer on the upper division of the North Branch Canal. Many of us have been acquainted with Mr. F. since he first entered on his duties, at his present station—and from personal knowledge, we recommend him, as well as for his moral worth, as for skill and competency in his profession.

At the time he commenced his duties on the North Branch, the public mind was much excited, and our political opponents were looking for the same course of policy to be pursued towards them that had been so liberally bestowed upon our political friends in the northern section of the State by Ritner's administration—To the credit of the State be it said, they were disappointed. Mr. F.—though a stranger, by his courteous bearing and general deportment, at once secured the confidence and esteem of all deserving men.—The old contractors, however, not satisfied with justice, made complaint to the Legislature that injustice had been done them in the measurement of their work, and a remeasurement was ordered to be made by Mr. Foster and the former engineer. The result showed that Mr. F. was perfectly correct, and he was honorably sustained in all he had done.

The Democracy of Pennsylvania, which we have the honor to represent, are anxious to retain in the service of the State a man of such estimable moral and professional character, and in view of any reduction in the Engineer Corps, do most respectfully urge the continuance of Mr. Foster.—Mr. F. is most emphatically a business man, and will add strength and credit to any administration that shall continue him in its service.

With much respect,
We have the Honor to be—
Truly your friends & fellow citizens—

James R. Snowden,   Asa Dimock.

Forty-six more names are signed to the petition.

Owing to lack of funds, however, work on the canal was suspended in the summer of 1842 although William stayed on until September, going over the line of survey and laying plans for future construction. He clung to Towanda, for he had learned to like the place and the people.

Eliza Foster started for home on May 24, 1842, and the day she left Paradise, Thomas Wick died in Youngstown. His death was unexpected, for he was seriously ill only two days. On Monday, Henrietta dispatched a messenger who arrived in Allegheny at three o'clock Tuesday morning, asking her father to come at once. Wm. B. Foster, Sr., left on the six o'clock stage, and arrived in Youngstown at eleven that same morning, but Thomas had already passed on. In the words of his truly sorrowing father-in-law, Thomas "resigned up his spirit to that God who gave it, without a groan or a struggle." William's father wrote him on May 25:

I found Henrietta greatly distressed, but was much relieved by my arrival, and is pretty calm and resigned today. She informs me that every kindness and attention has been given her by old Mr. and Mrs. Wick, as well as by every male and female belonging to the whole connection, without a single exception.—The funeral will take place this afternoon, and I hope to start home on tomorrow evening, in order to meet your Mother, who we expect at Pittsbg. on Friday evening.

Eliza Foster describes the situation as she found it on her return.

Youngstown June the 11 1842

My dear William,

I am again in this place, invited under sader circumstances than has ever yet been the inducement for me to visit this painfully remember'd spot.

You have already been aprised by your Father of the decease of Thomas Wick, of which I was ignorant, untill I arived at our home in Alleganey. I remained at home one week, during which time I was surprised with the arival of Charlotte and Caroline; which would have induced me to stay at home at this time, had not the force of duty been paramount to all other considerations; the distress of your sister Henrietta call'd for all the consolation I, as a mother, could summon to communicate to her brused heart.

She has three children; consequently has made up her mind to continue here under the care of old Mr. and Mrs. Wick, who are kindly disposed toward her, as have they all been during the trying scene through which God in his wonderfull providence has permited her to pass. Though heavy laden with sorrow, her mind and body are both in a healthy condition, and she seems to be alive to the duties of her widowhood; if it were not for the loneliness of a desolate spirit, which must be felt by every sensitive person who loses a companion so ever preasent as a husband; she has borne the whole scene with a patience and resignation which surprises every body.

She begs me to say to you that she will write, as soon as she is able to sustain herself through the effort it will cost her to refrain from tears, when she atemts to communicate with a brother who has pased through a simmilar heart rending trial. She also requests that I will intreat you to make her a special visit, when you can be spared from your arduous employment.

I shall stay one more week and return with your Father, who is to come down to go with Henrietta to Warren court, in relation to the few effects Thomas has left. I shall find Charlotte and Caroline on my return at the house, as they intend to stay some three or four weeks. [These ladies were relatives of Eliza Foster's from the South.]

I am, my dear son, quite well, which I know will give you much satesfaction to be asured of. I requested Pa shortly after I arived at home to give you every infermation respecting my jurney and safe arival, and defer'd writing to you myself untill I would get here, being very busy during the week I stayed at home, what with attending to some business for Henrietta, and the coming of the ladies mentioned above, I could not write. As this is the fourth letter I have writen to you I will expect to hear from you before I write again. I have nothing more to say that I can well communicate by letter, but much to tell you when I shall once more have the pleasure of seeing you, which I trust will be before very long.

I am, my dear son, now as ever, your efectionate

Mother,

Eliza C. Foster.

Perhaps the reader has noticed the strange rules, or absence of all rules, that govern Eliza Foster's spelling, especially in letters written under the strain of excitement or emotion. When writing to the younger boys, she is particularly careful, but to her son William she writes as she feels. When her mind and hand are tired, it shows very plainly in her penmanship. She usually does not double a letter where a single one will suffice, as in the word *arive,* but above is the only instance where she misspells *affectionate.*

Henrietta and her affairs were the chief concern of all the family during the summer of 1842. Her mother, father, and Stephen spent a great deal of time with her, for she was only twenty-three, and still young enough to feel helpless in the face of her loss. Mother and Father Wick were extremely fond of her and the children, but longing for her own home and her own people almost overwhelmed her at times. The first few weeks after Thomas' death, she was sustained by the necessity of getting his rather tangled business affairs in order, and making secure for her children their inheritance. In this she was assisted by her father, who stayed with her until all was settled to his own satisfaction. He reported his progress to William:

June 23, 1842. Old Mr. Wick requested that Henrietta should administer on her late husband's estate, and the laws of this state require that letters of administration shall be granted by the court, not as in Pennsa. by the Register of Wills. The Court met in Warren on Tuesday 21st. inst. and the letters have been granted to Henrietta, Robert W.

Taylor, Esqr. and Uncle Struthers, her Bondsmen. Mr. Taylor will direct her in all her business; of course he will keep all straight. The law here also requires that the administrator shall give five days notice, of the time of taking inventory and appraisement of deceased personal estate; and we have appointed Monday the 27th. for that business.—Doctr. Manning, Frank Barclay and James McEwen, appraisors.

I can't leave until after the inventory shall have been taken, and expect to get home in about a week. Your mother arrived at home on the 27th ult. the same day I return'd from Thomas' funeral at this place. She remained there only ten days, when she came out here, and is with us now; she will return home with me, and we intend taking with us Henrietta's second little daughter, Eliza. I suppose she will fall to our share.—Henrietta is as comfortable as I could expect, you know there is a good deal of elasticity in her composition.

Old Mr. Wick requested that I should go to Warren, Pennsya. & settle up all Thomas' business in that country; and I have agree'd to do so. It will be necessary for me to take out letters of administration there, as the laws of Pennsylvania do not recognise the authority of an administrator in another State, to appoint by power of attorney.

If you wish me to do anything for you while at Warren, you will have time enough to write me at Allegheny, as I can't leave in less than two weeks after I get home, which will be about three weeks from this time.

The old people and all the connections are very kind to Henrietta, and I feel a strong hope that her future situation will not be so desolate and cheerless as it otherwise would be. She received a letter from you day before yesterday, which was very consoling to her feelings.

I believe I mentioned in my last letter to you that Mr. Wick told me that the house and lot, and the farm which Thomas occupied belongs to his children.

From the tone of some of the present legislature, I apprehend that you, or any other engineer, will not be long retain'd in service, but "sufficient for the day is the evil thereof"—we must not repine.

The house and lot and farm which Wm. B. Foster mentions so casually were situated in the heart of the present-day business section of Youngstown, and proved to be a splendid legacy to Thomas' children. But at that time, Youngstown was only a sleepy little town where "Father Wick sat in his own front door exactly as he use'd to do, and Doctor Manning rode along the street with precisely the same benevolent aspect as in other times."

While the members of the family in Allegheny had their thoughts centered on Henrietta and her problems, Henry, though not indifferent to his sister's trials, was far removed from the scene of trouble and pursued his interested way in the new circle in which he found himself. His affair with Selina had received "somewhat of a setback" from the young lady herself, for she informed him that although she reciprocated his affection, she "did not want to get married"—with the last phrase underscored, and upon consulting his father as to what he thought of the matter, Henry was somewhat dashed to learn that pretty Miss Skinner was six years older than he—in fact, two years older than his sister Ann Eliza. However, Henry was blessed with the same "resilient nature" as Henrietta, and when he resolved to forget his cousin from the Eastern Shore, it proved to be not a very difficult task, for Washington offered plenty of distractions, as a letter to Brother William, dated June 30, 1842, reveals.

You did not state whether there was any probability of Snyder and Lizzy Goodwin making a match of it, but presume that nothing further has transpired since I left Towanda. I am very glad to hear that the new Church is ready for divine service, and am very sorry that you are obliged to leave it just at a time when it is in successful operation, after having undergone so much in endeavoring to establish it, but we know not what a day may bring forth & our hopes blasted.

I presume that you have heard of the Veto of the Postponement Bill & have no doubt there is considerable confusion today in Congress in consequence of it. I enquired of Irwin yesterday how they received it, to which he replied that it was expected he would Veto it. I understand the President agrees to sign a bill should the duty be 50 pr. ct. provided that amt. is necessary to support government, if they will repeal the distribution bill, but will not agree to distribute the proceeds of the public lands among the states and increase the Tariff to make up for it.—Huzza for John Tiler! I say he is not so easy headed, or beheaded as they think for. Too much old Hickory in him.

While seated in John Butler's room yesterday afternoon at Fuller's Hotel, Mr. Bosler the Marshal came in, to whom John introduced me. After conversing a short time, he invited John & I to take a ride out through Georgetown with him, which we did & found him quite a fine old Gentleman.

Mr. W. Robinson of Allegheny has been here & left a few days since for England to negociate a loan for the U. States.

The principal amusement at present is promenading in the Capitol & President's grounds to the music of the Marine Band, on every Thursday & Saturday Evening at 6 o'clock, and as I want to go up to the Capitol this evening I am writing this in a great hurry, it being about the time the music commences.

I received a letter from Ma yesterday written at Youngstown, stating Pa was out there likewise attending to dear Sister Etty's affairs.

Mrs. Patten's daughter is here, a very pretty girl, jet black hair & eyes. I visit Mrs. Eaton's frequently and find her and her two pretty Daughters extremely agreeable. Ex-V-Presidentess, you know.

Henry's friend, Mrs. John H. Eaton, was the charming Peggy O'Neill who had been the cause of much storm and stress in the life of Andrew Jackson when he was President. His open championship of Mrs. Eaton when Washington scandal-mongers and political enemies endeavored to drive Major Eaton from Jackson's cabinet, drew down on the President's head a deluge of abuse both personal and public. Andrew Jackson's dearly beloved wife, Rachel, had been the victim of most malicious slander because she had been divorced from her first husband; consequently, "Old Hickory" despised and repudiated the busybodies who came to him with scandalous stories about Mrs. Eaton when Jackson appointed Major Eaton as Secretary of War. As a result, all sorts of rumors were spread about the influence of Mrs. Eaton over the President of the United States, but he stood firm, and refused to countenance any disparagement of Margaret Eaton or John H. Eaton in his presence.

Another cause for criticism of Mrs. Eaton was that her father had been a "tavern-keeper"! It must have been very distressing to the suddenly elevated daughters of stable-boys and mule-skinners to find themselves expected to associate in Washington society with a lady who was not at all ashamed of her forebears, either of her father, William O'Neill, the tavern-keeper, or her uncle, Richard Howell, governor of New Jersey!

Changing only a few names, Henry's account of a day in Washington in 1842 could quite aptly be used to describe the same scene today. Visitors still drive out through Georgetown to view the same houses passed by Mr. Bosler and his young friends on their afternoon ride, and the Marine Band still plays for the entertainment and enjoyment of all. Mrs. Eaton, and her "two pretty daughters," Virginia and Margaret Timberlake, are gone, but their reincarnations are still holding court, and dazzling young treasury clerks in the same old way. Major John H. Eaton, and William B. Foster had met while Eaton was Secretary of War, not Vice-President, as Henry indicates. The acquaintance was revived by Henry, and the connection became closer in 1846 when General Eaton went before Congress to plead the cause of his old friend Foster in his government claim.

Henry's letters reveal that he has dropped the old fashion of ending with a *k* such words as *musick, physick,* and *frantick,* approved in *Walker's Dictionary,* that "recognized lexicon" of Mr. Stockton's academy. Although their children had adopted new methods of spelling, William and Eliza Foster clung to the old way, and spelled *color* with a *u,* and *music* with a *k* to the end of their days. *Walker's Dictionary* is a fine combination of learning and rare humor, qualities which evidently appealed to the accomplished Aaron Burr, who recommended Walker to his daughter Theodosia as the "final authority." Stephen was still using *Walker's Dictionary* for reference in 1842, but he had also discarded the old style spelling.

When Henrietta's father and mother left for Allegheny at the end of June, believing they had done all they could for their daughter for the time being, she, in her loneliness, turned to Brother William with a plan which it must have cut him to the heart to upset. William, unbeknownst to any of his family, had been making plans of his own which could not be set aside. Although Henry had found "just the girl" for Brother William in Washington, and his mother was sure that none could compare with Ann Eliza Anderson of Allegheny, William quietly went about getting a wife of his own choosing, and ultimately satisfactory to them all. Since he had given up all thought of Mary Ann Overton, William had found one who he felt was in every way qualified to take Mary Ann's place in his affections. This was Elizabeth Smith Burnett, a young widow who lived at Nippenose Bottom, in Lycoming County, not far from Williamsport, where William frequently made his headquarters. We do not know the circumstances of William's meeting with the pretty young widow. She was the daughter of Abijah Smith, of Brooklyn, New York, a gentleman of considerable wealth and standing who had interests in Towanda. Perhaps the reason William did not tell his parents of his approaching marriage was because he had confided to them so much of his unsatisfactory romance with Miss Overton that he felt another love affair would seem like an anticlimax. Whatever his reasons for silence might have been, in early September his mother as yet knew nothing of William's plans.

Henrietta's letter to William shows her bewildered and dismayed by the blow Fate had dealt her. She was suffering a nervous let-down after the strain of the last few years of nursing, anxiety, and childbearing. Brought up a petted and sheltered girl, with no responsibility, she suddenly found herself the head of a little family who looked to her and her only to uphold them. The difficulties of her situation were entirely mental; no actual want or privation threatened her. But her loneliness was overwhelming, and the whole world seemed a dark place indeed.

Youngstown July 2, 1842

My dear brother,

I received your very affectionate letter which was written at Towanda some time ago, and should have answered it long before this had my mind been settled long enough to have written a letter that you could have made any sense of, and even now I cannot promise you much of a letter. It seems to me that my mind never will be right again.

Do you not think you can possibly come out and see me? Oh, I am so dreadfully lonely—how delighted I would be to see you. Besides that, I want to consult you a little about my future plan of living, for I find since Thomas is gone the *world* cares but little what is to become of me. Father and Mother Wick are very kind to me indeed, but still I am alone as it were, for my education and way of thinking is so entirely different from the people here, that I feel like a stranger among them. It is my wish (if it were possible) to live near or with some of my own blood relations. I have laid out several plans for myself, but cannot make up my mind which one to pursue. I have a good deal of nice furniture, Piano, Sideboard, beds, beding & bedsteads, Glass & China, which would enable me to keep house comfortably in any place. I should like to have some one of my brothers live with me and provide everything we needed to live on, and there is none of them in a situation to do so but yourself. Oh, how I wish that you would give up canaling and settle in Pittsburgh in the way I have mentioned. It is more than I can do to take care of three little children, attend to my house properly and provide everything to keep the house going too. I have everything to do myself, not a creature to do an errand for me—to be sure, I have a girl to do my kitchen work, but you know that the girls in this country are very particular about what they do.

I did think at first that I would try and keep house alone here, but I find that my spirits become so completely depressed, and I feel such a sense of dreary loneliness, that it would not be prudent for me to do so. If it were not for my little children, I should find it hard to live at all from one day to another—everything appears so horribly to me.

I could live here in Youngstown very contentedly if I only had some person to attend to things out of doors for me, and who would feel for me when my grief is heavy and one who would take care of me when I am sick, and there is no one else but a brother who would do all this. Now if you could come to Youngstown and live, we might be company for each other.

It is probable that some time during the fall I shall go and make Ann Eliza a visit if God in his Mercy should spare the health of myself and children untill that time. Ma said she could keep the two little girls with her, and I would have the care of none but the baby, and he is so very good that he would not be much trouble to me if I should go.

Ma stayed with me two weeks—she and Pa both left on Tuesday last, and I am now all alone, no Husband, no brother or sister, Father or mother—not a relation near me, and a widow with three little children. Do you not think, my dear brother, that my situation is a pitiable one? I know you can simpathise with me, as you have met with a similar loss, but if you had been possessed of Mary nearly six years, and every failing (if she had any) had become a virtue in your eyes, and she had then been taken from you, then indeed would you have missed her. If any of my children were only large enough to talk to me about Thomas, it would be a great comfort to me, but they are not, and all they say only makes me feel worse.

Do, my dear brother, write to me immediately and give me some of your opinions on what I had better do. God knows that if it were consistant with his will I would gladly lie down in peace by the side of my departed husband, and rest from all trouble, but for some wise purpose he still prolongs my days, and all I can do is patiently to wait his Divine pleasure. I have no doubt but that all things will work together for good in the end.

If you can possibly come and see me, I wish you would, for you can say a great many things that you cannot write, and I want so badly to see you. Mother Wick sends her love to you. There is nothing new here, everything goes on in the same old way. Write to me soon, for I shall look anxiously for a letter from you untill I get one.

Your affectionate sister,
Henrietta.

When Henrietta's mother returned to Allegheny, one of the visiting cousins went to Youngstown to keep the lonely girl company, but she was almost as much of a stranger to Henrietta as her husband's family, and gave her little consolation. In the meantime, Eliza Foster took to her bed for two weeks, for she was exhausted with traveling, excitement, and visitors. The ladies from the South, with their small boy (who was a terror) still "hung on," waiting the rise of the river to take them to Louisville where they planned to visit other relatives. Henry grew anxious at not hearing from home, and wrote William on August 2, 1842:

Have not heard a word from home for more than three weeks, notwithstanding they are indebted to me a letter from there. I begin to feel quite uneasy, fearing some of them are sick, and delay writing, for the purpose of informing me favorably if possible when they write.

I suppose you receive all the Congressional news as fast as it transpires, from the newspapers. The Senate are still on the tariff, & the House on private bills.

I am boarding at present at Mrs. Milligan's opposite the Treasury, at $20 a month. We have a gentleman who was on the exploring expedition boarding with us, who amuses us very much relating his adventures.

Mrs. Patten's daughter, Miss Gay, was married not long since to a Doctor from New York City, who has taken her there. As for myself, I have become entirely out of that way of thinking for the present, and have stopped all communication with Selina.

In a report made by an investigating committee to Congress of the number and qualifications of the clerks, my name stands thus—

> Henry B. Foster, Salary $1000, attentive and
> a good clerk.

The Theater is open and we have Mrs. Fitzwilliams & Mr. Buckstone performing, both of them very good. Buckstone is equal to Hill in a comedy.

Henry had received a small raise in his salary after the investigating committee submitted its report, and doubtless this was what prompted him to move to a more convenient, if a trifle more expensive boardinghouse. In a city where some members of Congress paid the staggering sum of fourteen dollars a week for board, Henry's expenses were modest indeed.

As for Morrison, his mother reported on August 14, that he had had a small "lift in the salery way. He is now to get four hundred and fifty a year. Mr. McCormack thinks that little enough." Morrison was now nineteen, Henry twenty-six.

Dunning had his headquarters at home in Allegheny, but there was "nothing new" with him. His love affair is not mentioned again; it seems to have gone the way of all his sentimental adventures—it died of his lack of interest.

Henry had been fifty dollars in debt to William ever since coming to Washington, and he now began to repay his brother by signing over to William a debt owed him in Towanda. All the boys kept strict account of their borrowings from each other, always giving their notes. They did not hesitate to use these notes in payment of their own obligations, and there were never any hurt feelings over these transactions. It was a sensible and businesslike way for brothers to deal with one another, fixing on each a sense of his own responsibility.

Washington City, Augt. 18th, 1842

Dear Brother,

Enclosed you will find power of Attorney, which I hope will prove satisfactory, & am very sorry to hear that it is probable that you will not be under employ longer than the first of next month. However, it may result for the best, you certainly could not save much at a salary of $1500. I will send you $20 on the first day of October, provided nothing occurs to prevent it more than I now anticipate.

The young man who robbed his fellow clerk of $600 occupied the room immediately opposite to ours in the Land Office—is about twenty-one years of age. After taking the money, he left for Baltimore, where he was detected by endeavoring to pass one of the Treasury notes he had taken. The person who lost the money did not have him arrested, and no other individual cared about it. So he was left to go at liberty & is now I believe in Baltimore, but has lost his situation as clerk in our office, of course. It is supposed he will not return here again.

The Lower House of Congress have been discussing the merits of the different reports on the Veto presented by members of a committee appointed to report on the subject, two of which you will find in the paper I send you. There is no knowing what will be done yet, no time fixed for adjournment.

I have become very generally acquainted here now & am enabled to pass my time very agreeably indeed. I attend Church usually at Apollo Hall, where we have a very fine preacher & a pleasant congregation (Episcopal, of course,) & have just commenced the formation of a choir of which I am a member. It reminds me very much of our old choir meetings at Towanda. Then we meet for practicing on Wednesday afternoons in St. John's Church, for the purpose of having the assistance of the Organ, we not being sufficiently supplied with the ready to afford one yet. The reason I attend at the Apollo is that the preacher is the best in town, is a new one, the congregation is new, the Choir is new & *I am new* in this place.

When you visit Towanda tell Lizzy Goodwin I am very much obliged to her for the paper she sent me containing a story in which Henry Foster was an important personage! I derived considerable benefit from the perusal of it & will endeavor to profit by it. Give my respects to all who inquire for me, but none other, remember me to Mitchell, Piatt & Gamble when you see them.

> & believe me your affct.
> Broth. in haste
> Henry.

Henry's customary closing, "Broth. in haste" must have made his older brother smile. Henry was a busy young man, but still he always managed to make out a "middling long letter," anxious as he was to share with William the details of his new life. Everything that transpired in the capital in these days interested the Fosters, and the Democrats all over the country in general. In their revulsion against Van Buren, they had supported General Harrison, the Whig

—now he was dead, and John Tyler, elected as a Whig, but actually not one, was giving his own party no end of trouble. He was in favor of state's rights, and strongly opposed to the United States Bank. Naturally, this was gratifying to William B. Foster, who had been reluctant to desert his party, but believed firmly that a great principle was involved. It was not a case of brother against brother in the Foster family, for they all voted together, but it was a case of old friend against old friend in their social circle, and many bitter enmities sprang up between erstwhile boon companions. Men who had lived, laughed and wept together from boyhood were calling each other "scoundrels" and "miserable caitiffs." Happy neighborhood associations that had endured for years were broken up, for the partisanships of the Harrison-Van Buren contest were so violent that one must be either flesh or fowl; no halfway convictions were tolerated.

While the men of the family could divert their thoughts with politics, this escape was not possible for Eliza Foster. The troubles and problems of her children were her first concern. Henrietta's situation distressed her so greatly that her generally cheerful outlook on life became "browner and browner" as her letter to William proceeded. In her present state of mind, she even questioned the motives of the good people of Youngstown in their half-hearted support of Mr. Eton, the Episcopal minister, deciding gloomily that they attended his church solely to spite another denomination, the "Deciples"!

Youngstown September the 3d 1842

Dear William

Having written a short letter to you from Alleganey, soon after my illness, telling you the news in as few words as poseble, I thought as I have since made a change by coming here, I would inform you of it.

I left home this day week, in company with Stephen, to stay some time with Henrietta in order by degrees to reconcile her to living here. I believe your Father has closed the house as to the living part, and will only sleep in it. The aditional expence of three persons living on us for the last three months has made it nesesary to close up for a while—indeed I do not know how long they would have hung on if we had not come to that determination.

Henrietta and her children are charmingly fixed as to comfort and good health. While we are here, we pay her too dollars a week apeace board. I will stay with her untill the weather becomes colder than is good for me.

I have heard nothing new from Ann Eliza or Henry. Morison and Duning are both in good health.

Traveling is now reduced so very low between Pittsburg and this place that coming backward and forward is not felt. Too dollars is the extent of the cost of the jurney for one person.

I understood that you intend to be out in September. If so the time is nigh at hand. Henrietta anticipates considerable pleasure from your visit, and is daily wishing that you could retire from every employment and live with her. You know she is always so very sanguine, that she never fails to wish, however improbable it may be that the wish may be realized; it is happy for her that she is so; I suppose while she is yet young all such like glowing hopes will buoy her up and assist her to forget her bereavement, and other trials through which she had pass'd.

When she gets to be as old as I am all such flattering fixtures in her imagination will be shorn of its dazling tints; and the shadows in the landscape of life will become browner and browner, untill they are put on with so heavy a brush as to become almost black. She will find that no design of a woman can ever be put in practice without money or influence; that all her care and watching and labour has only been spent for the bennefit of others; that if she were to give her body to be burn'd it would not produce one martyr in her cause, such is the force of all powerfull selfishness; even the grace of our Lord and Saviour, in this generation of pride is not suficient to produce a thoughrough freind, independent of the opinion of those in whose eyes they wish to apear fair.

Mr. Eton, the Episcopal Church minister preaches here every three weeks; he is begining to get some few hearers, but they are such a strange people here, they do every thing from a pleasure of contradition, and nothing by virtue or principle. The only reason why they do not oppose the Church, is for fear of favouring the Deciples.

There are quite a number of new buildings puting up here at this time and a spirit of improvement seems to have commenced; which will be apt to bring strangers here. The Church will be apt to get on under present auspices.

I ask'd little Mary what I should say to her uncle William, Oh nothing she said, only that she had a new frock.

I know of nothing here of interrest to tell about. There *is* an incident or accident worth relating, with comments, but such things cannot be trusted to paper; therefore, when we see you the whole story can be develloped, and other explanations had better be defer'd untill then also.

I am, dear William, still your affectionate Mother,

E. C. Foster.

If William's mother had only felt that she could trust the incident, or accident, to paper that it might have been preserved! Whatever it was probably engrossed the family at the time, and now the event has slipped into the past as though it had never been. Eliza Foster seldom relayed any scandal to her children, but sometimes a little neighborhood gossip was too good to keep to herself. When she did relate it "with comments," they were to the point. Of one proud Allegheny family, who had been extremely overbearing since their head had been elected to a government office, she wrote, "They have had a small let-down lately in the way of a marriage—or rather, in too long putting one off!" which proves what Mary Wick frequently affirmed, "Grandmother Foster was nobody's fool!"

XV

WILLIAM B. FOSTER, Jr., and Elizabeth Smith Burnett were married at the home of George Crane, in Nippenose Bottom, by the Reverend John B. Clemson, on September 22, 1842. Elizabeth had a little boy, Robert, who, we believe, was three or four years old when she married Brother William. Although his marriage came as a complete surprise to William's family, it was a very pleasant one, for Elizabeth immediately won all their hearts. Her brother, Giliad, and sisters Lavinia (who married J. Edgar Thomson, afterwards William's associate on the Pennsylvania Railroad) and Crissie, also became great favorites with the family in Allegheny, and they all visited back and forth at frequent intervals.

The foregoing letter from Eliza C. Foster, dated September 3, 1842, is the last we have of her letters addressed to her son William.

It is certainly not the last one he received, but is the last in a package he evidently tied together just before his marriage to Elizabeth. The rest of Eliza Foster's letters to William have disappeared, but this particular package was carefully preserved by Robert Burnett, and thoughtfully forwarded to Morrison Foster in 1890.

In October, 1842, Stephen's mother returned to Pittsburgh but Stephen stayed on with Henrietta until December. His father sent Henrietta money for Stephen's board, and arrangements seem to have been made to have Stephen continue his studies with a certain Mrs. Rockwell, who was paid by the quarter. A dollar bill, which William B. Foster enclosed in a letter to Henrietta on October 29, for Stephen "to buy Powder and Shot" clearly indicates visits to Poland where a boy would need powder and shot if he wanted to go "coon" hunting with Uncle Struthers, or traipse along with the old man and his hounds through the October woods and fields in quest of rabbits and squirrels.

By remaining in Youngstown, Stephen missed a torchlight parade on the evening of November 8, and several performances of their favorite tragedian, Augustus A. Addams, who nineteen-year-old Mit declared enthusiastically was "the greatest of them all!" Had Stephen been at home, he would have gone to Old Drury with Mit and Dunning in November to see Mr. Addams play in *Virginius; Damon and Pythias* with Mr. Addams as Damon, and Mr. Jamison as Pythias; and *William Tell*. Stephen reached home, however, in time to see the elder Booth in two of his great roles, *Richard III*, on December 5, and *King Lear* on December 10. While Junius Brutus Booth was playing with his company in Pittsburgh, he took a house for himself and family where he could entertain his friends and admirers in the princely fashion he loved. William B. Foster attended several of the merry parties which gathered in the home of the famous actor after the evening performances. Pittsburgh's notables of the day were well represented at these informal suppers. Wine flowed freely, and sounds of revelry could be heard far into the night. Sometimes at these gatherings, the great Shakespearean actor would announce that he had a special treat for his friends. Whereupon, two of his small children would be roused from their beds and brought downstairs. At this date, Edwin Booth was nine

years old, his sister Asia seven, John Wilkes three and a half, and
Joseph two and a half years old. It seems most likely that Edwin and
Asia were the precocious little Booths their father called upon to
entertain the company. Junius Brutus Booth, "the younger," was
seventeen or eighteen years old at this time. Standing in their
night clothes in the middle of the littered table, the sleepy children
went through whole scenes from *Richard III, Hamlet,* and *Macbeth*
for the edification of their father's guests. William B. Foster was
amazed at the perfection of their performance and their remarkable
memories; but after a while, he said, the little actors' heads would
start to droop, they would stumble on their lines, and hold onto
each other in an effort to keep on their feet. A sharp command
roused them; they would struggle on a while longer only to succumb
again in a few moments. At last, the guests would cry for mercy for
the children and Booth then would permit them to drop into someone's arms where they slept till the party broke up at dawn.

Morrison's account books show that the young gentlemen of the
Foster family moved in a veritable social whirl during the fall and
winter of 1842 and 1843. Their father started for Washington and
Baltimore, and must have had excellent going, for he was home by
November 19, and set out for Youngstown where Henrietta's affairs
kept him occupied for several days. On December 3, he and Stephen
returned to Pittsburgh with Henrietta and her three children. Little
Mary and Lidie loved to stay at Grandma's where they received a
great deal of petting and spoiling. Mary Wick, whom her young
uncles called "Siss," said it used to be a fight to see which one would
sleep with Grandma. Eliza Foster was short and fat and warm and
comfortable, and Mary remembered vividly the nights she was the
lucky one to cuddle up beside that beloved grandparent.

Young Mitty was very gay that winter and spent a deal of money
for carriage hire and theaters. After the thirteenth of December,
the carriage items changed to "sleighing" ($1.50 per evening for
horse and sleigh) and he even purchased sleigh bells of his own!
One week shows $1.75 for the theater, and five cents to church!
(Oh, Mit!) Dickens' *Notes* cost him $1.25, the *Life of Wellington,*
fifty cents, *The Last of the Barons,* fifty cents, and a portrait of
Andrew Jackson, three dollars. Mrs. Harding's party and Emily

Irwin's marriage to R. B. Butler were important events. By January 1, 1843, Morrison "owed Ma, $7.00, Etty $5.00, and Steve $6.00." We are glad to say that these items are all drawn through with a pencil, and marked *Paid*. His second cousin, Mary Evans, appeared to hold first place in his heart. He wrote to her very often while she was away on a visit to Youngstown, and never failed to make a note of it when he received her reply; and "swarrys" at the Evans' home were frequent occurrences. "Pa" started for Erie in December, 1842, a week after his return from Youngstown, and made stagecoach journeys here and there all winter long.

Christmas Day of 1842 was not cold, and Steve and Mit got up at five in the morning to attend services at the Catholic church. Then Mit reports that he was sick from December 28 to January 4, 1843, and very cold, freezing weather set in. On the morning of January 21, General Cass arrived at eleven o'clock to be received by the officials of the two cities (William B. Foster represented Allegheny), and left at five on the steamboat *Belmont*.

Sleighing and festivities lasted all winter; then on March 11, 1843, when the river was high, Morrison left Pittsburgh for Memphis, on the steamboat *Lancaster*, on his first business trip for Pollard McCormick. His duty was to buy all the cotton he could, and sell all the yarn he could, and collect debts that required personal calls. He established drawing accounts in banks in Louisville, Nashville, Memphis, and New Orleans, and for a young man not yet twenty years old, he was given great responsibility, for he handled large sums of money, and used his own judgment about the quality of the cotton he purchased.

Looking over the long list of names of the steamboats on which he traveled, one is impressed with the immensity of the river commerce of those days. The railroads had yet not penetrated into the West and South, and the Ohio and Mississippi were the great highways of the nation. In three years, Morrison traveled on an amazing number of boats; he made frequent trips on the *Ben Franklin,* the *Hibernia,* and the *Lancaster,* which plied between Pittsburgh and Louisville. It is no wonder he loved the ever-changing and enthralling life of a cotton merchant. Here is the list; maybe some of these boats traveled the rivers well into the time of old rivermen yet

A western steamboat of the 1850's
From *Lloyd's Steamboat Directory and Disasters on the Western Waters*
(Cincinnati: James T. Lloyd & Co., 1856)

"Steamboat Wooding at Night," by H. Lewis

From *Das Illustrirte Mississippithal*, von H. Lewis (Düsseldorf: Arnz & Comp. [1855-1857])

living—the *Lancaster, Duc d'Orleans, Little Ben*, the *Pike No. 1*
and *No. 2, Little Pike, West Tennessee, Monongahela*, and *Allegheny Belle, Montgomery, Hermitage of Nashville, Walnut Hill,
Eclipse, Dunlap*, the *West Point*, the *Mayflower, Brunette, Minstrel,
Columbiana, Juniata, Wheeling*, the *Clipper*, and the *West Wind,
American Eagle, Edwin Hickman, Belle of the West*, the mailboats
Ben Franklin and *Telegraph* (the latter to go down in history in
Stephen Foster's "Oh! Susanna": "I jumped aboard de Telegraph,
And trabbelled down de riber"), *Hibernia No. 1* and *2*, the *Diamond* and the *Diadem, El Dorado, Majestic, Lancet, Missouri,
Rodolph*, the *J. M. White* (fastest boat on the western rivers—New
Orleans to St. Louis, in three days and twenty-three hours), the
*Lebanon, Aliquippa, Queen City, Mountaineer, Grace Darling,
Kate Aubrey, Olive Branch, Maria, Diana*, and *Salina*, the *James
Madison, Sam Leay, Pike No. 7* and *Pike No. 8*, the *Mail, Colorado,
John J. Crittenden, Princess, Sam Dale, Santa Fe, Robert Fulton,
Rockaway, Chalmette, Caroline E. Watkins, Countess, Duchess*, the
*Magnolia, Northern Light, Jamestown, Empire, Bulletin, Buckeye,
Fashion, Union, Silas Wright, Cumberland, Loyalhanna, Cinderella, Atlantis, Niagara*, the *Nominee*, and the *Keystone State*.

When the rivers were high, the steamboatmen worked frantically
to make the most of their time, for many a fine boat, loaded with
disgusted passengers, was left high and dry on a sand bar or stuck
in the mud when the water dropped. Morrison always recorded the
stage of the river; it was something every businessman regarded
anxiously. The fast passenger boats might just make their destinations—but Mit's cotton, following on slower freighters, was sometimes held up for weeks by low water.

Morrison's account book shows that he bought a blue coat from
Steve for ten dollars on February 22, and attended a temperance
concert the same evening. The life of the Foster brothers was a
strange mixture of circuses and temperance rallies. Contemporary
newspaper accounts state that the "rich entertainment" at the Temperance Ark in Allegheny, on the evening of Washington's Birthday,
1843, produced in cash $126.48. The board of trustees pronounced
the musical program "masterly," the address of William Elder, Esq.,
"able," and the audience "large and intelligent." But they presented

their thanks to Thomas Town, of Cincinnati, who gave a "short, pertinent address." Some disgruntled listener, who signed himself "Auditor" next day in the *Chronicle,* expressed his dissatisfaction with what had been advertised as a "musical treat." He seemed to think "Belshazzar is King" was rendered out of tune and out of time, and that "Cherry Ripe" was simply awful. Possibly these somewhat-less-than-musical offerings impressed Morrison in the same way, and nullified the good effects of the able and pertinent temperance addresses; at any rate, on his next trip, Mit brought back from New Orleans "One cask of London B. Stout, and One ditto of Scotch Ale" for his employer, Mr. McCormick, and thereafter when he went to New Orleans, he procured for Mr. McCormick something better than Pittsburgh offered in the way of cheer. At New Orleans, the "best Irish whiskey" was selling for $2.50 per gallon in 1843. But, for himself, we are glad to say, Morrison's expenditures were for nothing stronger than books, theaters, dioramas, and circuses.

On his second trip, Mit had the good fortune to travel from Natchez to Memphis on the steamboat *Eclipse* with his favorite, A. A. Addams. He needed something pleasant to remember during the discomfort at the end of the journey caused by low water—six days from Cincinnati to Pittsburgh in the July heat, changing midway from the *West Point* to the *Mayflower* when the former became stuck in the mud. In Morrison's photograph album there is a picture of Mr. Addams which shows a distracted looking person with a thick mop of hair sticking up on end. We hope he assumed a milder aspect when traveling, otherwise he would have scared every child on the boat into convulsions. (His picture may be found opposite page 202.)

In the midst of his business notes, Mit mentions the fact that a "comet appeared about the 1st of March, until the 23rd." Surely this was a favorable omen under which to start his new ventures.

The money of the country still was issued in a complicated way; bookkeepers had a hard time of it in the '40's. Going down the river, and passing from state to state, the value of the firm's money rose and fell according to the state in which it was issued. After stopping at Louisville to transact some business, Morrison proceeded on March 17, by the steamboat *Duc d'Orleans* to Memphis, where he says he

Gave $5000 check for $4950—1 per ct. Kentucky funds
Got $203 Tennessee for 200 Kentucky—1½ per ct.
Got $909 Tennessee for 900 Kentucky—1 per ct.

His time was not all spent in business, however; he made some pleasant acquaintances and was invited to the wedding of Miss Park, whose father, John Park, was one of the McCormick company's best reciprocating customers in Memphis.

Morrison left Memphis on April 13, 1843, on the *Joan of Arc,* with 155 bales of cotton for Mr. McCormick, stopped at Evansville where he did a deal of trading, then on to Louisville. Under date of April 19, 1843, his notebook states:

Left Louisville on SB Little Ben at 11 AM—reached
    Cinti. next day at 6 AM
Brought Frank Johnstons Band from Madison.

At Cincinnati, Morrison stopped long enough to buy fifteen bales of cotton from Captain Church, and proceeded home on the steamboat *Monongahela;* he reached there April 23. Probably this short trip was intended as a trial of Morrison's ability, for nearly all his future trips were to New Orleans, and finally extended to New York and Boston by way of the Gulf of Mexico and the Atlantic. On May 27, Morrison was on his way south again; this time bound for New Orleans.

Frank Johnson's Band was composed of ten colored musicians—a most unusual thing in the 1840's. They were a notable organization and in 1835 performed in London where the reviewer for a London paper mistook them for American Indians; however, he praised them for their excellent performance, stating:

A selection from De Berriott was most singularly, but cleverly executed by three violins and a violoncello, and the "sang froid" with which the performers went from one instrument to another was most remarkable; for having laid down the fiddles, they took up the key'd bugles and other wind instruments. They performed our national anthem in good style and with much enthusiasm, as though it had been their native Yankee Doodle. The leader is an expert musician, and a few good lessons would place him infinitely beyond comparison with many of our pseudo-practitioners.

When Morrison traveled with the band on the *Little Ben,* they were on their way to Pittsburgh and Allegheny, where they had one of the cruelest experiences of their career. On Friday, May 12, 1843, they gave a "Grand Soiree Musicale," at Philo Hall, which was well received by the audience and inspired "rapturous applause." The *pièce de résistance* of the evening was "The Battle of Prague," by Kotzwara, one of those descriptive compositions which contain a great deal of heavy cannonading, trumpet calls and cries of the wounded. To quote their own advertisement,

> By skill unsurpassed and efforts unceasing,
> We aim at the art of constantly pleasing.

The following Tuesday, Frank Johnson and his band filled an engagement at the Temperance Ark in Allegheny where William B. Foster and his friends recently had been holding such fruitful and enthusiastic temperance rallies. The advertisement of this concert read as follows:

> This far-famed and deservedly popular company per-forms at the ARK in Allegheny, this, (TUESDAY) eve-ning, for the benefit of the Ark, which is still in debt for its erection. The lovers of good music should not fail to be there, as a rich treat is offered in the Programme— and the friends of Temperance cannot aid the Cause better than by attending the Concert.—Tickets 25 cents to be had at Messrs. Schwartz, Mitchell's & Sergeants.

On the evening of Tuesday, May 16, 1843, the friends of temper-ance and good music assembled within the Ark, but outside, a gang of white hoodlums soon began to make themselves obnoxious by expressing in the only way possible to their type, their superiority over the inoffensive and talented colored musicians. A contempo-rary account states that the mob was composed in main, not of "potato foreigners," but of "native born subjects and sons of Aristo-crats." The same account continues:

On Tuesday night [May 16, 1843] some of the rowdies of Allegheny were guilty of a most shameful and unprovoked attack upon the mem-bers of FRANK JOHNSON'S Brass Band, for which there can be no excuse, particularly as the attack was made upon persons who are strangers and are therefore entitled to hospitality rather than unprovoked assault.

During the evening, the mob on the outside of the Ark, in which the Band were performing for the benefit of the temperance cause, were with some difficulty kept quiet, and after the performance had closed, WM. B. FOSTER, Esq., the Mayor of Allegheny city, advised the members of the band to remain within the building, and he went out and appealed to the better sense of the mob in a short speech, after which he conducted a portion of the band through the crowd, the remainder intending to await the arrival of a carriage from the city.

At the corner of the Diamond and Federal streets, the mob again collected and Mr. FOSTER made them another speech; after which he conducted another member of the band through the crowd. They went on and shortly after, the carriage with the other members overtook those who were on foot, and at the corner of Federal and Robinson streets, near the bridge, they were assaulted in the most brutal manner with brick-bats and stones, by which a deep gash was made in the forehead of one of those who were on foot, and one of the men in the carriage together with the driver were also struck with the missiles. The mob was mostly composed of boys and young men, but we were not able to say who threw the stones. It is the opinion of many persons in Allegheny city that there are persons at the bottom of the matter who are dissatisfied at the method in which matters in regard to the Ark have been conducted, and they have encouraged this attack. We hope that the city authorities of Allegheny will sift the matter to the bottom for if such outrages are suffered to pass unnoticed it is impossible to say where they will end.

We are happy to learn that no serious damage was done to the instruments of the band.

In the morning the blood on the pavement near the bridge where the assault was committed stood in pools, so profusely had the wounded man bled. He was taken into the toll-house and his head bound up, after which he proceeded to his lodgings.

We hope it may never be our lot to record another similar outrage.

Next Thursday morning, four of the bullies, Logan, Vickars, Stephenson, and Fitzsimmons were brought up before Mayor Foster on the charges of riot and assault and battery, and gave bail in the sum of two hundred dollars. The paper states that the "Mayor's office was crowded to suffocation, and from the interest manifested in the investigation, it would seem that citizens of Allegheny are determined to ferret out the ringleaders in this disgraceful proceeding, and mete out to them speedy and retributive justice." The speedy and retributive justice was not without its farcical aspect. When the rioters came to trial before the next court, the jury returned a verdict of "not guilty and the defendants pay the cost of prosecution"! As the news reporter of the case commented, "this was probably done 'by way of an example,' as the sea captain said when he hung one of his own men to frighten some pirates"!

Fortunately, the innocent and ill-treated colored musicians were not entirely crushed, and in a few days the newspapers advertised a "Grand Quadrille Party" to be held at Bonnafon's Saloon, where "Frank's band, though partially disbanded, the other night, will be in full tune again."

About this time, the Foster boys made the acquaintance of a picturesque character known as Dan Rice, born Daniel McLaren, of Girard, Pennsylvania, who was then beginning his career as a circus clown. We do not know just when or how Morrison met Dan, but it was probably while the latter was working in a Pittsburgh livery stable, of which he was even then part owner, when he was seventeen years old. Dan's father had been a lawyer and friend of Aaron Burr, but the son at no time had any liking for the law and early became a professional jockey. In 1843, he was traveling with the old original John Robinson Circus. Gil Robinson, son of the famous John, said that Dan Rice was the greatest clown that ever lived, and Earl Chapin May, a present-day authority on American circus history, declares Dan Rice was the "clowning sensation of the nineteenth century." There wasn't anything he couldn't do—he could dance, sing, tumble, juggle iron cannon balls, ride and train wild and tame animals, and quote Shakespeare while he rode his beautiful white horse around the ring. His rise to fame was meteoric. From 1850 to 1880, Dan Rice and his horse, Excelsior, were household words from the Atlantic Ocean to the Rio Grande. Dan became owner and manager of a big wagon show and also operated a giant showboat, which actually operated around Northern and Southern gunboats on the western rivers during the Civil War. During the 1850's, the public was enthralled by Dan Rice's bitter war with

Dr. Spaulding, his erstwhile manager, who operated a rival show. Morrison was involved repeatedly in this affair by frequent calls from Dan for quick financial assistance in waging his campaign. At one time both Dr. Spaulding and Dan operated showboats called the *Floating Palace* in competition with each other. Dr. Spaulding won out in this matter, so evidently he had a prior right to the name. In 1858, Dan Rice's circus was at Niblo's Garden Theatre, New York, and two years later, he owned the Walnut Street Theatre, Philadelphia. In the early 1880's the fortunes of Dan Rice declined, and he toured the West with W. C. Coup's Monster Show and gave temperance lectures in small town halls of Kansas. The friendship between Morrison and Dan endured for fifty years, and when Dan retired and was living in Florida, he and Morrison exchanged many affectionate letters.

It has been claimed that in 1844 Dan Rice was drawing a salary of one thousand dollars a week, but from his own letter, we know Dan was earning only $25 a week in 1843, so he either had a remarkable raise in salary in one year's time, or press agents were even then given to cheerful exaggeration. Nevertheless, his progress was exceedingly rapid. One of Morrison's earliest letters from Dan shows that the famous clown's spelling was as original as his "nigero" songs and dances.

Harrisburgh, June the 17, 1843

To—Morerson Foster,
     Pittsburgh, P. A.

My Dear Met,

I take my pen in hand to informe that I am Well An A doing Well, and I hope that this Letter will Finde you in the same Way. I have had a long jorney of it an am most tirde out.

I rote to Gorge a Bout to Weekes Ago and tolde him to direct his Letter to Carlilse P. A. But I did not go thare, An so I rote to the Postmaster At that place to direct the letter to Reading P. A. and you tell Gorge that if he dont heare frome me in A Bout A Weeke he must right to me at Reading, fore I expect to Be thare the Forth of July and you must right to me as Soone as you can.

We are doing A Big Bisiness. I am making money pretty fast, I am geting tow salerreys, A Bout twenty five dollors A Weeke. I am clowning an also my nigero singing an Danceing is drawing good houses.

——turn over——

I think that Weel be Back With the show in the fall. Give my Best respect to All of my friends and Gorge in Perticular an tell them that I am A going it With A perfect rush.

I Remane   Yours

DANIEL

I expect that Gorge is marred.

RICE

While Dan was "agoing it with a perfect rush" in the circus, Morrison was "agoing it" with an equally perfect rush buying cotton in Nashville, Tennessee, on the day that George M. Evans was "marred" to Emily Page; both of George's cronies missed the wedding festivities on June 1, 1843.

Eliza Foster had all her children, except Ann Eliza, with her that summer for a few weeks at least. Dunning still had his headquarters in Allegheny, and in August, Henry came home for a visit. On August 9, Morrison and Henry walked to Lawrenceville, to visit the house where they were born, now the home of Malcolm Leech and his family. Henrietta and her children traveled back and forth frequently between Youngstown and Allegheny, and William and Elizabeth also were with the family in Allegheny in July. On July 13, 1843, the first child of William and Elizabeth, Charlotte Frances, was born in her grandfather's home. William wrote to Ann Eliza to tell her the great news, and said the baby had blue eyes, and hair the color of Dunning's and William's which was red. William also reported that they had had a "pretty full house" all summer. In the latter part of May, Thomas Clayland and his sister Charlotte (Mrs. Samuel Pettigrew), with her youngest child, arrived; and part of the time, they also had James Pettigrew with them, "a stout lad larger and older than Stephen," said William. James soon secured work in a warehouse in Pittsburgh and went elsewhere to board. Although it was the time of year that we expect children to enjoy their vacations, William told his sister that "our little boy"

"Maria Bach Waltz"—one of Stephen Foster's early attempts at composition

Manuscript of Stephen Foster's first song, "Open Thy Lattice, Love"
Probably composed in 1843. Copyrighted December 7, 1844

(Robert Burnett, William's stepson) and little Mary Wick were going to school together in Allegheny.

XVI

SOMETIME during the year 1843, Stephen composed his first published song, "Open Thy Lattice, Love." The music only is his, and the poetry is by George Pope Morris who, in 1843, was one of the editors and publishers of the *New Mirror* of New York. Mr. Morris' partner in this magazine was Nathaniel Parker Willis. "Open Thy Lattice, Love" was published by George Willig, of Philadelphia, and entered for copyright in December, 1844. The title page reads:

OPEN THY LATTICE LOVE

Composed for and dedicated
to

Miss Susan E. Pentland

of Pittsburgh

by

L. C. Foster.

Lines from the New Mirror.

Stephen's own copy of "Open Thy Lattice, Love" preserved in his bound album of songs, now in the Foster Hall Collection, shows the *L* changed to *S* in what appears to be Stephen's hand. When W. C. Peters published a second edition of "Open Thy Lattice, Love" in Cincinnati several years later, Stephen's initials were given correctly.

Morrison Foster's recollection of his brother's first song was that Stephen produced it when he was sixteen years old. But recent discoveries by the staff of Foster Hall show that the verses of "Open Thy Lattice, Love" appeared under the title "Serenade" in the *New Mirror* for October 14, 1843, and Stephen had reached his seventeenth birthday on the preceding Fourth of July. But these verses by George Pope Morris previously had been set to music by Joseph Phillip Knight, under the title "Open Thy Lattice, Love." This edition was published by C. E. Horn, of New York, in 1840; another edition, published by Firth & Hall, appeared in 1843 or 1844. The words in both of these editions are slightly different in one or two places from the "Serenade" in the *New Mirror* of October 14, 1843, and the words used by Stephen in his song are precisely the same as the "Serenade" of that date. Although this indicates that Stephen was seventeen when he composed his first song, the fact remains that Morrison was at home during the year 1842, and part of 1843, and would have been familiar with all the music at which Stephen tried his hand. One edition of "Open Thy Lattice, Love" had been before the public since 1840, and Stephen might have been well acquainted with the song, and composed a new melody for it quite a long time before he found the lines in the *New Mirror,* and when he was still, as his brother Morrison said, sixteen years old.

On the back of Stephen's original manuscript of "Open Thy Lattice, Love" which has been handed down in the Robinson family, another of Stephen's early efforts has been preserved. This is a little waltz, never published, dedicated to "Miss Maria Bach." It has a Swiss or Bavarian-like swing to it, and the theme is quite as good as many that have been used and elaborated by older and more experienced composers. Perhaps Maria Bach was an Allegheny neighbor, or a young school friend at Athens. In spite of his shyness, Stephen readily made friends with anyone who sympathized with him in his devotion to music. Frances Welles, of Athens, Maria Bach, and little "Siss" Pentland did not share the fate of the despised "Emiline" whom he once had robbed for the sake of a tortoise-shell cat.

Susan (or "Siss") Pentland was the daughter of Captain Joseph Pentland, U.S.A. She was born in Council Bluffs, Iowa, and came to Pittsburgh to live when she was about five years old. Her father was a brother of Ephraim Pentland, for many years prothonotary and then judge.

William was not yet settled but was thinking favorably of running for the office of canal commissioner, a move highly approved by his father and friends, who were sure he would be elected. William's property in Allegheny produced some income, as there were two frame houses on the lots back of the newly erected Methodist Protestant Church. While William was in Allegheny in 1843, he started building another house, a three-story brick, under the supervision of E. W. Stephens, from whom he had originally purchased the property. His accounts show that the tenants, including his parents, were all supplied with outside bake ovens, which the landlord was expected to keep in good repair. William also derived a small income from coal mines in the region of Pottsville, Pennsylvania, in which he owned one-quarter interest. These paid him about four hundred dollars a year, so all in all, he did not have to depend on election to any office for his entire income.

Two letters to Morrison from William, written in August and September, 1843, show Brother William in a happy frame of mind; and well he might be, with a new wife, a new baby, and the prospect of election in the fall to a position he knew he could fill.

Canal Packet Boat "John Hancock,"

6 miles above Blairsville, 8/2 oclock P.M.

Wednesday, August 30th, 1843

My dear Brother,

At 9½ oclock this morning the boat reached Warren & I found all my little ones on board, quite well & glad to see me.—Elizabeth delivered me two letters, one of which was particularly acceptable, as it contained one hundred Dollars which I had dispaired of receiving until after my return. The letter informs that probably a hundred or so of Dollars more may be soon remitted & if so, if by mail, open the letter & see the amount & acknowledge the rect. of it.—If by private hands, do likewise. —If the bearer asks a receipt for it, then you give no other receipt; that is, you need not acknowledge the receipt to Messrs. Struthers, Johnston & Brown unless you receive by mail.—Anything you receive, keep sacred & untouched, because I had to borrow from the Exchange Bank, & must be saving all I can get from that source to meet my note in Bank.— Please take out all my letters & papers & pay postage (which I will repay you) and keep them together until my return.

On the next page, I give you an order on Mr. Stephens for Seven Dollars and one on Godfrey [a tenant] for Fifteen Dollars.—out of both, pay Henrietta eight dollars, balance I owe her. Tell Henrietta I would remit the money by mail, but it might be lost, & I know the seven dollars you can get from Stephens the moment you ask.—You may dun Godfrey pretty hard, because he was to have raised me some money on the evening I started & failed to do so.

On the boat I picked up a paper, the New York American, containing an article headed "Opinions of the Revd. Mr. Carey." You know that it was his ordination that Messrs. Smith & Anthon protested against because, as they alleged, he held the doctrines of the Romish Church. How far those two gentlemen are sustained let this article answer.—You will see that he denies any such doctrines. In fact, he sticks exactly to the true doctrines of the "Protestant Episcopal Church" and this fair expose of Mr. Carey's opinions places Messrs. Smith & Anton in rather an awkward position.—They have raised a great smoke & the whole matter will recoil to their disadvantage & cause no injury to the Church. —Preserve this paper as I want to retain the article.

Elizabeth desires me not only to return her thanks to you & all for your kindness in aiding her to get off, but her kindest love; she says she felt sorry when it came to the point of starting, that she had not remained.

With much love to Ma, Henrietta & all, I remain

Your affectionate brother,

Wm. B. Foster, Jr.

Mr. Morrison Foster,
care of Wm. B. Foster, Esqr.
Allegheny City, Pa.
By Capt. Hildebrand.

———

Towanda   Bradford County, Pa.

22   Sept. 1843.

My dear Brother,

Having a little leisure, I have thought it as well employed in giving you some account of my travels & doings as in any other way. After reaching Harrisburgh, I sent Elizabeth & family on to Paradise, where we met again on Sunday before last with our Brother Henry & Elizabeth's brother Giliad.—I reached Mr. Buchanan's on the Thursday previously & both brothers arrived on Sunday morning early.—It was quite a family meeting at the christening of our little Charlotte Frances.— You know the prayer book requires, for a female, two God-mothers &

so Elizabeth & Sister Ann Eliza stood up along with me, and the dear little thing behaved admirably. She was entirely quiet.—She was the sixth baptized by Mr. Buchanan on that day & at the same (afternoon) services.—Ann Eliza looks in much better health than when I saw her last fall. Her youngest child, Edward, is a prodigy for size & a beautiful boy.—Mr. Buchanan looks more robust & healthy than I ever saw him, and all their children look healthy & well.—James is a large boy & can take the horse to water, besides has made good progress with his books.

I am expecting to hear from Elizabeth every day—have not heard from her since we parted at the Railroad, a week ago last Monday.— She & her brother, Robert, the babe, and Katherine went one way & Henry & I the other. I parted with Henry at Lancaster, he taking cars to York, & I pursuing my way on to Harrisburgh.—

Say to Pa that on reaching Wilkes-Barre, I saw his old friend & acquaintance & also my friend, Mr. Hollenback, who was gratified with my success & glad to see me.—He said at once, we claim you as a Northern man.—

I send you by this mail a Lycoming County paper which places me exactly in the right position.—I was kindly met and greeted in Towanda by numerous friends who claim, in addition to my long residence among them, that I shall always make my home in this county. I am under obligations to them, and shall probably do so, for some years at all events.

You may inform any person who inquires for me that I shall visit Allegheny about the middle to 20th of October and tarry two or three weeks.

I almost forgot to mention that Elizabeth charged me to send *Mother*, as she calls her, Three Dollars.—You will please collect of Godfrey and hand MA three dollars.

As I requested in my former letter, I wish if any money comes from Warren or elsewhere for me, that you would be very careful of it, as election expenses, added to my other engagements, will require all I can rake & scrape together.

A few days before I left home, I engaged with Mr. Chislett for a pair of *Marble* mantels similar to those in the house he occupies—just step in and see them, they are nearly like those in the house you are in— the same quality of marble, but I think those in his house are a little shade better than those where you are.—Please see him & have them ready for Derby & Evans as soon as they are needed for the parlors.— Write me how they progress, & I wish you and Pa to give a little attention that the work is well done.—I think Derby will see that it is so done, and any conversation you have in regard to it, you will have with Derby, as he is the boss on the work, while Evans attends in the shop, If I only had half the money now which my Allegheny property will have cost me when the new house is finished, I could buy in this county property much more productive. But at all events, that cannot get worse, and must with the increase of population in the City, increase in value.—

As to the prospects of election, I find everything flattering as far as I can hear.—There has been no attack from any quarter, but from that vile, anti-Masonic sheet, the Telegraph, at Harrisbg. edited by Fenn, and his squibs are mere reiterations of slander published in 1839 at the time I beat them out in the measurements so awfully, on the North Branch Canal.—In this region, where the facts are known, it will be rather a benefit to me than otherwise.

In this County, there was a workingmen's party started last year & they have a press located at Athens.—They claim to be neither Whigs nor Democrats, but are composed of men from both parties. They polled about eight hundred votes last year.—This year, they have organized again, & have a full ticket for County officers. They have a Canal Comm. ticket with my name at the head of it, & I have not yet met with a Whig with whom I was acquainted, but what he said he would vote for me.— This county has about two to three hundred democratic majority on a close contest; but everybody tells me that they shall not be satisfied with less than one thousand majority for me, & convince the people elsewhere that they at least recognize me as a Northern Man.—I cannot say myself, but my friends assure me of a tremendous majority.

I sent you a paper with the full canal Comm. ticket correctly printed —I have sent similar papers to every county, either to a friend or a Democratic editor—I think all will be straight so far as that is concerned.

I want you, my dear brother to write me frequently & let me know how the matters go, both political and domestic, how the new house progresses, &c. &c. Give much love to dear Ma & Pa, Etty, Stephy & the children, and believe me ever your affectionate brother,

William

Don't forget Dunning when he reaches home, & tell him he must write to me also.

Mr. Morrison Foster,
    care of P. McCormick, Esqr.
       Pittsburgh, Pa.

In October, 1843, William was elected a canal commissioner, in company with his friends James Clark and Jesse Miller, on the Democratic ticket. It was the custom to draw lots for the length of term they were to serve, and William drew the three-year term, James Clark two years, and Jesse Miller one year. William's majority in the state was 14,531, and in Allegheny County, 1,128, a cause of great rejoicing to his father, for William triumphed over an ancient adversary, a neighbor who had sniffed at the possibility of William's having a large majority.

Elizabeth and William set up housekeeping in Towanda in a house on the river bank, at Weston and River streets, and William resumed his place there in the little Episcopal Church he had helped to establish. His enthusiasm for the church and its problems and controversies was very sincere, or he would not have been concerned so greatly about the troubles of Reverend Mr. Carey. The Fosters did their share of entertaining, too. In the reminiscences of Mildred Rahm Smith, of Towanda, she states that one of her older relatives told her that "Louise Overton was invited to a party given by Mrs. Barclay Foster. She was, girl fashion, greatly interested in Mrs. Foster's gown, and thought it very low in the neck. The fashion at that time was off the shoulders." (We know, of course, another reason for Louise Overton's womanlike interest in Mrs. Barclay Foster.) Perhaps Elizabeth did startle the ladies of Towanda with some of her advanced styles. She had come just recently from visiting her family in New York; her father owned a summer home at Kingston-on-the-Hudson, a very fashionable suburb of New York, and Elizabeth was up on all the latest "tricks" when she returned to Towanda.

Morrison was traveling regularly on the river now. His next trip in 1843 was to New Orleans in November, and straight back again; he arrived home on the steamboat *Allegheny* on December 10. This winter journey resulted in a $14,400 order placed with Burke, Watt and Company, commission merchants of Carondelet Street, whose chief officer was the notable Glendy Burke. The famous steamboat, later immortalized in song by Stephen, named for Glendy Burke, was not launched, however, until 1851. Her first captain was J. M. White. Morrison's impression was that Mr. Burke's name originally was Glen D. Burke, not Glendy; as he personally knew Glendy Burke, it would seem that he had some authority for this belief.

With Morrison and Dunning gone, the family in Allegheny would have consisted only of Mother, Father, and Stephen, but Henrietta and her children were still with them. Stephen received a great deal of help and encouragement from his sister Henrietta. It is quite unlikely that Stephen had to go to any of the neighbors to find a piano on which to practice, for on May 20, 1844, the family bill from Shackleford's Dry Goods Store lists one "piano cover," along with such items as blinds, gloves, cassimere, vest pattern, etc. Either they had their own instrument, or Henrietta had brought her piano from Youngstown.

Mit's six dollar debt to Stephen was paid in a roundabout way —Mit paid "to Pa" six dollars which Stephen owed his father. This method of settling his debt must have drawn protests from Steve, for the item appears several times thereafter, and finally on January 19, 1844, Mit set down in large writing, "S. C. Foster, To Cash, $6.00. Call this settled!"

On several occasions in the early 1840's, Henry Russell, an English singer, pianist, and composer of popular sentimental songs, came to Pittsburgh. He created a sensation in this country, and great crowds stormed the theaters to hear him. He did not write the words to his songs, but chose verses with a homely appeal which all classes could understand, and set them to melodies that seemed exactly suited. The air to "A Life on the Ocean Wave" has become such a classic that we accept it as part of nearly every musical setting that accompanies a nautical scene on stage or screen, without thinking of the composer. Morrison said, "He was the best ballad singer I ever heard—his concerts were performed by himself alone. He accompanied himself most brilliantly on the piano." "Woodman, Spare That Tree," "The Old Sexton," and "Cheer, Boys, Cheer" are still sung and enjoyed today. His concert must have made a deep impression on Stephen; perhaps Russell was the first good professional pianist he ever had heard, and the fact that Russell was the composer of the songs he sang seems to have inspired Stephen to try great things himself.

On February 7, 1844, Morrison made note in his diary of the death

William B. Foster, Jr.'s home in Towanda; and his children, William B. Foster, III (taken in Dresden) and Charlotte Frances Foster (Mrs. Henry Reed)

The steamboat *J. M. White*. From *Fifty Years on the Mississippi,* by E. W. Gould
(St. Louis: Nixon-Jones Printing Co., 1889)

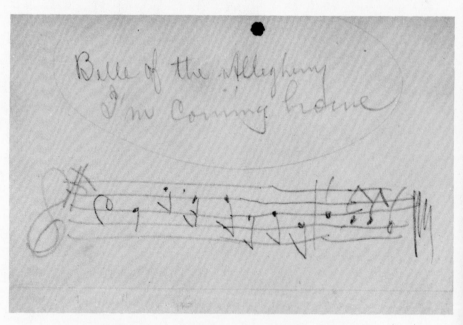

An unpublished fragment from Stephen's notebook

of his young friend Oliver Ormsby Evans; and on March 16, he set
down the fact that his employer's wife, Mrs. Pollard McCormick,
had passed away "at 4 o'clock A.M." He must have been deeply
affected by these events, for both entries are enclosed in a wide black
border made with pencil. On March 19, Morrison started again for
New Orleans on the steamboat *Hibernia*. Nothing of undue interest occurred on this trip, except that a few miles below Memphis,
the boat laid by because of high winds, and "all hands went ashore
and fought chickens the whole day Saturday." In the South, chicken
fighting was the principal indoor and outdoor sport of masters and
slaves, and many boatmen carried their gamecocks with them, fighting them up and down the length of the river. Stephen did not
publish "Don't Bet Your Money on de Shanghai" until March,
1861, which shows that he still carried with him the memory of
some unwieldy old Shanghai rooster up against a "little chicken
in de middle of de ring." While the feverish excitement of the
Negroes who had chickens to fight might have amused Stephen and
Morrison, it is not likely that the cockpits made any other appeal
to these boys, at whose kindly hands no dumb creature ever was
known to suffer abuse.

Morrison left New Orleans on July 10 on the famous *J. M. White*.
She was not large, but was the fastest boat on the rivers. The *J. M.
White* was built at Elizabeth, Pennsylvania, and was equipped with
very powerful engines designed by Billy King. On this trip, Morrison recorded that she made Natchez in twenty-five hours, and St.
Louis in "4 days and 12 hours" which was thirteen hours longer
than her record run. At St. Louis, Morrison changed to the *Lebanon*,
which took him up the Illinois River to Ottawa, Illinois, in two
days; from there to Chicago was a journey of thirty-six hours by
stagecoach. (The canal connecting the Illinois River with Lake
Michigan at Chicago was not completed until April 19, 1848.)
Morrison left Chicago on Saturday, July 20, "bound home by way
of the Lakes"; this was his first voyage on those great waters, and
therefore worthy of special mention in his account book. The trip
was brightened by a real adventure, too, for on the night of Tuesday,
July 23, the steamboat *Nile* was "run into by the Steam Propeller
Oswego, 40 miles below Detroit," and so disabled that she had to be

towed back to the Detroit River by the *Julia Palmer,* and thence
by the *Missouri* to Detroit where, next morning, the passengers
abandoned the unfortunate *Nile,* and took passage on the steamboat
St. Louis bound for Niagara Falls. In Buffalo, Morrison heard Ole
Bull play on July 26; then he started home via Erie by stagecoach,
to land in Pittsburgh on August 2, in the midst of the broiling
presidential campaign of James K. Polk versus Henry Clay.

The race for governor of Pennsylvania was a hot one, too—
Francis R. Shunk, the Democratic, or Locofoco, candidate against
Markle, the Whig, and Dr. Francis J. LeMoyne, pioneer abolitionist
of Washington, Pennsylvania. The Democrats were derisively called
Locofocos after the gas was turned off at one of their meetings by
their landlord who was a Whig, and they had to continue the
convention by the light of locofocos, or friction matches. The Whigs
had called themselves "Coons" ever since the hardy-pioneer, log-
cabin, coonskin-cap campaign of William Henry Harrison.

In 1844, Mr. Shunk was practicing law in Pittsburgh in partnership with James Findlay; he was a great friend of William's. The
state election was held on October 8 while Eliza Foster was on a
visit to Harrisburg. She made a journey "to the Eastward" particularly to see Ann Eliza, who was expecting another child. The baby
(Henrietta) did not arrive until December 23, 1844, and in the
meantime, Eliza Foster went over to Harrisburg and paid her first
visit to William and Elizabeth, who were staying in a popular
boardinghouse near the capitol. As a number of members of the
legislature made their homes there also, it created much pleasant
excitement around election times. Morrison's mother gives him the
election returns first thing.

Haresburg   October the 9th 1844

Dear Morison,

I drop you a few lines to let you know the Boughrough vote, too hundred and thirty for Shunk. William will write you when the County is
returnd.

Heard from Ann Eliza yesterday, she still continues rather better.

I have had a very pleasant time here if the rest of the world would
go on as well without me. I am only affraid they are spoiling me. I received your Father's letter telling me that Etty and the children returnd

all well. I hope that I shall hear that you are all at home together, prop-
ing each other up. Life is short, and I have discovered that the asocia-
tion of kindred friends is the highest enjoyment this uncirtain life can
aford.

William is waiting to endorse my lines. I am my dear son very affectionately,

Your devoted Mother.

Love to your Father and Etty and Stephen. If Duning is at home remember me to him. Little children not forgotten.

By the end of the week, triumphant Democrats were crowing all
over the state, and country editors were issuing extras in the shape
of dodgers, about eight by eight inches in size, jeering at the defeated Whigs. Here is a sample, issued by the Clarion, Pennsylvania,
Democrat on October 10, 1844. It contained the official returns of
the county, and these comments were made:

Has not little Clarion done nobly? She pledged herself for a *thousand*.
She has redeemed her pledge, and she throws 96 *into the bargain*. Yet
a great many Democratic voters were not out. *They will be out on the
1st of November, and the majority for POLK & DALLAS will be increased to TWELVE HUNDRED.* Mark that, and let our neighbors
"Register" it as soon as their nerves are settled. Poor coons! they would
allow us only from 3 to 500—some of them threatened to run us "an
even race."—and now to swallow 1096, after all their splendid meetings
and parades, their costly banners, their imported orators, their cunning
misrepresentations and foul slanders, (to say nothing of Gen. Reed's
documents and *dollars,*) oh, what a bitter pill!

Morrison had to leave for the South on November 1, but his boat,
the *Aliquippa,* did not start until eight o'clock in the evening, and
so he was able to cast his first vote for James K. Polk and George M.
Dallas. The candidate for Vice-President was a brother of their old
family friend, Judge Trevanion B. Dallas, who recently had died.
Judge Dallas' youngest daughter, Mary, to whom Stephen dedicated
two compositions in 1850, was only about ten years old at this time.
Then, there was Catherine, who married James O'Hara Denny,
and Matilda, who married Eugene Borda. Their brother, Alex
Dallas, and the Foster boys were comrades in one of the jovial political clubs that marched in torchlight procession and serenaded

under windows for the Democratic candidates. One of the members was Robert Peebles Nevin, a talented, musical young gentleman, later destined to become the father of a famous Pittsburgh composer, Ethelbert Nevin. During the Polk and Dallas campaign, Bob Nevin composed a rousing song that was a great success, not only in the Pittsburgh district, but all over the country. The following excerpts from "Our Nominee" show that it possessed all the swing and spirit that a marching song required.

> Three jovial Locos sat one day,
> By an alehouse door in the month of May;
> Said one as he seized his cup, said he—
> "Let us drink a health to our Nominee.
>   Our Nominee, ha! ha! ha! our Nominee,
>   We'll drink a health to our Nominee."
> For they loved a joke, these Locos three,
> And they laughed, ha! ha! they laughed ha! ha!
>   they laughed as they quaffed to their Nominee.

*　*　*　*　*

> "The wager's won," the horseman spoke;
> "For the man we'll run is JAMES K. POLK!"
> "And who is he?" said the jovial three.
> "Why, James K. Polk—of Tennessee."
>   "James K. Polk! ha! ha! ha! of Tennessee?—
>   The very man we thought would be!"
> 'Twas a right good joke for these Locos three
> And they laughed, ha! ha! they laughed, ha! ha!
>   they laughed as they quaffed to their Nominee.

Another song was written by W. H. Attree, and was sung to the tune of "Little Pigs Lay," the same tune used for "Tippecanoe and Tyler, Too." The copy of this old dodger preserved by Morrison is tattered and torn, creased and almost in shreds from being passed from hand to hand. The marching clubs serenaded under the windows of all their friends, and the young nieces of the Vice-Presidential candidate, and also their cousin, Sophy Wilkins, must have been highly gratified with the skill with which the author secured a rhyme for Dallas.

I tell you, boys, it is no joke—
The nomination of James K. Polk—
For, with him we'll beat Harry Clay,
    Clay, Clay,
    Gone by is his day!
And with him we'll beat Harry Clay!

When we did choose George M. Dallas,
The Coons they all cried out, "Alas!
That ticket will beat Harry Clay—
    Clay, Clay—
    Gone by is his day!
That ticket will beat Harry Clay!"

The next verse must have been reserved until they got around the corner; for never, under the windows of young ladies of the 1840's, would this have been tolerated!

Clay said to Polk—('twas very wrong)
"Go home, G-d d-n you, where you belong!"
Yes, this was said by Clay—
    Clay—Clay,
    Gone by is his day,
'Twas wrong in Henry Clay!

'Twas indeed wrong in Henry Clay, and very foolish, too. Such language was enough to defeat any candidate, except Andrew Jackson. And we can imagine that as the *Aliquippa* steamed down the Ohio that night, Mit was lulled to sleep by the rhythmical churning of the paddle wheels as they beat out the triumphant refrain:

Clay—Clay—
Gone by is his day—
'Twas wrong in Henry Clay!

XVII

IN the early part of the year 1845, William B. Foster, Sr., lost both of his brothers. Alexander Foster, the attorney, had moved to Harrison County, Ohio, and died there on January 23, 1845. (See Appendix I.) James Barclay Foster, the brother who had joined with William B. Foster in the temperance cause, died in Baldwin Township, Allegheny County, on February 6, at the age of seventy-seven. He was an elder of the Bethel Presbyterian Church, eight miles south of Pittsburgh where the Pittsburgh temperance speakers had held such successful meetings in 1841. James was the only one of his brothers or sisters with whom William B. Foster seems to have been in close contact through the years. James B. Foster was married three times and had twelve children, but was survived by only two of them, John K. Foster and Ann Foster Miller, both children of his first wife, Mary Kincaid.

Morrison returned to Allegheny on December 12, 1844, and was not sent out on the river again until the following May. Therefore, he was in town to witness, on April 10, 1845, the most disastrous conflagration in the history of the city. In later years, Morrison spoke of this fire as a most terrifying thing; flaming brands were carried for miles by the high winds, and all who lived near the river, as the Fosters did, were in great danger. In *Allegheny County: Its Early History and Subsequent Development,* J. W. F. White describes it thus:

The fire commenced about noon of that day on the southeast corner of Ferry Street, in some frame buildings. The weather had been dry for a week or two, water was low, and a scarcity of supply in the water pipes. High winds prevailed at the time, and increased, as is always the case, as the fire spread. In a few minutes the buildings in the square where the fire originated were all aflame, and the sparks flying set fire to other buildings, widening and spreading before the fierce winds, until one-third of the city was enveloped in a tempest of fire. In the appeal of the citizens to the Legislature for relief for the sufferers, prepared by Messrs. Cornelius Darragh and Wilson McCandless, it is said, "The burnt district comprised most of the large business houses and many of the most valuable factories—The loss cannot fall short of six or eight million dollars. The bridge over the Monongahela river was entirely consumed. The magnificent hotel, erected at a vast expense [in 1841], known as the Monongahela House, is a ruin; cotton factories, iron works, hotels, glassworks, and several churches are prostrated in the general desolation. It is estimated that not less than eleven hundred houses were destroyed, the greater number of which were buildings of a large and superior kind."

The Legislature passed an Act appropriating $50,000 for the relief of the sufferers, authorizing the return of certain taxes, and exemption for two years to persons who had suffered in the burnt districts.

From adjoining counties relief also came, in clothing, provisions and money for the sufferers. The donations in money amounted to $198,-873.40. The number of applicants for relief was 1,011. Four insurance companies were swamped by their heavy losses, and could pay only a small percentage.

Eleven years later, we learn from "The Great Baby Show," a campaign song written by Stephen (with two verses by Morrison), that one of the contributors to the relief fund was Senator James Buchanan, who gave $500 to the sufferers. Said Mit reproachfully, in one of his verses, on the ingratitude of the Republicans of 1856:

> In the year '45, when the fire laid us waste,
> Old Buck gave us five hundred dollars in haste.
> They then took his money, and lauded his name,
> But he's now "Ten Cent Jimmy," their banners proclaim.

Recalling the Pittsburgh fire in later years, William Wellington Bradshaw, who lived with his widowed mother and two brothers, Robert and George, on Robinson Street between Federal Street and the East Common, and attended the Rev. Joseph Stockton's academy with Morrison and Stephen, said that Steve and Mit Foster and himself were among the band of Allegheny boys and men who turned out with all the volunteer fire companies to help fight the flames. Mr. McCormick's great brick cotton warehouse stood on Water Street, near the Monongahela House, directly in the path of the fire. Morrison succeeded in saving the books, but the warehouse with all its contents, which included thousands of pounds of cotton lately received from Glendy Burke and other Southern dealers, went up in smoke. Dr. Andrew N. McDowell, the Foster's family physician, and father of the girl Stephen afterwards married, also lost three brick warehouses located in the same doomed section of the city.

But, such was the indomitable spirit of the Pittsburgh people, that within three months the newspapers reported that almost the entire business district had been rebuilt, and the "new Pittsburgh arose from the ashes of the old." Mr. McCormick was amongst those who immediately commenced erecting new warehouses. His factory, on the Allegheny side of the river, had not been harmed by the fire.

After the publication of "Open Thy Lattice, Love," Stephen tried his hand at an entirely different style of composition—plantation melodies. He had lately been given a small position in Mr. McCormick's new Hope Warehouse, checking cotton bales as they were rolled up the wharf directly from the steamboats into the building. Here Stephen watched with sympathy and interest the cheerful colored roustabouts singing as they "worked all night in the wind and storm, and worked all day in the rain." His first negro melodies were not written for professional minstrels, but for his own circle of young friends.

Their club, the Knights of the S. T. (Knights of the Square Table), was not officially organized until 1847, but the boys congregated in the evenings to sing and make merry at the homes of the different members. With the exception of George Evans, none of the Knights was married, but there was a great deal of pairing off with the girls of their acquaintance. Stephen, so far as we know, had no special attachment at this time—he enjoyed them all, especially if they could sing or play. His favorites seem to have been Siss Pentland and Mary Keller. Morrison was equally impartial though he wrote oftenest to his cousin, Mary Evans. The Keller girls, Rachel, Mary and Margaret, lived on Penn Street when Stephen first knew them, and their home was a favorite gathering place for the glee club. We do not know whether or not there was any romance between Mary and Stephen, but he had a strong affection for her, or he could not have written the touchingly beautiful verses of "Where Is Thy Spirit, Mary?" a song he composed in her memory and presented to Rachel Keller after Mary's death in December, 1846. "Where Is Thy Spirit, Mary?" was not published until 1895, long after Stephen's death. Stephen's second published song, "There's a Good Time Coming," with verses by Charles Mackay, was dedicated to Mary Keller; it was entered for copyright on October 9, 1846, so Stephen was not denied the happiness of bringing Mary a copy of the song he had dedicated to her.

Morrison Foster's account of the writing of Stephen's early minstrel songs is as follows:

Susan Pentland and Rachel Keller Woods (1858), Stephen's friends

The five "nice young men."

First, there's Charley the elder, the sunday-school teacher,
    Who laughs with a groan,
    In an unearthly tone,
    Without moving a bone
    Or a feature!

Then Charley the younger, the Illinois screecher,
    Who never gets mad,
    But always seems glad
    While others are sad;
Though his face is so long that it would'nt look bad
    On a methodist preacher.

There's Andy, who used to be great on a spree,
Whose duels (as he calls them) all fit to a T:
    But people do tell us
    He's got just as jealous
    Of Latimer as he can be.
    They say that he wishes
    The sharks and the fishes
Would catch him and eat him when he gets out to sea.

And Bob, that smokes seventeen tobies a day, —
He's liberal, however, and gives some away.
    Bob's been to college
    Picking up knowledge
But now he's got home and I hope he will stay.

We will wind up with Harvey, the bluffer, the gay.
He can play on the fiddle (or thinks he can play)
    Harvey's mind
    Is inclined
    To all that's refined,
    With a count'nance so bright
    That it rivals the light
Of the sun that now cheers us in this sweet month of May.

       — Pittsburgh —
          — May 6, 1845 —

By Stephen C. Foster —

Charles P. Shiras
Charles Robin
Andrew L. Robinson
Robt P McDowell
J. Harry Davis

In 1845, a club of young men, friends of his, met twice a week at our house to practice songs in harmony under his leadership. They were J. Cust Blair, Andrew L. Robinson, J. Harvey Davis, Robert P. McDowell and myself. At that time, negro melodies were very popular. After we had sung over and over again all the songs then in favor, he proposed that he would try and make some for us himself. His first effort was called "The Louisiana Belle." A week after this, he produced the famous song of "Old Uncle Ned." "Uncle Ned" immediately became known and popular everywhere. Both the words and melody are remarkable. At the time he wrote "His fingers were long like de cane in de brake," he had never seen a canebrake, nor even been below the mouth of the Ohio river, but the appropriateness of the simile instantly strikes everyone who has traveled down the Mississippi.

The following verses describing several members of the crowd show that Steve had a happy sense of humor, and "Five Nice Young Men" gives us a glimpse of the characteristics of each of these jolly fellows.

First, there's Charley the elder, the Sunday-School teacher,
   Who laughs with a groan,
   In an unearthly tone,
   Without moving a bone
   Or a feature.   [Charles P. Shiras]

Then Charley the younger, the Illinois *screecher,*
   Who never gets mad,
   But always seems glad
   While others are sad;
Though his face is so long that it wouldn't look bad
   On a methodist preacher. [Charles Rahm]

There's Andy, who used to be great on a spree,
Whose *duds* (as he calls them) all fit to a T.
   But people do tell us
   He's got just as jealous
   Of Latimer as he can be.
   They say that he wishes
   The sharks and the *fishes*
Would catch him and eat him when he gets out to sea.
      [Andrew L. Robinson]

And Bob, that smokes seventeen tobies a day,—
He's liberal, however, and gives some away.
Bob's been to college
Picking up knowledge
But now he's got home and I hope he will stay.

[Robt. P. McDowell]

We will wind up with Harvey, the *bluffer*, the gay;
He can play on the fiddle, (or thinks he can play)
Harvey's mind
Is inclined
To all that's refined,
With a count'nance so bright
That it rivals the light
Of the sun that now cheers us in this sweet month of May.

[J. Harvey Davis]

Pittsburgh May 6, 1845.

Charles P. Shiras lived with his mother on Hemlock Street a few blocks from the Fosters. Charles had a great deal of literary talent and contributed poetry and prose to various magazines. At one time, he edited his own weekly journal called the *Albatross,* which was strongly antislavery. Morrison said that Shiras possessed undoubted genius, but his poetry was too heavy and sombre for Stephen's style of music. "Annie, My Own Love" was the only published song written by Shiras to which Stephen set the music; but Shiras wrote the verses and Henry Kleber the music of a composition published in 1850, "My Mother, I Obey," which Godey's magazine described as a "comical and very pretty song."

Charlie Rahm, the Illinois screecher, who lived across the Common, was a good singer; the Rahms's friendship with the Foster family has endured unto the third generation.

Andy Robinson married Siss Pentland in 1849. He belonged to the aristocratic and wealthy Robinson clan, termed "that formidable dynasty" by Eliza Foster; but there were no airs about Andy.

Stephen himself best describes Bob McDowell, and we see a cheerful, smoking college student. Stephen must have been fond of Bob, for he says, "Now he's got home, and I hope he will stay." Bob did stay until he heard the news of the assault upon the Union; then

Captain Robert P. McDowell, with forty men under his command, marched across the mountains from Harrisburg to Washington and reported, ready for duty, to Secretary Stanton, only six days after the firing upon Fort Sumter.

J. Harvey Davis furnished the violin part for the mixed ensemble of flute, guitar, piano, violin, and voices, and probably flatted cheerfully on occasion, a habit most distressing to the precise Stephen.

The club survived for many years. They arranged their own duets and quartettes, and this practice was of the greatest value to Stephen. Up until 1845, Stephen had not tried his hand at any minstrel songs, so far as we know. He was of such a dreamy and romantic nature that songs of a sentimental character appealed to him greatly. It is possible that it was about this time that Stephen composed an air for Eliza S. Carey's verses, "Sadly to Mine Heart Appealing"; it was not published, however, until 1858. Maybe Stephen submitted the song to George Willig and it was not accepted, for it is not nearly so good as "Open Thy Lattice, Love." Robert P. Nevin said that it was composed about the same time as "The Tioga Waltz."* It is likely that "Sadly to Mine Heart Appealing" was an early composition, for, with its little triplets at the beginning of each measure, it seems to be written for the flute, and Stephen at first expressed his musical ideas through the medium of the flute or clarinet.

Sister Ann Eliza had great confidence in Stephen's ability to compose religious music, and desired that he write some pieces for use in her husband's little church. Published music was too expensive for their small congregation; it was beyond Stephen's small resources also. Believing that he could not compose satisfactory organ music, he borrowed some from his friend, Mr. Mellor, which he copied and sent to Ann Eliza.

On August 31, 1845, the Reverend Mr. Buchanan resigned the pastorate of St. John's Pequea Church and devoted all his time to the new church, All Saints, at Paradise, and the little stone Christ Church at Leacock. When the Buchanan family first removed to Paradise, they made their home at the Spread Eagle Hotel, but soon moved to a large house in Paradise purchased for his brother Edward

*Robert P. Nevin, "Stephen C. Foster and Negro Minstrelsy," *The Atlantic Monthly*, November, 1867.

by Senator James Buchanan. In the following letter to Ann Eliza, Stephen mentions Henry's plan to come to Pittsburgh and allow Stephen to go to Washington and work in Henry's place for a while; there is nothing to indicate that the exchange of positions ever took place, however. At this time, Stephen was employed at Mr. McCormick's warehouse.

Pittsburgh   Sep. 15, 1845

My Dear Sister,

In one of your letters you expressed a desire that I should compose for you some organ music, but as I have no knowledge of that instrument I have thought it advisable not to expose my ignorance. I have, however, seen Mr. Mellor who has promised to lend me some music that he thinks will suit, which I will copy and send to you.

Henry has written home saying that he would like to change places with some person until he may have time to come to Pitt. and rest himself, and as it would be a very pleasant change I have thought of taking his place in Washington. If I do so I will, no doubt, have an oppertunity of visiting you. He seems to think that there is no chance of advancement in the office which he now holds and if he can get a good situation here he will let me make a perminent stay at Washn.

We have received one letter from Dunning since he left us—I suppose he visited Paradise on his way east—he had not, when he wrote, visited Philadelphia, where (as you must know) his true-love is staying.

I am writing amidst the bustle of the Hope ware-house—you must therefore forgive my haste.

We are all well excepting little Tom, who has had quite a fever but in [is] now getting better.

Love to all—,   Your affectionate brother

Stephen.

Little Tom, Henrietta's youngest child, was then between four and five years old. Grandma and Grandpa generally had one or more grandchildren staying with them through the summer months. And Dunning's truelove was undoubtedly Anne Robinson, the only girl for whom we know Dunning cared at this time.

Pollard C. McCormick, Morrison's employer, and also Stephen's, was married on May 14, 1845, to his second wife, Sarah K. Shoenberger. Morrison attended this wedding at eight o'clock in the evening at the Shoenberger residence in Lawrenceville, and next day left for a long journey, the longest, so far, of his career. This time we may be sure that Eliza Foster watched his departure with an anxious heart, for it was the first time any of her flock had set out for the open sea. Morrison was filled with pleasurable excitement, and chafed impatiently when the *Diadem* was delayed at Louisville for sixteen hours, and then ran aground at French Island where she crowned the mud with her sparkling beauty for four, long, blistering days. Consequently, they did not reach New Orleans until the fifth of June. Mit accomplished a deal of business there, and, on the thirteenth, set sail for New York on the ship *Louisa,* which, in company with the schooner *Fanny,* was towed to the mouth of the Mississippi by the *Claiborne.* (Morrison never failed to mention the names of the boats he traveled on—even ferry boats—they seemed to have a never-ending charm for him.) This was his first experience on a sailing vessel—the passenger boats on the Great Lakes were already propelled by steam. The *Louisa* made the Tortugas on June 23, and anchored at quarantine outside of New York on July 2, "nineteen days from New Orleans." Next day, he went up to New York and registered in grand style at the Astor House. But he saw little of the city or of the fashionable hotel he had chosen, for he spent the Fourth of July with Lavinia Smith and her father at their home in Kingston. Then he did some strenuous visiting within the next two weeks. To sister Ann Eliza's at Paradise on July 9, then to Harrisburg, on Saturday, July 12, where he stayed four days with Brother William, then to Baltimore and Washington for a glimpse of Henry.

Morrison left Washington on July 19 and proceeded home by way of Uniontown and Fayette Springs where he took the steamboat *Louis McLane* on the Monongahela and steamed into Pittsburgh at five in the evening of July 21. What a lot of talk there must have been when the traveler returned! A journey like that was not often made by a young man in moderate circumstances. And considering the large amount of ground and water that he covered, and the time deducted for visiting and business, the old-time means of transportation made a very respectable showing.

A tragic accident occurred that summer, which, coming so soon after the great fire, must have made Henrietta and her mother feel as though Judgment Day were near at hand. The Foster home in Allegheny was next door to the Methodist Protestant Church, which stands on the corner of Ohio Street and the East Common, now Union Avenue. In fact, William built his larger house on ground he bought from the church. Many an evening, Eliza Foster slipped in to join her Methodist friends at prayer meeting. The Reverend Charles Avery, pastor of the church, was widely known and respected for his benevolence and philanthropy.

On the evening of the thirteenth of August, 1845, several workmen had been called in to repair a patent gas apparatus that had been in successful operation for over a year in the basement of the church. This was before the formation of the present gas company. Some members of the congregation volunteered to help the workmen raise the gasometer out of the pit where it was installed. The leak was soon repaired, and the workers were ready to go home when someone went back into the building for a walking cane he had forgotten. It was growing dusk, and believing that all the gas was out of the building, he lighted a candle. The resulting explosion demolished the whole inside of the church. Mr. Herron, the sexton, and Mr. Eyester and Mr. Russell were horribly burned and died that same evening. The entire neighborhood rushed to the assistance of the victims, several of whom had to be dug out from under the beams and plaster that had fallen upon them. The injured men were carried into neighboring houses, and the Fosters' home being the nearest to the church, undoubtedly it was Eliza Foster's sad duty to receive these sufferers and give them what relief she could until carriages arrived to take them to their homes. Mr. Karns and Mr. Williams, members of the church, who were severely burned, eventually recovered, but Charles Brown, after lingering ten days, finally succumbed to his injuries, bringing the death toll to four.

All Merry
All Happy and Bright
1846-1854

LATE in 1845 or early in '46, Dunning went into partnership with Archibald Irwin, Jr., in a steamboat agency and commission business in Cincinnati. They established an office at No. 4 Cassilly's Row, which was located on East Front Street, overlooking the steamboat wharves on the Ohio River. Dunning made himself at home at the Broadway Hotel, at the corner of Broadway and Second Street. Morrison gave the new firm of Irwin & Foster as much of Mr. McCormick's cotton business as he could —but instructed Dunning on January 29, 1846, not to ship any cotton to the Hope factory at more than fifty cents a bale for freight. It was the business of the steamboat agents to secure the best rates possible for their customers, and pick out the fastest and cheapest boats. Eliza Foster went to Cincinnati to visit her son Dunning in February, leaving Stephen and Morrison at home; but Henrietta was there with the children, and there was no lack of entertainment and music when she was at home. Wm. B. Foster, Sr., made a trip to Washington in January, but before he left, he had been very active in behalf of his son William, for next November would come again the election for canal commissioner and William B. Foster was taking no chances in the primaries with William's opponents, the "Kickapoos." The senior Foster was now sixty-six years old, and brought all his old-time fire and zeal to any business he undertook, especially if it had to do with politics. When his children wanted anything done right, they called on Pa. He spent no time fooling around, but planned his campaign carefully and issued his commands emphatically, as the following instructions to Morrison indicate. The "Dutch," properly called Germans, whom he mentions, were and still are thickly settled in Allegheny City, east of the parks.

Jany 21, 1846

Dear Morrison,

I was in hopes that you would be at home, and have put off starting to the last day that I can.—

I go to Washington for Mr. George Cochran of this City, to give testimony before the committee on Claims in a case he had submitted them of considerable amount, and can't tell when I will return.

I wish you to give the enclosed memorandum to George Robinson; and give all your attention to getting our friends to turn out to the meetings on the 7th of February, in order to secure delegates who will be favourable to the nomination of William for Canal Commissioner.— J. K. Moorehead will be down with all his forces at the 4th Ward in Allegheny, to appoint delegates who will oppose William's nomination.

You must stir up our friends to go early; Wm. Davidson and Reuter will do for our delegates; but I wish you and George to call on Reuter, and consult with him. He can bring out more Dutch than any other man; if he promises, he will play true.

You will see the names in my letter to George who must be reminded to attend early; you can wake up all hands about the factory, and see Ed Cassilly, and John Solens and Sam Henderson if he is about. Ed can take an old cock down who lives in the Brick house at the locks, etc. etc.

You must stir up your young friends to attend in this Ward.—Mr. Gordon in Allegheny will give you all his help. See old Saml. Woods, and put him up to trap. Don't let the Kickapoos out-General you and George!

Mr. Cochran pays my board and travel.

Your affectionate father,

W. B. Foster.

About this time, the North Branch Canal Company had been revived, and the officers asked William to resign his position as canal commissioner and become chief engineer again and help push their work to completion. But William recognized before his father did that the transportation system of the future was not more canals, but more railroads, and his interest in his re-election even to the office of canal commissioner was not wholehearted. Already he had been offered a position by the newly organized Pennsylvania Railroad Company, as an associate engineer on the new line to be cut through the mountains from Harrisburg to Pittsburgh.

After receiving the nomination for canal commissioner, in which (according to Mr. Fry, a partisan of William's, from Norristown, Pennsylvania) "all opposition was foiled," William, nevertheless, was defeated at the election in November. It must have been a great disappointment to his father, and to such loyal followers as, for example, Charles Kugler of Lower Merion, Montgomery County, who had written on February 7, 1846, to Thomas J. Gross, a member of the House of Representatives:

I will endeavor to attend the County meeting, and use my feeble exertions to defeat the machinations of the opponents of Mr. Foster and the Governor. It must be apparent to every reflecting mind that experience is highly essential, to the judicious management of any important measures, and when the evidence is clear that we have men who unite with experience honesty of purpose, why should we displace them to give place to some selfish aspirant?

William B. Wilson, of the Pennsylvania Railroad Company, in a sketch of William's life which appeared in the *Pennsylvania Railroad Men's News* for August, 1897, states:

That year, 1846, was not a good one for a Democratic nominee in Pennsylvania, and the Whigs elected their State ticket and nearly every state Senator and Congressman. [But the Democrats re-elected Governor Shunk.] He [William] had been nominated for a re-election at the State election in October, 1846, but was defeated by the Whig candidate, James M. Power, a very reputable man. Mr. James Clark, who had been so long and favorably connected with the public works, said on that occasion, "I would rather, if I owned the public works, pay William B. Foster, Jr. thirty thousand dollars a year, than lose his services as Canal Commissioner. The loss of him can never be repaired."

The Pennsylvania did not offer William thirty thousand a year, nor anything near it, but it offered him an opportunity to engage in an undertaking that fired him with enthusiasm. His term with the board of canal commissioners expired on January 12, 1847, and he entered immediately on his new duties, under J. Edgar Thomson, the chief engineer. With William, as an associate engineer, was Edward Miller, and the principal assistant engineers were James E. Day, Charles Cramer, Samuel K. Kneass, and Stother Hage. His old friend, Jesse Miller, was now Secretary of the Commonwealth.

Early in the year 1846, Morrison had a new responsibility added to his list. He was appointed guardian of Henrietta's children, and it was his duty to look after their property in Youngstown, securing tenants, collecting rents, etc. Henrietta had leased their house in Youngstown while she and the children were living in Allegheny, and it was often a painful process to extract from the tenant the twenty dollars a month due the children. But Morrison persevered, writing numerous sharp letters and visiting Youngstown several times a year to fulfill his obligations as guardian. The "old gentleman," Thomas Wick's father, had recently died leaving a ninety-five acre farm (the one to which Thomas had occasionally taken his family between the closing out of one business venture and the opening of another) to little Mary, Lidie, and Tommy. In May, 1846, as Morrison was unable to secure any other tenant, William B. Foster himself rented the farm, and put it all out on shares. Although he made barely enough to cover the rent that he paid to his grandchildren, it was a good investment, for it took him to Youngstown frequently, and there he became interested in buying some property and bought one house in partnership with Morrison and William. This was all sold later to good advantage when he was stricken with paralysis and unable to attend to any business.

On May 13, 1846, war with Mexico was declared, and sometime during the year, Morrison joined up with the Third Regiment as a corporal, and was soon accorded the rank of sergeant in Company 7, under Captain Thorn. Dunning, in Cincinnati, began to get the war fever. A large encampment of soldiers was stationed outside the city, and the popular pastime of the day was to walk out to see them drill. He was feeling exceedingly downhearted about his prospects of winning the favor of Annie Robinson, who had captured his heart on his last visit to Pittsburgh. Annie was away at boarding school, and poor Dunning was discouraged at what he felt was the fickle nature of boarding-school misses in general. Morrison passed through Cincinnati in June, and told Dunning then that he hoped to secure a better situation for Stephen with Mr. McCormick, regarding which, Dunning confided in a letter to Ann Eliza, dated June 26, 1846, "I hope he may succeed, if we get Stephen comfortably situated it will be a great object gained."

In 1846, we first begin to hear of some other genial spirits—Dick Cowan, Cust and Tom Blair, Bill Denny, Dan Beltzhoover, John Duncan, and Bob McKnight; and the girls they loved and serenaded "when hopes were buoyant, hearts were young"—Mary and Lizzie Irwin, Sophy Denny, Louisa Bell, Mary Anderson, Julia Murray, Annie Robinson, the Dallas girls, the Wilkins', the McDowells, the Ogdens, and the Shoenbergers. Invitations, in tiny envelopes sealed with a wafer and a silk ribbon, came to "Mr. Mit Foster," or "The Messrs. Foster," written in dainty feminine script, or elegantly engraved with "Gen'l and Mrs. Robinson," or announcing that "Mr. and Mrs. Wm. Wilkins" were "At Home." All the parties were not formal, however. J. Cust Blair, with a grand flourish to his signature, sends the following invitation addressed to

MORRISON FOSTER, ESQR.

4th Corporal Company 3 of the 3C Regt. Penna. Militia,
& Boss No. 2 of the Hope Cotton Mill—

Dear Mit,

I am requested by the higher powers to request the pleasure of your agreeable company out at our house in the country tomorrow evening. Come early before dark.

Yours with all the trimmings,
J. Cust Blair.

Sept. 17, 1846

The wittiest and most irresponsible member of this goodly company was Richard Cowan. According to his own account, he spent all his time imbibing spirituous liquors, and heckling his Presbyterian friends against whom he held a most unreasonable grudge. His letters to Mit are of a decidedly ribald nature, and certainly would not have been approved by Eliza Foster if she ever read them, which I doubt. Richard Cowan was sent to the Legislature of Pennsylvania in 1852—probably on account of his legal ability, certainly not for his godliness. It was said that he had a way with women, and if Eliza Foster secretly disapproved of the young man, she probably forgave him a great deal on account of his infectious genialty. Gentle little Stephen had a formidable rival when Dick Cowan started to call on Jane McDowell, but somehow or other Stephen won.

After the Pittsburgh fire, Dick advertised in the Pittsburgh papers: "Richard Cowan, Atty. at Law, will devote himself particularly to collections and all claims entrusted to him will meet with the most prompt attention." Amongst a long list of references appended appears the name of "Messrs. Irwin & Foster, Cincinnati."

The following letter written from Bedford Springs, on July 11, 1850, is a mild sample of Richard Cowan's style. "Sir George Armstrong" was the fraternal name applied to Morrison by the Knights of the S. T.

I have been sojourning here but for a short time, as thou knowest, O Armstrong, and as yet have spent my time offering up prayers at the shrine of St. Crockford, and also in making gifts of gold pieces for masses for my soul after death, and for thy soul, O brother Armstrong. I have also drunk of the water of the Holy Well and am strong and sound.—The barbarian Hutchison is now doing penance for his manifold sins, and swalloweth copious libations of holy water and brandy.— There are also some respectable but ungodly men here from divers parts of the earth, and also some seemly and devout women, which maketh me right glad.

While at my devotions yestereve, I did feel a sudden qualm—a sinking of heart, and my soul was disquieted within me. Methought at first that it had pleased some unruly devil to enter my body and I was sore affraid —but while I was pondering upon these things, I heard footsteps of men approaching my cave, and Lo, there stood before me two Heathen Priests with spectacles upon nose and with white cloths about their neck, and clad in black raiment. Their noses were red as though with drink— their eyes were turned upwards and their hat brims were broad. I crossed myself and uttered a pious ejaculation; when they incontinently disappeared from my sight; whither they went, no man knoweth. They are of the order called Presbyterians! They do infest this Holy Place each year—and by Saint Dunstan, do give us of St. Crockford's great trouble, though God wot, they dare not venture within our cloisters, no, truly!

The Astrologer waxed drunk last night while quaffing wine with Friar Watson—commonly called Friar Tuck—when retiring to his dormitory, which he did in an unseemly and boisterous manner— he stopped at the door of my cell and kicked in one panel, for which I will mulct him in sundry drinks. The barbarian Hutchison was drunk and noisy, as also was Duncan of Whitehall!

Go to Lockwood and tell him I did not receive my Home Journal, and tell Scully if you see him, to enquire about those shoes at the express office, and send them on by the first person who may come.

On Sunday night last, we reached Stantler's, and here John Duncan was discovered by me, sitting alone and reading a *bible*—and wearing the self same look that Captain Cuttle did when occupied in a similar manner.—

Give my love to any one who enquires for me—excepting Jno. Lee!

John Lee was his tailor!

II

WHILE Stephen was working at home on his music and Morrison and Dunning were busy with steamboats and cotton, Henry was still plugging away at his desk in the Treasury Department, now apparently well satisfied with Washington. He was glad to see his father when the latter arrived in February, for Henry loved his home folks, as his letters reveal. He fully justified his father's estimate of his character—"So good and so virtuous a man! So obedient a child, and such a kind and loving brother!" Soon after he reached Washington, Wm. B. Foster addressed a few lines to Morrison.

Washington Febry 5th, 1846

My Dear Morrison,

Your letter of the 30th ult. came limping along to Fuller's Hotel last night about ten o'clock, and after the Western mail had closed on my letter to your mother. I don't know where it has been fooling around so long. It was not in this City until last night, as I enquired at the

Post Office yesterday.—However, I was delighted to get it even so late.

I am a good deal surprised at the amount of Reinhart's [the grocer's] bill, and cannot account for it being so high; I supposed it would amount to about 50 dollars, but it is a fact that we cannot get along for less, in our mode of living.

Tom Flood told me before I left home that Wm. was charged with being unfriendly to the right of way, and I told William of it when I saw him; he said it was false, and had been put in circulation by his enemies.—He promised to write to Megraw or some other of his friends at Pittsbg. and put it all straight; I have written him today & told him what you say & urged the necessity of attending to it.—

I hope to go before the Committee here tomorrow; if I do, I shall return in a day or two to Harrisburgh to attend to claims before the Legislature of Thomas Flood & Thos. Makewen—if you should see either of them, you may tell them so.—From Harrisburgh I must take a short ride to see Sissy Anny and will hurry home to help out in our domestic treasury department.

Don't forget to write me the result of the delegate-election on Wednesday next. Address me at Harrisburgh.

I visited the President a few evenings ago in company with Henry D. Foster [a cousin from Greensburg]; but I did not attend his levee last night.—He is mighty polite entirely.

Keep good heart; all I trust will yet go well with us. I can bear any disappointment while my good children stick by me & reverence their dotingly fond mother.

With much love to all, I remain,

Ever your affectionate father,

Wm. B. Foster.

Henry sends his love to all.

William B. Foster did not remain in Washington until his own claim was presented to Congress by General John H. Eaton on February 26; but he returned there in April to learn that his friend's "kind interference" had been in vain. In the meantime, Henry had been trying to get an appointment for Stephen to West Point. The latter was now almost twenty years old, restless and dissatisfied at the warehouse. The other boys were all earning a living and helping with the "home treasury department." Although Stephen kept himself occupied with his music, he did not yet recognize it as a way to earn his living. He always had been favorably inclined to either the Army or the Navy—probably because all he knew about either he had gained from romantic literature. Stephen's health, as Henry admitted, undoubtedly never would have withstood the rigorous training at West Point. Although Henry was grieved at what he felt was governmental injustice, "young McK." might honestly have been appointed because he was more fitted for a soldier's life than Stephen was.

Washington City, March 16th, 1846

Dear Brother, [Morrison]

I received your acceptable letter of the 12th inst, & it seems that the appointment to West Point resulted (I can scarcely believe it possible that there is so little justice in our Government) in that of young McK. & had I not been under the impression that you would be informed of that fact by some of his friends, I should have informed you some time since. However, I make no complaints, hoping that it may result for the best, as I doubt very much whether Steve's health would have permitted him to remain at the Point had he received the appointment.

William received quite a flattering vote from the delegation, notwithstanding Sam Black thought it necessary to have a *Western Man.*

You may imagine my surprise yesterday morning while returning from church, I saw Lieutenant Warner a little in advance of me in company with, as I supposed a strange lady & was endeavoring to make out who she was, when upon overtaking them I found it to be no less a person than Miss Ogden & a little in advance of her, I perceived Miss Stevenson in company with Lucy Jesup. I walked down to the General's door with Warner & Co. where they all got into a carriage and drove off to Coleman's Hotel, where they put up. Miss Jesup was quite polite entirely.

I had a delightful ride on horseback on Saturday afternoon last in company with Miss Kuhn who lives with Genl. Tomson. I had a pleasant combination rarely met with, delightful weather, a fine horse & agreeable companion. We rode first to the Navy Yard, next to Georgetown & then up to Col. Bamford's. Mrs. B. requested me to ask Pa to do her the favor of inquiring of Mr. Thos. Bakewell whether he has the salt cellar she left with him two years since in the form of a silver frame to have filled with glass, if so, to send her it the first opportunity. The price of filling was to be $2.00, which she will pay to me & I to Pa.

I hope my dear Mother was pleased with the peaches I sent her by Pa.

Tell Steve not to be discouraged & to try to get at some employment as soon as possible.

Calhoun spoke today in the Senate—was for giving the notice & compromise.

With much love to Ma, Etty, Steve, Pa & the children, in hopes that God may permit us all to meet again before another year passes over,

I remain
Your affect. Brother Henry.

P.S. How was Dunning's health when you heard last?   In haste

On October 9, 1846, Stephen's next song, "There's a Good Time Coming," was copyrighted by Peters & Field, Cincinnati. William C. Peters of this firm, formerly a music teacher in the Foster home, had opened a branch store in Cincinnati in 1839; his name appears in the Louisville directories from 1832 until 1848, and he had another branch music store and publishing house in Baltimore. The words of the song are by Charles Mackay; they had been published in the London *Daily News,* and reprinted by many American newspapers, but Mackay's name does not appear on Stephen's edition, only the statement that the "Lines" are "from the London Daily News." Newspapers of the day copied and recopied many columns of popular verse without seeming to be under the least obligation to mention the name of the author. It is a long song—eight verses— and Stephen made it still longer by introducing little arias here and there suited for the flute. He dedicated it to Mary D. Keller, who doubtless played it over and over for him while he selected the little trills that appealed to him. It is a very good song and has quite a swing to it. Stephen indicates tempo and expression by imposing foreign musical terms. In order to play "There's a Good Time Coming" properly, the performer must regard these instructions—*pia e scherzando, ritournelle boiteuse, ritardando,* and *en boiteux.* Stephen flattered his public immensely when he assumed that they would have the slightest idea what these phrases meant. It is interesting to contrast the flowery terms employed by Stephen in this youthful effort with songs which made him famous later. "Old Folks at Home" carries no instructions but the simple "Moderato," and "My Old Kentucky Home" is sufficient unto itself with only "Poco Adagio" before the introduction.

Mary Keller, the youngest of the three Keller sisters, died suddenly on the following December 26, 1846, at the age of twenty years and five months. She was within a few days of being exactly the same age as Stephen. When she died, her parents, Samuel and Prudence Keller, were living on Penn Street, but had formerly lived on a farm in Lawrenceville not far from the White Cottage. William J. Rose (Bill Rose of the Knights of the S. T.), who afterwards married Mary Mahon, wrote a touching obituary in Mary's memory; he alludes to a romance in her life, but sheds no light on the object of her love.

But a few days ago, she was in the full flush of health, bright with the promise of life, and her very last errand upon the street was connected with the choice of the attire in which she was expected soon to stand, not at death's, but at the bridal altar!

Her death was a shock to the entire Foster family, and possibly left a deep scar on the heart of the susceptible and affectionate Stephen. Mary's own copy of "Mary of Argylle," signed with her name, was carefully preserved by Morrison, and it may be that this is the "old time ballad" to which Stephen refers in the verses he composed in her memory, and presented to her sister, Rachel.

Where is thy spirit, Mary?
   Dwells it in the air?
Friends thou hast forsaken
   Fondly deem 'tis ling'ring there!

I heard an old time ballad,
   Low and plaintive was the strain,
So pure and clear I seem'd to hear
   Thy gentle voice again.

She who sang was lovely,
   She was innocent and fair,
And I said, if angels guard us,
   Thy sweet spirit lingers there.

In the fall of 1846, we find William B. Foster writing to Morrison from the home of his nephew, John Struthers, Jr., who lived on a farm near New Castle, Pennsylvania. Uncle Struthers had died the year before, at the good old age of eighty-six. The reason for appointing Morrison guardian to Henrietta's children becomes apparent, for she was now being courted by Jesse Thornton, of Warren, Ohio, and there were legal restrictions which prevented her continuing as guardian to her children if she married again. On his frequent visits to Youngstown, Wm. B. Foster, Sr., looked after Henrietta's interests as well as his own. His letter shows that Stephen was still at home, but Stephen left shortly to join Dunning in Cincinnati.

Near New Castle, Octr. 31, 1846

Dear Morrison,

I came home with John Struthers in his Buggy from Youngstown on yesterday; and would return today, but the weather forbids, as it is a continued rain. He will take me up tomorrow.

I wish if Major Herron should arrive at Pittsburgh, you would write and inform me immediately, as I wish much to see him, and would hurry home for that purpose. If you should see the Major, ask him in my name to tarry a few days.

Doctor Bane informs me that old Mr. Wick took a Bond from him and from each of his sons binding them to the faithful payment of $30 annually for the use of Henrietta's children until they shall arrive at Lawful age, as the old man calls it in his Will.—And that the old man had also a lease with each of them for their Land and House & Lot in town. These papers must be in the hands of Henry or Hugh Wick, and the Doctor thinks you as the guardian of the children, ought to have copies of these documents which concern the children, and thinks you had better ask for them yourself for that purpose. As we expect Dunning to come out, if you can spare the time, it might be well for you to accompany him.—Write & let us know when we may expect you.

Should the weather be fine, we expect mother to come along. Tell me how her eyes are getting; I am quite uneasy about that.—

Your affectionate father,

With much love to Ma & Stephy.   W. B. Foster.

On the return trip from New Orleans in June, 1846, Morrison notes in his diary:

Hibernia grounded at Wheeling bar—got on board Steamer *Santa Fe*, came to Steubenville [there was a girl in Steubenville] staid there all night & came over home in the stage, Monday June 30th. Same night, went to Jim McKnight's wedding.

He did not go down the river again for his firm until April 20, 1847.

In the meantime, Henry returned home for a visit during the summer of 1846; while there he fell in love, this time in earnest. Although he had known Mary Burgess nearly all her life, she had been very young before he went to Washington, and evidently he did not consider her as a matrimonial possibility at all. Her mother was one of the Ledlies, of the old firm where Henry had worked so long. Mary was a dainty, fairylike girl, and on meeting her again, Henry succumbed immediately. Their courtship was a short one —he was back in Pittsburgh for his sister Henrietta's marriage to Jesse Thornton on January 5, and for his own wedding on January 12.

So, 1847 was ushered in with two weddings in the family, followed by many parties for the two couples, especially for Henry and Mary; and then, the departure from home of all the children. Late in 1846, or early in the year 1847, Stephen left home for Cincinnati, and started work as a bookkeeper in the office of Irwin & Foster. Although Morrison had enlisted in the Third Regiment the year before, his company was not called to Mexico, and Eliza Foster watched him leave for his next Southern trip, on April 20, with a prayer of thankfulness that it was on the business of peace he was leaving home. But she was not to be easy in her mind very long, for in a few weeks Dunning arrived in Pittsburgh to say good-by to his mother and father, as he was leaving for Mexico with General Scott's army. Morrison, fortunately, returned in time to see Dunning before he left. It must have been a shock to his mother, for the war in Mexico was a vague, faraway affair to her. Dunning, with Richard Cowan and Bill Blakely, belonged to Capt. Alex Hays' company, the Jackson Blues, commanded by Captain Hays and Captain William Carlton. They left home on June 4, and on June 9, Dunning wrote to Morrison from Cincinnati.

Cincinnati, June 9th, 1847

Dear Brother,

I enclose you herewith sundry due bills, notes, etc. due me, all amounting to Twelve hundred & seventy six dollars, which you will retain until I come back or until paid. Attached to the note of James Hughes, you will find a deed for a lot of ground in Newport, Ky. which you will return to him when his note is paid—the rest of the claims I presume will not be paid for some time, but in case you can get any of them, it would not be amiss.

In case any accident should befall me, I wish all the resources I have in this world settled up as soon as possible and converted into cash, the whole amount to be safely invested for the benefit of our dear Mother, as long as she lives—after her death to be applied to the benefit of our Father, as long as he lives, should he survive Mother. (I mean that it shall be invested so as to secure the interest.) After the death of both, let it go as the law directs, as I have no preference among my brothers and sisters. As this will be the only document showing my wishes, I am sure, my dear brother, that you will endeavor to see it faithfully performed, and I doubt not that Pa and all the family will cheerfully concur in the disposition I have made.

All my clothes you can have; my watch give to Stephen, in case it should ever reach you. Any small trinkets that may be found in my personal baggage, distribute as you may see proper to the different members of the family. The Emerald gold ring I have left with Stephen, give to Ma. As these are the only directions given about my affairs, attend to them. I neglected to mention that in case I should die in Mexico, I wish my body brought home if it can be found, pay the expenses out of any property I may leave. I hope, however, that it will not be found necessary to comply with the last wish expressed, as I expect to be able to bring my own body home.

I leave tomorrow in company with Dick Cowan. Give my best love to all the family making inquiries about me, and above all to our good Mother, whom may God bless and preserve until I see again.

Your brother,

D. M. Foster.

With all of her boys away from home, and Pa frequently absent, Eliza Foster decided to move into a house in Youngstown which Mr. Foster had purchased recently, and give William a chance to rent his house on the East Common to some one else. For the next two years, she did very little housekeeping, but took a well-earned rest, staying when she returned to Pittsburgh, at different family boardinghouses and the St. Charles Hotel, at the corner of Wood and Third streets, which must have been a favorite dwelling place of the Fosters for they stayed there so frequently.

Shortly after Dunning's departure for Mexico, Morrison started on his summer vacation, arriving in Baltimore on June 14, 1847. He traveled from Baltimore to Philadelphia with a party of Pittsburgh friends, Mr. and Mrs. Robert McKnight, Mary Irwin, and Sophy Denny, daughter of Dr. William H. Denny. At this time, Morrison was growing increasingly fond of a sweet singer in the Trinity Church choir, Julia N. Murray. She was the daughter of William B. Foster's old friend, Magnus Murray, and Catherine Wilkins. One of Julia's sisters was Mrs. John B. Guthrie, wife of the Mayor of Pittsburgh in 1851. (The writer of these Chronicles remembers their son, George W. Guthrie, also a mayor of Pittsburgh, and a mighty fine one, acting as a pallbearer the day that Morrison Foster was buried from the same Trinity Church in May, 1904.) Julia was one of the belles of Pittsburgh. Her lovely portrait, painted by J. R. Lambdin in Philadelphia in 1849, is reproduced in these pages through the courtesy of Julia's daughter, and namesake, Julie Murray LeMoyne (Mrs. William B. McIlvaine, of Hubbard Woods, Illinois). Although Julia was kind and gracious, Morrison rather despaired of ever winning her love. He continued to correspond with Mary Irwin and Mary Anderson, and the girl from Steubenville whose soul was full of poetry, and who wrote him long rhapsodies on the beauties of "friendship," addressing Morrison as "thee"!

Morrison visited Henry in Washington, and on June 18, Henry took him to call on President Polk. Mit does not say, but, in all probability, the President was "mighty polite entirely," which all the Presidents seem to have been in the 1840's. Mary, Henry's wife, glad of the opportunity for company, returned with Morrison to Pittsburgh for a visit to her mother. On the way, they stopped at Paradise and spent June 20 and 21 with Siss Anny and her family. Ann Eliza, like the good older sister that she was, had a long, serious talk with Mitty on this occasion. She was greatly concerned about the state of his soul, and feared he was becoming too devoted to a worldly and frivolous life. Ann Eliza was an ideal minister's wife, consecrated, devout, enduring all things, and complaining never. She looked up to her husband as to an oracle, referring to him always as Mr. Buchanan. Already the mother of seven children, she was the child of her own mother in devotion to duty, but she accepted all her trials with more meekness than Eliza Foster, who, even though she said she "submitted to her lot," protested "with comments"!

Mary and Morrison came home by way of Duncan's Island where they visited three days with William and Elizabeth, who were spending some weeks in that pleasant place. Duncan's Island was a spot of great natural beauty and the pride of the Pennsylvania Canal system. In his history of Pennsylvania, Sherman Day tells what the place was like in 1843.

Duncan's Island is the name now applied to the flourishing settlement at the mouth of the Juniata, fourteen miles above Harrisburg. . . . The river here is nearly a mile in width, and is crossed by a wooden bridge, on the Burr plan, resting upon many piers, the whole constructed with an elegance and strength equal to, if not surpassing, those of any public work in the country. A dam across the river just below the bridge creates a pool, upon which boats cross by means of a double towing-path, attached to the bridge. The canal continues up Duncan's island, diverging at its upper end into the Juniata and Susquehanna divisions. The Juniata division then crosses the Juniata on a splendid aqueduct, with wooden superstructure, and continues up the right bank to the rope-ferry, twelve miles above. There is also a fine bridge across the mouth of the Juniata. . . . About half a mile above the village, Mrs. Duncan, the accomplished widow of the late proprietor of the island, still resides in the family mansion, where the traveller who chooses to tarry in this delightful region may find accomodations—not in a hotel, with its bar and bottles, and blustering loafers; but in a comfortable, well-furnished gentleman's home, with its quiet fireside, and books, and intelligent society, and sociable tea-table.*

On June 25, 1847, Mary and Morrison boarded a canalboat at Duncan's Island and after three days' leisurely travel, they reached Pittsburgh, a distance of less than two hundred miles. It was a delightful journey through the beautiful Pennsylvania mountain country, but this mode of travel was soon to be supplanted by the railroad. The canal ended at Hollidaysburg where the passengers spent the night, and at five o'clock the next morning, began their journey over the mountain by way of the Allegheny Portage Rail-

* Sherman Day, *Historical Collections of the State of Pennsylvania,* 1843.

road. This was a series of remarkable inclined planes, called the slides, which took canal passengers over the thirty-six miles of mountains between Johnstown and Hollidaysburg. At Hollidaysburg, the travelers changed from the canalboats to little cars which were hauled up and lowered down the Allegheny mountain slopes by means of cables; then, across the level areas, horses took the cars to the next incline. The canal began again at Johnstown and followed the course of the Kiskiminetas and Allegheny rivers to Pittsburgh. When Mary and Morrison made their journey, jointed packet boats had come into use. These could be divided in the center, and hoisted up over the mountains in two parts, thus enabling the passengers to stay in their places all the way. When the divided canalboats reached the bottom of the slide on the other side of the mountains, the two parts were hooked together again, and the boat proceeded along the canal without the passengers being disturbed in the least. Locomotives were beginning to displace horses on the level stretches, and it was soon but a step to an uninterrupted railroad as William, Jr., had been amongst the first to perceive.

A few extracts from a letter Morrison received from Ann Eliza after he reached home show how concerned his sister was about what she considered his exceedingly precarious spiritual state.

Paradise August 1847

My dear brother,

As I find I will have to wait in vain to receive a line from you, I have concluded that the only way I can get to hear from you is to write myself, expecting of course to receive an answer in a short time. We have heard through Pa of the safe arrival of Mary and yourself in Pittsburg.

The cars came along I believe very soon after I left you at Leamon Place. Did you get your dinner eaten before they came? We felt quite lost for a short time after you all left us. The children yet frequently say to me "Don't you wish Uncle Mitty would come back again?"

I have been thinking about you a great deal my dear brother since you left us, and have not failed constantly to offer up my feeble prayers in your behalf. I will be much pleased to hear that you have procured the books we spoke of, or some others of a serious and instructive kind, and still more to hear that you are taking into serious consideration the subject of our conversation while you were here.

It is scarcely necessary for me, my dear brother, to talk to you about the *unsatisfying* nature of all purely worldly pursuits; your own heart has, I have no doubt, taught you this long since—that, even if they could satisfy, they are short lived and uncertain. . . . I do not doubt also that you have frequently felt the great importance of turning your thoughts and heart to God and His service as being the only things which are to last forever.

All then that remains for me, my dearest brother, is to urge you—to beg and entreat of you—to think of these things, to meditate upon them frequently and diligently, to withdraw yourself by force from the petty trifling vanities which are frittering away your time and thoughts, and make a great effort to "strive to enter into the Kingdom of God." The great means by which this effort is made are as you know, prayer—consideration—reading the Holy Scriptures—and other religious books, and resolutely endeavouring to keep out of the way of temptation. If you *faithfully*, however imperfectly persevere in the use of these means, you need not fear but that those pious dispositions, of the want of which you complained to me, will be given to you. . . . Do not let the "World's dread laugh" deter you, it will respect you the more while it laughs and tries to hinder you.

We are all at present in good health and moving on in the old way. James is paying a visit just now in Lancaster to his cousin James Lane.

Give my love to Mary and to any other member of the family you may see. Let me hear from you soon, and remember me always as your

Sincerely attached sister,

Ann Eliza.

Sometime during the summer, Eliza Foster had moved over to Youngstown and from there she addressed her next letter to Morrison.

Youngstown August the 23 1847

My Dear Son,

I am a thousand times obliged to you for the kind letter you addressed to me from Harresburg, and the one previous, but truly, my dear Morrison, I have not dared to write since I came here, my eyes have been so bad. They feel a little stronger this cool day, therefore, I will afford myself the very great pleasure of droping you a line; your father started for Erie on Friday last, consequently I have no one with me but little Mary and the girl, yet I am not lonely. James Richards stays at night, and the house is so delightfull I would never get tired keeping it in summer, how it will be in winter remains to be tried.

Cincinnati about 1846, when Stephen Foster began work there. Cassilly's Row, which housed the firm of Irwin and Foster, is the long block of buildings at the right. From *Robinson & Jones' Cincinnati Directory for 1846*

Cincinnati in the 1850's—Broadway, about Fourth Street, near Stephen Foster's residence
From *Western Scenery; or Land and River, Hill and Dale, in the Mississippi Valley,* by William Wells
(Cincinnati: Otto Onken, 1851)

The neighbourhood is the best I have ever liv'd in, and nothing can excede the beauty of the spot for shade and verdure. If I had some of my boys here, I would not wish to do better than to make my home here the rest of my days, but this may not be, as Pa says he is trying to sell it.

I am glad you had a pleasant trip. Have you been well since you came home? Poor dear Duning, what perils is he going through by this time, when shall we hear from him again. Was Henry quite well looking when you parted with him? Have you seen any one who has seen Stephen since you came home? I wish the weather was as cool at Cincinnati as it is here at this time. I have to sit with a shawl on whilest I write. How is it where you are, if you are too warm and can leave, you had better come here. I have three beds and a cot well fitted up, so you see, I am pretty well off.

Mr. Thornton has Etty nicely pack'd in cottage stile, with a nigro to wait on her. I think she will be able to get along without much more of our help.

How did Sissy Ann look, and what did she say. I know she was delighted to see you.

Did Mrs. Murray go to Bedford Springs? They were all very kind to me when I was up, while you were away. I left them all at Mrs. Thomson's under very kind feelings.

You have call'd on Elizabeth more than once I trust, how respectfull the dear child was to me. I was there on the evening of the fourth of July. Mrs. Harmer Denney and Anne Robenson were both there.

You may expect to see Pa in Pittsburgh as soon as he returns, when I expect Mary with him. Now, dear son, I can find nothing more to say to you. May every hapiness attend you, that can be realized from the knoledge of your worth, be as religious as you are moral and dutifull, and never depart from the course of life you have commenced, so may your after years be crown'd with peace.

I am, my dear son Morison, your truly affectionate Mother,

Eliza C. Foster.

III

BY this time, Stephen found himself fairly well settled in Cincinnati and working regularly at his desk at Irwin & Foster's. Their office in Cassilly's Row was near the largest steamboat landing in Cincinnati. Stephen could see the river from the office windows, but even when he did not watch it, he was ever conscious of the river's near presence, for the whistles of the steamboats sounded in his ears all day long. Stephen's lodgings probably were first with Dunning in the Broadway Hotel, a stone's throw from the wharf, and later at Mrs. Griffin's in Fourth Street, so he was never, day or night, out of sound of the mighty stream. Although possessed of a nervous temperament that was exceedingly sensitive to noise, the fact that Stephen did not move his lodgings to a place farther back from the river indicates that the "woo-hoo" of the steamboats was not noise to him, but rather music to his ears. Dunning was absent, but Stephen had plenty of friends in Cincinnati if he wished company, the Marshalls, the Cassillys, the Febigers, and the Millers, besides the various companions he picked up for himself at Mr. Peters' music store. He was awakening to the fact that he could write songs that people enjoyed singing though he still was unaware of just how good his songs were. In Cincinnati, he became acquainted with William Roark, of the Sable Harmonists, a popular minstrel troupe, who were perhaps the first to introduce "Old Uncle Ned" on a professional program. His friend, Mr. Peters, had requested copies of "Lou'siana Belle" and "Old Uncle Ned" for publication, and doubtless Stephen gave him at the same time, "What Must a Fairy's Dream Be?" a fanciful little song wholly unlike Stephen's minstrel melodies. Furthermore, Mr. Peters thought so well of the commercial possibilities of the compositions of the promising young Pittsburgher that his firm produced another edition of "Open Thy Lattice, Love," probably with the permission of George Willig who had published the first edition in 1844. A notice of Stephen's song was recently discovered by Dr. Raymond Walters in the Cincinnati *Gazette* for June 10, 1847:

> "Open Thy Lattice, Love."—This is the title of a sweet little melody for the Piano, just published by Messrs. Peters & Field. It is composed by Mr. S. C. Foster, whose spirited air of "A Good Time Coming" published two or three months ago, has become a decided favorite.*

*Raymond Walters, *Stephen Foster, Youth's Golden Gleam*, Princeton University Press, 1936.

"What Must a Fairy's Dream Be?" was copyrighted by W. C. Peters on October 18, 1847, and was dedicated by Stephen to Mary H. Irwin, the daughter of the Hon. Thomas Irwin, who lived at the corner of Grant and Diamond streets, Pittsburgh. Mary was one of the pretty girls admired by the Foster boys. The verses of "What Must a Fairy's Dream Be?" are of a style that must have delighted Stephen's romantic mother.

> What must a Fairy's dream be,
> Who sleeps when the Mermaid sings?
> Would she rob the night of her jewels bright
> To spangle her silv'ry wings?
> Rock'd on the wind 'bove the land and the sea,
> What can the dream of a Fairy be?

Already Stephen's compositions revealed his gift for musical words and phrases, lines that blended with a light, lilting air that was delicately suited to his fairy theme. Back in Pittsburgh, A. Andrews, enterprising proprietor of the Eagle Ice Cream Saloon, was attracting patronage by giving musical entertainments for the enjoyment of his customers while they consumed their ice cream. Mr. Andrews' establishment must have been an exceedingly popular place, and a letter to Morrison Foster from Robert P. Nevin, dated July 21, 1865, shows that Mit and Bob were in attendance on an important occasion. He says in part:

Do you recollect, many years ago (it must be some twenty or more) when the old "Eagle Saloon" was in operation here, and "Kneass" its star performer, of a premium of some sort being offered for the best original "Ethiopian song" that should be composed for the occasion? Do you remember, furthermore, that your brother Stephen produced one of his earliest compositions on that occasion, which was received with rapturous applause? I can't recall all the circumstances, but recollect well the fact that you were present, from your stating to me at the time that you thought I was in the list of competitors, altho I was not. Was not the song "Uncle Ned?" What was the prize offered?

Together, Morrison and Robert Nevin revived their recollections of the old Eagle Saloon, and the following account by Robert P.

Nevin was published in *The Atlantic Monthly* for November, 1867, entitled "Stephen C. Foster and Negro Minstrelsy."

A certain Mr. Andrews, dealer in confections, cakes, and ices, being stirred by a spirit of enterprise, rented, in the year 1845, a second-floor hall on Wood Street, Pittsburg, supplied it with seats and small tables, advertised largely, employed cheap attractions,—living statues, songs, dances, &c.,—erected a stage, hired a piano, and, upon the dissolution of his band, engaged the services of Nelson Kneass as musician and manager. Admittance was free, the ten-cent ticket required at the door being received at its cost value within towards the payment of whatever might be called for at the tables. To keep alive the interest of the enterprise, premiums were offered, from time to time, of a bracelet for the best conundrum, a ring with a ruby setting for the best comic song, and a golden chain for the best sentimental song. The most and perhaps only really valuable reward—a genuine and very pretty silver cup, exhibited night after night, beforehand—was promised to the author of the best original negro song, to be presented before a certain date, and to be decided upon by a committee designated for the purpose by the audience at that time.

Quite a large array of competitors entered the lists.... Morrison Foster sent to his brother Stephen a copy of the advertisement announcing the fact, with a letter urging him to become a competitor for the prize. These saloon entertainments occupied a neutral ground, upon which eschewers of theatrical delights could meet with the abetters of playhouse amusements,— a consideration of ruling importance in Pittsburg, where so many of the sterling population carry with them to this day, by legitimate inheritance, the stanch old Cameronian fidelity to Presbyterian creed and practice. Morrison, believing that these concerts would afford an excellent opportunity for the genius of his brother to appeal to the public, persisted in urging him to compete for the prize, until Stephen, who at first expressed a dislike to appear under such circumstances, finally yielded, and in due time forwarded a melody entitled, "'Way Down South, whar de Corn grows." When the eventful night came, the various pieces in competition were rendered to the audience by Nelson Kneass to his own accompaniment on the piano. The audience expressed by their applause a decided preference for Stephen's melody; but the committee appointed to sit in judgment decided in favor of someone else, himself and his song never heard of afterwards, and the author of "'Way Down South" forfeited the cup. But Mr.

Kneass appreciated the merit of the composition, and promptly, next morning, made application at the proper office for a copyright in his own name as author, when Mr. Morrison Foster, happening in at the moment, interposed, and frustrated the discreditable intention.

On the margin of Mr. Nevin's magazine article, Morrison Foster has made the following penciled note:

It was at the Court of Judge Thos. Irwin, U. S. District Judge, in whose family I was a frequent visitor. I explained the circumstances to Judge Irwin and the two vagabonds were fortunate in being permitted to leave the court unpunished. I had just previously taken a copyright for Stephen.

The two whom Morrison termed "vagabonds" were presumably Messrs. Kneass and Holman.

The following items from 1847 Pittsburgh newspaper columns that recently have come to light at Foster Hall add chapters to the story of the contest in the old Eagle Saloon. The prize song, "Wake up Jake, or the Old Iron City," was afterwards published by W. C. Peters, with authorship credited to George Holman.

The following announcement is from the *Daily Commercial Journal* (Robert M. Riddle, editor and proprietor) of Tuesday morning, August 31, 1847.

ALL THE WORLD AND HIS WIFE
RUSHING TO SEE AND HEAR THE VOCALISTS
—UNPRECEDENTED POPULARITY—THIRD
ENGAGEMENT—ONE WEEK MORE.
SILVER CUP PRIZE!

Andrew's Eagle Ice Cream Saloon   Admittance 25 cts.

The troupe of Vocalists having run two engagements at this temple of Pleasure with the most marked approval of overflowing assemblages every night—at the urgent solicitation of the Manager, have been prevailed upon to remain a few days longer. They will accordingly appear EVERY NIGHT THIS WEEK, in an entirely new selection of Solos, Duettes, Trios, Quartettes, Quintettes, sentimental, patriotic, comic, &c., with Ethiopian Melodies and Extravaganzas.

A PRIZE OF A SILVER CUP

will be awarded to the author of such original words of an Ethiopian Melody or Extravaganzas—to be set to music by the present Troupe, as shall be decided the best by the spontaneous voice of the audience at the TRIAL CONCERT, MONDAY EVENING, Sept. 6.

Competitors for the prize must hand in their pieces to the Manager, on or before FRIDAY NOON, Sept. 3, to afford time for the adaptation of suitable music to each piece which may be offered.

On Wednesday morning, September 8, 1847, the *Daily Commercial Journal* carried the following item under "Local Matters."

THE EAGLE SALOON was crowded on Monday night by a brilliant audience, to hear the songs offered for the silver Prize Cup. Ten songs were offered to the audience, some of them exceeding clever. The audience, by a large majority, awarded the prize to a song written and set to music by Mr. Holman, the tenor singer, whose vocal talents we have had occasion, heretofore, warmly to commend. It should be a satisfaction to the disappointed to know that they, at least, have been defeated by a gentlemanly and excellent man, aside from his professional merit. The cup was presented by Mr. Shanon, with appropriate remarks, to which Mr. Holman replied pithily as follows:

"Ladies and Gentlemen: With your approval, I believe I take the cup, and hope I could take many such without taking a cup too much." [The newspaper does not tell us what sort of a prize the audience awarded "Mr. H." for his pithy acceptance speech!]

The same issue of the paper prints the Eagle Saloon's advertisement, giving their own version of the presentation of the prize cup.

FOUR NIGHTS MORE!
AND POSITIVELY THE LAST OF THE ENGAGEMENT OF
THE VOCALISTS!!
ANDREW'S EAGLE ICE CREAM SALOON

Admittance 25 Cents.

This and every Evening this Week.

GRAND MUSICAL ENTERTAINMENT!

Public desire continuing very great to hear the new Prize
Song of "THE OLD IRON CITY," written by Geo.
Holman, Esq., which took the silver cup by the almost
unanimous voice of the audience, the same will be sung
every evening this week during the entertainments,
together with one or two other of the pieces submitted
for the prize, and which have been stamped by popular
approval—all of which songs have been *copyrighted,*
and can only be heard, as originally produced, at the
Eagle Saloon.

The entertainments of every night will be choice
and amusing.

In the *Daily Commercial Journal* for "Saturday Morning, Sept'r
11, 1847," the Eagle Saloon's advertisement announces the possible
presence of a distinguished visitor, and, in spite of the late unpleas-
antness in Judge Irwin's courtroom, two of Stephen's compositions
are listed for presentation.

Last Night of the Vocalists.

GRAND GALA CONCERT!

Vice President Dallas!!

ANDREWS' EAGLE ICE CREAM SALOON.

Admittance 25 Cents.

This evening, Saturday, Sept. 11, will appear for the
last time

MRS. PHILLIPS,   MISS BRUCE,
MRS. SHARPE,   MR. KNEASS,
MR. HOLMAN:

When will be produced—

> "The Old Iron City"—Prize Song;
> Away down Souf:　　　　"
> Allegheny Belle;　　　　"
> SUSANNA—A new song, never before given to the
> 　　　public;
> Picayune Butler;
> The Floating Scow;
> The gal wid the blue dress on, &c;

With a choice selection of other songs, &c.
> *Vice President Dallas is expected to be present.*

Whether Vice-President George M. Dallas put in an appearance or not, I have not learned, but Morrison undoubtedly was there, as he would have been eager to hear Stephen's songs performed in public, even by The Vocalists who had tried to claim the copyright for one of them. Morrison was staying alone in Pittsburgh at the St. Charles Hotel, and was there from June 25 to November 29. He spent many evenings with friends of "the S. T." in places such as the Eagle Saloon, for the mild entertainment they afforded, a way of "frittering away his time" deplored by Ann Eliza; but Mit's diary shows that he devoted plenty of time to reading such worthy works as *The Battle of Life,* and Thiers' history of France and Napoleon which should have met with his sister's approval.

And maybe The Vocalists at Mr. Andrews' Eagle Saloon rendered the last stanza of "Oh! Susanna" the way I never have heard anyone sing it in these days, but the way Stephen intended it to be sung, and as it was sung by the young members of the Knights of the Square Table in 1845 and '46 before the public took "Susanna" to their hearts.

> I soon will be in New Orleans,
> And den I'll look all round,
> And when I find Susana,
> I'll fall upon the ground.
> But if I do not find her,
> Dis darkie'l surely die,
> And when I'm dead *and bear-i-ed,*
> Susana, dont you cry.

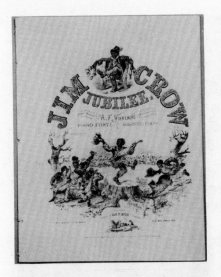

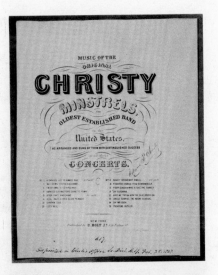

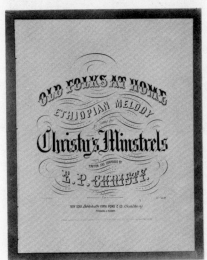

Early editions of Foster songs

"Memphis, Tennessee," by H. Lewis

From *Das Illustrirte Mississippithal*, von H. Lewis (Düsseldorf: Arnz & Comp. [1855-1857])

Another of Stephen's compositions, "What Must a Fairy's Dream Be?" had been sung at the Eagle Saloon on August 19, 1847, two months before it was entered for copyright by Mr. Peters. It was sung by Miss Bruce in a grand "extraordinary musical entertainment" on the evening of August 19, and, the program states, for the first time. It is likely that The Vocalists brought the manuscript of this song, and also a copy of "Oh! Susanna" with them from Cincinnati, having received them from Stephen himself. Later in life, Stephen wrote to Robert Nevin regarding "Oh! Susanna," "Imagine my delight in receiving one hundred dollars in cash! Though this song was not successful, yet the two fifty-dollar bills I received for it had the effect of starting me on my present vocation of song-writer." It was probably many years before Stephen realized just how successful from a financial standpoint "Susanna" was to the publisher. Mr. Peters is said to have made more than ten thousand dollars from Stephen's rollicking tune, with its nonsensical, happy-go-lucky words, and from the plaintive but equally popular, "Old Uncle Ned."

On September 14, 1847, General Scott occupied Mexico City, and an armistice was declared. The troops began to return home, many more of them weakened with fever and dysentery than from wounds. Morrison was in Memphis, Tennessee, on December 10, when Dunning and Dick Cowan passed that river town on their way to Pittsburgh. Dunning recently had been seriously ill. The meeting of the brothers will have to be imagined because it is not described by Morrison. Four days before that, he "wrote by Telegraph to Father" from Louisville that Dunning was on the way home. Knowing the brothers' deep affection for each other, we can easily reconstruct the scene at the Memphis wharf—Morrison anxiously waiting on shore for the *Jamestown* from New Orleans to whistle for the landing; Dunning on the boiler deck, still very weak, attended by debonair but devoted Dick Cowan, eagerly scanning the welcoming crowd for a first glimpse of Mit, as the gangplank is thrown out to the wharf boat. A joyful recognition, and perhaps half an hour together; then handclasps and good-bys, some waggish valediction from the graceless Dick, and the *Jamestown* heads north again.

Two red-letter days indeed that week for solitary Morrison! On December 11, the steamboat *Northern Light* docked at Memphis on her way down to New Orleans, and Mit had a short, happy visit with another friend from home, pretty Catherine Dallas, now Mrs. O'Hara Denny. That evening, Mit wrote to Pa and Mrs. Dallas, too, that he had seen the wanderers, and all was well with them.

While he was away this time, Morrison missed the wedding on December 21 of his best friend, Tom Blair, to Miss Virginia Dike, of Steubenville, close friend of the little lady named Hannah with whom Mit kept up an exalted correspondence for a time.

Morrison's only entry for Christmas Day, 1847, spent at the Planter House in New Orleans, was that he "wrote to Etty." He was back in Cincinnati by January 9, having arrived on the steamboat *Fashion*. The name evidently put some notions in the young man's head (that, and the prospect of numerous pleasant calls to be made when he reached home); in Cincinnati he ordered a new coat from McElevy, the tailor, just around the corner from Dunning's office, and shirts from Sheppard's. His bill at the end of the year with Mr. McElevy amounted to sixty-seven dollars! A prodigious sum for the erstwhile economical Mitty. And an entry of nine dollars for two daguerreotypes made in New Orleans matches a letter from Mary Anderson, written at Bedford Springs, July 29, 1848.

I long to see you so much, you cannot tell how many times I have wished and wished again for just one peep at your sincere face. I now have your Daguerreotype before me, which I think a most excellent likeness. I am a thousand times obliged to you for it. Mrs. Pennock handed it to me the other evening in the ball room, when I was dancing with Dick Cowan. I had a presentiment as to the contents of the parcel, so I opened it and let Dick share my pleasure. We turned it over and over again, and perhaps we didn't talk about you a little!

IV

DURING 1847 the first records appear of the organization known as the Knights of the Square Table, that jovial club whose sign was a fish, and whose motto on their fraternal writing paper was "Hereof Fail Not!" Each member had a fraternal name.

Morrison was addressed as "Sir George Armstrong." His office in the order was Grand Pantler and Commissary. Richard Cowan called himself "Shiras"; why this was so, when Charles P. Shiras was a member of the club, I don't know, unless it was because the name brought Dick a pleasant reminder of a brand of sherry wine. "Sir George Breed" was the title given to James Kerr. Stephen and the "Five Nice Young Men" were members, and others who were either members or familiar friends were Alex Dallas, Dan Beltzhoover, Jim O'Hara, and Bill Denny, Tom and Cust Blair, Davie and Algernon Bell, Jack and Brady Townsend, Overton Carr, Will Anderson, Sam Magaw, Oliver Barnes, Joe Brown, Tom Watson; the three Bradshaws, George, Bob, and Bill; Robert McCargo, John Duncan, Alex Murray, J. Harry Reed, H. S. Bateman, R. Biddle Roberts, Brady Wilkins, and John Scully. Favorite belles of these gay beaux were Ginny and Annie Crossan, Annie and Lib Ogden; Mary, Margaret, and Rachel Keller; Mary and Lizzie Irwin, Julia Murray, Hattie Wilkins, Mary Anderson, Mary Phillips, Lizzie Harding, Mary and Margaret Stevenson, and Louisa Bell; the Dallas girls, Molly, Matilda, and Catherine; Caroline, Annie, and Sophy Denny; Annie Robinson, Mary Mahon, Susan Pentland, Sophy Wilkins, Martha and Margaret Shoenberger, and the six daughters of Dr. Andrew N. McDowell.

Dunning Foster and Dick Cowan were amongst the lucky ones to be sent home from Mexico shortly after the armistice was signed, but others of the Knights were not so fortunate. Dan Beltzhoover, and a fellow volunteer, H. B. Field (a newcomer to Pittsburgh), were still languishing in Texas and Mexico, and Dan expresses his disgust at the situation in a letter dated December 15, 1847, to "dear Mit," written from Fort Polk, Point Isabel, Texas.

. . . About a week ago I was ordered to relieve Major Scott in command of this Port. I am now stationed here for God knows how long, with only thirty men. The place is the loneliest place on earth, plenty of time for meditation. All other officers who have been here before me since this became a secondary line, have actually been forced to hard drinking to pass away the time, and I fear I would take to it too naturally enough if I had not promised a certain one to be very discreet and temperate.

Why have you not written to me? I hope you are not jealous because I have sent a letter to you for Jule Murray (bless her heart)? I hear that Jule is engaged, if so, advise the gentleman to volunteer for Mexico, and when he gets out here I'll attend to him for both of us. . . . I have the blues continually, but what of that? I've had them with little intermission for years. In heaven's own good time, I shall be relieved and sent to a better post; until then I must wait, sometimes cheerfully, but generally in no very good humor.

Field went to General Scott's column. I have never heard of him since. I would like to send Miss Mary Stevenson better news, but I must tell the truth.

. . . The countersign at Fort Polk this blessed evening is *Murray*. Give my love to Jule. I am very anxious to hear from her. I will inclose a note for her. No, I take my "Bible oath" I wrote this letter merely for the pleasure of writing to you. If you don't believe me, you need not give her the note.

We have had no mail for twenty days, the last mail brought General Taylor's leave, and he has been in New Orleans for two weeks.

. . . The yellow fever has returned to Matamoras. Col. Temple of the 10th Infantry is dying or dead.

. . . I hope Congress will do something for us this winter. Anything is better than doing nothing. I go to two drills a day just for occupation.

Give my love to *all* the girls. Ah, me, I wish I could see them all again, but somebody must suffer, why not I? So you have lost Ginny Crossan! Hope Annie is able to take her place. I used to be engaged to Annie, according to report. I wonder if it would be so yet.—Write to me, Mit, and send me some Congress news if you get hold of any papers.

From Mexico, Morrison received a letter from Lieutenant H. B. Field, dated March 30, 1848. It is addressed from the "Citadel, City of Mexico."

Dear Sir,

Your favor dated Jany. 28th came to hand in due season, and I was delighted to hear once [more] from one of my old Pittsburgh friends, from whatever cause. Since I left you, variable indeed have been the scenes—from the greatest exposure and hardships of a campaign to the luxuries of a palace; from eating fresh Beef without salt or spices, to the richest delicacies of a Mexican nobleman's table; from almost nudity to being draped like a gentleman; from the angry and exciting strife of Battle to the pleasures of a sociable evening in a beautiful Senorita's parlour—all of this for the love of the profession, and I trust not as many have done, "leaving their country for their country's good!"

My health for the past few weeks has not been good—the confounded chills and fever have nearly used me up, and as for getting outside of many of those "big drinks of brandy and water" often, is out of the question, as the liquor here and all that is brought here is most horrid —enough to excite one's olifactories with disgust, and make your bowels gush out with anguish!

I would like exceedingly to spend a short time in Pittsburgh during the armistice as nothing is doing here. I think I could get up some fun there. I had no idea that I had become so much attached to the place. It was not in reality the town, but the many people so kind, hospitable and generous—and *the* one not so soon to be forgotten. However, I suppose I might as well forget as in all probability there is no use to remember any more than many others, as a friend. I cannot easily forget the many marks of kindness shown me by all the family. I am perfectly satisfied that if I had not lived quite so fast at times while a resident of Pittsburg, matters would have stood different—perhaps it's all for the best.

I have not seen John Wilkins for some days. He is quite well, as fat as a Trojan, and I think is quite content. Saml. Black, Tom Denny & Alex Hays left a few days before your letter arrived—the two latter go home, having resigned. They will give you all the news.

Congratulate Tom Blair and his lady for me, and say to them I wish them all the happiness imaginable. Remember me kindly to all good friends, and tell Annie Robinson not to be in too great a hurry about shuffling off her maidenhood, as many a Hero will return from the wars in due course of time, upon any one of whom that she may fancy she can bestow her smiles, and Dimes to a very good advantage, for a poorer set of Devils never will return to the United States again.

I would like, and I can almost fancy myself dropping in at some of your "accidentals" and having a spree such as we were wont to have in bygone days. Say, for instance, at Mr. Ogden's. True, there would be a vacancy; still I can imagine a pleasant party, for I consider Miss Lib rather a fine lady, certainly a very sociable one; and then one of those Sunday afternoon lounges out at Mr. Shoenberger's, a glass of wine and cigars, etc. etc. Hot punches are not very fashionable here, the weather being rather warm, but I think if I was in Pittsburgh, it would not take long to set Hughey [Hughey Harrold, a barkeeper] brewing at least one. However, all this resolves itself into one peculiar fact, that of an impossibility.

If you wish to go through the motions, go round into 4th St. and borrow my countenance of Miss Mary [Mary Stevenson]. Go round by all means and give my very best love to Misses Margaret & Mary and remember me kindly to the family.

Tell Dr. McDowell that he must not forget that man that said, "An' its drunk I am, yer Honor." Doubtless the Dr. has many stories to relate on me. I liked the Dr. so well that I should not be offended if he did exaggerate a little—if not too great an exposition!

Please to tell John Duncan to take good care of my dog, as I shall call or send and get her if we should be so fortunate as to have peace declared in the course of time. By the way "Peace stock" is rather on the decline of late—yet we have some hope, and if we can be on our winding way home by next fall, I for one, shall be content. Col. Geary told me the other day that he should apply to have me go to Pittsburg to muster them out of the service. I hope he may succeed.

Remember me to all friends at the St. Charles and in Pittsburg. I should be pleased to hear from you again, and Believe me,

As ever,

To—
    Mit Foster, Esq.
Yours truly,
H. B. Field.

Lieutenant Field's dreams of a reunion at Hughey's bar with old-time boon companions, and a more sedate but happy meeting with "*the* one not so soon to be forgotten," Mary Stevenson, were realized at last, but they did not endure for long. The young officer was amongst the unfortunate members of the Third Regiment of United States Artillery who perished when the steamer *San Francisco,* bound for California, was lost on December 24, 1853.

Morrison returned home about the middle of January, 1848, and remained the rest of the winter in Pittsburgh, boarding with his mother and father at the St. Charles Hotel, at the corner of Wood and Third streets. Eliza Foster was glad to have Mit at home to take her to the concert, of their friend Robert P. Nevin, given the evening of January 27 at Dr. Swift's church in Allegheny, the First Presbyterian. Mr. Nevin was the director of the quartette which consisted of Miss Irwin, soprano, Miss Stockton, alto, Mr. Nevin, bass, and Mr. Kleber, tenor; from the next day's paper, we learn that "the clear, bold thrilling notes of Miss Irwin's voice in the 'Prayer of Moses in Egypt,' blending with the deep bass of Mr. Nevin, united with the clear, musical second of Miss Stockton and the tenor of Mr. Kleber, produced a concord of sweet sounds that would have pleased the most fastidious lover of harmonies."

Henry Kleber, Stephen's teacher and helper, was now established in Pittsburgh as a piano and voice instructor, and gave frequent musical soirees in Wilkins Hall which were reported to be fashionable, elegant, and *recherché* affairs. *Recherché* was the overworked adjective of the '40's, as *colorful* is today. In addition to these activities, Mr. Kleber was agent in 1848 for Nunn & Clark's grand and square pianos at Wardwell's Furniture Rooms, 83 Third Street, and was engaged in composing and publishing many excellent songs and piano compositions. Professor Henry Rohback was another local celebrity of marked ability. In 1848, Professor Rohback published a rondo entitled "L'Etoile" dedicated to Mrs. Wilson McCandless and Mrs. William McClure, who, in old White Cottage days, had been Sarah and Lydia Collins.

Events not quite so recherché were happening in other musical circles in 1848; the newspapers reported that Stephen's friend, Frederick Blume, music and piano dealer, was arrested and fined for abusing and beating his wife, Charlotte, and the general opinion of Mr. Blume seemed to be that he was a "cowardly blackguard"! Thus did the artistic temperament in Pittsburgh assert itself in different ways.

William B. Foster was busy with various undertakings, principally the collection of soldiers' claims from the government, including back pay, pensions, and warrants for bounty lands to which veterans of all the wars were entitled. These land grants consisted of plots ranging from forty to one hundred and sixty acres according to individual cases. Investigation of each claim by an authorized person was required before a grant could be secured. Eighty acres seem to have been the standard allotment to soldiers of the War of 1812; one John Clark who served in the Seminole and Creek war (enlistment 1839-'44) received 160. The allotment to Mexican War soldiers who had served twelve months or more was 160 acres of land, or one hundred dollars in treasury scrip bearing six

per cent interest. Those serving less than twelve months were entitled to forty acres, or twenty-five dollars in scrip—but no bounty
lands were given to volunteers "as were accepted into service, and
discharged without being marched to the seat of war"; they were
supposed to smell a little powder at least, before they were eligible
to compensation.

Claims were also filed for the children of Revolutionary soldiers
who had not received the allotment to which they were entitled.
Many of these veterans never went to look at their land, but sold their
claims as soon as they were handed to them. During the year 1848,
Wm. B. Foster, in partnership with William Larimer, Jr., bought
up $1,478 worth of land warrants ranging from $75 to $110 each.
There was little profit to be derived from the resale, however, as
all the grants within a reasonable distance had been taken up long
before by the Revolutionary and 1812 veterans, and government
lands were now pushed west as far as Iowa, and other remote sections
unfamiliar to most potential buyers. Some agents were able to buy
up large quantities of these claims and hold them for speculative
purposes which caused a lot of talk in Congress about the scandalous
profits being made from the sale of bounty lands, but we have no
record of Mr. Foster ever reaping great profits, scandalous or otherwise. We do know that he lost frequently by advancing back pay to
clever heroes who had already collected it. For example, of one
J. Moore, he says, "The Rascal recd. pay from Maj. Vanners, $21.00.
By which I lose amt. paid, $13.00." Probably, Private J. Moore
moved on to pastures new, and played the same little trick on
sympathetic soldiers' agents in other towns. Another item reads,
"Cash paid out to and for Mrs. Flower, $38.20. She is dead, and this
is lost."

V

ELIZA FOSTER thoroughly enjoyed staying at the St. Charles
Hotel. She was relieved of household cares, and found time to
"step her way" of an afternoon out Penn Street to call on her old
friends much oftener than she could when she was taking care of
the house on the Common. Jane Wilkins Dallas, widow of Judge

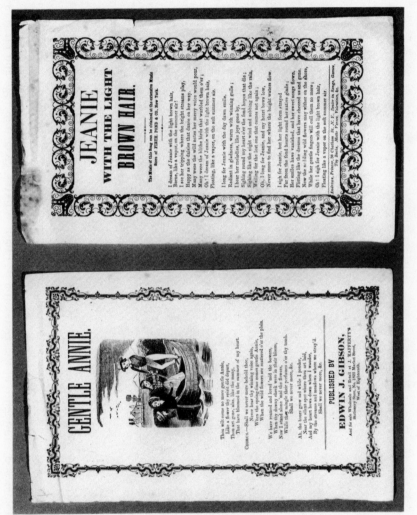

Broadsides of the 1850's

"Homewood," residence of the Honorable William Wilkins, erected in 1836 and razed in 1924

Trevanion B. Dallas, lived out the Butler Road just beyond Lawrenceville in a charming story-and-a-half house called "Elm Cottage," covered with vines, and set back from the Allegheny River in a grove of huge forest trees. This homestead was afterwards the residence of Mrs. Burgess, and Henry and Mary Foster made their home there for many years.

During the winter of 1848, Alex Dallas, one of the "Knights of the S. T." and Mrs. Dallas's only son at home, was seriously ill for several weeks, and either Morrison or his mother went out and stayed at night with Mrs. Dallas and the girls, Mary and Matilda.

A brilliant social event of February, 1848, was the wedding of Sophy Wilkins to Lieutenant Overton Carr. That it was a special affair is evidenced by Mrs. Foster's purchase of a two dollar and twenty-five cent handkerchief the day before the wedding. At no other time on record did economical Mother Foster's bill at Mrs. Davidson's New York Store, No. 2 St. Clair Street, show higher priced handkerchiefs than the two-for-seventy-five-cents variety!

The splendid mansion in which the wedding was held was "Homewood," the residence of Honorable William Wilkins. It stood in the middle of a park of six hundred acres, and the actual location of the house was at the present intersection of Edgerton and Murtland avenues in the section of Pittsburgh known as Homewood. This beautiful home, with its lofty porches and imposing pillars, was razed in 1924. The following account of the wedding is taken from Eliza Foster's "Sketches and Incidents."

On the 22nd February, 1848, at four o'clock in the afternoon, three persons entered a carriage to wend their way over muddy roads to "Homewood," the seat of Judge William Wilkins.

Two of them were ladies, and the other a young gentleman rather above the middle height with dark complexion and brown eyes, wearing his beard pointed according to the fashion at that time, without mustache or whisker.

The rain kept a continual patter on the roof of the carriage during the whole of their seven mile ride to "Homewood;" calculated to dampen the gaiety of almost any party so situated. But not so with the present occupants of the vehicle, whose spirits were heightened by the prospect of a brilliant wedding party which was the object of their ride upon this dismal day; and they were also amused and consoled by observing the numerous other carriages that lined the road, destined for the same place, looking likewise wet and muddy enough.

The cloak and hood that enveloped the youthful person of Miss Susan Fulton could not hide her sweet smile and laughing black eye from Mrs. Foster, as she made her appropriate remarks upon her own discomfiture in relation to the mud having bespattered her white muslin dress, and her uncertainty whether in her haste she had not forgotten her fan and gloves and some other things.

Mr. Morrison Foster was encumbered with some several such articles for his mother, as well as a boquet he was carrying to present to a young beauty in her teens whom he expected to meet at the wedding.

The carriage dragged along until six o'clock, when it came to a stand waiting for a full half hour for those ahead of them to alight in regular order. At length the party alighted, and the two ladies escorted by a servant up stairs into a handsome dressing room already crowded with ladies finishing their toilettes. This was very soon done by the two in question, and attended by young Mr. Foster, who rejoined them at the door of the room, they descended the stairs, and entered the saloon. The soft light from many a wax candle shed its rays upon the full length portraits which graced the walls, and was reflected back by the immense mirrors reaching to the ceiling.

After paying their respects to Mrs. Wilkins, the mistress of the house, the minute observation of Mrs. Foster immediately divided every object of attraction separate and apart from the other. There were but few in the room when she entered. The first person who addressed her was Mary M. Dallas, a little lady in her fourteenth year, fair and sprightly, with luxuriant flaxen hair, blue eyes, beautiful mouth and white even teeth. She was the daughter of the lovely Jane Wilkins and the late Judge Trevanion B. Dallas.

"Come this way, Mrs. Foster," said she smiling, "the bridal party will enter from the eastern parlour."

"Thank you, love," rejoined Mrs. Foster, "Then I will take my stand nearby where I can better observe them."

Young Mrs. James O'Hara Denny [Catherine Dallas], another daughter of Jane Wilkins, was adorned in white satin muslin and Brussels lace dress and drapery. She was rather above the middle height, and the downy white plume she wore gave effect to the graceful motion of her person, as she gaily chatted with her cousin, Mrs. W. W. Irwin. The latter was a lady of superior talents and showy exterior. She was dressed in white silk with a becoming wreath on her head. She had but lately returned from abroad, her husband having been Charge des Affaires to the court of Denmark.

The next moment, the eyes of Mrs. Foster rested upon the familiar figure of Mrs. Jane Dallas, many years older than when last she wrote of her, but still very handsome. She was clothed in black velvet, with her dark hair brushed smoothly back under a head dress of Valenciennes lace. Mrs. Foster lingered some time with this group, for the rooms had not yet commenced to fill, though a goodly number of persons were scattered about.

Miss Fulton and young Mr. Foster joined the beautiful Julia Murray [daughter of Magnus Murray and Catherine Wilkins], who was immediately encircled by several admirers. Like a true belle, she treated all with equal suavity and condescension.

Soon there entered Mrs. Collins, and her two daughters, Mrs. McClure and Mrs. McCandless; also her grandson, John Duncan, son of the deceased Margaret Collins; along with him came Miss Mary Evans, the daughter of Valeria Collins, attired in pink crepe with a rose of the same colour in her brown hair. Here also were Mrs. Robinson and Mrs. Denny, Mrs. Shaler, Miss Shaler, also Mrs. Craig and her daughter and son, descendants of Major Neville B. Craig, Mr. Richard Cowan, a grandson of Major Kirkpatrick, lovely Miss Mary Mahon and many others.

The Revd. Dr. Upfold took his stand, and all eyes were turned toward the door of the eastern parlour. Soon the bridal party entered [including] Mr. Duncan and Miss Beelen, Miss Stevenson, Mr. Robinson, Mr. Cust Blair with Miss Annie Robinson, and Mr. Alex Murray with Miss Wilkins. Lastly appeared the bride and groom, Lieut. Overton Carr and Miss Sophy Wilkins.

Dr. Upfold was clad in his robes and proceeded with the ceremony after the forms of the Episcopal Church. When he inquired, "Who giveth this woman to be married to this man?" her aged father, who stood by her side, replied, "I do."

The venerable Judge William Wilkins still retained his graceful figure, and erect, commanding form though his hair was now white as snow from length of years, and long service in public office, for he had held high positions in the councils and cabinet of his country. The mother looked on with swelling heart, proud of her daughter and proud of the father that dignified the scene. Her own native grace and failing beauty were forgotten in the joy that animated her. Her children were now all grown, for the youngest, (the first bridesmaid) was near nineteen years old.

The ceremony over, the bride was kissed and caressed by numerous friends and relatives. The musicians in full band now struck up the gay quadrille, and the handsome Alexander Murray led forth the bride, his cousin, to grace the head of the dance, and soon the floor was filled with light-footed girls and beaux, while others chatted merrily round, or looked with admiration at the dancers.

Tom Blair and his lovely bride were there, and the pretty blackeyed Sophy Denny, the affianced of the handsome Brady Wilkins; also the young beauty in her teens, Mary Mahon, with her boquet presented by young Morrison Foster. [So that's where the flowers went, Mitty!]

As Julia Murray met Brady Wilkins to balancez [yes, that's the way it's spelled] in the dance; with her little hand, she crushed and broke an elegant fan that she held, which had been presented to her by Morrison Foster. The latter saw the act, but said nothing. He danced the gayer, and seemed devoted the most of the evening to Miss Mahon.

Julia Murray was importuned to dance by two gentlemen, one at each elbow, Mr. Brown and Mr. Eugene Borda. Looking at her card, to discover where their names came in, she said, "No, Mr. Brown, you are very much mistaken, it is the dance after the next. I am engaged to Mr. Foster for the next set."

"Mr. Foster must have been very early then, indeed, Miss Julia," replied Mr. Brown, "for I am sure I requested that pleasure as you passed through the hall."

Without replying to this remark, Julia addressed herself laughingly to Mr. Borda, saying, "I am afraid we shall not have a dance together this evening."

"Impossible, Mees Murray," said the Frenchman, "I ask you long time before ze grand entree, you could not be engaged all zees time!"

"Oh, oui, Monsieur, I have indeed!" said she, casting a merry glance toward young Mr. Cowan, who appeared to be enjoying the scene vastly a short distance off.

After a promenade and waltzing, the second set of quadrilles filled the floor. Mr. Morrison Foster led out Julia Murray, vis a vis to Miss Anne Robinson and Mr. Harry Reed, an old lover of the latter.

"I never tore the fan purposely," said Julia to Mr. Foster, as they danced forward, "Respect for your feelings, no one has more than I have."

After a while her voice was again heard, in answer to some remarks in an undertone of Mr. Foster. "I suppose you are tired of the purse I made you; if so burn it—I would carry the boquet holder, if I had any flowers to put in it. So you are angry, Morrison! well, I suppose we will not have our annual ride this year on the third of April!"

Dear Eliza Foster! With what an eye for romance did she watch her boy as he flitted from one lovely maiden to another—one carrying his flowers, the other his broken fan.

The quadrille was ended and the music changed to a polka. In this dance nothing could exceed the graceful elegance of Miss Annie Robinson as she moved with exquisite exactness to the time of the music.

It was also delightful to observe young Mrs. Denny, whirling round in the waltz with that ease and measured graceful step which distinguished her. Fourteen months before, she became the bride of Captain James O'Hara Denny, he the grandson of General James O'Hara and of Major Denny; she, the granddaughter of General John Wilkins and the daughter of Jane Wilkins Dallas. One week after their nuptials, he left his bride and home to serve his country on the far distant plains of Mexico, where he still was, in command of his company.

Mrs. Foster now took her seat in a quiet corner with Mrs. Upfold and Mrs. Beelen. Here also was Mrs. Hutchinson, the eldest daughter of the host, who, though looking delicate, had always been remarkable for loveliness and gentle ladylike behavior.

Judge Wilkins soon offered his arm to Mrs. Upfold, and led the way to the supper-room. Every luxury and delicacy were tastefully arranged upon two long tables, which were now surrounded by beauty and fashion. Miss Mahon and young Mr. Andrew Robinson were enjoying themselves in one corner, in a subdued tete a tete, as he helped her to candied grapes and other delicacies. She was a pretty little creature dressed in pink with frills of the same colour. Miss Robinson stood near gaily chatting with her cousin Harry Murray, a handsome young gentleman, with black eyes and hair, and as high minded and honorable as he is handsome.

Time flitted by, and it was a late hour before the party found themselves on their way home.

Evidently, Miss Murray's rather broad hint on the night of the wedding did not fall on barren soil, for her annual ride with young Mr. Foster took place as usual on April 3, 1848. Julia got her flowers, too, to put in the empty bouquet-holder. Let Mrs. Foster describe the scene:

It was the third of April. A young lady of marvelous beauty stood equipped for a ride. A hostler soon led two rather gay animals to the door of Mrs. Murray. Mrs. Foster, who at that moment stepped in, asked Julia if she was not afraid to mount so fierce and spirited a horse.

"Oh, no!" said she, gaily, "I am quite accustomed to riding Snip!"

"Won't you stay the evening, Mrs. Foster?" said Mrs. Murray.

"No, not at present," replied she, "I set out for my usual afternoon walk to prevent me from being drowsy. But I will stop on my return and remain the evening with you."

Mr. Morrison Foster here made his appearance, and assisted Miss Julia to mount Snip. He threw himself into the saddle and the young couple rode quietly forward and were soon out of sight.

In the evening, they returned, looking the gayest of the gay. Julia carried in her hand an elegant boquet which had been procured for her by Mr. Foster.

Mrs. Murray, and her married daughter, [Mrs. John B. Guthrie] were engaged in some preparations for attending the wedding of Brady Wilkins and Sophy Denny [the daughter of William H. Denny] which was to take place the following week.

"What is going on this evening?" said Mrs. Foster, observing that the rooms were being unusually lighted up.

"Oh, not much," observed Mrs. Guthrie, "Julia and her friends have a musical soiree."

"Will young Mrs. Denny be here?" asked Mrs. Foster.

"Yes," replied Mrs. Guthrie, "we have persuaded her to come round. There is no use in her staying at home forever, looking out so anxiously for O'Hara Denny. If he did come down with the last train from Mexico to Vera Cruz, he could not get here yet."

Before long, singers and performers began to assemble.

Miss Mary Irwin was the prima-donna of the evening. The music was enchanting, and Julia Murray having a sweet voice, bore her part with great taste. When the programme was ended, they danced to the piano, and closed the evening merrily.

A few days afterward, Morrison Foster left home for a journey to the south, and Mr. Alex Murray took his departure for the ocean, regretting to leave behind him Miss Susan Fulton.

Following is one paragraph from a lengthy and romantic description of the return of young James O'Hara Denny on the steamboat *Telegraph,* and the touching reunion of young Mrs. Denny with her soldier-husband:

She flew to the door to look for him, and immediately came back again, seeming not well to know whether to remain in the parlour or out in the hall. Before long, however, Mr. Harmar Denny came in presenting his son, O'Hara. This young gentleman was tall, straight, and elegantly formed with black hair and eyes and beard, with all the manly bearing of Major Denny, his grandfather. He had been doing a soldier's duty for sixteen months, having left the sweet girl he was now about to meet, a few days after their marriage. How was she to receive him, as a lover or a husband? Between these conflicting feelings, she came forward, pale and agitated, gave him her hand, and her head quietly fell upon his breast. Mrs. Guthrie and Mrs. Foster immediately rose and withdrew, rejoiced to see the happiness of their young friends complete.

The question as to whether James O'Hara Denny's reception was that of a lover or a husband does not seem to be answered.

"When do you go to Cincinnati to visit your son, Mrs. Foster?" asked Mrs. Murray.

"Next week," replied Mrs. Foster.

"Tell your son Dunning," said Julie, "that if he stays much longer away from Pittsburgh, we will not acknowledge him."

"Oh," said another young lady, "I suppose he will not come until Miss Annie Robinson sends for him!"

"I think," said Julia, "that my commands would have more effect upon him than those of Annie Robinson. He might at least have come to see us after being all the way to Mexico, and nearly losing his life there!"

The manuscript for 1848 ends abruptly here, when Eliza Foster was called suddenly to Cincinnati by the serious illness of her son, Morrison. All these trifling little events, set down in story form, were of the greatest importance and interest to the little granddaughters, Mary and Lidie Wick, to whom Grandma read many of these chapters just as she finished them. They were enchanted with the love-making, the balls and parties, the handsome belles and beaux riding round on "gay animals," especially when these romantic heroes and heroines were their own young uncles and their friends. If some of the "Knights of the S. T." had known of the affecting love scenes in which they played a prominent part, I think they would have left town.

Another glimpse into that long-ago world of youthful happiness and heartaches is revealed in a package of beautiful old handmade valentines preserved by Julie Murray LeMoyne (Mrs. William B. McIlvaine) of Hubbard Woods, Illinois, the youngest daughter of lovely Julia Murray. The majority of these charming epistles, bright with silver birds, lace, and pink rosebuds, were meant to twit Julia on her fickleness of heart. In 1847, it is evident that the little lady gravitated uncertainly between Mit Foster and Joe Brown, J. Cust Blair and James O'Hara. When she finally settled on Jim for a time, Mit concocted a dire prophecy of the situation in which Julia could expect to find herself ten years hence; on St. Valentine's Day, 1847, he sent her "A Vision of 1857":

> "I dreamed a dream in the midst of my slumbers"
> "And as fast as I dreamed it was coined into numbers"—
> Methought the dark veil of the future was raised,
> And into its depths unobstructed I gazed—
> Before me a snug looking cottage appeared,
> And a garden where Morus Mult'caulis was reared.
> On one side a river ran rapidly past,
> While on 'tother, (as slow as the river was fast)
> Pennsylvania's canal, was still there, and unpaid for
> And tax payers (as now) wondering what it was made for.—
> By a ferry the river's clear surface was stirred,
> And Guyasuta's forge hammer contagious was heard.—
> Having no lack of impudence, when wide awake
> Sleep appeared not a jot of it from me to take;
> But into the midst of that house snug and nice,
> Transferred the subscriber in less than a trice.—
> Now what I saw there if you'll patiently wait,
> I'll as quickly as possible try to relate.—
> Close by the fire, in an easy arm-chair,
> Sat the lord of the house, with long yellow hair,
> There were chairs, tables, bedstead, a cradle, &c;
> And to keep his head warm when inclined for to go forth,

Julia Nancy Murray, to whom Stephen Foster dedicated
"Wilt Thou Be Gone, Love," from a portrait by J. R. Lambdin, 1849

"Julia's Valentine," sent to Julia Nancy Murray
by Richard Cowan about 1851

A white hat; which though now somewhat rusty and old,
Was as good *as the new* one to keep out the cold.
I did not disturb him, but waited to see,
Who, of all these nice fixins, the mistress could be.
Nor had I staid long, when a voice at the door
Which recalled to my mind one known well of yore
Sighed out in a tone which your pity would move,
"Oh! of what use are riches, without there is love"*—
I turned round to see, who bewailed thus her doom
When the fair belle of 5th Street entered the room.
Not as she now appears; lively, and glad,
But sorrowful, pale, dejected, and sad.—
I wished to see more; but as you will know it
Dreams always shut down, when you want them to go it.
Thus 'twas with me! for a jerk and a crash
Knocked the house and the garden, to almighty smash;
Guyasuta's bright fire went out in a minute,
As if a young torrent had just been poured in it.
The tilt-hammer flew with a kind of a slant,
And lit on the shore of the river beyant,
(Where Uncle Sam sends his big guns to be proved
And pays so much money for having them moved,)
Then a darkness ensued; such as that which ('tis said)
Shrouds the regions where howl the impenitent dead,
Or with which, a large stack of black Cats is o'erspread,
And I woke with a start, and a feeling of dread;
But collecting my senses soon thought, what a fine
Subject this would be, for your

Valentine

To Miss Julia N. Murray

*and Vice Versa—Whats the use of love without riches—

"Guyasuta" was the historic home of Jim O'Hara's grandfather, General James O'Hara, and was named for the Indian chief, Guyasuta, whose remains were interred on the farm. This great estate was located on the north bank of the Allegheny River near Sharpsburg, a mile or so above the Lawrenceville arsenal on the opposite side of the river. A portion of Guyasuta is now maintained as a bird sanctuary by the Boy Scouts of America.

Jim O'Hara's garden of "Morus Multicaulis," whatever they were, was a favorite subject of jest and is mentioned in three of Julia's valentines. One of these, a seriocomic effusion apparently in the handwriting of Tom Blair, contains these verses:

> See'st thou, fair maid, the Morus Multicaulis
>   And him, the chosen one, with spade in hand,
> With spacious hat & manly figure, tall as
>   Those interesting plants which round him stand?
> From twelve months back,—that sight—how't would appal us
>   But now behold thee there, with features bland
> And placid, happy face; wherein we view
> Not what has been, but that which will be—you.
>
> *Is* this—oh *can* this be—the widow Foster?
>   —And yet, who *am* I, that should thus complain?
> Would I, in this her love, have wished to've crossed her
>   —xxx Miss Julia, here the effusion did remain
> Unfinished, for my wandering muse had lost, or
>   More properly—had dropped—her rightful strain.
> For this I will confess, in accents meek
> The whisky Punch was strong, & I was weak.

Another, from an unknown sender, depicts Morrison fervently gazing at a demure damsel in a pink dress while in the background looms a large warehouse bearing a huge sign "Hope Yarns." Below are these verses:

> Mit Foster was as gay a boy
> As ever said his prayers,
> His heart was big, & full of joy
> His face was full of hairs.
>
> I'm speaking now of what Mit *was*,
> He's *now* another creature;
> How easy 'tis to guess the cause
> That changed his every feature.
>
> In talking state affairs one day,
> I said, "be careful of *that Julia*,
> She's a sweet creature in her way,
> But look out! or she'll fool you."

Ah! little did avail my words,
All useless was the warning;
They flew into his ear like birds,
And out the other ere next morning.

He courted her, he sported her,
At concert and at Blitz's,
He adored her, he assured her
That he didn't love in *fits as*

Blair & Cowan & some more do,
Or like Brown & Squire O'Hara,
And when he could afford to,
He said that he would marry.

Alas! Alas!! my poor friend Foster
You courted, almost won & lost her,
I now believe as it was said by "some un"
If you're hunting *faith* don't look for it in woman.*

The marriage of Sophy Denny and Brady Wilkins occurred on April 11, 1848, and was followed shortly by two more weddings of other young friends close to the hearts of all "Square Tablers"— Marian McDowell and John Scully on April 27, and Martha Shoenberger and John Duncan on May 2. Morrison made note of all three ceremonies, but was unable to attend any of them because he started for the South on April 7. Besides Morrison Foster and sundry other small fry, the *Clipper No. 2* was honored this trip by the presence on board of two important military figures of the day, Brigadier General Shields, and Major Stockton.

This almost proved to be Mit's last journey down the river or anywhere else. On May 21, he came down with malarial fever in New Orleans and took to his bed in the Planter House. There he remained ten days, and we don't know how he managed, nor who took care of him. He started north on the *Magnolia* on June 8, but became so ill that he had to leave the boat on June 14 at Evansville, Indiana, where he was placed under the care of Dr. Morgan. The captain of the *Magnolia* took the news to Dunning in Cincin-

*These extracts from Julia's valentines have been reproduced through the kindness of Julie Murray LeMoyne (Mrs. William B. McIlvaine).

nati, and the latter immediately came down to Evansville and took charge of his sick brother. Mit was able to leave there with Dunning on June 25, but they had to quit the boat at Louisville, and Mit could not proceed for four days. In the meantime, his mother had been notified and was there with Stephen to greet her sick boy when he and Dunning disembarked at Cincinnati from the *Ben Franklin* on the first of July. At this time, Dunning and Stephen were making their home at Mrs. Griffin's on Fourth Street, a few blocks from the offices of Irwin & Foster, and a short walk from the home of Mrs. Marshall on Third Street. The entire family had been appraised of Morrison's serious condition by what Ann Eliza called the "unsatisfactory language of the telegraph." But Ma took him in charge at Cincinnati, and on July 11, they were able to leave for Pittsburgh on the steamboat *Niagara*. Morrison never was too sick to jot down the name of the boat.

An idea of the effect of the Chartist uprising on the cotton market, and the condition of business in general in 1848, can be gleaned from a couple of letters to Morrison from his employer, Mr. McCormick. These are included here because they may be of interest to students of commercial history in the United States.

Pitts. May 5th, 1848

Mr. M. Foster,
    Care Messrs. Johnson & Smith,
      Nashville, Tennessee
Dear Sir,

Your last letter is to hand; the *Loyal Hannah* has not arrivd. I think it advisable to buy *good* cotton even if you have to pay five cts. The market may stiffen with next news, since the Chartists trouble is over (which was a humbug as to power) & the poor Irish will probably do nothing but talk, & even if they should try their hands, it will not retard manufacturing operation in England. There will no doubt be some fighting on the Continent; *it* will decrease the consumption of cotton among the belligerents & will proportionably revive the English establishments. A large demand must arise for coarse cotton & woolen goods.—The information by the *America* is not cheering for such places as Manchester, for they admit manufacturing to be *very* dull, and yet, in the same breath, claim an advance of 1/4 ct. on cotton. This figure must have been forced, for it is in contradiction to the other part of the news.

However, I think it would be impolitic to wait longer. If you cannot operate where you are, without delay I would advise you to go to Memphis, or farther if deemed advisable, and authorize Messrs. Johnson & Smith to buy for you by Drfts. on us 5 to 600 Bales if it can be bought for 5 to 5¼c. per pound.—

I have just recd. a letter from Mr. Kraft in Memphis, he quotes—middling, 4½—middling fair 5 & 5¼—plenty there, but owners disposed to hold on; should you find yourself compelled to go to N. Orleans you would require your drfts. converted, in which event try & see if you cannot get hold of as good a lot of Red River cotton as you did a few years since, on as good terms as you can by Mississippi or Tennessee. It was the best spinning cotton we ever had. We have now on hand here some three or four hundred Bales at 6½, so you see we have had no difficulty in getting along & aplenty offering to us. Write if you intend leaving Nashv.

Yours Respfly.   P. McCormick.

May 11th, 1848

Dear Sir,

It will require us now to be exceedingly active if we wish to make a proffitable years work. Much will depend on your exertions. Can you not make arrangements with one, two, or three houses in Nashville to purchase for you as *rapidly* as *possible* 10 or 1200 Bales.—you might tell Mr. Corry that we are entirely free from debt, with our Mill. City Property here, & Phila. property which would in ordinary times sell for $350,000; this is no small backing. In any event, please present him my sincere thanks for his kindness to our interest there. If you could arrange it for 1500 Bales, so much the better. You might then proceed with your funds to Memphis & see if Mr. Kraft could not buy 2 to 500 for you, on even 60-day Bills, then go to New Orleans with your cash if you find you can lay it out to more advantage. See Messrs. Burke Watt & Co. as soon as possible. You can get them to purchase for you & draw on us as before (if they can't do better.) All your purchases I think should *now* be made without delay & you know the value of even ⅛ to us in the cost.

Telegraph me when you can so as to let us know your locality. I shall write you at Memphis, care Mr. Kraft & New Orleans, Messrs. B. W. & Co. [Burke, Watt and Co.] I would not come back with *less* than *Three Thousand Bales*. We can work it out; once through, you should hurry

back to help us out here. If your cotton does not cost you more than 5¼
or 5½ here, you will make a pretty penny, worth indeed struggling for.

Yours Respectly.
P. McCormick.

Morrison's accounts show that he was able to purchase only 835
bales, then his sickness put an end to all business negotiations for
that trip. But he managed to do an exchange business of over $24,-
000 before he gave up the struggle and went to bed.

Eliza Foster's days in Cincinnati were not all clouded by anxiety.
Her good friends there relieved the strain of her nursing with frequent calls and kind attentions. At this time, Stephen was working
on a song which he dedicated to Sophie Marshall; the sweet melody
and sentiment of "Stay, Summer Breath," must have pleased his
mother as well as Sophie. It is a light, fanciful little song like "What
Must a Fairy's Dream Be?" and reveals the unaffected and ingenuous
disposition of the young composer. "Stay, Summer Breath" was
advertised on July 15, 1848, by W. C. Peters, as "just published."
Although it never became famous, it probably lived its little hour
in the drawing rooms of the day.

On July 17, 1848, Ann Eliza directed a letter to Morrison in care
of Dunning, as she did not know that he had already left for home.
Although relieved to hear of his physical well-being, its contents
show that she was still far from easy about her brother's spiritual
state.

Through the kindness of Henry, I was kept constantly in possession
of the last news from you, and it has been, I hope, with unfeigned
gratitude to God that I have lately received such encouraging accounts
of your improving health. As you may imagine, the first news of your
illness conveyed in the concise and unsatisfactory language of the Telegraph was very distressing to me. Through the mercy of God, in answer
to our prayers, you have I trust been restored once more to health and
I for one feel deeply that this new mark of His favour towards us calls
loudly upon me to devote myself with renewed diligence to His service,
and I hope that as a family, we may be enabled to "shew forth our
thanks not only with our lips, but in our *lives*."

For yourself, my dear brother, I trust and most earnestly pray that the
goodness of God thus manifested to you may constrain you to turn
away from every sinful pursuit and every idle vanity, and give yourself

up soul and body a living sacrifice to Him who died Himself for you.

I have been much pleased to hear that our dear Mother was with you and hope you will soon be able to accompany her home. When you are strong enough, I think a journey across the mountains might be of service to you. You may be well assured that such an opportunity of seeing you once more would be hailed with delight by us all.

Tell Ma, we are all in our usual health—poor Charlotte continueing very delicate. I wish I could hear more frequently and more particularly about Ma, I am often very anxious about her. Give much love to dear Dunning and Stephen and tell them I never forget to include them very particularly in my prayers. Hoping to hear very soon from you all, I remain your sincerely attached sister,

                                                    Ann Eliza.

Mr. Buchanan (whose interest in you was particularly manifested during your sickness) joins me in affectionate remembrances.

Just before Morrison took sick on May 21, 1848, in New Orleans, W. C. Peters had published "Old Uncle Ned," and C. Holt, Jr., of New York issued an edition of "Oh! Susanna." It is doubtful if Stephen said very much to either Morrison or Dunning of the number of manuscript copies of these songs which he had given away to his minstrel friends, nor of how many publishers he allowed to have copies with "neither permission nor restriction in regard to publishing them," to quote his own words. These are contained in a letter to William E. Millet, written about a year later, which shows that Stephen gave little or no thought to his rights as author and composer of the songs he handed out so freely to singers and publishers. The letter is dated May 25, 1849, at Cincinnati.

Mr. Wm. E. Millet

Dear Sir

I hasten to acknowledge the receipt of your favor of the 21st inst. and to give you what information I can touching the subject of your inquiry.

I gave manuscript copies of each of the songs "Lou'siana Belle"— "Uncle Ned"—& "Oh, Susanna" to several persons before I gave them to Mr. Peters for publication, but in neither instance with any permission nor *restriction* in regard to publishing them, unless contained in a letter to Mr. Roark accompanying the m.s. of "Uncle Ned"—although of this I am doubtful. Mr. Peters has my receipt for each of the songs.

The only information which I can give you in regard to dates, as my memory does not serve me, must be in copying the years named on the title-pages of the Cincinnati publications, from which I infer that "Lou'siana Belle" was copyrighted in 1847—the others in 1848.

If I see Mr. Roark (who lives in our city) I will give you further information in regard to the letter which I wrote him. I have the honor, sir, to subscribe myself

Very Respectfully Yours

Stephen C. Foster.

By this time, minstrel shows all over the country were singing "Uncle Ned" and "Susanna." In 1848, the famous Southern Sable Harmonists' songs were published in a special edition by Millet's Music Saloon, 329 Broadway, New York, with pictures of all the minstrel troupe on the cover page. William Roark, who seems to have been Stephen's special acquaintance, is pictured with long curls, like little Lord Fauntleroy. The caption of "Old Uncle Ned" claims this song was "Written & Composed for Wm. Roark of the Sable Harmonists by S. C. Foster of Cincinnati." We know this is not strictly accurate—"Uncle Ned" was written and composed for the Knights of the Square Table, but the Sable Harmonists were possibly the first to sing "Uncle Ned" professionally in public. This Millet edition was copyrighted May 16, 1848; also published in the Sable Harmonists' special edition in 1848 were Stephen's "Lou'-siana Belle" and "Oh! Susanna" which were advertised for sale at Mellor's Music Store in Pittsburgh.

Another song in the Sable Harmonists' 1848 list lately has been discovered to be the work of Stephen Foster, "Way Down South in Alabama." This song is included in many minstrel anthologies without any composer named. But in the collection of the late Maskell Ewing, Jr., of Philadelphia, a grandson of Ann Eliza Buchanan, there is a bound volume of Stephen's songs collected by Ann Eliza, and in that book there is a copy of this song, entered for copyright in 1848 by W. E. Millet, with the usual elaborate cover page showing all the Sable Harmonists, and on the inside it states "Music by S. C. Foster—Arranged by Frank Spencer." It undoubtedly is a hitherto unknown Foster song, the melody only of which was composed by Stephen. This air is spirited and lively.

Frank Spencer possibly was a member of the Sable Harmonists' troupe. His name appears as the author of the words of a song called "Young Folks at Home," music by Hattie Livingston, published in 1852 by Gould & Berry of New York, and "written & composed expressly for Wood's Minstrels—Minstrel's Hall, 444 Broadway." The author of the words of "Way Down South in Alabama" is not known—they are of the typical waggish minstrel style.

It is too bad that Stephen did not compose an accompaniment to this tune himself, for Frank Spencer's, even though it contains possibilities, is poorly constructed, and shows but a meagre knowledge of composition. It is likely, however, that the minstrel arranger only suggested the theme to be followed by the musicians, and, like "swing bands" of the present day, each member carried the song along in his own original way, producing quite as pleasing an effect as a carefully worked out score. On the whole, Stephen's melody and Spencer's suggested arrangement of "Way Down South in Alabama" are very appealing, and the song is recommended to modern orchestras for revival. The prospect of going back to Alabama always seems to inspire song writers to introduce the pleasant sound of train whistles into their compositions. Stephen's melody contains a long-sounding "Ah-Hoo" in the chorus which is almost exactly the same in tune and rhythm as in two popular songs of a few years ago, "Alabamy Bound," by Green, De Sylva, and Henderson, and Irving Berlin's "When That Midnight Choo-choo Leaves for Alabam'!"

The discovery that "Way Down South in Alabama" was composed by Stephen C. Foster leads one to wonder how many of the anonymous minstrel songs of the late 1840's might not be Stephen's also. C. Holt, Jr., of New York, got out three editions of this song without giving Stephen credit. It is not improbable that the unassuming young composer frequently jotted down melodies for his minstrel friends which he did not consider worth mentioning even to members of his own family. Morrison Foster does not include "Alabama" in his list of Stephen's early compositions, but it must be remembered that Morrison was ill for many weeks during the year 1848, and it may have been that Stephen considered his contribution to the minstrel show too inconsequential to note.

Stephen's compositions were rapidly gaining favor all over the country, and without doubt Morrison brought a bundle of his brother's music back to Pittsburgh with him from New York, to present to the several young ladies amongst whom he divided his attentions, not to mention bouquets and "elegant fans." One of these belles was Mary Anderson, who played the piano and sang, and was a pupil of Henry Kleber. In 1853, Mr. Kleber dedicated a very charming but difficult song, "Spring is Coming," to Mary Anderson. It is described on the cover as "brilliant," and if her teacher composed it for Miss Mary's own performance, it shows that she must have been an exceptionally fine singer.

On July 29, 1848, Mary Anderson addressed a letter from fashionable Bedford Springs to "Mr. Mit Foster." It is the same letter in which she expressed her great pleasure at receiving Morrison's "most excellent likeness."

My dear Friend,

Do not think for one moment that I have forgotten you. I intended answering the letter you wrote from Nashville, but was told by everyone that it would be useless, as you would be on your way home before my letter could reach you. I then put it off until I heard of your illness, and then, O, how I regretted not having written instantly, but then Alas! I feared it was too late, for from all acounts, I feared we had met for the last time. I mourned you as one passed away forever; but thank Heaven that is all over, and you are safe once more. I long to see you so much, you cannot tell how many thousand times I have wished and wished again for just one peep at your sincere face.

Mary then thanks Morrison for the daguerreotype, and continues:

I had a letter from Jule [Julia Murray] the other day; she tells me that you are recovering, and that everybody goes to see you. Perhaps you think I should not like to be one of your visitors. However, I shall soon be home, and then you can come to see me, and we will have some more long talks, like those we had last winter.

Bedford has not been very gay this season, but still I have had a very pleasant time. Beaux have been plenty lately, such as they are, and with Joe Brown and Dick [Cowan] to call upon in a case of emergency, I am in a very good way. I am rather melancholy today, however, as Dick Stevenson left this morning, and I saw a great deal of him; we became great friends, I feel quite lost today. We had a most delightful ride on horseback yesterday evening, but Alas, it is all past. One would think I was in love to hear me talk, but as you happen to have a different belief, I shall let it rest.

How are you and Jule getting on? I hope you have concluded to look upon her as an old and good friend. You must tell me everything when I return. And now for another friend? How is Cust? I have heard nothing of him since I left. Davie Bell wrote to me not long since, and I shall answer his letter very soon. How are Brady and Jack Townsend?

I wish, if you are able, that you would write to me. I should be delighted to hear from you. I make a last request that you will let *no* one see my letter, above all people do not let *Cust* see one letter of it. I have a particular reason for making the request.

The dressing bell will ring in a few minutes, and as I wish my letter to go tomorrow, I shall send this off directly. Do write to me if you feel able. Tell Will [her brother] that I shall write tomorrow, Sunday, my letter day. I am going to town tomorrow to sing in the *Catholic Church*. And now, good-bye, for I must stop. Believe me ever

Your sincere friend,
Mary H. Anderson.

Singing around the old square piano in the evening was the principal social diversion of all the friends of Stephen Foster and his brothers. There was music wherever Morrison, Stephen, and Dunning went. Mit possessed an agreeable low baritone, and he copied the verses of many a song that he found on his travels. In Cincinnati, he made the acquaintance of a young actor named James G. Drake, who was the author of "Tom Breeze," a favorite ballad of the day. This sailor tune possessed a lusty swing that found high favor with the basses and baritones of 1848. Poor Drake died in 1850, only thirty-four years old. The first verse of "Tom Breeze," as preserved in Morrison's diary, is:

> Here's a health to thee, Tom Breeze!
> Tom Breeze, of the mountain billow;
> May grief sit lightly on thy breast
> As feathers neath thy pillow.
> Let the tide of fate roll on,
> Revealing joy and sadness,
> I'll pledge to thee and thine, Tom Breeze,
> A cup brim full of gladness!

By the middle of July, 1848, Morrison and his mother were back with Pa in their homelike rooms at the St. Charles Hotel. Mit was too weak to attend to any business, but time did not hang heavily on his hands, for, as Mary Anderson said, everybody called on him, rejoiced to find him still in the land of the living. When he finally set out, on October 9, to return those calls, he had thirty-two names on his list! He covered the list in three days, which was a pretty good record for an erstwhile sick man. One call was on Jane McDowell, whose hospitable home had become a favorite gathering place for the club, not only on account of the six girls, including Mrs. Scully, but because Dr. McDowell was a genial host to his daughters' young friends. He was undoubtedly interested in hearing from Morrison the latest news of William's progress, for the good doctor was amongst the forward-looking Pittsburghers who had organized a pioneer railroad company called the Pittsburgh and Connells-ville Railroad, whose charter was issued as early as 1837. This char-ter had been taken over by the Pennsylvania, and the outcome of their work was of great concern to the men who had originally pro-moted the venture. William's headquarters were now at Lewistown, midway between Harrisburg and Altoona, which meant that he and his fellow workers were pushing the railroad westward at a rapid rate.

This was a presidential year, but there was little excitement in the Foster family, as Brother William was definitely out of politics for a time. His father troubled to preserve only the returns of Alle-gheny County because his cousin, John K. Foster, had been elected to the office of county auditor. General Zachary Taylor, the Whig candidate, and hero of the Mexican War, was almost as popular with the Democrats as with the Whigs. Martin Van Buren had formed a new party called the Liberty Party, or Free-Soilers, and the success of the Democratic candidate, Lewis Cass, was hindered by this defection, as well as by the people's enthusiasm for General Taylor.

However, Morrison missed the pre-election days' uproar in Pittsburgh, for as soon as he had made his calls, he and Ma started on October 12 on a trip to the East. They arrived in Lewistown, "by canal boat packet," on October 15, and visited with William and Elizabeth and their two children, Lottie and Willie, three more days, and then went on to Philadelphia. Morrison and his mother stayed for several days at a popular boardinghouse conducted by Mrs. Levely while Ma made calls on old friends and relatives. And one evening Mit took his mother to an Italian grand opera then playing an engagement in Philadelphia. The Americans were introduced to "real Grand Opera, just like Paris," when the Astor Place Opera House, of New York, opened in November, 1847, with *Ernani*. The programs show that Madame Biscaccianti, later a friend of Morrison's and Stephen's, sang in *La Somnambula* that season. Catrina Barilli-Patti, mother of Adelina Patti, was a member of this company. Morrison did not attend the Astor Place Opera House when he reached New York early in November, 1848, but he took in the museum, a diorama, and two theaters in one week. His accounts show eleven dollars expended for an overcoat, but nothing paid for white kid gloves, that insignia of the "silk-stocking gentry" required of all who attended performances of grand opera at Astor Place. An advertisement appearing in a Philadelphia paper for January 25, 1847, gives one an idea of the strict requirements for grand opera in those days, even for members of the chorus.

> WANTED IMMEDIATELY.—Some ladies choruses for the Italian opera; none to apply but those who are more or less acquainted with music, to call at Mr. Willig's Music Store, Chestnut St.

While Morrison continued on his way to New York and Boston, and the mill town of Lowell, Massachusetts, Eliza Foster went out to Paradise to visit her daughter, Ann Eliza. There were seven little Buchanans now; the youngest, Marie Lois, born in 1847, her grandmother had never seen. Morrison joined his mother on November 11, 1848, at "Mr. Buchanan's in Lancaster County," and stayed with his sister for several days. As Eliza Foster desired to visit a while longer with her little grandchildren, she did not accompany Morrison when he left Paradise, on November 15, for Baltimore and Washington. Morrison stayed four days with brother Henry, seeing the sights of the capital, then started home on November 20, arriving in Pittsburgh on the twenty-third. His mother reached home early in December, and soon thereafter the family gave up their rooms at the St. Charles Hotel, and on December 7, according to Morrison's account book, "commenced boarding at Miss Hetick's."

Although he was not in New York very long, Morrison was there long enough to catch a disease that might have proved more disastrous than malaria—that was the gold fever. Gold had been discovered in California, and the whole country was in a state of wild excitement. New York was probably the most feverish spot, for there the would-be millionaires were being outfitted with gold-digging equipment, and crowding onto vessels that would take them to Panama, or even the whole way to California, down around the Horn. There had been no official announcement yet of the gold discovery when Mit was in New York, but plenty of unofficial, firsthand stories were to be heard, and every newsboy was singing Stephen's song set to new words!

> Oh, California!
> That's the land for me—
> I'm going to Sacramento
> With my washbowl on my knee!

On December 18, Mit's diary states he "wrote to William and Dunning"; he does not say on what subject, but Dunning's reply tells us that!

Cincinnati Dec. 29, 1848

Dear Brother,

I received your letter of 18th inst. by due course of mail, and glad to learn that your health has at length become good. Your notion of Gold Hunting is very good, but I cannot advise you to undertake the journey, and more especially as you would be obliged to go without money sufficient to give you a good start. I have had the fever slightly but am now recovering slowly—that there is gold and plenty of it, I have no doubt and that a young man with proper industry could make a fortune I cannot doubt either; but whether the expense and change of climate and perfect estrangement from everybody for whom you feel any interest would compensate for the accumulation of riches to be left for others to enjoy, is a question that I cannot so easily satisfy myself about. You must expect to undergo many hardships that you do not dream of in a trip so full of uncertainty and adventure. If I had nothing to bind me to home and could leave without creating a pang in the breast of any person I should leave behind me, I would start immediately and undergo all the hardships and troubles of the trip merely for the adventure; but as I am now situated, I cannot reconcile it to my mind that I should be evincing a proper respect for the feelings of my good parents and friends who have laid us under so many and lasting obligations. These are the only considerations that will prevent me from going to California and the Gold Diggin's, and they are weighty reasons with me.

It would be out of my power to give you much assistance in money in case you make up your mind to go, but what I can do I will do with pleasure, and wish you all the luck that an honest and intelligent adventurer could have befall him, and while I cannot say Go, I shall not offer any objection, if you make up your mind to undertake the trip.

I shall now turn from the bright picture of Gold and riches to the dark and desolating one of Cholera, that sweeps alike the rich and poor, teaching man that there is a power above more potent and powerful than all the glittering wealth of California. It is not yet in Cincinnati, but is *hourly expected*. The Captain of the *Saint Cloud*, Jubez Smith, will be here tonight a corpse, having died in a few hours. He was a good and worthy man, and his death has thrown a gloom over our house, where everybody loved and respected him. Peace to his ashes! If there is a place beyond for the honest and noble-minded, he is there, and happy.

The accounts today are such as to deter boats from leaving for New Orleans. The *Diadem, George Washington* and *Alhambra* are loaded, but will not start until we get better accounts. Business is very much affected, also. Pork is declining rapidly, and will go a good deal lower unless the health of New Orleans improves.

I cannot determine what time I will visit Pittsburgh, but will do so as soon as possible. Give my best love to Ma and Pa and my respects to all our friends.

Your brother,

D. M. Foster.

This is the first letter to Morrison that shows evidence of being mailed enclosed in an envelope; heretofore, as was the custom, the sheet of paper had been folded and sealed with a dab of red wax. Letters from small towns like Paradise still came in the old way, with the postage rate written in the right-hand corner by the postmaster, but the large towns had been supplied with that convenient little innovation, the postage stamp.

Strange to say, in Dunning's next letter, written barely two weeks after the foregoing, he completely reverses himself and scoffs at the idea that there is any danger of cholera in Cincinnati. This is accounted for by the fact that Stephen had come back to Pittsburgh in December or January, and had taken Dunning at his word (or pretended to do so) that Cincinnati was soon to be swept by pestilence, and was not a safe place to which to return. Already, Stephen was straining at the leash, and in his music saw release from the intolerable bookkeeping. But Dunning was a practical and sensible brother, and, in ninety-nine cases out of a hundred, would have been right in insisting that Stephen stick to the "bird in hand." That Stephen's case was the exception, Dunning could not know, and neither could anyone else. The publication of two or three good minstrel songs did not indicate genius.

Dunning's advice to Morrison in regard to California was wise, for his younger brother was entirely unsuited to a life of exposure and physical hardship. But lately recovered from malaria, Morrison in all likelihood would never have reached the gold fields, but would have succumbed to one of the diseases that wiped out scores of amateur prospectors who tried to pierce the jungles of Panama, or cross the burning sands of the great American desert on their way to California.

Cincinnati   January 13, 1849

Dear Brother

I have received your letter of 9th inst. and am very much surprised to learn that you are indebted to me in the sum of fifty dollars, but as you say it is so, I shall not dispute your word. I do not know of any better purpose to apply this Godsend than in the way you propose and therefore desire that you should use it as you suggest. I am very glad to learn that you have abandoned the California gold speculation, as I feel confident that it is not an undertaking that would yield profit enough for the deprivation of comfort that you would be naturally subjected to. I agree with a letter writer in those parts that a full stomach of good food is better than full pockets of gold dust.

We have not the slightest apprehension about Cholera here—it is all a *bugbear*. Stephen need not stay away on that account. I would have liked very much to have been at the wedding of Isaac Pennock and Lizzy Grant, as they are both friends whom I highly esteem, and wish them all the joy and happiness that it is possible to fall to the lot of an honourable gentleman and an amiable and accomplished lady; this you can say to them for me.

We had quite a time last night at Mrs. Marshall's when we had a masked party, and an interesting and amazing one it was. All characters from the Roman Senator to the "bat" in the play of "Fair One with Golden Locks" were there to speak for themselves. My character was a Mexican soldier with the last remnants of a uniform and less of a face, all of which gave us a pleasant evening and most agreeable entertainment. I have entered considerably into the fashionable world again and may now be put down as one of the beaux (not b'hoys) of Cincinnati; which reputation I do not covet, but as I am amused I shall not quarrel about names. We have a party almost every night.

I am sorry that Jane McDowell is not with some of the young ladies that go into society, as I fear she will not have as favourable an impression of our people as she would have were she to see more of them. Mr. Stewart's family is not generally visited by people that would interest her much; however, she appears to enjoy herself very well, and does not complain in any way. She is, by the way, a very sensible and interesting young lady. I have a good deal of sport out of her and Lidia, and give them some strong doses of news from Pittsburgh, which they swallow with a good grace. They often sigh over the friends at Pittsburgh and wish to be with them, but as yet I have not heard them set a time to go up. They say they will go up when I do, but as that is a very indefinite period, it is not very conclusive as to the time they will be in Pittsburgh.

I shall avail myself of the first favourable moment to visit you. I am very anxious to see you all once more.

Give my love to Ma & Pa and believe me to remain

Your affectionate brother,
D. M. Foster.

VI

IT is likely that Stephen's first real friendship with Jane McDowell began in Cincinnati while Jane was visiting there. Dunning's letter was effective in returning Stephen to his desk at

Irwin & Foster's, and he was back in Cincinnati in February. It was natural that he and Dunning should drop around to Mr. Stewart's frequently to call on the young lady whom Dunning found "sensible and interesting." But Dunning also enjoyed the large parties, given by the fashionables of the city, which were not to Stephen's liking. He preferred the atmosphere of Mr. Stewart's quiet, old-fashioned parlor where he found a sympathetic companion in the girl from home.

Jane was born December 10, 1829. She came from a Scotch-Irish pioneer family whose background was practically the same as the Foster family's. We are indebted to Mrs. Virginia S. Fendrick, of Mercersburg, Pennsylvania, for the following information concerning the McDowells. Jane's great-great-grandfather, William McDowell, settled in Franklin County (Peters Township) in 1737 when the country was still a savage wilderness. During the Indian forays of 1754-55, at least part of the family fled to the Susquehanna. William McDowell died in 1759 and is buried in the old Donegal churchyard in Lancaster County, Pennsylvania. His son, William McDowell, married Mary Maxwell, daughter of Major William Maxwell and his wife, Susanna, and they had a large family, amongst them John, born in 1751, and Andrew, born in 1761. Dr. John McDowell was president of St. John's College at Annapolis, Maryland, in 1799 when George Washington sent his young stepgrandson, George Washington Parke Custis, to the school, and introduced him to Dr. McDowell with the following letter:

Consequent of a letter I have received from Mr. Stuart, I have been induced to confide to your care the young gentleman who will deliver this letter (George Washington Parke Custis.) You will find him intelligent, truthful and moral, and I have reason to hope he will live to justify the best expectations of his friends, and to be useful in the councils of his country.

Dr. John McDowell is buried in the old Waddell Presbyterian graveyard, now Spring Grove, near Mercersburg, Pennsylvania. His monument is inscribed as follows:

Underneath this marble is deposited the body of John
McDowell, Doctor of Laws, once principal of St. John's

College, in the State of Maryland, and late Provost of the University of Pennsylvania. Distinguished for learning, integrity and piety. Respected by the world, esteemed by his friends and beloved by his relations. He closed a life of useful labours on the 22nd day of December in the year of our Lord, 1820, and of his age the 69th.

Judging from the records, compiled by Mrs. Fendrick, Jane was a lineal descendant of Dr. John McDowell's brother Andrew. Andrew was also a learned educator of early days. He was graduated from the medical department of the University of Pennsylvania in 1787, and for a brief period was professor of Latin and Greek in the university. Dr. Andrew McDowell then settled in Chambersburg, Pennsylvania, where he remained in active and successful practice for forty years. He finally relinquished his practice and removed to Mercersburg where he died at the home of his son, another Dr. John McDowell, on January 13, 1846. Dr. Andrew McDowell was married on May 9, 1793, to Agnes McPherson, and of their family of about eight children, Andrew Nathan McDowell, Jane's father, also followed the family profession and attained a reputation in Pittsburgh as a fine physician. In 1824, Dr. McDowell married Jane Denny Porter of Chambersburg, a young lady who was an intimate friend of Charlotte Susanna Foster. It is interesting to note that the same minister, the Rev. David Denny, of Chambersburg, who married Stephen's father and mother, also performed the ceremony for Jane's parents. In 1826, Dr. and Mrs. McDowell, accompanied by Mrs. McDowell's sister, Miss Porter, removed to Meadville, Pennsylvania. Writing from Meadville to Charlotte Foster on March 3, 1826, Abby Barlow, the wife of Judge Stephen Barlow of that place, reported that the Meadville folks were "very much pleased" with the doctor and his lady and predicted that Dr. McDowell would "do very well" in Meadville. However, Dr. McDowell did not remain there long, but moved to Pittsburgh where he established an extensive practice early in the 1830's.

Dr. McDowell died very suddenly on May 7, 1849, leaving his wife and six daughters, Marian (Mrs. John D. Scully), Agnes (Mrs. Cummings), Mary, Elizabeth, and Alice (who did not marry), and Jane Denny McDowell.

Another loss sadly noted in Morrison's little diary was the death on January 15, 1849, of Catherine Dallas, as they still called her, and her newborn infant. It will be recalled how romantically Eliza Foster described the reunion of Catherine and her soldier-husband, Captain James O'Hara Denny, on his return from Mexico only the year before. In her reminiscences, Mrs. Foster expresses her deep sorrow at the death of this young wife, who was the daughter of her long-time friend, Jane Wilkins Dallas. Small wonder that in so many of his melancholy songs, Stephen Foster grieves for lost forms he called his own—loved ones, dear ones, who bloomed in the summer of his heart only to vanish one by one.

Lately, Stephen had been branching out in his musical field, and endeavoring to compose parlor pieces more suitable for young ladies to play for their friends than his rather rowdy minstrel songs. "Santa Anna's Retreat from Buena Vista" (copyrighted December 30, 1848, by W. C. Peters, Louisville) is written on this pattern, and might just as suitably have been named "General Scott Occupies Mexico City." There are some military effects produced by descending with the left hand in heavy octaves and twinkling along high up in the treble with the right. It probably made a very effective piano solo during an evening devoted to music in the home, when Grandma asked one of the girls to "play something lively." But it was the product of the composer's hand only—it no more originated in the heart of Stephen Foster than the neat lists of figures he set down in Irwin & Foster's ledgers. Irresistibly, he returned to his true medium, and his heart and soul sang out as he set down the plaintive, mourning verses and melody of "Nelly Was a Lady"; but so little was he aware of its superior beauty that he called it a "miserable song" and told Morrison to tell Gil Smith to take "10$, 5$ or even 1$ for it," and "make a donation of the amount to the Orphans Asylum, or any other charitable or praiseworthy institution."

There is no striving after effect in this simple song—it is composed within a range of only six notes and holds within that narrow compass all the beauty and pathos which more skilled composers often try to express by introducing long, mournful swoops from high notes down to low notes and vice versa. Even the few measures of melody which Stephen uses for an "introductory symphony" fit the song infinitely better than any of the modern elaborate arrangements one frequently hears of "Nelly Was a Lady."

Stephen's song was entered for copyright in Pittsburgh on December 5, 1848, more than seven months before it was recopyrighted on July 18, 1849, by Firth, Pond & Company. Remembering their experience with "Away Down South (Whar de Corn Grow)" and the extensive pirating of "Oh! Susanna" and "Old Uncle Ned," either Morrison or Stephen himself registered the song. It is described in the record as an "Ethiopian Melody written and composed and arranged for four voices with piano-forte accompaniment and symphony." Stephen C. Foster is "Claimed as Author."

About two months afterwards, February 6, 1849, a song was copyrighted by Firth, Pond & Company in the court of southern New York, entitled, "Toll the Bell for Lovely Nell, or My Dark Virginia Bride, A Favorite Ethiopian Song & Chorus by Chas. White." Charles T. White was a very famous minstrel man of the 1840's, and, in 1848, was manager of a minstrel theater called the Melodeon at 53 Bowery, New York City.

The next chapter in the story logically seems to be contained in the second paragraph of a letter from Stephen to Morrison, and it shows that "Nelly Was a Lady" was another in the number of Stephen's compositions around which complications arose.

Cincinnati   April 27, 1849

Dear Mit

You must be tired waiting for an answer to the many favors which I have received from you not the least welcome of which was that, introducing to my acquaintance Signor Biscaccianti and his accomplished lady. I called on Madame B. and was as much delighted by her conversation and agreeable manners as I was subsequently by her singing at her concerts. She spoke very affectionately of you and the ladies who accompanied you on the occasion of your visit to her, as if you had been her own brother as well as mine. Her concerts were very well attended here, indeed such was her encouragement, notwithstanding the formidable opposition carried on at the theatre by Mr. Macready, that she expressed an intention to return after she should have made a visit to Louisville where she is now singing.

In writing to Gil Smith please say that I am very much grieved at having been the cause of so much trouble and humiliation to him on account of a miserable song, and tell him that if he has not already burned the copyright (as I certainly should have done) he may give it to Mess. Firth & Pond any time that he may be in the neighborhood of No. 1 Franklin Square. If they will give him 10$, 5$ or even 1$ for it, let him make a donation of the amt. to the Orphans Asylum or any other charitable or praiseworthy institution. Mess. F. & P. have written to me for the song.

I did not read the articles which I marked in the Atlas but supposed them to be written in the usual style of the editor whom I consider the most powerful and talented writer in the West, therefore you must not blame me if he treated of Kamtchatka or Noatka Sound. I merely desired that you should have a touch of his quality.

Tell Ma she need not trouble herself about the health of Cincinnati as our weather here is very healthy the cholera not having made its appearance. There is something about letter writing which so runs away with my hand that my ideas can find no interpreter. I think I must study phonography which will probably remove this blind bridle *orthography*, and give my brain a lighter harness to work in.

With love to all, your affectionate brother

Stephen

Mr. M. Foster
Care P. McCormick Esq.
Pittsburgh, Pa.

This letter from Stephen was presented by Morrison Foster to Louis J. Cist, of St. Louis, a private collector of rare manuscripts, particularly of famous musicians. In his letter of thanks to Morrison, dated March 1, 1865, Mr. Cist says:

. . . I resided in Cincinnati during the time your brother was there, & when the letter you have sent me was written, altho' I regret to say I never made his acquaintance. I have often seen him on the Street, & at the Counter of the "Ohio Life Ins. & Trust Co" (of which I was Teller from 1846 to 1851), and can recognize his likeness in the Photograph you have been kind enough to send me. . . .

When Morrison sent Stephen's letter to Mr. Cist on February 27, 1865, he wrote:

. . . Who the editor of the Atlas was at that time you will perhaps remember. Stephen's estimate of his ability may have been too high, but I know you will consider the fact that my brother was quite young then.

. . . The song Stephen refers to had been sent to Gilead A. Smith Esq a connection of ours in New York to be by him delivered to a person who had requested Stephen to send him a song for public performances. Mr. Smith after calling several times, failed to find the person, and so informed my brother. Hence the latters irritation. I well remember that this very song was "Nelly was a Lady" one of Stephens best compositions. It afterwards sold in immense numbers and to a profit of several thousands of dollars.

I also inclose you a photograph of my brother Stephen, copied from an original ambrotype (the only correct likeness of him extant) which I beg you will do me the honor to accept. The letter I send is one of the few left of a great many I once had but I was so unfortunate as to leave most of them in Philadelphia several years ago and have as yet been unable to find them. You will believe me when I assure you that to no one but yourself (and for the use you wish to make of it) would I part with it.

There seems to exist here a little confusion in Morrison's mind as to just what the actual mission was that Gil Smith had performed for Stephen in regard to "Nelly Was a Lady," for Morrison says "song" and Stephen specifically states "copyright." The natural deduction from these different items of information is that Stephen was acquainted with the minstrel leader, Charles T. White, and, at White's request, sent him the manuscript of "Nelly Was a Lady." The song proved successful, and on February 6, 1849, Firth, Pond & Company copyrighted it under the long title, crediting it to Charles White. On learning this, Stephen probably called their attention to the fact that he was the rightful composer, had already taken out a copyright, and sent a copy of the registration to Gil Smith to deliver personally to Firth, Pond & Company. The publishers seemed anxious to give Stephen due credit for the song, and it was entered by them in the district court of southern New York the following July 18, 1849, under the title "Nelly Was a Lady," and the title page states it was "Written & Composed by S. C. Foster."

This was the beginning of Stephen's association with Firth, Pond & Company, of New York, and a little further light is shed on "Nelly was a Lady" in the following letter from the publishers to Stephen, dated September 12, 1849.

S. C. Foster, Esq.
Dear Sir

Your favor of 8th inst. is received and we hasten to reply. We will accept the proposition therein made, viz. to allow you two cents upon every copy of your future publications issued by our house, after the expenses of publication are paid, of course it is always our interest to push them as widely as possible. From your acquaintance with the proprietors or managers of the different bands of "minstrels," & from your known reputation, you can undoubtedly arrange with them to sing them & thus introduce them to the public in that way, but in order to secure the copyright exclusively for our house, it is safe to hand such persons printed copies only, of the pieces, for if manuscript copies are issued particularly by the author, the market will be flooded with spurious issues in a short time.

It is also advisable to compose only such pieces as are likely both in the sentiment & melody to take the public taste. Numerous instances can be cited of composers whose reputation has greatly depreciated, from the fact of their music becoming too popular, & as a consequence they write too much & too fast, & in a short time others supercede them.

As soon as "Brother Gum" makes his appearance he shall be joined to pretty "Nelly," & your interest in the two favorites duly forwarded to your address, say 50 copies of each.

We remain in the hope of hearing from you soon.

Very truly yours,
FIRTH, POND & CO.

Stephen's accounts show no income from either "Nelly Was a Lady," or "My Brudder Gum," and it is evident that the fifty copies of each, mentioned by the publisher, were all he ever received.

Madame Biscaccianti, whom Stephen mentions in his letter to Morrison, was a granddaughter of James Hewitt, founder of one of the most notable musical families in America. Her uncle, John Hill Hewitt, was the composer of many beautiful ballads of the day, amongst them "The Knight of the Raven Black Plume," and "The Minstrel's Return from the War." But he is probably best remembered for the Civil War song, "All Quiet Along the Potomac

THE FIRST PRESIDENTIAL RESIDENCE.—OCCUPIED BY GEORGE WASHINGTON.—FRANKLIN SQUARE, NEW YORK,
JUST BEING DEMOLISHED.—(SEE PRECEDING PAGE.)

THE opening of the Bowery to Franklin square will cause the demolishment of most of the "oldest remaining houses in the city." The vicinity of Franklin square at the close of the last century was the aristocratic portion of our city. The "Walton House," which faces it on the east side, is now one hundred years old, and still, in spite of the luxury of the present time, retains a degree of magnificence that forms no unfavorable contrast with our best palatial mansions. Chief-Justice Jay lived at the head of Cherry street, and many of the most distinguished members of the first Congress had residences in the vicinity. At this moment (May 29th, 1856) the workmen are taking down "the first Presidential mansion," so familiar in comparatively modern times, as the music store of Firth Pond & Co. This building was erected for Walter Franklin, a rich merchant and Quaker; on its gable-end were originally the following significant letters and figures:

W. F.

1770.

DeWitt Clinton, George Clinton, and John S. Norton, married daughters of Franklin. Mr. Genet, the French Minister to this country, who created so much mischief in his day, married the daughter of S. Osgood, who married the widow of Walter Franklin. Genet's wife was born in this house, as were also probably the wives of DeWitt and George Clinton. When the Government of the United States was organized, the national capital was New York city. Washington, who was sworn into office in this city on the 30th of April, 1789, selected this house for his private residence, and was much complained of for "going so far out of the city" at this time he attended religious service in St. George's Chapel in Beekman street, where he was a communicant. In later days this residence has been dedicated to the circulation of music, and the buildings in the neighborhood, under the "logic of events," have degenerated into stores and boarding-houses. Quite recently, the magnificent pile of iron, known as Harper's book establishment, has shed a splendor on the west side of Franklin square; and as soon as the Bowery, the widest and finest laid-off street in the city, reaches this classic locality, we see no reason why Franklin square should not again assume its primal grandeur, different in kind, but grandeur still.

FIRST PRESIDENTIAL RESIDENCE—OCCUPIED BY GEORGE WASHINGTON. FRANKLIN SQUARE, N. Y., JUST DEMOLISHED. (SEE PAGE 414.)

First headquarters of Firth, Pond & Co., Stephen's publishers

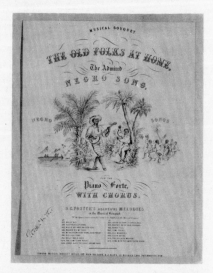
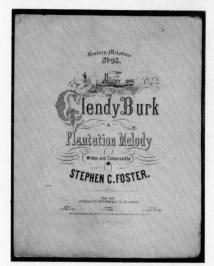

Early editions of Foster songs

Tonight," for which Hewitt wrote the music only. Madame Biscaccianti's first concert in Pittsburgh was given at Apollo Hall, on March 30, 1849; she was assisted by J. L. Hatton, pianist and vocalist, and by Signor Biscaccianti, who performed "two of his favorite solos on the violoncello," the newspaper said. Perhaps Morrison was introduced to this lady by Henry Kleber, who was the local manager of almost all of the celebrities who came to Pittsburgh to perform musically. Madame Biscaccianti continued her concerts in Pittsburgh until April 5, after which she departed for a tour of the western and southern cities—Cincinnati was probably her first stop. We can be almost sure that the ladies who accompanied Morrison to call on the singer were the Misses Mary Anderson, Mary Irwin, and Julia Murray.

VII

IN every large family where several of the children are married, there is always something turning up in some one of the households to make life interesting, and the Fosters' was no exception. On October 10, 1848, Henrietta added another son to her flock, and named him for her father, William Foster Thornton. At that time, Mr. Thornton was in business with a Mr. Canfield in a general store in Warren, Ohio. Mr. Canfield left the partnership in February, 1849, and Jesse assumed the entire management. About the same time, a fire in the store caused great excitement, but Henrietta replied to her father's anxious inquiries that no one was hurt and little damage resulted. Although the weather was bitterly cold, none of them suffered any ill effects. Henrietta was more concerned about her father than about the fire. In her girlhood days, she had not been filled with serious religious zeal like sister Ann Eliza; her nature was lighter and more inclined to frivolity; but of late years, she had been drawn into church work and church life, and her anxiety for her father and brothers approximated Ann Eliza's. William B. Foster's continued indifference to what she considered his spiritual danger, in face of approaching old age and not very robust health, alarmed his conscientious daughter to such a degree that she felt she must make another appeal to him before it was too late. The most striking thing about her letter to most readers, I think, will be the pen portrait she paints of the lovable qualities of Wm. B. Foster in his seventieth year, and the tender regard in which he was held by his children.

February 19, 1849. My beloved husband has been brought by Divine Mercy into the fold of Christ. He has become a member of the Church, and of course you may know, a consistent one. . . . Oh, that I could see *all* my beloved family in the same saving state! Oh, that you, my dearly loved father, could be persuaded to set to work in good earnest, preparing for that change which, sooner or later, must come. You are now an old man, and instead of being left like a leafless stalk, alone in the world, wifeless, childless, and forsaken, look around you and say, if you are not blessed beyond all description. A devoted wife, affectionate and dutiful sons and daughters, grandsons and granddaughters—not a *"black sheep"* in the whole flock, not a deformed, or sickly one, not a knavish or dishonest one, not a broken-hearted, or dejected one amongst them all. And added to all these, is a competency sufficient to provide *all* the necessaries of life, and many of the luxuries. If an earthly friend could have bestowed such rich gifts upon you, you would wish your life were seventy years longer, that you might devote it all to his service; your gratitude would know no bounds.

When I think of your many virtues, your kind and endearing ways, your benign and cheerful countenance, your affectionate and tender voice, your disinteredness, your industry, your patience, and your affectionate forbearance, what a gush of tenderness comes over me, what an overwhelming feeling of love for my own dear father! Then, too, arises the prayer in my heart, "Oh Lamb of God, that takest away the sins of the World, have mercy upon him!"

When we, your children are together, how often have your many loving ways been the theme of our conversation, and when we are separated, how constantly the subject of our thoughts. But with what joy could we look forward to the future, were you numbered amongst the followers of Christ. . . . do, dear father, give up all your doubts, and pray for true holiness, pray to your Heavenly Father to remove your indifference, to give you a realizing sense of your own sinfulness, and utter inability to save yourself, and your need of a Saviour.

Tell my dear brother Morison, that I am greatly in hopes to hear that at the Bishop's next visitation he will be amongst the Candidates

for Confirmation. He is now come to that age when it is time for him
to relieve dear Ma of the responsibility she took upon herself at the
time of his Baptism, and that he must be careful, or the world will soon
choke all the good seed that was sown in his heart last summer when
on his sick bed. God was indeed good to spare both those dear boys
to us, and they, nor we, cannot be too thankful for it. "Praise the Lord,
O my Soul, and all that is within me, praise his holy name."

I beg, dear Pa, that you will forgive my earnestness, and attribute
it to the right cause, that is, a sincere and devoted love for you all.
I do hope to see dear Dunning and Mitty out here soon. Give much love
to dear Ma and the boys, and accept for yourself the most sincere and
affectionate love of your daughter,

Henrietta.

Warren, Feb. 19th, 1849.

There is no affectation in these frequent entreaties which were
received by the Foster men from their womenfolks. They sprang
from the depths of their gentle hearts. The natural laws of cause
and effect never shook the unquestioning faith of the devout wives
and mothers and sisters of that day and age. They discerned the
hand of a personal God in the smallest domestic joys and worries,
and although both Ann Eliza and Henrietta had families of their
own to cause them care and anxiety, they still found time to give
plenty of thought to their father and brothers in the old home.
The latter may not have heeded the loving warnings, but they
cared enough for the writers to preserve their letters carefully.

The family at Pittsburgh left the St. Charles Hotel and moved
to the Misses Hettick's private boardinghouse at 85 Penn Street,
on December 7, 1848. Dunning was with them frequently, as Irwin
& Foster did considerable business with Pittsburgh firms, and
Stephen, in Cincinnati, attended to the Foster end of the partnership when Dunning was away. Henry, with his wife and baby girl,
Birdie, returned to Pittsburgh in May, 1849, with Henry looking
for a position. When President Taylor assumed office, he made a
thorough cleanup of Democrats, and Henry, in company with all
the clerks appointed by Walter Forward, received a letter of dismis-
sal issued by Thomas Ewing, new secretary of the interior. With
what mingled feelings of pride and exasperation must Henry and

the whole Foster family have listened to the bands playing "Old Zack's Inauguration Grand March" (entered for copyright April 6, 1849) in which, as proclaimed on the title page, "is introduced the admired Ethiopian Air of Uncle Ned, composed for the Piano Forte and respectfully dedicated to the Whigs of America by J. C. Beckel."

All the appointees under the new administration did not meet with the approval of Henry Clay, however, and there was so much friction between him and President Taylor that it became a subject of general speculation how long they would remain friends. As early as February 10, 1849, Morrison made the following note in his diary:

W. W. Dallas & M. Foster bet J. C. Blair & A. Washington 10$ that President Taylor & Henry Clay quarrel politically before the expiration of the next session of Congress.—Referee, R. Cowan.

Mit probably lost his bet if he meant that the President and Mr. Clay would come to an open break. Somehow they managed to keep the peace, notwithstanding the fact that the President was opposed to Henry Clay's compromise measures. General Taylor died suddenly on July 9, 1850, as though, as Meade Minnigerode says, "There was a fatality that pursued the Whig Presidents."

On May 1, 1849, Morrison joined up again with the Pennsylvania Militia, in Captain John Herron's company, the Duquesne Grays, but to his mother's great relief, he was not called for military duty, and did not get the taste of a soldier's life which he seemed to crave.

Morrison's old friend, Dan Beltzhoover, was now stationed at Fort Columbus, in New York Harbor, where he found himself almost as greatly bored as he had been at dreary Point Isabel. Julia Murray still seems to be the main subject of Dan's thoughts.

Fort Columbus N. Y. Harbor
Feb. 8th, 1849

Dear Mit,

Officer of the day; the weather as cold as Greenland; all the other officers at a party in the city; all my music old; too soon after dinner for a drink; I would not have any excuse for not answering your letter, even if such an excuse were desired.

Your letter, which I had been led to expect, gave me much pleasure and your confidence in my sympathising with you and other friends, in the loss your society has sustained, was not misplaced. Mrs. Denny I knew but slightly, but I admired and esteemed her very much. Miss Keller I never knew, although I have serenaded her, and almost loved her from the reports I have heard of her. Miss Irwin I have heard much of from our friend Miss Jule Murray. I hope she will not follow the others, but remain a long time to gladden you with her charming voice, which Jule speaks of in such ecstacies.

Some day, I hope to be with you again in Pittsburg. God knows when. And sometimes I think I would rather never go back, than go and see the changes that must have taken place. Of all my old friends, I can think of but four who have not married, died, or gone off to other places. Jule Murray and Hettie Wilkins are the last of my lady acquaintances unmarried. I had forgotten Annie Crossan. Mit, believe me, I suspect, and always have suspected you of a fondness for Jule. I wish I could know that it was so, and hear of your engagement or marriage. She is a noble girl, one in a thousand! I would stake my life on it. I am in love with her myself. I confess it freely, but for her own sake and yours and others who love her, I confess as freely that she does not even approach to loving me.

You ask me how I spend my time—very tediously. Once in four or five days, I have a tour of guard duty. On other days, nothing to do. I play the violin sometimes, read sometimes, go to the opera, but most of the time, we are all on a spree. The other officers are often to parties, etc. but although always invited with them, I never go. I care nothing for society, and in fact get more morose, and *excentric* (as others say of me) every day. Jule Murray might help me, confound her, but I tell you she will not, and besides I want her to be Mrs. Foster.

California and Gold, and the great Prize Fight are all the talk now. People go to California daily by ship loads. The Herald has at least half a column of names every day. Don't Go!

The news from Congress has given us a little life. If they can only break the treaty and let us go back to Mexico, we will forgive everything else.

Do you ever see my 'big brother' in Pittsburg? Remind him of my whereabouts, and that I am still in life.

Jule told me you are to have a musical soiree, and I half promised her a quartette for the occasion; but I have done nothing towards it yet and am so confoundedly stupid I fear I will not be able to send one.

Remember me kindly to her, and do not let my magnanimous resignation of her heart & hand to you be lost.

I hope that, having opened a correspondence at last, you will not fail to keep it up. On my part, I shall take the greatest pleasure in answering your letters, and in writing to you at all times.

With the kindest regards towards you, your father & family, and my Pittsburg friends,

I remain, dear Mit,

Very truly yours,

D.M.B.

How did you find out that Jule Murray ever wrote to me?

In spite of Dan's "generous renunciation," matters were not yet settled between Julia and Morrison; the latter still wrote impartially to Mary Irwin and Mary Anderson, but it was well known to all his friends that Julia Murray was his first choice. The little lady in Steubenville had grown rather wearing with her long letters on the beauties of true friendship. She came down from her romantic perch long enough to urge "dearest Mit" to spend a few days in Steubenville, remarking sarcastically, "Surely *Julia* can spare you *that* long." As we do not know the author of these letters (they are signed simply Hannah), I hope the reader will not consider it in bad taste if we quote a few choice paragraphs from the pen of this little "gifted female."

Mit, dear Mit, I do believe that unkindness would kill me.—Deprive me of *sympathy,* take away from me the sweet flowers of *affection,* and my very existence becomes a burthen—and never, never did I so *utterly* feel the want of it as now. Would that I could this moment seat myself at thy side, and reveal to thee *as in days past by,* every thought and feeling that dwells within. . . .

Let perfect *Candor,* and perfect *confidence,* be the brightest link in the chain which binds us together. But, Oh! let not the poisonous breath of suspicion breathe upon it lest its *beauty* fade away. But, come *what may,* I shall ever treasure the *past,* as carefully as does "Queen Victoria" her most glorious diadem.

I, like you, have been at a loss for a name by which to designate my feelings towards you, and I *cannot* call it anything but *love*. Start not, dear Mit, it is not a love which asks *all,* but 'tis a love as *pure,* as *deep,* as *lasting,* as that of a sister. 'Tis love without its *jealousy,* without its *selfishness,* and *such* dearest, if you will accept the offering, shall it ever be.

You may marry her whose image now reigns in your heart, and *I, too,* may link my fate to that of another, yet we cannot cast from us the *memory of the past.* We cannot cease to feel the fetters that bind us each to the other. There dwells not within my heart a feeling so pure, so exalted, so unselfish, as the *affection I have for you.* It is my boast, and my pride, and though I learn to love another as *deeply,* as *wildly,* as ever *man* was loved by *woman,* yet the feeling you have inspired in my heart, can *never* cease to be, or change in the slightest degree.

I know that it is unnecessary to repeat such assertions as these—I know that you *cannot* have a *doubt* of my friendship for you, yet I do *so love* to explore its depths, to dwell upon its intensity, and to go over and over again, those vows which bind us together.

A most annoying habit women have, of going "over and over again" sentimental utterances a man would "fain forget." And the guileful, guileless, little letter writer dwells upon the past with a most distressing and painful persistence.

Everything is so still and calm around, I know it must be very late; it was after the tenth hour when I commenced writing, so I think upon the whole, I had better prepare for the *arms* of *Morpheus.*—Oh! Mit, how *vividly* at an hour like this, does the memory of the *past* steal o'er me; once again I am by thy side, in that *well-remembered parlor,* where so *oft* we met and parted.—Again I listen to the tone of thy dear voice, and turn quickly round, half *expecting* to meet the gaze of thy dark serious eyes, bent full upon me.—It is indeed an hour to woo the heart to dreams of the joyous past; but, I am wandering, when I had ment to stop.—

I have so many things to tell you—but I vow I will keep them to myself, if you do not come to see me soon. Good night, dearest and best, I go to dream of thee!

As a writer of strictly sisterly letters, little Hannah, you do well, very well indeed!

Eliza Foster also had succumbed to Julia Murray's charm, and she declared that the Trinity Church choir did not sound the same when Julia was not there to sing. Julia returned Mrs. Foster's regard and even presented the older woman with a little tribute of her affection in the form of verses. As in the drawing rooms of

London and Edinburgh, it was the custom in those days, even in prosaic Allegheny, for the ladies to write poetry on every conceivable subject. Eliza Foster possessed a decided talent for simple, homely versifying, generally in a religious vein. Julia, desiring to please Morrison's and Stephen's poetic mother, set forth her admiration in the following lines:

June 2nd. 1849

TO MRS. FOSTER

Unto our Poetess I would fain
    Attempt a simple song,
But that I fear my artless strain
    Might seem to her too long.

I feel thy worth, I know thy mind
    Has beauties rich and rare
And that thou wilt but be refined
    By troubles thou dost bear.

Like Venus that bright evening star
    Whose rays console the sad
I long for thee when thou'rt afar
    And feel I would be glad

If I could see thee ever near
    To comfort and advise
I'd know no shame and feel no fear
    And bid adieu to sighs.

They see the *star* and think of heaven
    And long to be at rest,
To *me,* thy kindly *look* is given
    I feel that I am blest.

O love me ever and forgive
    Sins though they many be
That I may learn how best to live
    By living just like thee.

                      JULIE.

On November 21, 1849, "Summer Longings" was copyrighted by W. C. Peters' Baltimore house. This was probably the last song

Morrison Foster about 1849

Manuscript of "For Thee, Love, for Thee," copyrighted June 10, 1859

that Stephen published on a small cash or fifty copies payment basis. In December, 1849, Stephen secured a contract from Firth, Pond & Company, of New York, to pay him two cents a copy royalty on all future songs, and he also made a contract with F. D. Benteen, of Baltimore, which shows that Stephen finally had awakened to the commercial possibilities of his musical compositions, and had ceased to hand out the work of his brain and heart to others for them to reap all the benefit.

"Summer Longings" is doubtless more familiar to most readers by its first line, "Ah! my heart is weary waiting, waiting for the May." The words are by Denis Florence MacCarthy, a poet and teacher in the University of Dublin. The verses were reprinted in this country in the *Home Journal* without giving credit to the author, and Stephen set them to melody, probably struck by their sad appeal. He dedicated this song to "S. P. Thompson, Esqr." Dr. Raymond Walters, President of the University of Cincinnati, has discovered that S. P. Thompson was one of the young men who lived with Dunning and Stephen at Mrs. Griffin's boardinghouse on Fourth Street.

Mr. MacCarthy's verses in the *Home Journal* made a sentimental appeal to another American composer of the same period. We find the song described in *Godey's Lady's Book* for April, 1850, as a "very sweet and plaintive ballad that cannot but please" with music by Saroni, published by Edward L. Walker, 160 Chestnut Street, Philadelphia.

Dunning spent May and June boarding with his family in Pittsburgh and returned to Cincinnati in July, at which time Stephen went to visit sister Henrietta in Warren. In June, Eliza Foster had all her sons "by her"; even William came to Pittsburgh for a month's stay, and the Foster family all boarded at Mrs. Lynch's. After Dunning left, they moved on July 17 to Mrs. Thompson's. This lady conducted a popular boardinghouse in Lawrenceville not far from the old White Cottage where Malcolm Leech now lived. Mrs. Thompson had an interesting clientele drawn from military and professional circles, and Eliza Foster was very happy there. She was surrounded by old friends and neighbors and heard all the latest news of Pittsburgh, and especially of the "Arsenal" society.

Three weddings took place in June, 1849, which would have drawn Dunning and Stephen home even if business had not. On June 5, little Siss Pentland was married to Andrew Robinson, and on June 19, J. Cust Blair and Anne Robinson were married. So far as we know Annie was the only girl with whom Dunning was ever really in love. What his feelings were at that wedding, we can only guess. Stephen was always attached to Susan Pentland in a brotherly fashion, but there is no evidence of a love affair between them, present-day moving pictures to the contrary notwithstanding. At the wedding of Cust Blair and Annie Robinson, Mit "stood up" with Cust, who was then his closest chum. On June 27, "sweet little Louisa Bell," at one time ardently admired by Henry Foster, was married to J. B. Shepley, of St. Louis. Eighteen hundred forty-nine was a happy year—a year of weddings and peace and full of glowing promise for the children of Eliza and William Foster.

But maybe it would not have been so if Stephen and Dunning had not come home for the weddings in the early summer of 1849. They both proved to be very poor prophets when they wrote to Morrison that there was no danger of cholera in Cincinnati, for that summer the city was afflicted with the worst epidemic in its history. Letters of Harriet Beecher Stowe, who lived in Walnut Hills, Cincinnati, reveal the horrors of those days.* Writing to a relative on June 29, 1849, Mrs. Stowe says:

. . . This week has been unusually fatal. The disease in the city has been malignant and virulent. Hearse drivers have scarce been allowed to unharness their horses, while furniture carts and common vehicles are often employed for the removal of the dead. The sable trains which pass our windows, the frequent indications of crowding haste, and the absence of reverent decency have, in many instances, been most painful. . . .

July 1. . . . Yesterday, Mr. Stagg went to the city and found all gloomy and discouraged, while a universal panic seemed to be drawing nearer than ever before. Large piles of coal were burning on the cross walks and in the public squares, while those who had talked confidently of the cholera being confined to the lower classes and those who were

*Charles Edward Stowe, *The Life of Harriet Beecher Stowe,* Cambridge, Riverside Press, 1890.

imprudent began to feel as did the magicians of old, "This is the finger of God."

On July 26, the Stowe's little son Charlie died of the cholera, and Mrs. Stowe wrote to her husband, Professor Calvin Ellis Stowe, who was away from home at that time:

... I write as though there were no sorrow like my sorrow, yet there has been in this city, as in the land of Egypt, scarce a house without its dead. This heartbreak, this anguish, has been everywhere, and when it will end God alone knows.*

The cholera was followed by smallpox, and it is a mystery that Stephen and Dunning escaped; they had daily contact with traders, roustabouts, and travelers, coming and going from the wharves to the steamboat agency. Professor Stowe, who was a teacher in Lane Theological Seminary in Walnut Hills, wrote on February 6, 1850:

... During the three months of June, July and August last, more than nine thousand persons died of cholera within three miles of my house, and this winter in the same territory, there have been more than ten thousand cases of small-pox, many of them of the very worst kind. Several have died on the hill, and the Jesuits' college near us has been quite broken up by it.

That her boys were spared to her, though so closely exposed to these dangers, surely would have been credited by Eliza Foster to her prayers raised in their behalf to an all-merciful Providence.

In letters to Morrison from his young associates, Stephen's name is not mentioned very often, as he was away from home the greater part of 1848 and 1849, and he was younger than most of the Knights of the Square Table. But when Stephen did come home, there was one girl he went to see quite regularly, Martha A. Morse, known as Marka to Stephen and the Foster family. A little note from Stephen to Marka is still cherished by Martha's daughter, Lettie M. Christian, of Aspinwall, Pennsylvania. Stephen admired her greatly —called on her and took her places, even to see his cousin Annie Evans when she was ill. Why they drifted apart we do not know.

The course of true friendship did not always run smooth amongst

*Lyman Beecher Stowe, *Saints, Sinners, and Beechers,* New York, Bobbs-Merrill Company, 1934.

the Knights of the Square Table any more than it does anywhere else. Misunderstandings and little quarrels arose between the young members every now and then. A letter to Morrison from Mary Anderson (who was then visiting in Philadelphia), in reply to one Mit had written Mary from Nashville on November 10, 1849, reveals that there was still a feud on between Mary and Cust Blair although the latter was now a settled old married man of five months' standing.

Philadelphia, November 23rd. 1849

Good morning, Morrison! Gude morning, as our friend Sherry would say. I hope you feel better about the eyes than I do, as mine are decidedly sandy, the effects of sitting up late and getting up early—but to the purpose. Many thanks for your friendly and most interesting epistle, notwithstanding the *effectionate terms* which you see fit to commence with, for as Cust politely informed me once, "they all go for nothing, a mere matter of form, etc. etc!" To these remarks I always answered, "speak for yourself, if you please, as I flatter myself there are some young men who have a sincere affection for me, and mean all they say." Talking of Cust, I suppose you have heard that he & Tom have sent in their resignation to the Club. *W.H.Y.???* Alas! that we should so soon be brought to this. I had a long letter last evening from Sheriff Bell, and also one from mon frere, Guilluame. Their lamentations over their loss are *loud* and *deep both*. I am glad and they are mad, etc. I begin to think I am a wicked wretch, what is your opinion on that subject?

All my correspondents speak of the horrible stupidity of Pittsburg; Mrs. Kemble stirred them up for a few days, and then all again was quiet. Mary Phillips was married on Wednesday morning in church, and in the evening danced her friends in Grant Street. Sam Magaw is in Pittsburg with his new wife, a Norfolk gal, and Jane McDowell is engaged to some chap near New Lisbon. Will wonders ever cease? Will and Dick Cowan have concluded *not* to *fraternise!* There, I know you are astonished at *that*!! But with this wonderful piece of news, I must stop, for the present as it is time for Chestnut St. Sunday afternoon 6 o'clock.

You will think that I am indeed busy from the fact of my letter being so long on hand; but you know how it is when one is absent from home. Talking of home, I had a long letter last evening from our darling Mary Irwin, who writes in good spirits, and seems to be enjoying herself very much, notwithstanding the absence of her two devoted admirers, *Mitty* & *Molly*. But as you and she correspond as a matter of course, I need not attempt to give you any Pittsburg news.

But were you not delighted to hear of the re-engagement of the Pittsburg *Troupe Operatique*! I am charmed with the idea of singing again, only wait until I get back to Pitt, won't I screech! On Tuesday evening, Benedetti & Truffi are to give a concert in the Musical Fund Hall. I wish you were here that we might enjoy *la musique divine* together. On Wednesday morning, we go to New York, and then Hurrah! for the Grand Opera, with Maretsek at its head. The new Prima Donna, Signorita *Bertucci* (you see, I am up to all sorts of French & Italian) is said to be superior to Laborde, and in my opinion, that is *high praise,* so I should like to judge for myself, and on my return, I shall try to tell you what I think of New York, as seen in the winter, my visits heretofore having been made in summer.

I have just returned from church, and feel rather fatigued. Mary Sites is full length on the lounge, regarding me with looks of love, & sending any quantity of kind messages to you—but, there goes the tea bell, au revoir!

I commenced this letter so long ago that I am almost ashamed to send it, but I suppose you would rather have it than none at all, so I shall send it off. I am waiting for a visit from Jack Townsend & perhaps I shall not be glad to see him. We did not get off to New York this week, but go on Monday. I hope you will write soon again & I shall try to make my next epistle more interesting.

Good-bye; take good care of yourself & believe me

> Truly your friend,
> Mary N. Anderson.

Cust and Tom Blair's dignified withdrawal from the club was not for long—they would have missed too many good times if they had remained outside permanently. Tom Blair was back again, a most enthusiastic member, the following year.

In July, 1849, Stephen visited Henrietta in Warren and then went back to his desk and his minstrel shows in Cincinnati; William returned to his family at Lewistown where the headquarters of the westward-driving railroaders were still located. Dunning also returned to Cincinnati, and Henry, being out of regular employment, helped Morrison and made frequent trips to Washington for his father and Major Larimer with whom William B. Foster,

Sr., was transacting a very fair business in his soldiers' agency. Major William Larimer was an experienced exchange broker. Morrison found plenty for Henry to do because Mr. McCormick had added the Sarah Furnace to his various interests, and Morrison now had full charge of the Hope Cotton Mill. In fact, Mit was at home almost a year without making any business trips, and did not find time to start South until October 29. This time, he spent almost two months in Nashville, doing a great deal of buying and selling, and running up a bill of thirty-one dollars for telegrams alone!

One of Morrison's reports to Mr. McCormick gives an idea of a cotton buyer's problems in the year 1849. The entire country was in a state of unrest and unsettlement over the slavery question, which both the Whigs and the Democrats had been trying to ignore during the recent presidential campaign. California was about to be brought into the Union; the North wanted it admitted as a free state; the South, as a slave state. California already had a law forbidding slavery. Henry Clay had not yet come forward with his compromise measures, and President Zachary Taylor was opposed to, rather than in favor of, an extension of slave territory although he was a slaveholder himself.

Nashville Dec. 20, 1849

P. McCormick, Esq.

　　Pittsburgh

　　　Dear Sir,

I have drawn on you this day for Two thousand dollars (2000$) at 4 mos. favor James Correy, Cashr. and tomorrow 21st. will draw for One thousand (1000$) more, which please protect.

I have bought and have ready for shipment 112 bales. The prices paid range from 9.10 to 9.15.

It is impossible to get the market down in a proportional degree with the decline in Liverpool. Everybody here is impressed with the belief that in consequence of the fine weather which prevailed up to the middle of this month, the bulk of the crop is already picked out, and that the months of January & February will begin to show a vast falling off in receipts compared with the same period last year. The buyers therefore look on the present decline as only temporary and *principally* caused by a misapprehension of these facts as yet in Europe. They are all buying prospectively in expectation of still higher rates than have yet been paid, a month hence.

The receipts in Nashville now amount to 16,000 bales against 5,000 this time last year. The high prices induce planters to send in every bale as soon as it is ready. There is more selling, and less storing of cotton than I have ever seen in this place.

I am not buying now, as there are too many purchasers in the market. Several new ones commenced today and the competition is strong among them. 9.20 is freely paid, and some sales have been made at 9¼. In a few days the most of them will be out of the market, and I *think* I can then buy on better terms. We will receive no more accounts from Europe till the 1st January. In the meantime, I will buy the remainder of your order as corrected, say 150 bales in all. My impression is that the next accounts, if they do not bring an advance, will at least show no further decline. I would like therefore to go on and buy the 250 bales as first ordered. Please let me know by telegraphy whether I shall do so. There are no boats here now for Pittsburgh. The first one that comes I will ship on.

What do you think of the conduct of Mr. Wm. I. Brown of Indiana? He gets well abused by all parties here.

I am beginning to be afraid that if they don't come to an understanding soon at Washington the Union will *dissolve itself* and I will suddenly find myself turned into a foreigner.

Yours very respectfully,

Morrison Foster.